CONTESTED
NATURE

CONTESTED
NATURE

*Promoting International Biodiversity
Conservation With Social Justice
in the Twenty-first Century*

edited by

STEVEN R. BRECHIN
PETER R. WILSHUSEN
CRYSTAL L. FORTWANGLER
PATRICK C. WEST

STATE UNIVERSITY OF NEW YORK PRESS

Published by
STATE UNIVERSITY OF NEW YORK PRESS, ALBANY

© 2003 State University of New York

For information, address State University of New York Press,
90 State Street, Suite 700, Albany, NY 12207

Production, Laurie Searl
Marketing, Jennifer Giovani

Library of Congress Cataloging-in-Publication Data

Contested nature : promoting international biodiversity with social justice in the twenty-first
century / edited by Steven R. Brechin . . . [et al.].
    p. cm.
Includes bibliographical references and index (p.).
ISBN 0-7914-5775-3 (alk. paper) — ISBN 0-7914-5776-1 (pbk. : alk. paper)
   1. Protected areas—Social aspects—Developing countries. 2. Protected areas—Political
aspects—Developing countries. 3. Biological diversity conservation—Social
aspects—Developing countries. 4. Biological diversity conservation—Political
aspects—Developing countries. I. Brechin, Steven R., 1953–

S944.5.P78C65 2003
333.95'16'091724—dc21

                                                                    2002044774

10 9 8 7 6 5 4 3 2 1

CONTENTS

PREFACE

In 1991, Patrick C. West and I edited a well-received volume on the social dimensions related to international biodiversity conservation entitled, *Resident People and National Parks* (University of Arizona Press). It was an early attempt to highlight the social considerations and consequences of nature protection activities throughout the world, including some of its darker tendencies. Since that book was released, human population has increased dramatically; there are one billion more mouths to feed since 1991, from 5.3 to 6.3 billion. Most of these people are found within the economically impoverished but biologically rich tropical countries of the developing world. Like most of us, they want only a better life for themselves and their families. While the number of animal and plant species has decreased rapidly, the number of protected areas, IUCN categories I–V, designed in part to protect them, has skyrocketed from slightly less than seven thousand in 1991 to more than twenty-eight thousand in 2000, protecting around 6.4 percent of the world's land areas, up from 4.8 percent in 1991 (these figures do not include the hundreds of marine protected areas, biosphere reserves, World Heritage Sites, or wetlands of international importance). These noteworthy events have been compounded by a myriad of commercial and other economic development related activities and schemes, large and small, which have placed even greater demands on scarce natural resources and ecological systems. As a consequence, the growing demands on the earth's limited capacities have only intensified. Access to nature's bounty is being contested at many levels by many sources. The future will only bring more competition over access, not less.

This challenge of finding the right balance between protecting nature and providing for the needs of poor people and economic development in impoverished countries has been also marked in recent years by the incredible explosion of books and articles on this critical subject. This explosion only attests to the urgency and complexity of the matter. In spite of greater social enlightenment and humanization related to protected area creation and management in the more recent years, there is a long road ahead to more seamlessly blend the two together, the needs of humans and those of nature protection. The question for the editors of this volume has never been whether or not we should protect biological riches for nature's sake or for posterity's, but how.

The case for selective nature preservation is extremely strong, but so is the case for protecting the rights and fulfilling the needs of people, especially among the poorest of the poor, or the dispossessed, as we call them. It is our position that in spite of all of the recent efforts in the international conservation movement to progress in that direction, the movement's detailed understanding and appreciation of the sociopolitical aspects of nature protection remains underdeveloped. We hope this new volume will add to the strong foundation of the literature being established by a wide range of scholars and practitioners and add support to the efforts by many for making conservation practices more socially just and hence effective. As we argue throughout this volume, social justice and effective nature protection, go hand in hand.

Some members of the international conservation community argue that attempting to integrate local people and community needs into conservation efforts is a waste of time, finances, and human resources that actually diminishes conservation's effectiveness, not enhances it. We could not disagree more. Instead of agreeing with the view that integrating local human needs into the conservation has failed, we argue that it has not yet been fully embraced.

The essential argument of this book is that nature protection is more a process of politics, of human organization, than of ecology. Although ecological perspectives are vital, nature protection is a complex social enterprise. Many conservation biologists, who are among the most dedicated to protecting the world's most endangered ecosystems and species, naturally highlight their perspectives and disciplinary views. While these views are fundamentally important, they are by themselves insufficient for comprehensively addressing nature protection problems. The effort to better protect biological diversity will require more financial resources to be sure, but conservation requires more attention to developing the proper political, organizational, and institutional capacity for carrying out the work. It is the sociopolitical realm that enhances or diminishes conservation efforts. The volume's chapters elaborate on the basic ingredients for pursing conservation in this manner.

Over the years, the senior editors of this volume have been criticized by some for focusing too narrowly at the local level, worrying about local people and communities when the more critical concerns come mostly from the large-scale issues of government policy and economic actions. To set the record straight, we too believe that macro-level concerns, such as the actions of the state, market forces, and international activities and policies are crucial to the future of biological conservation. It has always been our view that biological conservation can only be achieved through sound national and international level policy and support, as well as the involvement and acceptance of local people and communities directly affected by conservation efforts. To emphasize the point, the conservation community cannot succeed by focusing on only one level without focusing on the others. Effective biological conservation requires proper international and national policies, finances, and actions as well as political will. While we tend to address the more local considerations, we recognized that these activities must fit comfortably within the broader context. But the processes are linked. To build capacity at the local level encourages capacity building and coordinating efforts farther up the scale as well as vice versa. Empowering the local and linking up with the extralocal so knowledge and resources can be exchanged is essential for the future of biodiversity conservation.

Many argue that nature protection and the needs of people and development are locked in a zero-sum game; we only must make the tough decision on the winners and losers. While we do not fully reject this view, we do argue it is essential to make the decision-making processes and management efforts more fair and inclusive, that social justice enhances the conservation effort rather than diminishes it. If we are to succeed at protecting nature, it is essential for all players involved in the effort to embrace the notion of conservation as social and political process. We must more fully understand the politics generated from the practice itself.

Social justice relates locally to biodiversity conservation efforts in a number of ways. The most basic is the way some members of the conservation community view local people as threats to biological conservation. Their numbers, activities, and needs make them easy targets as identifiable threats. In sum, the argument goes, a single species, Homo sapiens, is taking over the world, threatening nature. As a consequence, it is often logically claimed that Homo sapiens must make sacrifices in the name of protecting our biological heritage. Although an attractive point that carries some validity and one that is easily agreed with, especially at this level of abstraction, it ignores the obvious sociological reality of the vast differences among people: culturally, geographically, religiously, economically, politically, and most importantly, on the amount of power they possess. One needs to be careful with such sweeping views of the human threat to conservation. While there, it is also our argument that Homo sapiens can be the conservation community's greatest ally. In fact its future success ultimately depends on that relationship. A greater appreciation for a sociological view is essential; not all of humanity will be called upon equally to sacrifice their needs in the name of global biodiversity conservation. We must become more aware of which groups pay the personal costs for the conservation mission and which groups receive its benefits. Those that are called upon to make sacrifices in the name of biological diversity should be fully and honestly involved in that decision-making process and be allowed to negotiate for compensation in return for their participation. As we have argued before, conservation will not succeed in the long run if it is built on the backs of the poor. It must maintain the moral high ground or it will lose its soul.

One of the more cutting edge issues in modern day biological conservation is defining success. Many writers decry the failings of biodiversity conservation, but empirical evidence presented in a recent *Science* article also shows that parks and other forms of protected areas generally work in protecting biological diversity when compared to other land uses. Success here, however, may be viewed by some as only in relative terms. But to those conservationists who condemn the decline if not the demise of biodiversity because these efforts involve people and communities in the conservation effort, we ask: unsuccessful compared to what? A world without people? Although most of us would like to see a world of fewer people, demographic reality states we will see a world of at least ten billion in the coming decades before declining. Effective enforcement of parks and protected areas is necessary. However, park boundary enforcement, which is a central theme in a growing number of publications by frustrated conservationists, to us should not simply mean police action that one group imposes on another—conservation officials to local people or other potential user groups. Rather, enforcement must be based upon an understanding achieved among the stakeholder groups. Police action may be needed, but it should be based upon rules established through legitimate negotiations and consent among relevant stakeholders, such as park officials, local communities, national agencies, international environmental groups, and so on. Everyone must be on the same page at least, if not on the same team. Simple monetary reimbursement to local people for loss of access to needed resources, while sometimes useful, will rarely be a completely reciprocal substitute to the full and legitimate involvement in the political decision-making process related to how conservation affects their lives. Likewise, the benefits from ecotourism will never be sufficient to compensate all impacted groups in all places. Other approaches to constructive local relationship building must be pursued.

Specific areas can be and should be set aside with limited or even no access to all user groups. But how these areas are created and managed remains the fundamental issue. The political process of nature protection must be recognized and local people and communities must be fully and honestly engaged as essential stakeholders in the effort. This is precisely where the sociological concept of legitimacy comes into play. Oddly, the word has been rarely associated with nature protection efforts or found in the vast literature on the subject. In order for biodiversity conservation efforts to be successful over time, among other concerns, those actions must be viewed as legitimate by local people affected by them. Legitimacy, which is defined in the volume's first chapter, requires sincere involvement in the political discussions and management options of protected area management. Legitimacy demands co-management or stakeholder collaboration in the conservation practices, which then facilitates social justice, which then in turn generates a climate for conservation effectiveness at the local level and beyond, one park at a time.

Before wrapping up this preface I must recognize the tremendous contributions of the other co-editors. When Pat West and I embarked on this project several years ago we enlisted the support of two very bright and talented graduate students, Peter Wilshusen and Crystal Fortwangler. As we worked on this project together, their contributions became so outstanding we made them co-editors of the volume. This book's topic overlapped significantly with their dissertation research interests and hence the match between their respective independent projects and this common one was simpatico. We cannot begin to outline their influence. With fresh perspectives, detailed understanding of the most recent literature, first-rate editing skills, and unmatched energy, they greatly enhanced this work in ways that encouraged us to refocus the book to its present thrust. Their fingerprints are found on every page. During this process they rapidly rose from graduate assistants to inspiring collaborators. The future is bright for them both and for the fields of inquiry they represent.

I must comment also on the broader contributions of Patrick C. West. Although Pat continues to be very active on the topic of social justice and resource management as is illustrated by his involvement in this volume, the other co-editors and I, who are his current or former students, feel the need to recognize his pioneering work in this area that goes back to early 1970s. As a natural resource sociologist, Pat first rubbed elbows with this particular subject when he became a resource person to the International Parks Seminar, an innovative training program sponsored jointly by the U.S. National Park Service and the School of Natural Resources, The University of Michigan (as it was called at that time). The seminar brought together rising stars from the park services from developing countries to interact with North American experts as well as with each other. The challenges faced by these young park professionals in their respective countries were daunting on a number of grounds, political, financial, human resources, and many more. A common concern and one less addressed directly by the seminar had to do with park service interactions with impoverished local people and communities in countries lacking well-established democratic institutions and related political values. This experience with the International Park Seminar planted the seed for our 1991 book. The other co-editors and I would like to openly express our deep appreciation to Pat for his pioneering work in integrating the concerns of social justice and natural resource issues and for inspiring several generations of scholars dedicated to this largely neglected topic.

To conclude, in Pat's introduction to our 1991 volume, he made use of a famous quote by a philosopher from long ago: "that the greatest and most troubling conflicts are not between good and evil, but between good and good. In the conflict between good and evil the solution is simple—seek the triumph of good over evil. But in the conflict between good and good, the balancing of conflicting moral imperatives is painful and trying, and without clear implications for correct course action" (p. xix).

While this quote still has relevance to the people and parks debate today—the good of protecting biological diversity and the good of protecting social justice and human rights—it also reflects a changing view. The conflict between these two "goods" continues today but more so in the minds of conservation stakeholders than it should. Perspective framing is a powerful sociological concept. The people-biodiversity conservation nexus needs to be reframed as an essential opportunity for promoting conservation sustainably, not simply as a threat to it. The future success of biodiversity conservation rests on our abilities to establish the human infrastructure necessary to organize the effort, and the human relationships among all interested groups to make it work. In the broadest terms, people are indeed the essential problem to conservation; they are also its only solution. To make use of one of Martin Luther King Jr.'s famous quotes: "We must learn to live together as brother [and sisters] or perish together as fools." This wisdom applies aptly to biodiversity conservation today as well.

STEVEN R. BRECHIN
JULY 2002
URBANA, ILLINOIS

Acknowledgments

There are too many individuals and organizations to thank properly for helping us bring this book to completion, but we must mention a few. Our colleagues at the School of Natural Resources & Environment, the University of Michigan provided a stimulating atmosphere for this work. Here we must recognize Ivette Perfecto, Brian Maguranyanga, Grant Murray, Christopher Thoms, Juliet Erazo, Jesse Buff, Denise Mortimer, Barry Rabe, Steve Yaffee and the Ecosystem Management Center, Osmany Salas, Jennifer Rennicks, and Lisa Curran, now at Yale University. A very special acknowledgment must be given to Heather Plumridge for her researching and editing role in pushing this manuscript forward. The product is much improved because of her efforts.

A special thanks goes to Tom Rudel of Rutgers University for his endless interest in this project over the years and for making us think even harder. We also need to recognize Max Pfeffer at Cornell University as well. Don Field encouraged the development of the precursor to this book, and along with Fred Buttel, also at the University of Wisconsin-Madison, encouraged the development of some of the book's important themes in its later stages. We would like to thank our contributing authors for their patience and professionalism in constructing this volume. Our decision midstream to radically reorganize the project unquestionably improved the final product but delayed its production. We thank them for remaining steadfast with us.

We are most grateful to the School of the Literature Arts & Science, the University of Illinois at Urbana-Champaign for its support of a subvention for this book, helping to make it more affordable to many more readers.

Finally, additional thanks must be passed along to our acquisition editors at SUNY Press, Dale Cotton, especially Ronald Helfrich, and more recently Michael Rinella, and senior production editor, Laurie Searl. We thank each of you for supporting this project and for guiding us through the publication maze. We too must thank the Press's anonymous reviewers who provided us with outstanding, detailed, and balanced critique of our earlier drafts. This book has been considerably improved by their efforts and contributions. As always, we remain responsible for any inaccuracies or follies that may remain.

At a more personal level we each would like to thank our family and friends for their support throughout this project and beyond. Steve Brechin must thank Nancy Cantor, Madeleine Cantor Brechin, Archibald Cantor Brechin, Diane Eddy, Frank Brechin, and Elva Brechin, Richard Cantor, and Andrea Lilienthal Cantor, Aaron and Marjorie Cantor for their love and support, and finally to his old friend David Harmon, Executive Director of the George Wright Society. Peter Wilshusen would like to thank Cláudia Carvalho Wilshusen and João Pedro Wilshusen for their patience and support throughout the long life of this project. Crystal Fortwangler thanks PJ Saliterman, Lewis and Judith Fortwangler, Lewis and Darla Fortwangler, Richard (1918–2001) and Jeanne Morgan, and Vittorio Falsina (1962–2001). Patrick West thanks Sally West who has eagerly supported his work on social justice, and Heather West for reminding him who the social justice radical of the family really is.

Chapter One

CONTESTED NATURE

Conservation and Development at the Turn of the Twenty-first Century

PETER R. WILSHUSEN, STEVEN R. BRECHIN,
CRYSTAL L. FORTWANGLER, PATRICK C. WEST

During the second half of the twentieth century, the world witnessed the emergence of a global environmental movement dedicated, among other things, to curbing unprecedented rates of species loss and habitat destruction. Now at the beginning of the twenty-first century, we still face an alarming downturn in the diversity of life found on the planet in spite of key gains in policy development, political participation, financial support, and program implementation. The need to act decisively and quickly is indisputable. At the same time, it is important to recognize that most areas considered to be high priority biodiversity "hotspots" (Myers 1988) are also social and political "hotbeds." These rural areas in countries such as Colombia, Brazil, Indonesia, Madagascar, Mexico, the Philippines, and the Ivory Coast may feature high levels of poverty, insecure land tenure and landlessness, unstable and/or undemocratic political systems, and histories of state-sponsored repression. While the conservation movement is certainly not responsible for these conditions, individual interventions aimed at nature protection can exacerbate rather than alleviate social justice problems. As mechanisms of resource control, conservation programs tie up natural areas that are highly sought after by resource-dependent agrarian communities. A number of other groups also have interests in these biologically rich areas including drug cartels, guerrilla factions, pharmaceutical companies, international development banks, the military, tourism agencies, and oil and mining companies to name just a few. Thus, nature is contested on numerous levels under highly complex social and political conditions.

The purpose of this book is to analyze in depth the politicized nature of conservation programs and to explore how local conflict and resistance often develop in response. Even those approaches labeled as "people-oriented" conservation generate complex political relationships and challenges that can frustrate biodiversity protection efforts and detract from sustainable human development. Although practitioners recognize this political complexity, it rarely enters into the problem analyses that inform conservation policy (Blaikie and Jeanrenaud 1996; Ghimire and Pimbert 1997; Peluso and Watts 2001; Zerner 2000). As a result, it is important to study the politics of conservation in order to identify specific factors that tend to aggravate social justice problems and to explore how conflict and resistance hinder the conservation imperative.

This volume is intended as a reader for upper level undergraduates, graduate students, and practitioners who wish to explore these issues—especially those interested in conservation biology, environmental and natural resource sociology, cultural anthropology, human population-environment dynamics, international rural development, and protected area management. It is structured around conceptual chapters and supporting case studies that analyze the politics of conservation in specific contexts. The central theme of the book is that, regardless of approach, conservation interventions transform local and regional political landscapes in complex ways. Whereas numerous analysts argue that parks are "under siege" by an array of social threats, we find that the opposite also holds—rural agrarian communities often experience irreversible social and cultural impacts from conservation programs. Therefore the question arises, how can conservation initiatives operate in ways that ameliorate rather than aggravate social justice problems in these communities? We argue that the conservation with social justice question is primarily a matter of human organization. Therefore, the conservation community's responses to the question posed above will have to focus internally on the fundamental concepts, methods, and modes of organization that govern action. To encourage this process, we present a synthesis of conceptual tools centered on strengthening organizations, crafting institutions for collaboration, and establishing politically constructive social processes; all elements that aid in the formation of social capital. When applied fully, these tools will increase the likelihood that conservation organizations will carry out programs in ways that advance social justice. In general, we hope that this book will incite constructive debates about contemporary approaches to biodiversity conservation and their social justice implications as well as generate creative ideas for pursuing the conservation imperative in ways that protect both nature and human dignity.

DOWNWARD TRENDS FOR NATURE AND PEOPLE

By even the most conservative estimates, progressive degeneration of ecosystem structure and function with its associated loss of species is occurring at an alarming rate, stemming from a range of human activities. Most sources point to the increasing number of species extinctions as a clear indication of a biodiversity crisis. Using data from the 1996 IUCN Red List of Threatened Species, Tuxill and Bright (1998, 41) estimate that some one thousand species are lost each year. The 2000 IUCN Red List of Threatened Species suggests that this trend may be worsening. Compared to the 1996 report, this more recent assessment concludes that the number of critically endangered species has increased—mammals from 169 to 180 and birds from 168 to 182. Two key groups—primates and freshwater turtles—suffered sharp downward turns. The number of critically endangered primates has increased from thirteen to nineteen and freshwater turtle species in the same category rose from ten to twenty-four (IUCN 2000:1).[1]

By most accounts, habitat loss and degradation represent the leading threats to species. The 2000 IUCN Red List notes that changes in habitat affected 89 percent of all threatened birds, 83 percent of mammals, and 91 percent of threatened plants that were assessed (IUCN 2000:2). Studies on conversion and reduced quality of forested lands present worrisome trends on habitat loss. While many of the world's temperate forests have been significantly altered over the last two centuries, the last 30–40 years have seen major changes in the amount and quality of tropical forests. Estimates suggest that one-fifth of all tropical forest cover was lost between 1960 and 1990. In terms of forest quality, both timber harvesting and atmospheric pollution continue to affect forest cover, species composition, and age stratification (Abramovitz 1998, 22–23). Recognizing the rate and extent of species decline, ecologists including Norman Myers have identified twenty-five biodiversity "hotspots" that may house as much as 44 percent of vascular plants and 35 percent of all species in four vertebrate groups, covering just 1.4 percent of the earth's surface (Myers et al. 2000). Given this concentration of biodiversity in such a small area, conservation planners propose that "hotspots" should receive highest priority for species protection efforts.

In addition to the disturbing ecological trends described above, the majority of developing countries in tropical regions face significant social, economic, and political challenges that complicate both nature protection initiatives and the ideal of social justice. Several gross indicators for countries where biodiversity "hotspots" occur suggest that adult mortality prior to age forty, adult illiteracy, population without access to basic services, and income distribution vary by region (Table 1.1). Countries such as Madagascar and Ivory Coast in the Africa region present higher levels of adult mortality prior to age forty, adult illiteracy, and population without access to basic services compared to countries in Southeast Asia and Latin America. One can also discern differences within regions. For example, within Southeast Asia, Indonesia faces more acute development challenges according to the indicators shown in Table 1.1 compared to the Philippines. In the case of Latin America, Colombia and Mexico show percentages on par with the Philippines while Brazil is comparable to Indonesia. The Latin American countries stand out for their highly unequal income distribution compared to the other countries. Brazil in particular features an income distribution ratio that is more than twice as high as Madagascar and more than four times greater than Ivory Coast. It is important to recognize also that all of the countries shown in Table 1.1 currently face some level of violent unrest that offers stiff challenges to stable governance.

In addition to the political and social indicators mentioned above, global population dynamics present some important trends. According to recent estimates, in 1999, the world became home to six billion people. By the year 2050, this number is expected to increase by nearly one-third to almost nine billion. Available data suggest that 90 percent of these new people, some 2.7 billion, will be living in the world's poorest regions where the greatest indices of biodiversity are found (United Nations 1998).

While the biodiversity "hotspot" countries mentioned above show high population growth and fertility rates, trends suggest that these numbers are decreasing (Table 1.2). Perhaps the most pressing threat to biodiversity and communities related to population dynamics is large-scale, uncontrolled migration. Homer-Dixon (1999) presents a model that suggests how resource scarcity is linked to unplanned migration, ecological degradation, and violence. He estimates, for example, that land scarcity has strongly contributed to the migration of twelve to seventeen million people from Bangladesh to northeastern India. Similarly, Brechin et al. (1993) note how government transmigration programs in the Indonesian province of South Sumatra led to the massive relocation of some 296,775 people between 1980 and 1987. They indicate that many of these migrants were forced to invade protected forests for lack of other alternatives. Case studies from Guatemala, Ecuador, Indonesia, and Sudan document environmental impacts from migration including deforestation, soil erosion, and desertification (Bilsborrow 1992). Refugee populations fleeing war, ethnic violence, and political instability have had heavy impacts on protected areas (McNeely and Ness 1996).

The sources mentioned above suggest that social injustice related to political and economic factors such as unequal income and land distribution, forced relocation, and rural violence lead to environmental degradation. At the same time, several cases indicate that conservation programs generate complex, often irreversible, negative social impacts. Ghimire and Pimbert (1997, 7), for example, refer to a 1993 study stating that some 600,000 tribal peoples had been displaced in India (20 percent of the country's total tribal population) as a result of protected area establishment and management. Similarly, Geisler (chapter 13) documents social impacts that resulted from the forced relocation of rural communities resulting from the expansion of Los Haitises National Park in the Dominican Republic. In other cases, press reports suggest that conservation activities have served, in part, as a front for authoritarian measures aimed at controlling strategic rural areas. In Burma, available information points to links between the military and conservation groups in creating the Myinmoletkat Nature Reserve, a move that apparently has served to protect the interests of transnational oil companies (Associated Press 1997; Faulder 1997; Levy and Scott-Clark 1997). More subtle negative social impacts stem from restrictions placed on community resource access and use. These state-mandated controls are typically viewed as arbitrary and illegitimate by affected rural communities and thus produce a range of violent and nonviolent reactions (Bryant 1997; Ghimire and Pimbert 1997; Neumann 1998; Peluso 1992).

THE EVOLUTION OF PROTECTED
AREAS MANAGEMENT APPROACHES

While national parks were still an oddity in most countries at the turn of the twentieth century, by 1998, approximately 6.8 percent of the world's land area (854.2 million hectares) was listed in one of the World Conservation Union's (IUCN) protected area categories sanctioning limited, if any, human use (these include IUCN categories I–IV, which account for 64.8 percent of all protected areas). If all IUCN protected areas are taken into account (categories I–VI), this figure increases to 10.2 percent or 1,327 billion hectares globally (Cox 2001).[2]

National Parks and Resource Control

Although protected areas play a fundamental role in maintaining biological diversity and ecological integrity, their creation and management tend to reflect the political environment in which they are embedded. We find that the history of nature protection and parks often emerges out of colonial and authoritarian rule as instruments of natural resources control (Guha 1997; Marks 1984; West and Brechin 1991). Rather than assigning blame, this understanding of conservation's past helps to explain why local resistance and skepticism of national parks remain close to the surface in most areas around the world.

TABLE 1.1
Human Poverty Indicators for Selected Biodiversity "Hotspot" Countries

Country	Adults not surviving to age 40 (%) [1998]	Adult Illiteracy (%) [1998]	Population w/o access to basic services (%) [1998]			Income distribution (%) [1987–98]		
			Safe Water	Health Services	Sanitation	Richest 20%	Poorest 20%	Ratio Rich:Poor
Madagascar	21.8	35.1	32	—	—	5.1	52.1	10.2:1
Ivory Coast	37.0	55.5	58	40	61	7.1	44.3	6.2:1
Indonesia	12.3	14.3	26	57	47	8.0	44.9	5.6:1
Philippines	8.9	5.2	15	—	13	5.4	52.3	9.7:1
Colombia	9.8	8.8	15	13	15	3.0	60.9	20.3:1
Brazil	11.3	15.5	24	—	30	2.5	63.8	25.5:1
Mexico	8.2	9.2	15	9	28	3.6	58.2	16.2:1

Source: (UNDP 2000)

TABLE 1.2
Demographic Trends for Selected Biodiversity "Hotspot" Countries

Country	Pop. (million)	Annual Growth Rate (%)		Urban pop. (%)	Pop 65+ (%)	Total Fertility Rate (%)	
	1998	1975–1998	1998–2015	1998	1998	1970–1975	1995–2000
Madagascar	15.1	2.9	2.6	28.3	2.9	6.6	5.4
Ivory Coast	14.3	3.3	2.0	45.3	2.5	7.0	5.6
Indonesia	206.3	1.8	1.1	38.3	4.5	5.1	2.6
Philippines	72.9	2.3	1.7	56.9	3.5	5.5	3.6
Colombia	40.8	2.1	1.6	74.1	4.6	5.0	2.8
Brazil	165.9	1.9	1.1	80.2	4.9	4.7	2.3
Mexico	95.8	2.1	1.3	74.0	4.5	6.5	2.8

Source: (UNDP 2000, United Nations 1998)

As numerous observers have noted, rigid restrictions on human settlement and resource use stipulated under the most commonly applied protected area categories have generated numerous resource access and use conflicts in "developing" countries with sizable rural populations. Historically, protected area designations frequently occurred via authoritarian policies in which rural communities were forced off their lands and denied access to resources essential to their economic and cultural well-being with minimal consultation or compensation (Ghimire and Pimbert 1997; Hough 1989; West and Brechin 1991). For example, numerous parks in East Africa and Southeast Asia were set up in the late nineteenth and early twentieth centuries as game and recreation parks for ruling elites (Grove 1990; MacKenzie 1988). In sum, early approaches to nature protection were largely advanced and controlled by elites and treated local people as the main threats to high priority natural areas rich in biological diversity.

Despite major advances in reducing the social impacts of establishing protected areas, governments and international conservation organizations continue to create new parks by less than democratic means. For example, in 1989 the Mexican government established the Calakmul Biosphere Reserve in the southeastern state of Campeche without consulting local communities, some of which were located within the newly gazetted protected area. While politically expedient, the creation of the reserve greatly altered local power relationships and increased levels of conflict. Community members claimed they knew nothing about the reserve until a year after it was decreed when researchers began performing ecological studies. Faced with land-use restrictions, farmers adopted a militant attitude, threatening to kill anyone claiming to be an "ecologist." In the end, the government and local communities achieved a political détente but management activities have been very limited due, in part, to local resistance to conservation programs (Haenn 1997). Similar stories emerge from countries throughout the developing world.

Community-Based Conservation and Local Participation

The 1982 World Congress on Parks and Protected Areas marked a turning point in conservation practices by encouraging approaches that promoted greater local participation and sustainable use of resources (McNeely and Miller 1984). Since the early 1990s these "people-oriented" strategies have been organized under the rubrics of community-based conservation (CBC) and integrated conservation and development projects (ICDPs). The logic governing this approach suggested that if local people had a stake in management and their livelihoods were somehow linked to conservation, then they would support and comply with protected areas management restrictions. Ideally, these incentives would translate into decreases in park boundary encroachment and illegal poaching. Based on this reasoning, large-scale environmental protection programs began promoting conservation with development. Numerous projects focused on multiple strategies such as compensation for denied access to resources in the form of park employment, social services, fuelwood plantations, and marketing assistance (Furze et al. 1996; Wells and Brandon 1992; Western et al. 1994). Following the biosphere reserve approach, protected areas were conceptualized as comprising different zones, including a "buffer zone" housing "sustainable use" projects with local communities (Batisse 1982).

In recent years, the community-based approach has come under attack with respect to both its underlying assumptions and performance record. In particular, critics argue that while communities have received economic benefits from projects, the integrated approach has not strengthened protection of biological diversity. They suggest that by focusing the bulk of resources and attention on small numbers of communities in and around protected areas, community-based projects tend to create mini development poles that in some cases vastly increase local populations and resource use demands. At the same time, emphasis on individual protected areas and buffer zones means that regional ecological corridors and broader political and economic forces have been left largely unattended (Brandon et al. 1998; Kramer et al. 1997).

Numerous studies have critically examined ICDPs and related approaches to better understand their underlying assumptions and implementation shortfalls (Brandon 1997). One line of research, for example, examines the diversity encased in the term *community* (Agrawal and Gibson 1999, chapter 6). The success rate among community-based and integrated conservation and development projects varies (Larson et al. 1997; Wells and Brandon 1992). In many cases, projects have been hampered by a combination of poor design, inefficient implementation, weak local participation, institutional changes, and regional political dynamics. Recent studies on ICDPs in Indonesia (Wells et al. 1999) and community-based conservation in Nepal and Kenya (Kellert et al. 2000) conclude that interventions in these countries do not offer biodiversity protection at a sufficient scale or degree to guarantee species survival. Numerous community-based projects, however, have emerged as qualified successes in terms of strengthening local institutions and reducing destructive land use (Galletti 1998; Western et al. 1994, chapter 14).

The Regional Approach to Conservation

From an ecological point of view, protection of ecosystem structure and function will best be achieved at the eco-regional or landscape level (Dinerstein et al. 1995). The overarching logic of this approach suggests that conservation programs should focus at the regional level rather than individual protected areas and their buffer zones. This shift in scale was produced by the realization that parks as islands are insufficient to guarantee the long-term survival of many species, especially large mammals. In addition, analysts have argued that the most serious threats to biodiversity come from macro-level sources such as national and international policies (Kramer et al. 1997). As Gezon notes with respect to the latest phase of conservation planning in northern Madagascar (chapter 11), the eco-regional approach makes sense from an eco-logical perspective but produces stiff organizational challenges and largely precludes local participation in decision making.

Conservation Through Private Acquisition

A fourth approach to conservation, which has received less attention than the first three strategies, entails private acquisition of land for nature protection (chapter 8). Although this type of intervention is gaining in popularity among conservation planners, it has not been widely studied. In Belize, for example, a number of factors allowed the NGO Programme for Belize to become the owner of the Rio Bravo Conservation and Management Area in 1989, a reserve which covers 92,614 hectares (228,800 acres or 4 percent of Belize's terrestrial area). Compared to state-run protected areas, co-management arrangements, or community concessions, private ownership in the Rio Bravo case generated clear and largely uncontested tenure and management rights. Programme for Belize owns the reserve in trust for the Belizean people and thus enjoys tax-exempt status (Wallace and Naughton-Treves 1998). In this regard, then, private acquisition appears to have worked well in the Rio Bravo case given low population density and undisputed property rights.

In contrast, South Africa presents examples where the creation of private game reserves has been used as a political strategy to thwart land reform in the post-Apartheid era. Evidence suggests that numerous white landowners changed the legal status of their farms and ranches to private game reserves, which are exempt from land reform under South African law. This shift in sta-tus effectively nullified land claims made by black smallholder farmers seek-ing to establish homesteads (Brinkate 1996).

Conservation as Politics

It is important to note that, while we present these four conservation strate-gies chronologically, they can and do coexist in conservation policy circles. At the same time, however, certain approaches receive greater financial, political, and technical support depending largely on their perceived effectiveness at maintaining biological diversity. Given that conservation programs do not take place in a social and political vacuum, we set out in this book to explore the complex human dimensions that govern protected areas management. More than a response to ecological complexity, "on-the-ground" conservation programs comprise reactions to social complexity where decision making is dominated by politics.

While attempting to make policy adjustments for greater ecological protection, shifts in conservation approaches have only partially responded to
the political dynamics that typically determine program success or failure. As
we noted above, whereas the community-based approach dedicated too little
attention to regional politics, the regional approach appears to slight the local
organizational dynamics that are the focus of most ICDPs and community-
based conservation projects. Thus, in this book, we propose to more fully
analyze the politics of conservation in order to offer recommendations for a
more balanced approach that maximizes both biodiversity protection and
social justice.

THE CHALLENGES OF JOINING
CONSERVATION AND SOCIAL JUSTICE

While most conservation practitioners promote the ideals of conservation and
sustainable development, the daunting ecological, social, and political challenges facing both of these areas have left many wondering if it is practical to
combine such a broad policy agenda (Brandon et al. 1998; Kramer et al. 1997).
The approximately fifteen years of experience from attempts at combining
nature protection and sustainable development have generated numerous
human organizational challenges that deserve continued examination in order
to further strengthen international biodiversity conservation policy. While
framed in terms of conservation and sustainable development, these challenges pertain to all of the conservation approaches described above. They
include social scientific uncertainty, low organizational capacity, rapid institutional change, weak local participation, and contravening understandings of
nature and conservation.

Social Scientific Uncertainty

While those working in conservation biology and ecosystem management
point to a significant degree of scientific uncertainty regarding ecosystem
dynamics and associated human impacts, social scientists from a variety of disciplines face immense challenges in predicting the social impacts related to
conservation interventions (chapter 13). Interestingly, both ecological and
social scientific uncertainty dictate more restrictive, cautionary approaches,
albeit with quite different results. Whereas "erring on the side of caution" in
ecological terms would suggest maximizing protection of high priority areas
with a minimum of human interference, strategies for reducing social impacts
from nature protection might translate into foregoing potentially socially disruptive conservation interventions. We will return to this apparent dilemma at
the end of this chapter.

Low Organizational Capacity

Regarding organizational factors, the most salient challenges center on questions of organizational structure and capacity. We find that a complex array of organizations participate in biodiversity conservation arenas including local agrarian associations, regional NGOs, international NGOs, state agencies, multilateral development banks, and international aid organizations, to name some of the most prominent examples. Although each of these organizations has an important role to play in conservation, they feature distinct structures, behavior, and even "cultures" that often clash in the context of a particular project. Organizations also feature different operational capacities based on the quality and quantity of resources they have at their disposal. Governmental natural resource management agencies, for example, often lack political power, administrative and technical means, and effective governance systems to both maintain protected areas and work with local communities. These conditions tend to engender partial or ineffective program implementation and at the very least make interorganizational collaboration difficult. We discuss organizational issues in greater detail in chapter 10.

Rapid Institutional Change

All organizations and conservation programs are embedded within an institutional environment, which comprises the broad array of formal and informal rules that govern action. Institutional "environments" typically manifest themselves as laws, policies, and programs, which in many nations tend toward political instability, frequent change, and unequal access to resources. These regional governmental programs, national rural development policies, constitutional amendments, and other institutional factors, in turn, shape local/regional decision making regarding land use. Thus, political processes far removed from rural areas where conservation programs take place often help produce barriers to both biodiversity protection and community development. The well-cited, now historical case of economic subsidies for cattle ranchers in Brazil offers an excellent example of this process.

Beginning in the mid-1960s, the Brazilian government established a wide range of subsidies to encourage large-scale investment in the Amazon region as part of a national development program. Under the program, a regional development agency operated by the federal government doled out projects to investors. As an incentive, these individuals and firms became exempt from paying federal taxes and received a three dollar rebate for every dollar invested from their tax liability. The subsidy program created a highly attractive investment arena in a place where development was otherwise a losing proposition. The regional development agency strongly encouraged development of large cattle ranches, which generated unprecedented rates of deforestation (Moran 1993).

Weak Local Participation

Closely linked to the organizational and institutional challenges mentioned above is the difficulty in generating strong local participation in conservation and development activities. Whereas organizational and institutional issues relate to the *structure* of biodiversity conservation interventions, the notion of participation focuses on the programs' decision-making *processes*. Studies of integrated conservation and development projects (ICDPs) note low levels of local participation (Wells and Brandon 1992). Common barriers to local participation include divergent goals among groups, knowledge differences, histories of domination, class, ethnic, and status differences (Wilshusen 2000). At the same time, examples suggest that local people can participate effectively in projects when outside groups work with communities from the outset, encourage local organizations, and develop regional support networks (Pimbert and Pretty 1995, chapter 5).

Contravening Understandings of Nature and Conservation

Underlying our approaches to biodiversity conservation is the manner in which different groups understand and define the task or problem of biodiversity conservation. Most observers ranging from farmers to conservation biologists agree that natural systems are being degraded and species lost. However, this wide spectrum of players presents very different ways of thinking and talking about nature that typically produce divergent conclusions about how to protect biological diversity. These divergent conclusions can represent opposing opinions, which draw on contravening empirical evidence and moral arguments. Within the scope of biodiversity conservation, for example, we often find conflicting logics about the role of humans with respect to protected areas. One view promotes preserving representative portions of our world's ecosystems free of human interference while another perspective sees sustainable use and controlled settlement as a more equitable way of maintaining ecologically valuable landscapes. While these two views are by no means mutually exclusive, they do mark a key philosophical separation regarding the relationship between humans and the natural world. As a result, conceptual differences among groups create tensions that impede concerted action on the ground. Moreover, as several of the chapters in this book illustrate, the challenge of problem definition extends well beyond the question of competing policy paradigms to encompass the different ways that diverse cultural groups understand and explain the relationship between humans and nature (chapters 3 and 5).

These and other challenges make any attempt at joining biodiversity conservation and social justice a very complex undertaking. At the same time, the urgency of both the biodiversity and social justice crises around the world increases the need to act quickly. Limitations in funding, organizational capacity, and political support make it necessary to focus our conservation efforts. Why, then, is it so important to pursue the complex task of pursuing conservation with social justice given all of these factors?

THE RATIONALE FOR BIODIVERSITY
CONSERVATION WITH SOCIAL JUSTICE

The most commonly cited rationales for protecting biological diversity constitute a combination of practical and moral arguments. The pragmatic conclusions forwarded in the 1992 Global Biodiversity Strategy, for example, point out that healthy and diverse ecosystems potentially offer highly marketable goods such as new pharmaceuticals, genetic banks for key agricultural crops, and ecological services such as flood control (WRI et al. 1992). In addition to these utilitarian reasons, many scholars argue that wilderness should be preserved as a social good in and of itself (Norton 1992).

We concur with the reasons for conserving biodiversity summarized above but would stress that, since conservation, by definition, requires restraint by resource users, biodiversity protection will only take place through human institutions such as laws, organizations, or cultural practices that control our behavior. While obvious, this point leads to a series of other important conclusions. The behavioral restraint implied by conservation can occur voluntarily or be imposed by outside forces. In practice, social control typically occurs through a combination of self and externally imposed enforcement. The key underlying concept in both cases is legitimacy. Legitimacy refers to any behavior or set of circumstances that society defines as just, correct, or appropriate. This logic by no means precludes enforcement but since "legitimacy" is socially defined, divergent beliefs about what constitutes a legitimate act are most likely to generate tension and conflict when they interface in the same political arena. For example, a group may follow customary practices codified in complex traditional institutional arrangements that govern resource use such as water for irrigation or fuelwood collection. Modern legal institutions that govern protected area management may include regulations that contravene these customary use practices. In the absence of concerted negotiation, enforcement of protected area regulations in such a situation might be viewed as illegitimate by local resource users. The result would most likely be noncompliance with the law (chapter 4). The line between legitimate enforcement and illegitimate coercion is often unclear. Since conservation and other agencies will likely never have enough resources to universally enforce the law and since confusion over the legitimacy of enforcement acts at times creates conflict, a more practical, long-term approach would be to negotiate agreements that participants view as legitimate and feasible. Since even the most well-intentioned intervention is to some degree an imposition of knowledge and practices, one means of reversing associated patterns of domination is to help construct authority (defined as "legitimate power") at all levels (Wilshusen et al. 2002). Concerted negotiation may not be feasible in all situations, such as when local representatives are unwilling or unable to participate.

In addition to this pragmatic argument, there are important moral reasons for elevating the importance of social justice within conservation policy thinking. If we accept that conservation is as much a question of human organizational process as it is ecological processes, then it becomes necessary to establish explicit moral parameters or boundaries for social responsibility. Such guidance would parallel the moral arguments in favor of biodiversity protection advanced by numerous conservation advocates. Beyond principles of basic human rights, which should guide all human action, probably the strongest direction in this regard emerges in discussions of justice. As we discussed above, what is considered as just by a given group constitutes the core of our definition of "legitimacy."

The notion of social justice that we propose is built on the right to self-determination, a principle that guides most international initiatives concerned with securing human rights for all people. By this we mean the right to participate at all levels of the policy-making process as equal partners, the right to self-representation and autonomy, and the right to choose one's political, economic, and cultural systems. These rights imply responsibilities entailing politically constructive participation. However, attempting to define these terms beyond specific cultural and social contexts risks imposing knowledge constructs incongruent with local understandings, practices, needs, and desires. At the same time, purely local definitions of justice may be too parochial to garner wide support from enough groups to allow large-scale collective action. One option is to undertake concerted dialogue and negotiation in the context of a specific intervention to shape mutually agreeable courses of action for both conservation and human dignity. Although it implies significant "start-up costs," this type of deliberative approach appears to have the greatest potential of generating a legitimate process that can account for social differences as well as changing ecological and political circumstances. It promotes constructive debate, compromise, and power sharing over the long term as opposed to intractable conflict and domination.

The ideal of social justice appears in numerous discussions on sustainable development usually in the form of policy statements calling for a combination of economic growth, social equity, and environmental protection (WCED 1987). These formulations are often too general to provide meaningful guidance for local application and do not consider the inherent political tensions among the three objectives (Silva 1994). In contrast, other observers suggest that groups must negotiate the meaning of sustainable development for each context in order to attend to diverse and often conflicting interests (Lelé 1991). At the heart of these calls for negotiating the "details" of sustainable development lies the question of governance. Governance in this case refers simply to arrangements for decision making and power sharing.

Thus, like the term *legitimacy*, the idea of "social justice" takes on tangible meaning in a particular context. This assertion has important implications in that it points to the conundrum of localism, which holds that justice is defined locally through customary or national laws and practices. While local traditions are fundamental components for delineating the boundaries of social justice contextually, local political actors potentially can manipulate them in the absence of checks and balances. For example, local community leaders may use social justice arguments to prevent the creation of a wildlife sanctuary to protect personal economic interests related to a mining concession with an independent contractor. Similarly, advocates of a protected area may claim that their plans to relocate surrounding communities are legitimate because they do not violate national laws. When confronted with the problem of localism, dialogue and consensus on transnational or transcultural referents for justice, even in general terms such as the 1948 Universal Declaration of Human Rights or the principles of Environmental Justice (Taylor 2000), provide some broad-based criteria for making judgments on questions of social justice.

In the end, both the pragmatic and moral positions focusing on legitimacy and social justice revert back to the ideal of self-determination for all participants, but particularly for those rural communities that depend on local natural resources. In other words, we must ask ourselves the fundamental questions: Who decides how biodiversity conservation will occur and at what social cost? and, Who benefits from biodiversity conservation? Our analysis in this book suggests that local resentment and resistance to protected areas will increase to the extent that conservation interventions marginalize those communities that live in greatest proximity to and often have the strongest dependence on and attachment to key ecologically valuable areas.

At the same time, conservationists have a special social responsibility to work in ways that promote increased social welfare in resource-dependent communities. Some recent analyses suggest that protected area programs cannot and should not assume responsibility for all aspects of social development at the community level (Brandon et al. 1998). While this is true to a certain point, we must also recognize that in most rural areas, outside projects significantly alter the local political landscape. In order to increase the chances of success and maintain a strong moral foundation, members of the conservation community must take responsibility for their actions and introduce mechanisms that can encourage greater social justice.

OVERVIEW OF THE BOOK

In the remainder of this chapter we present an overview of the book, which grapples with this immense challenge of how to pursue biodiversity conservation with social justice. In this sense, it comprises both an analysis of the political dynamics of conservation and an exploration of possibilities for strengthening human organizational capacity. Since conservation programs inevitably transform local and regional political landscapes in "developing" countries, adoption of the politically constructive approach that we propose will allow participants to work in ways that advance rather than detract from nature protection and the ideal of social justice.

The Contested Nature of Nature

The contested nature of nature manifests itself in complex ways. Since conservation interventions are highly "charged" politically, the analytical task of understanding conflict and resistance associated with protected areas management must focus on the actions of and outcomes produced by the diverse array of players that work to maintain the ecological integrity of the world's biologically rich areas (Wilshusen et al. 2002). Whereas the different conservation approaches summarized above—strict preservation, integrated conservation/ development, regional landscape ecology, and private acquisition—represent a range of strategies for safeguarding biological diversity, many of the actors involved and political processes are the same regardless of approach. As a result we can explore the different ways that political actors interact in the context of specific projects and identify several factors related to human organization that tend to impede biodiversity conservation efforts and work against agrarian communities' opportunities for achieving social justice.

By presenting a range of cases on the politics of conservation, we uncover the enormous social diversity encased in the term *local people* and suggest how the impacts of conservation programs favor some groups but more often dispossess others that depend most on access to and use of local natural resources. We deliberately chose the term *dispossessed* to convey several aspects of the inevitable social impacts that accompany conservation programs such as the establishment and management of protected areas. Again, rather than trying to assign blame, we focus on the dispossessed to show how conservation interventions tend to differentially disenfranchise groups in complex ways. The verb *dispossess* suggests that certain groups lose something valuable against their will. In extreme cases, as Geisler describes in chapter 13, protected area management programs forcibly remove long-term residents from their lands, creating "protected area refugees" in the process. In less extreme instances, conservation initiatives typically impose restrictions on access and use of local natural resources. Under such circumstances, agrarian communities often lose control over land but also may experience irreversible social and even emotional impacts associated with forced changes to long-standing cultural practices.

The first section of the book, "Politics, Power, and Social Justice in Biodiversity Conservation," analyzes the complex ways in which conservation interventions transform rural agrarian political landscapes. In this sense, it explores the types of social impacts that biodiversity projects occasion in rural communities as well as the power dynamics produced in the process. In chapter 2, Fortwangler explores human rights and social justice concerns associated with conservation practices past and present and traces the movement toward socially just protected area conservation. She provides a review of protected area-local people relationships that spans a range of practices and raises questions that promise to challenge us into the future.

In order to better understand the complex matrix of political relationships that underlie the conservation process, Wilshusen (chapter 3) offers a wide-ranging exploration of power in practice. Many scholars define power as the ability of one party to impose its will upon another despite resistance. He builds upon these understandings by exploring how organizations, laws, rules, language, everyday cultural practices, and other so-called "social structures" produce power effects by enabling some groups to achieve their desired goals while constraining others in the pursuit of theirs. He finds that local conflict and resistance associated with biodiversity protection initiatives surface not only as a result of conflicting interests but also when contravening institutional and cultural practices interface in the same political arena.

The case studies in this part of the book illustrate the different manifestations of power dynamics associated with conservation programs from a number of angles. In chapter 6, for example, Belsky provides a detailed analysis of the complex political and social divisions masked by the term *local community*. In her study of community-based ecotourism in Belize, she finds that the intersection of social factors such as gender, class, and political party affiliation divided community members and largely produced a progressive deterioration of efforts to join conservation and sustainable development.

In contrast, chapter 4, by Brechin, and chapter 7, by West et al., focus on institutionally based power by examining the ways in which national-level institutions and political action impacted local projects to develop protected areas in South Sumatra, Indonesia, and village-level ecotourism in northern Benin respectively. In the case of South Sumatra, Brechin suggests how modern laws for nature protection clashed with locally recognized customary law regarding access and use of natural resources during the 1980s. The contradictions between modern and customary institutions created ambiguities regarding the legitimacy of entering the forest and using its products in the context of regularly shifting protected area boundaries. The chapter on ecotourism in Benin illustrates how political maneuvering between an international tour operator and the government's tourism ministry allowed outside interests to secure relevant permits and thus prevent community-level actors from pursuing competing enterprises.

Chapter 5, by Wilshusen, in turn, explores how national level institutional change and the emergence of a broad-based social movement among black and indigenous communities facilitated new organizational approaches to biodiversity conservation in Colombia's Pacific Coastal region. In this case, participants took advantage of political opportunities to negotiate the direction of a regional conservation project, challenging the boundaries of conventional understandings regarding the relationship between humans and nature in the process.

The last two chapters of Part One explore the social and political issues surrounding private sector involvement in biodiversity conservation. In chapter 8, Langholz explores the perils and promises of privately owned protected areas from a number of perspectives, including social justice. In chapter 9, Dorsey explores the complex world of bioprospecting, the search for profitable chemical agents. Focusing on Ecuador, Dorsey argues that power differences and profit motives are too great to easily produce win-win scenarios for all involved, where the "losers" are typically local communities, national governments, and nature.

Conceptual Tools for Pursuing Biodiversity Conservation with Social Justice

Whereas Part One of the book analyzes the political dynamics associated with biodiversity conservation interventions, Part Two presents a set of conceptual tools and approaches for increasing human organizational capacity. The concepts that we present center on organizational design, performance, and learning; institutional design for collaboration; and deliberative decision making through dialogue and negotiation.

Like a myriad of other collective action problems, the biodiversity conservation objective is generally pursued through organizations and institutions. As we discussed above regarding the challenges of linking conservation and development, organizations are key actors in the process but they develop their own cultures and possess inherent weaknesses that define and limit their goals, strategies and performance. In Chapter 10, Brechin, Wilshusen, and Benjamin further explore these questions of organizational structure and behavior. They explore how to design and maintain organizational and institutional arrangements that are best tailored to the biodiversity conservation task. Among other things, Gezon's analysis of eco-regional conservation programs in Madagascar (chapter 11) illustrates both the organizational failings of past approaches and the persistent challenge of interorganizational collaboration in the context of current policies. Chapter 12, by Wilshusen and Murguía, presents a case study of a grassroots NGO network in Mexico's Yucatán Peninsula that has successfully established collaborative institutional arrangements for promoting community-based conservation and development at the regional level.

The concepts of learning and adaptation are central to the organizational and decision-making processes presented in this book. Whether framed in terms of organizational learning, social learning, or adaptive management, we emphasize the importance of constant evaluation and self-correction. This theme emerges in particular in Geisler's review of collaborative-adaptive assessment (chapter 13). Using the case of Los Haitises National Park in the Dominican Republic, Geisler outlines how the principles of learning, which are central to adaptive management, can be combined with participatory methods to reduce social impacts associated with protected area establishment and management. Christie et al.'s case study on collaborative, community-based coastal zone management in the Philippines (chapter 14) suggests that participatory approaches can successfully lead to improved ecological and social conditions.

CONSERVATION AT THE CROSSROADS

The conservation community stands at an important crossroads. Its members have tried different strategies, secured generous project funding, and made important conservation advancements. Yet it still has much to learn regarding the human organizational factors that largely determine the success or failure of biodiversity conservation endeavors. If the biodiversity conservation problem is largely a matter of human organization then our search for responses needs to focus internally not externally. This assertion points to the fact that conservation programs have yet to fully take advantage of a wealth of social theory and applied studies from disciplines such as anthropology, geography, and sociology.

By focusing problem-solving efforts internally to look at the concepts, methods, strategies, and modes of organizing, conservation practitioners and other interested parties can comprehensively consider how to continually adapt approaches to local circumstances and work in ways that advance rather than detract from the ideal of human dignity. Such a process will provide effective policy alternatives to the extent that it is grounded in contextual problem analysis. Further, concentrating on conservation as social and political process allows advocates of both nature protection and social justice to move beyond competing paradigms or approaches and constructively negotiate actions that respond to local desires, needs, and complexities (Brechin et al. 2002).

Earlier in this chapter we pointed to an apparent contradiction between the goals of maximizing biodiversity conservation and minimizing negative social impacts. Whereas maximizing biodiversity protection suggests minimizing human interference, reducing social impacts related to conservation programs would translate into forgoing potentially disruptive interventions of this kind. In practice, however, biodiversity conservation need not produce "zero-sum" outcomes where one objective is favored at the other's expense. At the same time we do not mean to imply that clear "win-win" scenarios will automatically emerge from conservation projects that incorporate social justice criteria. The key is ongoing dialogue and compromise (Lee 1993).

Our discussion in this chapter suggests that the only sound course is for the conservation community to work constructively with people at all levels, as difficult and imperfect as that may be. To proceed in this fashion will require that conservationists adopt a stance of open dialogue and concerted negotiation with a wide array of actors in diverse contexts ranging from rural villagers to government officials to international lending institutions. The notion of social justice carries a connotation of rights, which, as we have proposed, center on the principle of self-determination. It is important to remember that rights imply significant responsibilities for generating workable compromises that advance the nature protection imperative. Indeed, one of the main advantages of reorienting the social processes associated with conservation to incorporate social justice is that the agreements produced by dialogue carry greater legitimacy. At the same time, they offer a stronger practical and moral foundation for fair enforcement. Conversely, agreements that result primarily from force or domination tend to include contravening claims, minimal commitment, and enforcement that many times engenders intractable conflict.

Given the reasoning for explicitly joining conservation with social justice as we have discussed in this introductory chapter, one important question remains: What happens in "emergency situations" where the conversion of specific tracts of tropical forest or other habitats is happening so rapidly as to require tough decisions and immediate action? We certainly do not want to end up talking about protecting nature while the forest burns down around us. The "triage" approach being pursued by several conservation organizations to save ailing biodiversity hotspots (Dalton 2000) suggests that rapid response "emergency rooms" need to be the policy norm rather than the exception. For example, a proposed $150 million Critical Ecosystem Partnership Fund that emerged in 2002 out of a joint effort led by Conservation International, a Washington, DC-based NGO, promised to strengthen management of key protected areas for ecosystems in Madagascar, West Africa, and the tropical Andes of South America. It remains unclear, however, what types of protection strategies this initiative will pursue and how it will work with people living in these areas. In most cases when a government declares a "state of emergency," it suspends the civil liberties of its citizens until the threat to national order has been controlled. In hospital emergency rooms, highly qualified, well-equipped medical teams take all necessary steps to save patients that often arrive in critical condition. Both examples are analogous to proposals for protecting biodiversity advanced in recent literature on protected areas, but with one crucial difference. Governments that declare states of emergency or physicians that provide emergency medical services must ultimately respond to the citizens or patients they serve.

In contrast, it is unclear what degree of responsibility the international conservation community has to the broad array of groups that are impacted and served by biodiversity protection interventions. Consensus on the question of whom the conservation community ultimately serves has yet to be fully articulated and acted upon. Platitudes focused on the global community's needs are laudable but incomplete. The real test of biodiversity protection's future rests on the degree of legitimacy that the conservation imperative will take on for all impacted groups, but in particular those resource-dependent populations whose livelihoods and oftentimes survival depend upon nature's vitality. These groups—the world's dispossessed—remain a critical element to defining conservation success.

NOTES

1. Under the IUCN Red List system, scientists classify species into one of eight categories: extinct, extinct in the wild, critically endangered, endangered, vulnerable, lower risk, data deficient, and not evaluated. A total of 18,276 species and subspecies are included in the 2000 Red List. The list includes 5,611 species of threatened plants, many of which are trees. The total number of globally threatened plant species is still small compared to the total number of plant species due to the fact that most plant species have yet to be assessed for their level of threat (IUCN 2000).

2. IUCN's Protected Area Categories: Category I, Strict Nature Reserve/Wilderness Area; Category II, National Park; Category III, National Monument; Category IV, Habitat/Species Management Area; Category V, Protected Landscape/Seascape; Category VI, Managed Resource Protected Area (McNeely et al. 1994).

Part I

Politics, Power, and Social Justice in Biodiversity Conservation

Chapter Two

THE WINDING ROAD

Incorporating Social Justice and Human Rights into Protected Area Policies

CRYSTAL L. FORTWANGLER

Where do we stand in terms of achieving conservation with a "human face" (Bell 1987)? Some protected areas are co-managed by communities, conservationists, and governments to safeguard biodiversity and incorporate the elements of social justice (Western et al 1994; Stevens 1997a).[1] And there are examples where people have secured their right to remain in an area and use the resources (Horowitz 1998). Protected areas have provided real benefits to people, such as protected watersheds, safe harbors for wildlife, and protection from logging and mining interests. However, many protected area policies have ignored social justice and human rights, resulting in devastation or decreased quality of life for people living in the vicinity. These have often been protected areas with an "exclusive management" strategy, which separate the interests of local communities from protected areas (Borrini-Feyerabend 1996, section 1). Such an approach is often called the "Yellowstone Model" and is troublesome to many. The International Alliance of the Indigenous-Tribal Peoples of the Tropical Forest explains, "[O]f all the environmental problems facing indigenous peoples, some of the gravest threats come from protected areas . . . [these areas] have led directly to serious human rights abuses" (International Alliance 1999, 44). At times exclusive policies have even been detrimental to the resources that they were intended to protect (Drijver 1992; Lowry and Donahue 1994; Ghimire and Pimbert 1997).

This chapter examines the winding road toward socially just conservation that has emerged in response to injustices experienced by people in relation to protected area policies. It is an abbreviated history of the movement toward protected area policies with a human face. Despite such support, social injustices have occurred along the way and still do, as detailed in the second section. The final section explores issues of concern as we move forward in the quest for socially just conservation.

THE ROAD TOWARD SOCIALLY JUST CONSERVATION

Voices have been raising the flag of justice for at least a century[2] and responses have been widespread and diverse.[3] International bodies have prepared conventions, declarations, and strategies on incorporating human rights and social justice into the planning and management of protected areas. The movement has also found support in international and national agreements on basic human rights. In addition, a range of protected area management systems has also been implemented, moving beyond strict protection models. In the mid-1970s Biosphere Reserves were created and in the early 1990s Integrated Conservation and Development Projects (ICDPs) and Community Based Natural Resource Management (CBNRM) programs emerged as ways to incorporate both conservation and development through protected areas (Wells and Brandon 1992). Such approaches, however, have received criticism from both ends: some argue that overall conservation has been sacrificed for development while others point out that development has taken a back seat toward protecting biodiversity.

Three UN documents provide a foundation of support for the right of people living in or near protected areas to self-determination, to secure subsistence, and to take part in public affairs. The first document supporting basic human rights for all people is the Universal Declaration of Human Rights (UDHR), adopted by the UN General Assembly in 1948. The two other covenants specifically support the right to a natural environment and were signed in 1966: the International Covenant on Civil and Political Rights (ICCPR) and the International Covenant on Economic, Social and Cultural Rights (ICESCR). The ICCPR has been ratified by 148 states and the ICESCR by 143 states (Magin et al. 2001)—both are binding agreements for states that ratify them.

Support for socially just conservation can also be drawn from regional human rights charters.[4] The American Convention on Human Rights (adopted 1969) entered into force in 1978 (OAS 1969) and was later supplemented by the protocol of San Salvador (signed 1988) entering into force in

1999. Article 11 of the Protocol provides for the right to a healthy environment. In 1981 the African Charter on Human and Peoples' Rights was adopted and signed into force in 1986. It read in part, "All peoples shall have the right to a general satisfactory environment favourable to their development" (OAU 1981).

A specific declaration for human rights in relation to the environment was sounded at the first international conference on the environment held in Stockholm in 1972, establishing the United Nations Environment Program (UNEP). While the conference focused on human-induced environmental destruction and protecting natural resources, it was also concerned with ensuring that environmental policies did not curtail the ability of people to secure better living conditions and provided for the right of people to live "in an environment of a quality that permits a life of dignity and well-being" (UNCE 1972). A few years later the Cocoyoc Declaration identified economic and social factors that lead to environmental deterioration and stated that any interference in the ability of people to secure basic needs is a travesty (UNEP 1974). And in 1975, the IUCN passed a resolution supporting "traditional methods of living" and stated that reserves should not be implemented without adequate consultation with indigenous peoples (Colchester 1994).

In the years following Stockholm, calls for more socially just conservation grew, including the publication of the *World Conservation Strategy* in 1980 (IUCN 1980). The central theme of the strategy is that development must be based on resources that regenerate naturally and meet our needs indefinitely. Although the document did not address social justice or human rights vis-à-vis protected areas, it did recognize the need to reconsider conservation and address human needs in relation to conservation.

New conservation approaches promoting greater local participation and sustainable use of resources were announced at the 1982 Third World Congress on Parks and Protected Areas (WCPPA) held in Bali. Following the congress, discussions about human concerns and protected areas included examinations of how such areas could contribute to sustainable societies and the need to include cultural diversity as a fundamental requirement of humanity (McNeely and Miller 1984). Similar approaches followed, such as *Our Common Future* (WCED 1987) and *Caring for the Earth* (IUCN 1991)—both pressing for sustainable development and the right to participation in natural resources issues.

Throughout the 1980s numerous documents were adopted concerning self-determination and rights to natural resources. Article 1 of the UN Declaration on the Right to Development, adopted by the UN General Assembly in 1986, provided for the full realization of self-determination, including the right to sovereignty over natural resources. In 1989, the International Labour Organization (ILO) agreed on the Convention on Indigenous and Tribal Peoples, 1989, (No. 169), which affirmed the right of indigenous peoples to the use, ownership, management, and control of their traditional lands and territories (ILO 1989). It also called on governments to establish means through which people can freely participate in all levels of decision making. Although Convention 169 does not refer specifically to self-determination, it does include indigenous peoples' right to not be removed from their lands without their free and informed consent (Barsh 1994). And the World Bank adopted an indigenous peoples' policy in 1991, which called for the "informed participation" of indigenous peoples in development projects and for projects that ensure indigenous peoples benefit from development investments.

Movements that focused on social justice in relation to conservation continued to gather strength. Based in the UK, Down to Earth (DtE) started its Indonesian campaign for ecological justice in 1988, focusing on social and human implications of environmental issues. The World Rainforest Movement (WRM) established the Forest Peoples Programme in 1990. One of its activities is to challenge "conservation projects that are imposed on local people and do not recognise their land rights" (Forest Peoples Programme n.d.). In 1993, Rainforest Alliance established the Natural Resources and Rights Program "to integrate concerns for social justice, rights and culture with tropical conservation and environmental management, particularly in biologically diverse areas of developing countries" (Rainforest Alliance n.d.). Two years later WRM created Fern, a nongovernmental organization that advocates changes in European Union activities to achieve the sustainable management of forests and respect for the rights of forest peoples (Fern n.d.). And at the 1991 People of Color Environmental Leadership Summit Seventeen Principles of Environmental Justice were issued. The principles call for freedom from discrimination, right to sustainable use of land and renewable resources, right to equal participation at all levels of decision making, and self-determination for all peoples (PCELS 1991).

Social justice was again linked to biodiversity at the 1992 Fourth World Congress on Parks and Protected Areas in Venezuela (WCPPA), which declared that the "establishment and management of protected areas and the use of resources in and around them must be socially responsive and just" (WCPPA 1992). Like the ILO, the congress stopped short of recommending full decision-making power for peoples affected by protected area policies: "[I]n many cases, the continuation and development of human activities in protected areas should be accepted, insofar as THEY ARE compatible with conservation objectives" (WCPPA 1992).

Parallel to the IV WCPPA, representatives from twenty countries met in Malaysia in 1992 with the assistance of WRM. The meeting led to the creation of the World Alliance of the Indigenous-Tribal Peoples of the Tropical Forests and a Charter of the Indigenous and Tribal Peoples of the Tropical Forests. In contrast to the IV WCPPA, the charter explicitly addressed the issue of self-determination and the promotion of biodiversity conservation in relation to indigenous and tribal peoples. It insists that "there can be no rational or sustainable development of the forests and of our peoples until our fundamental rights as peoples are respected" (World Alliance 1992).

Also in 1992 UNCED's Earth Summit was held in Rio de Janeiro, Brazil. It still stands as the largest gathering of representatives of state, civil, and economic society on the environment yet organized (UNEP 2002). Among the achievements was the signing of Agenda 21, the nonbinding international agreement on actions to pursue following the summit. It emphasized active participation in decision making on land use and management, particularly for groups that have often been excluded. Agenda 21 also addresses indigenous people, calling for greater control over the lands and management of their resources, as well as "where appropriate, participation in the establishment or management of protected areas." However, it took a cautionary approach to indigenous rights, using tentative language such as "some indigenous people" and "may require" and "where appropriate."

Representatives of indigenous peoples held a meeting, the International Conference on Territory, Environment and Development, a week prior to UNCED at Kari-Oca, Brazil (International Alliance 1999). It was held by and for the world's indigenous peoples. More than 650 indigenous representatives participated in the conference. The attendees signed the Kari-Oca Declaration, declaring "indigenous peoples'" rights to self-determination and inalienable rights to their lands, territories, resources, and waters. They also asserted their responsibility to pass those on to future generations. In addition to the declaration, the meeting attendees adopted a 109–point Indigenous Peoples Earth Charter. A few years later, in 1996 at the International Meeting of Indigenous and Other Forest-Dependent Peoples on the Management, Conservation, and Sustainable Development of All Types of Forests, the Leticia Declaration and Plan of Action was adopted, recognizing the fundamental rights of indigenous peoples and that "human rights, sustainable forest management and peace are interdependent and indivisible" (Commission on Sustainable Development 1997). It also states that the interests of indigenous peoples and other forest-dependent peoples "should have priority in any decisions about forests" (Commission on Sustainable Development 1997).

The first global agreement on the conservation and sustainable use of biodiversity came into force in 1993—the Convention on Biological Diversity (CBD) (UNEP 2002, CBD 2002a). With 183 parties (168 signatures), it calls on parties to "respect, preserve and maintain knowledge, innovations and practices of indigenous and local communities . . . and promote their wider application with the approval and involvement of the holders of such knowledge . . . and encourage the equitable sharing of the benefits" (CBD 2002b). Indigenous peoples argue, however, they have limited access to the intergovernmental forum known as the Conference of the Parties, which implements CBD (International Alliance 1999).

Building off growing interest in relationships with local communities, support for indigenous peoples' rights in relation to conservation efforts continued to grow. The UN Working Group on Indigenous Populations completed a draft UN Declaration on the Rights of Indigenous Peoples in 1994, which is still under discussion. In addition to addressing equality and self-determination, the central concept is that indigenous peoples have the legal right of ownership of their lands, waters, and all related resources (Coulter 1994). And the draft Declaration of Principles on Human Rights and the Environment, submitted to the UN Sub-Commission on Prevention of Discrimination and Protection of Minorities in 1994, supports indigenous peoples' rights to control their lands, territories, and natural resources as well as to maintain their "traditional way of life" and to secure their means of subsistence. In 1996 at the World Conservation Congress in Montreal, IUCN passed a resolution recognizing the rights of indigenous peoples with regard to their lands and resources that fall within protected areas and the need to reach agreements with peoples prior to the establishment of areas within their lands or territories (IUCN 1996). The same year WWF International adopted a "Statement of Principles on Indigenous Peoples and Conservation." The document recognizes that indigenous peoples have "rights to the lands, territories, and resources that they have traditionally owned or otherwise occupied or used, and that those rights must be recognized and effectively protected, as laid out in the ILO Convention 169" (WWF 1996, also see Maffi et al. 2000). In 1997 the Inter-American Commission on Human Rights approved the Proposed American Declaration on the Rights of Indigenous Peoples. Among many other rights, it recognizes the right of indigenous peoples to cultural integrity, the right to development, and the right to environmental protection, and the full participation in conservation programs of their lands, and in the case of protected areas declared on their territories, the areas shall not be developed without their informed consent (OAS 1997).

In addition to a focus on indigenous peoples, increasing attention is being given to greater equity for all people living in the vicinity of protected areas. For example, the IUCN Theme on Local Communities, Equity, and Protected Areas (TLCEPA),[5] set up in 2000 by the World Commission on Protected Areas (WCPA) and the Commission on Environmental, Economic, and Social Policy (CEESP), seeks the "recognition of the rights of local communities in the development and implementation of conservation policies and strategies that affect the lands, waters and other natural and cultural resources that they relate to" (TLCEPA n.d.). TLCEPA lists ten "rights of local communities in relation to protected areas" as well as five responsibilities. And the draft Declaration of Principles on Human Rights and the Environment underscores that "all persons have the right to an environment adequate to meet equitably the needs of present generations and that does not impair the rights of future generations to meet equitably their needs." Moreover, it states, "everyone has the right to benefit equitably from the conservation and sustainable use of nature and natural resources for cultural, ecological, educational, health, livelihood, recreational, spiritual or other purposes. This includes ecologically sound access to nature. Everyone has the right to preservation of unique sites, consistent with the fundamental rights of persons or groups living in the area."

The movement to address social justice and human rights issues in relation to protected areas remains active locally. In Namibia, Hai//om San people have advocated for the return of ancestral land in the Etosha National Park and in Kenya the Ogiek and Maasai are protesting the excision of areas from the Mau Forest (Maletsky 1997; Digital Freedom Network n.d.). In Tanzania local activists have declared that national park policies violate human rights (Neumann 1995, 2000). Katu protested against plans to resettle them from Lore Lindu National Park in Central Sulawesi. They wrote to local authorities, appealed to the National Human Rights Commission, and held demonstrations (DtE 1998). And the Centre for Amerindian Rights and Environmental Law has launched a campaign to provide legal advice and training to Amerindians experiencing problems with the extended Kaieteur National Park (APA 1999).

International efforts are also pressing forward. In an attempt to build social concerns into conservation, the Social Policy Programme of the IUCN, as part of capacity-building activities, has developed a set of resources (Borrini-Feyerabend 1997). In 2000 a Policy on Social Equity in Conservation and Sustainable Use of Natural Resources was adopted by the IUCN Council Meeting. It calls for the "integration and promotion of social equity as a fundamental condition for sustainable conservation and natural resource use" (IUCN 2000). In April 2002, professionals attending the "Mobile Peoples and Conservation: Crossing the Disciplinary Divide" conference hosted by the Refugees Studies Centre at the University of Oxford and co-sponsored by WCPA signed the Dana Declaration on Mobile Peoples (WCPA n.d.). It states that conservation approaches should be adaptive and collaborative, any potential impact on mobile peoples must recognize their rights, and the implementation of biodiversity conservation should respect different knowledge systems. And the Fifth World Congress on Protected Areas will take place in South Africa in 2003. Its theme is "Benefits Beyond Boundaries." Proposed workshops include poverty alleviation and protected areas, importance of protected areas to communities, mainstreaming areas into the broader landscape, and traditional owners/local communities involvement in establishment and management.

THE ROADBLOCKS: SOCIAL INJUSTICES AND HUMAN RIGHTS ABUSES

Despite support for socially just conservation, it does not necessarily play out on the ground. At a recent international conference it was reported that the majority of communities affected by conservation (in Africa) continue to "suffer impoverishment, lack of access to resources and cultural collapse" (FPP 2001). The day-to-day responsibility for enforcing human rights and ensuring social justice in relation to most protected area policies falls under the watch of state and local governments. And although a state is party to international agreements, it may have its own definitions of human rights or social justice, perhaps advocating them in the same way, more so, or perhaps less so (Russell 2001). Or its policies may not even be clear (Robbins 2001). Some argue that ratification of human rights treaties by states is mostly a formal and sometimes empty gesture (Heyns and Viljoen 2001). Most of the violations mentioned in this section have taken place in states that are parties to the ICE-SCR and ICCPR.

Removals

People have been forced to relocate from their lands in order to create protected areas.[6] This can destroy the fabric of communities (Colchester 1987 and 1994; Râval 1994; Cernea 2000; Kent 2002; Maruyama 2002; Sugawara 2002) and elicit negative attitudes toward a protected area long after its creation (Akama et al. 1995). In his discussion of evictions from land to create national parks, Lewis argues, "In flagrant disregard of the [African Charter on Human and Peoples' Rights], the denial of land rights to hunter-gatherers is almost universal in Africa" (Lewis 2000, 19).

Most international organizations, conservation groups, and governments denounce forced relocations for communities that have "traditional" or "customary" rights of resources.[7] However, they still occur (Chatty and Colchester 2002). In Botswana, more than a thousand San were relocated from the Central Kalahari Game Reserve in 1997 to settlements on non-Reserve land (Hitchcock 2002). Before evicting most of the people, the government pursued a policy of "freezing development" in the reserve; it took much longer than necessary to repair roads, buildings, and boreholes and drought relief feeding programs were slower than elsewhere (Hitchcock 1996, 36). As of January 2002, the Government of Botswana did not plan on providing water to people still in the reserve, numbering about 550 in November 2001 (Hitchcock 2002). The UN Human Rights Commission has condemned Botswana for its "discrimination" against the Bushmen (Survival International 2002). Another example is the case of the Twa people located in the eastern region of the Democratic Republic of Congo (formerly Zaire), who were evicted from their traditional lands about thirty years ago to create the Kahuzi-Biega National Park (Lewis 2000). The Twa have been denied access to lands and now live in squatter camps on the margins of other villages in the area surrounding the park. Barume (2000) documents the rise in malnutrition and disease among the Twa due to such restrictions.

Fear and Torture

Protected area personnel have tortured and intimidated people to enforce policies (Peluso 1990; Areeparampil 1992; Guha 1994; Lowry and Donahue 1994; WRM 2000a; Kothari et al. 1995). Others have extorted money and goods from local people (Ribot 1996). These issues are likely connected to larger issues of oppression and torture in the society. Ethnic minorities in or near protected areas are especially vulnerable to such tactics, particularly when the enforcers are from a dominant group.

There are reports that protected area personnel beat people to achieve results. Survival International has tracked reports that pastoralists from the Rombo Group Ranch were severely beaten by rangers of the Kenya Wildlife Service when they were caught grazing their cattle inside the Tsavo West National Park in 1991 and 1992 (Survival International forthcoming). In another case, the Botswana Christian Council argues that wildlife and park officers tortured "Bushmen" suspected of hunting on their former lands (Kelso 1993). WRM reports that in India in both June and September 2000 the forest department and the police forcefully dislocated a total of eighty-one families from the Kolengere tribal settlement in Nagarhole National Park to a new site at Veeranahosalli at the fringes of the National Park. In response people tried to defend themselves and were beaten by armed officers (WRM 2000b). Hitchcock (1994) reports that many innocent people in Zimbabwe, Zambia, Namibia, and Botswana have been killed and tortured by those working for wildlife departments.

The use of fear or torture may appear during "negotiations" over protected areas. In 1991, government officials threatened to imprison community leaders if they did not cooperate with a proposal concerning Khunjerab National Park in Pakistan (Knudsen 1999). The villagers of Shimshal refused to agree to government terms and in order to make them do so, the government dispatched the district commissioner to the village who subsequently threatened to imprison the Shimshal spokesperson. Other villages may also have signed due to the implied use of force (Knudsen 1999).

Restricted Access to Resources

Restricting access to resources can be an effective way to protect biodiversity. At the same time, however, such policies often create difficulties for people that have relied on such resources for survival or their livelihoods (Colchester 1994). Some of the figures are dramatic: the establishment of most Tanzanian national parks has resulted in the restriction of access to lands and resources (Neumann 2000) and almost 23 percent of land in India had been placed under state management by 1980, resulting in the loss of land rights for an estimated three hundred million rural resources users (Poffenberger 1994).

And Gordon (1990, 8) explains that the "establishment of every game reserve in Namibia has involved interference in the rights of local people." There are certain resources that tend to become inaccessible once protected areas are created and policies are implemented, such as blocked access to grass, timber products, fuelwood, and trees. One or more of these resources has become more limited or denied at numerous protected areas in India: the Koyna sanctuary, created in the mid-1990s (Bokil 1999); Gir National Park (Råval 1994); the Tiger Sanctuary/Save the Tiger Programme (Morris 1987); and near Kanha, Nagarhole, and Bandipur National Parks (Gadgil and Guha 1992). At Chobe National Park in Botswana, Ts'exa have been denied access to fruit groves since the park was established in 1960 (Taylor 2002). Other policies stop or limit land cultivation, hunting, grazing, and access to migrating wildlife. For example, the creation of Khunjerab National Park in Pakistan curtailed customary rights of the Wakhi to graze domestic animals and hunt wildlife (Knudsen 1999) and the creation of Chobe National Park in Botswana blocked the access of the Ts'exa to seasonal migrations of wildlife (Taylor 2002).

In some cases protected area policies limit hunting to bow and arrow only, forbidding the use of guns or dogs (Gordon 1985; Hitchcock and Holm 1993; Colchester 1994; Survival International 1996). Goodland (1982) has called this "enforced primitivism," which is sometimes built into the protected area policies of states (Novellino 2000).

Participation

Local participation in the management of protected areas has varied from not at all to a fair amount (Wells and Brandon 1992; Pimbert and Pretty 1995; Borrini-Feyerabend 1996). But when participation does take place, it is not necessarily adequate (Rodriguez 2000). In general, participation in any type of public affair can be difficult for "indigenous peoples" and "minorities" to secure (Ghai 2001). Moreover, questions of participation generally refer to the implementation and management of protected areas; local people are rarely consulted about whether to create an area in the first place.

Despite much progress and considerable support, participation is still not guaranteed. In 1997, a survey of people living in an area proposed as a national park in the Bobo plains of Nigeria showed that almost half of the respondents were not aware of the plan (Gbadegesin and Ayileka 2000). In another case, the Nicaraguan government created the Bosawas National Reserve of Natural Resources in 1991 without prior consultation of 34,000 Miskitos and Mayagnas people in the area. They are still demanding such consultation and suspect that the government declared the area to profit from the natural resources within. They also consider it a violation of their rights to the land and its resources (von Humboldt 2000).[8]

THE WINDING ROAD INTO THE FUTURE

There has been considerable movement toward socially just protected area policies—and there have been numerous roadblocks. As we wind our way forward, we find as many questions as answers. Some of the debates and issues are discussed below.

Self-determination

Many people around the world are increasingly calling for or demanding rights to self-determination along with expanded autonomy and support for their efforts to maintain cultural integrity (Indigenous Alliance 1999; Bowen 2000; Assembly of First Nations n.d.; International Indian Treaty Council n.d.). The term implies a right to plot one's own course without interference from any external source (Peang-Meth 2002). IWGIA defines self-determination as the "right to participate in the democratic process of governance and to influence one's future—politically, socially, and culturally" (IWGIA n.d.). Self-determination has also served as the basis for colonized peoples to secure independence and as a foundation for indigenous peoples and ethnic minorities to secede or proclaim some independence and autonomy from states (see Peang-Meth 2002). IWGIA stresses that for indigenous peoples the term *self-determination* most often does not imply secession from the state (IWGIA n.d.).

If we evaluate protected area policies in terms of the right to self-determination, we find that numerous protected areas have been created and maintained without the participation or knowledge of people living in or claiming the lands, and regularly without their approval (see for example DtE 2002). Most protected area agencies, the states in which they lie, and many organizations are cautious about actively advocating self-determination for people in the vicinity of protected areas because it could mean the end of their control over the protected area. However, they may find it easier to support in cases where land is part of traditional or customary resource use (i.e., indigenous territory) or when it does not interfere with the conservation and sustainable use of biodiversity. For example, Principle 11 of the WWF Principles on Indigenous Peoples and Conservation recognizes indigenous peoples' right to decide on the type of technological and management system on their lands— but it only supports such application "*insofar* as they are environmentally sustainable and contribute to the conservation of nature" (WWF International 1996, emphasis added). Weber et al. (2000, 12) explain that the principles in part echo Article 10(c) of the Convention on Biological Diversity, which "means that traditional systems for environmental management and for the use of biological resources should be supported by conservation organizations *as long as* those systems contribute to the conservation and sustainable use of biodiversity" (emphasis added).

For those dedicated to securing self-determination for all peoples, however, the idea that a protected area can be created on lands claimed or occupied by peoples in the first place, particularly indigenous peoples, is unacceptable. One of the strongest supporters of people being able to plot their own
course in relation to protected areas is the London-based organization Survival International. It argues, "Protected areas should only exist if and where
indigenous peoples (and local people) want their lands to be part of such a
scheme. Parks and protected areas that deny indigenous peoples' territorial
rights and/or exclude indigenous peoples without their agreement should be
opposed and abolished" (Survival International forthcoming). The organization also points out that even though ownership and management of an area
by indigenous people may not ensure the sustainable use of resources, it does
not change the fact that the land is rightfully theirs. Similarly, Stevens (1997a)
has argued that indigenous communities should be able to refuse the designation of their lands as protected areas.

Implicit in the call for self-determination is the right to participation.
Many protected area programs have adopted "participatory" practices and the
principle of participation in decision making has achieved almost universal
acceptance (Magin et al. 2001). Like self-determination, however, securing
equal participation is not always easy. And agreeing on what it means and how
much there should be is challenging. Its purpose and role is even questioned;
observers debate whether participation is a means to realize biodiversity conservation or an end in and of itself (Drijver 1992; Little 1994; Dugelby and
Libby 1998). Others argue that providing opportunities for local communities
to participate in projects is not enough. For example, Wagner believes that a
community's role should be more authoritative such that external agencies
"should be requesting the opportunity to participate in local institutions of
environmental management" (Wagner 2001, 89). Still others are concerned
that many national agencies and international conservation organizations stop
short of power-sharing or power-ceding arrangements with communities in
and near protected areas (Alcorn 1994; Knudsen 1999; Neumann 2000). And
Pimbert and Pretty (1997) argue that participation is still seen as a way to
achieve other goals such that many conservation professionals limit the types
of participation they accept in protected areas management.

Different Peoples, Different Justices?

There is also the issue of recognizing differences between and among the
numerous types of people living in and near protected areas. Some of the
labels either given to or chosen by people include indigenous peoples, tribals,
aborigines, Indians, First People, natives, *adat* communities, minorities,
oppressed peoples, farmers, peasants, rural people, and resident peoples. And
in each locale there may be unique terms used to distinguish people as

"indigenous," often in relation to one another. For example, the expression "sons of the soil" is used in Indonesia and Malaysia to refer to Malays or "indigenous" Indonesians as opposed to Chinese and later immigrants (Bowen 2000). Should there be, and on what justification, different types of rights for different people in the vicinity of protected areas? Borrini-Feyerabend (1996, section 8) raises the issue by posing this question, "On what legal and ethical basis could national resources be exploited by local residents but denied to immigrants (e.g., those fleeing natural or social disaster from other parts of the country)? Who has the right to stop newcomers and declare that the "lifeboat is full"?" |Useb (2002:32), arguing on behalf of "indigenous peoples," asks if it is "appropriate to dispossess one group of people to meet the needs of another group?"

Most often it is people calling themselves or referred to as "indigenous peoples" who are best able to secure better conditions in relation to protected areas, drawing on a pool of international support, organized movements, and sophisticated networking. The term *indigenous peoples* is used to describe more than five thousand groups with an estimated population between 230 and 300 million. The most widely accepted definition of indigenous comes from the UN Working Group on Indigenous Populations, formulated in 1982; an abridged version being: "descendants of the original inhabitants of conquered territories possessing a minority culture and recognizing themselves as such" (Charles 1992 cited in Corntassel and Primeau 1995). A primary characteristic is that they are "preinvasion" and "precolonial" societies, designating all peoples who migrate later to an area nonindigenous (Peang-Meth 2002).

Of particular concern is whether any group of people living in an area prior to the establishment of an area should be afforded the same consideration as those with longer ties to a place, such as indigenous peoples. In a discussion on the right to self-determination, Peang-Meth (2002, 105) poses the question most directly: "New arrivals are not indigenous. But do they not have the same right to self-determination?" On the other hand, some indigenous peoples and supporters argue that indigenous peoples have special rights over others that have come more recently to an area—namely their special relationship to the land / area and their long-term experience of self-government (Bowen 2000).

A few observers have examined the needs and rights of all people living in and near protected areas (West and Brechin 1991; Nygren 2000a; Chatty and Colchester 2002). Ghimire and Pimbert (1997, 3) argue that "social development" for rural people living in or near protected areas is "crucial in its own right," pointing out that "rural people deserve to have access to the resources required to meet their basic needs, economic safety, and where possible, upward social mobility." And WRM (2002a, 4) argues, "long-standing inhabitants must have a voice in land use activities and changes."

Conflicting Rights?

Different emphases in international documents can lead to confusion or uncertainty in how to pursue protected area policies, for instance, the right to self-determination versus rights for nature. For example, Stegeborn (1996) points out that the creation of a national park in Sri Lanka was acceptable under the United Nations' World Charter for Nature but unacceptable when measured against the United Nations International Covenant on Civil and Political Rights, to which Sri Lanka is a signatory. The continuing challenge is how to balance both internationally binding human rights agreements and the mandates to protect biodiversity through protected areas.

Another area of concern is eminent domain. States often retain the right to eminent domain, taking property with fair compensation for the betterment of society. While the right to property is often protected, the law of states or international conventions also can provide for the subordination of property use for the interest of the larger society. Indeed, securing biodiversity conservation is often seen in this light, which for some justifies the need to limit the use of property or resources by people living in or near protected areas.

Framing the "Problems"

In addition to working out the details of socially just conservation, there is also a debate over how conservation "problems" are framed and discussed in the first place. Sometimes local people have been stereotyped as "rootless forest ravagers" (Nygren 2000b, 824), as "menace[s] to environmental conservation" (Geisler 2002, 80–81), and generally in need of conservation education. West (2001, 66) points out that at times people are "discursively produced as a threat" before solid data on their environmental impact is produced.

When reading conservation literature, there are often references to "invasions" of protected areas by "illegal squatters." Although at times people move to an area and illegally enter already established protected areas, often the "illegal squatters" are people that were living in the area prior to the area's establishment. They became illegal because the designation of the area changed; they are "yesterday's hunters, today's poachers" (Stegeborn 1996). Thus, in some cases, people living within their ancestral territories are labeled landless squatters, which is the case for Batwa who were living in what became the Bwindi and Mgahinga national parks in Uganda (Lewis 2000).

At times, conservation literature and discourse lacks sophisticated analysis and description of the people living in the vicinity of protected areas. Differences between subsistence practices and the relationships between land use and population are confused and terms misused (West 2001) and people are collapsed into general categories, such as "small-scale farmers," masking all social distinctions (Nygren 2000b:820). In the case of the Crater Mountain Wildlife Management Area, West argues that such misuse by NGOs limits the ability of those reading such literature to understand life in rural villages involved with the project and limits the NGOs own ability to understand local environmental uses (West 2001, 60). Ultimately, the narratives "become a reality and they become the filters through which future actions and practices are carried out" (West 2001, 61). Similarly, Nygren (2000b, 828) shows how viewing the relationship between local people and nature as destructive can provide justification to increase resource regulation, and Leach and Fairhead (2000) show how the production of certain forest use histories and deforestation discourses in Africa can be used to justify conservation agendas.

The collective outcry of numerous communities continues to fuel efforts to incorporate social justice and human rights into protected areas policies. As we secure biodiversity conservation and the protection of natural resources, we can also, as Zerner argues, "place nature management projects on the scales of justice" (Zerner 2000a, 17).

NOTES

1. The IUCN designates six protected area categories—from strict wilderness reserve to managed resource protected area. UNESCO has also developed the Biosphere Reserve. Within each state the actual management of a type of protected area may vary from the description offered by IUCN (Borrini-Feyerabend 1996).

2. Others have also explored connections between social justice, social movements, and the environment. See Hecht and Cockburn (1989); Gomez-Pompa and Kaus (1992); Merchant (1992); Kothari and Parajuli (1993); Johnston (1994); Cronon (1995); Sachs (1995); Guha and Martinez-Alier (1997); and Escobar (1998).

3. Early examples include Kitching's fight for an investigation into the creation of Serengeti National Park and the Maasai protest against its existence (Neumann 1998). Another was the work of Elwin who served as a "one-man pressure group for the rights of tribals" in India (Guha 1998, 326).

4. The earliest regional document signed was the Convention for the Protection of Human Rights and Fundamental Freedoms in 1950. The protection of property was secured in a later protocol (Council of Europe 1998).

5. Formerly the Task Force on Local Communities and Protected Areas, established in 1999.

6. Examples of forced removals include: Turnbull 1972; Gomm 1974; Marks 1984; Clad 1985; Fürer-Haimendorf 1986; Volkman 1986; Drijver 1992; Gadgil and Guha 1992; Alliance of Taiwan Aborigines 1993; Basappanavar 1993; Chandrasena 1993; Whyte 1993; Asiema and Situma 1994; Colchester 1994; Hitchcock 1994; Koch 1994; Lewis and Knight 1995; Nepal and Weber 1995; Neumann 1995; Sachs 1995; Hitchcock 1996; Stegeborn 1996; Stevens 1997b; Neumann 1998; Spence 1999; Survival International 1999; Lewis 2000; World Rainforest Movement 2000a; Abu-Rafia 2001; Down to Earth 2001; Jacoby 2001; Brockington 2002.

7. There seems to be less support for communities without historic rights and even those with secure rights might not avoid relocation. The World Bank's policy is that if "involuntary resettlement" is unavoidable, resettlement should be "executed as sustainable development programs" with assistance to improve or restore livelihoods (World Bank 2001). TLCEPA calls for "free and informed consent" of those affected with "long-term resettlement and rehabilitation measures" if under exceptional measures relocation is necessary (TLCEPA n.d.).

8. See Nietschmann (1997) for another case in Nicaragua concerning the Miskito Coral Reef Protected Area.

Chapter Three

Exploring the
Political Contours of Conservation

A Conceptual View of Power in Practice

PETER R. WILSHUSEN

This chapter explores the multiple dimensions of power. This is essential if one is to better understand the contested nature of biodiversity conservation in "developing" regions around the globe. By focusing on biodiversity politics, it presents a synthesis of theoretical concepts that can begin to explain both the positive and negative outcomes associated with conservation and development programs. In this sense, I attempt to provide a conceptual frame for this section of the book on social conflict associated with biodiversity conservation and contribute to the literature in political ecology.

First, I present political ecology as an overarching frame of inquiry for exploring the politics of natural resource access and use at multiple levels over time. While the political ecology literature offers diverse perspectives suggesting how extralocal factors shape local resource use, it lacks an explicit conceptual synthesis that joins the symbolic and material dimensions of power and domination. Second, I situate the discussion of power that forms the core of this chapter in the context of social theoretical debates regarding the dual nature of social structures as well as the material and symbolic dimensions of social phenomena. Third, I begin constructing a synthesis of perspectives on power, drawing primarily on the work of Weber (1978 [1968] and Lukes

(1974). Finally, I examine the social structural elements of power, looking at the ways in which institutions and cultural practices shape political action reflecting the writing of Friedland and Alford (1991) and Foucault (1972, 1980, 2000). The balance of power relationships among diverse groups in conservation and development arenas depends in part upon the degree to which institutions and practices enable some participants to advance their interests while limiting others in the pursuit of their objectives. Conflict tends to occur where competing institutional and discursive practices interface in the same political arena, creating contradictory claims to legitimate action.

UNCOVERING THE POWER IN POLITICAL ECOLOGY

Political ecology has emerged as a fast-growing and important research agenda for those interested in probing the social and political processes tied to environmental change. As such, it does not present one coherent framework or set of theoretical propositions. Rather, it presents related areas of intellectual inquiry drawing on perspectives from both the natural and social sciences (Blaikie and Brookfield 1987; Blaikie 1994; Bryant and Bailey 1997). The main question posed within political ecology concerns the political interactions and outcomes associated with environmental management, particularly in "developing" countries. The central emphasis on politics directs attention to the struggles among diverse actors over natural resource access and control (Carney 1996; Moore 1996; Neumann 1998; Peluso 1992; see also Vayda and Walters 1999).

Those writing under the rubric of political ecology generally agree on three fundamental tracts of analysis that consider scale, time, and, less explicitly, power. First, regarding scale of analysis, Blaikie (1985) proposes an integrated "place-based" and "non-place-based" inquiry, which begins with land-use activities in a specific local context and traces the larger social forces that impact land-use decisions. Non-place-based inquiry extends the scope of analysis beyond the local setting to the larger political economic structures and processes linked to regional, national, or even global systems (see also Vayda 1983). Second, a historical perspective offers an explanation of past events and processes of reproduction and change in order to better understand current conditions (Blaikie 1995).

The third tract of analysis, power, is central to understanding resource access and control but is implicitly incorporated rather than explicitly defined in most analyses. Taken chronologically, the political ecology literature presents three perspectives on power including Marxian political economy, actor-centered political analysis, and post-structuralism. Early works in political ecology such as Hecht and Cockburn (1989) focused on the political economic forces responsible for persistent rural poverty and ecological degradation. Building on insights from work in peasant studies (Wolf 1972, 1982), this perspective sheds light on the state and market forces that seemingly forced poor rural producers to degrade their lands. While this approach avoided laying blame exclusively with the victims of environmental degradation, it tended to grant excessive explanatory power to social structures.

Partially in response, more recent studies have focused on local political processes (actor-centered politics) tied to struggles for resource access and control. While some works emphasize resource control strategies used by the state and capitalist interests (Neumann and Schroeder 1995; Stonich 1993), others look more closely at internal community struggles (Moore 1996, chapter 6). To a certain degree, Bryant and Bailey (1997) have captured these arguments in their action-centered approach to "Third World" political ecology.

The third perspective on power emphasizes the symbolic realm, calling for a "post-structuralist" political ecology that can join the sensitivities of cultural studies with new social movements and related elements of civil society (Peet and Watts 1996).[1] Escobar (1995, 1996) in particular, suggests how understandings (discourses) of sustainable development shape power relationships by legitimating certain explanations and approaches to nature and economy to the exclusion of others. From this point of view, power is not so much the imposition of one actor's will upon another but instead the combined potential as well as the inherent boundaries present in discursive practices (including, most importantly, the historical "baggage" that these carry).

All three of these perspectives on power in the political ecology literature—political economy, action-centered politics, and post-structuralism—represent important conceptual anchoring points that I will refer to in the sections below. In attempting to synthesize different views on power, I seek to bridge the gap between the largely materialist understandings found in the political economic and actor-centered approaches on one hand and the predominantly symbolic perspective found in post-structural political ecology on the other. Before discussing different perspectives on power, however, it is first necessary to delve briefly into wider social theoretical debates on the dual nature of social structures as well as the material and symbolic dimensions of social phenomena.

CRITICAL SOCIAL THEORY AND THE DUAL NATURE OF STRUCTURE

How can one make sense of power dynamics? To start answering this question requires an understanding of a fundamental dialectical relationship between agency and structure. It posits that *agency,* which refers to transformative human action, and *social structure* (defined below) are mutually constitutive (Giddens 1984). In other words, social structures shape people's practices and people's practices produce and reproduce social structures. In the case of a government working to pass a new wildlife protection law, both agency and structure are important. On one hand, numerous citizens' groups and government organizations would work politically to draft proposals, gain support, and make alliances (agency). On the other hand, all these actors would be bound in their pursuits by existing laws, scientific knowledge, and conservation strategies (social structures). This relational focus suggests that agency and structure work in concert.

Sewell (1992, 19) defines structures as "mutually sustaining schema and resources that empower and constrain social action and that tend to be reproduced by that social action." The first facet of structure comprises the *schema*—cognitive cues, scripts, and/or procedures—that frames interpretation and action. Schemata operate at varying "depths" ranging from "shallow," consciously invoked procedures to "deep" metaphorical oppositions that enter into cognitive processes at a preconscious level (DiMaggio 1997). The second facet of structure encompasses human and nonhuman *resources*. They represent the media of power and are unevenly distributed. Examples of human resources are knowledge, physical strength, and dexterity. Nonhuman resources might include information, rocks, money, or legal codes. Social structures take on numerous forms but legal codes present a prominent example. Mexico's 1997 forest law regulates and promotes both natural forest and plantation management. The law presents procedures for establishing plantations ("shallow" schemata) that, in part, encourage large-scale production on private property ("deeper" schemata). In addition, it provides for resources such as funds (nonhuman resource) and technical knowledge (human resource) in the form of two government-sponsored programs.

This distinction is important because political actors may be relatively more aware of the boundaries of "shallow" schemata as compared to "deep" schemata. One would expect to see more active political bargaining or negotiation of ideas or organizing principles associated with "shallow" schemata and little or no intentional negotiation surrounding changes in "deep" schemata. Given this definition of structure, one further qualification remains that accounts for structural—and thus social—change. Rather than forming a monolithic unit, social structures are multiple and overlapping. As a result they feature contradictions that represent the source of social conflict. In response to these perceived contradictions, both concerted bargaining and routine activities generate contested arrangements wherein certain schemata and resources carry greater legitimacy and lines of access compared to others. More commonly, deep schemata and resources (structures) provide meaning for action in a way that is unquestioned and taken for granted, producing fractured, slowly shifting yet relatively stable matrices of power relationships (social order).

In addition to the mutually reinforcing relationship between agency and structure, political practices feature both a symbolic and material dimension.

The question of material versus symbolic interpretations of social phenomena lies at the heart of philosophical debates currently coursing through the social sciences and is fundamental to any consideration of power (Calhoun 1995). In many forms of political analysis, the historical and spatial boundaries of "the ways we think" are left unquestioned. In these approaches, our understandings of reality as those material conditions external to the human subject are considered to be universally the same for every person across time and space. Many scholars challenge this division between the material and the ideal as arbitrary, claiming that humans construct their understandings of phenomena in accordance with cultural practices (this perspective is often called "social constructivism" after Berger and Luckmann 1966). They argue that even our most basic explanatory concepts are human symbolic representations, mediated by cognition and situated in time and space. Those who adopt the latter view generally refer to their work as "critical studies" since it critiques those concepts, such as "modernity" or "progress," which tend to be taken for granted.

The difference between the materialist and symbolic aspects of power is best described by example. Materialist understandings of power relations focus on the more obvious "concrete" instances where, for example, a patrol of forest guards captures a group illegally cutting wood. While seemingly a routine and legitimate enforcement exercise, we cannot fully understand the power dynamics of this encounter without looking into the symbolic aspects that guide action. In this case, the symbolic side would include the laws, ecological knowledge, cultural practices, and other factors that lead to the intervention. The legitimacy of the act, therefore, depends largely on the symbolic realm of rules, cultural norms, and ideas among other things. For example, would enforcement be seen as equally legitimate if the wood cutters were illegally harvesting precious teak trees versus collecting dead branches for fuelwood? Understanding how and why such routine activities reflect and generate complex conflictual and nonconflictual power dynamics requires a specific set of concepts that can account for the historical contingency, relationality, as well as the material and symbolic dimensions of social phenomena.

POWER-OVER: CONFLICT, EXCLUSION, AND CONTROL

Lukes's (1974) widely cited "three-dimensional" perspective on power offers an initial framework for making sense of political processes and outcomes. His formulation represents a genealogy of contemporary conceptualizations of power beginning with simple democratic pluralism (one-dimensional) and extending to nonparticipation (two-dimensional) and manipulation of interests (three-dimensional). Although debate lingers regarding the voluntarist bent of the two- and three-dimensional approaches, each of these perspectives largely presumes intentionality on the part of social actors. In general, Lukes's materialist framework overlaps with the action-centered politics perspective and, to a lesser extent, the political economic view associated with the political ecology literature.

The one-dimensional approach holds that people recognize and act upon grievances in open political arenas on their own behalf or through their representatives. It assumes that politics generates observable conflict, which is the result of tensions among competing subjective interests (often referred to as "pluralism") (Clegg 1989; Lukes 1974). The two-dimensional approach to power represents a critique of key assumptions found in the pluralists' focus on participation in decision making. It emphasizes how "nonparticipation" and "non-decisions" play into political processes. Whereas one-dimensional explanations attribute nonparticipation to the disinterest or failings of the excluded party, the two-dimensional approach argues that certain issues are actively suppressed, leaving a broad range of potential participants outside the political arena (Bachrach and Baratz 1962, 1963). Although intentional acts of exclusion lie at the core of this concept, the two-dimensional view on power can also refer to institutionally based procedures or "rules of the game" that benefit some groups at the expense of others (Bachrach and Baratz 1970; Steinmo et al. 1992; Thelen 1999). I return to this institutionally based understanding of power below.

Lukes's (1974) own critique of the first two perspectives emerges as the three-dimensional approach to power. In this case, power extends beyond pluralism and nonparticipation to include circumstances where one group manipulates another group's perceived desires, possibilities, and strategies. Whereas the first two dimensions of power presuppose resistance based upon perceived grievances, Lukes argues that, in some cases, no observable conflict or reaction may occur since the affected party's conceptions of the issues at stake have been altered. Lukes's three-dimensional approach further recognizes that social structural forces and historical patterns create power effects that cannot be explained by "individualistic" or "behavioralist" interpretations (Gaventa 1980; Lukes 1974, 1986). This structural interpretation of the third dimension of power resonates closely with Gramsci's (1971) notion of hegemony, which contemplates a form of ideological control operating through traditions, myths, and conventional morality.

Like most treatises on power, Lukes's "radical view" has its roots in Max Weber's political sociology, relying largely on an "impositional" definition of the term *power* as well as the closely related concepts of authority and legitimacy. For Weber (1978 [1968]), power connoted the ability of one person to impose his or her will despite resistance. In this regard, he established a tight focus that highlighted observable episodes and outcomes wherein parties willfully act to resolve conflicts of interest. A number of key points follow from this definition of power. According to Weber, most if not all social interaction is political to some extent (Bendix 1960). Therefore, that which counts as "political" extends well beyond the conventional institutions associated with the state. Further, the concept of power is relational. As a result, it only takes on meaning when considering the advantage that one party holds with respect to another. Thus, social actors do not possess or gain power per se (although they employ "power resources") but occupy a position of advantage, disadvantage, or equality relative to others in a given time and place. At the same time, Weber made clear that most political interactions are not accompanied by overt conflict since social actors invoke different forms of authority to legitimize their claims. Authority is defined as *legitimate power* where *legitimacy* is "the property of a situation or behavior that is defined by a set of social norms as correct or appropriate" (Scott 1998, 305; Weber 1978 [1968]).

Weber's focus on authority as a reciprocal relationship in which one party possesses the "power to command" and another party has the "duty to obey" provides the core of his definition of domination proper (or "domination by virtue of authority") (Weber 1978 [1968], 943). In this sense, he saw domination as a continuous, structured pattern of control that does not necessarily require the exertion of power (c.f. West 1994). Weber identified a second form of domination emerging from a "constellation of interests that develops on a formally free market" (Bendix 1960, 290). This latter form was "based upon influence derived exclusively from the possession of goods or marketable skills guaranteed in some way and acting upon the conduct of those dominated, who remain, however, formally free and are motivated simply by the pursuit of their own interests" (Weber 1978 [1968], 943). Since Weber was largely concerned with the institutionalization of a distinctly modern, rational-legal order in society, he focused on domination based in established authority ("domination proper"). He thus placed less emphasis on domination through a constellation of interests such as market-based monopolies.[2] This is apparent in his extensive treatment of the bureaucracy as a modern organizational form (Weber 1978 [1968]). Weberian perspectives on power-domination inform numerous works relevant to this book's focus on the politics of biodiversity conservation, including critical studies of state bureaucracies that point to particular forms of domination. These works build on Weber's formulation by detailing cases in which informal authority, illegitimate power, and relationships of domination detract from common or public interests (Selznick 1984 [1949]; West 1982).

Peluso's (1992) historically informed study of resource control regimes in Central Java's teak forests offers a richly detailed account that illustrates Lukes's three-dimensional view of power and Weber's understandings of power-domination including threats, sanctions, and to some extent ideological control. She disentangles strands of rational-legal power by investigating the state's coercive or control organizations, noting their place within the state apparatus, their connections to other social groups, and their effectiveness.

Peluso (1992) characterizes state domination of agrarian communities in terms of land, species, and labor control. A fourth type, ideological control, is embodied in formal laws, official discourse, and past and present practices that instill fear.

Control of land and species was manifested in the state's formal authority to determine land and tree use as well as enforce laws aimed at protecting economically and ecologically valuable resources. Until the mid-1990s, Java's State Forestry Corporation (SFC) strictly controlled all activities on forested lands including mining, firewood collection, and research. As a quasi-military government organization, it carried out routine preventive measures such as patrolling and maintaining security checkpoints. The agency also regularly staged armed enforcement activities, such as raids and stakeouts, via three special police forces. Particularly in teak forests, the SFC placed tight controls on species classification, tenure, and marketing in order to consolidate land claims and guarantee a monopoly on the highly lucrative teak timber trade. In addition to controlling the distribution and planting of teak seeds and seedlings, the SFC dictated which agricultural crops farmers could plant between tree rows. The agency further controlled all aspects of marketing and transport of teak, including those trees grown on private lands. Regarding labor controls, the SFC regulated both formal and informal activities on forested lands. Field foresters managed all formal labor opportunities and since there was a significant labor surplus, they could threaten to refuse jobs for those villagers who did not comply with resource use rules. Seasonal forest labor jobs such as reforestation, logging, resin tapping, and log hauling provided important sources of income and thus were coveted by villagers. The SFC also controlled informal labor activities related to lime production, game hunting, and fuelwood collection via official permits and informal permission granted by field foresters.

Interestingly, Peluso (1992, 19) found that each state resource control strategy elicited parallel forms of resistance from forest-dependent villagers including reappropriation of land and species, tree sabotage, strikes and other work actions, as well as "cultures of resistance." Thus, despite its relative power advantages and wide-ranging formal authority, the state did not fully dictate resource access and use; villagers resisted consistently, if subtly, to what they perceived to be illegitimate control measures that ran against customary laws, practices, and beliefs. From the perspective of the state forest service, however, these responses represented forest "crimes" such as "squatting" on state land, "stealing" state-owned trees, and "sabotaging" state-run reforestation programs. They broke the law by striking and acted "ignorant" or "backward" by adhering to traditional cultural practices.

In Peluso's rendering, power-domination emerges primarily as an imposition of wills shaped by wider political economies. The control strategies employed by Java's State Forestry Corporation (SFC) helped maintain a timber economy that was Indonesia's second greatest foreign exchange earner after oil during the 1980s. This suggests that, in addition to the imposition of wills that forms the core of Weber's definition of power, institutional arrangements and cultural practices linked primarily to the state and the market enable and constrain action strategies. Institutional and cultural shaping of power relationships appears most clearly, for example, in Peluso's (1992) identification of "cultures of control and resistance," which suggest a set of routine practices that have remained generally stable over time despite institutional changes from a colonial to an independent state regime.

By conceptually exploring notions of power-domination as fields of force emanating from social structures, comprising institutional and cultural expressions, it is possible to see "accretions" of power relationships over time independent of episodes of conflict or control. Eric Wolf (1999, 5) has referred to this set of relationships as "structural power." He writes, "By this I mean the power manifest in relationships that not only operates within settings and domains but also organizes and orchestrates the settings themselves, and that specifies the direction and distribution of energy flows." To make greater sense of structural understandings of power requires a deeper examination of structural power's institutional and cultural expressions. In what follows, I pursue this line of inquiry drawing from two, related theoretical perspectives—institutional theory and post-structuralism—that fill out a conceptual framework for viewing political processes and outcomes associated with biodiversity conservation. First, I discuss how institutional arrangements enable and constrain human action both in material and symbolic terms. This follows a perspective typically referred to as "new institutionalism" (Powell and DiMaggio 1991). Second, I explore cultural expressions of structural power drawing primarily on theories of discourse found in the writings of Michel Foucault (1972, 2000) and prevalent in post-structural perspectives in political ecology (Escobar 1996; Peet and Watts 1996).

POWER IN PRACTICE: INSTITUTIONS AS CONSTRAINTS, CAPACITIES, AND CONTRADICTIONS

While questions of power are predicated upon human agency, a broad understanding of power dynamics necessitates an examination of how social structures enable and constrain action. The structural realm of power may comprise constructs such as race, gender, class, ethnicity as well as institutions such as the state, the market, family, or religion. While all of these manifestations of social structure can impact political relationships in a given context, together they represent routine formal and informal rules, norms, and procedures that inform action by presenting the basis for authority. In addition, diverse social structures produce identifiable but constantly shifting boundaries that position social actors in a particular arena. We find that institutions present certain "logics" and that contravening institutional logics produce conflict and social change when they interface in the same political arena.

Institutionally based power, then, is not so much the imposition of one's will as in the Weberian definition but more the enactment of everyday social practices linked to rules (or "schema" in Sewell's theory of structure) typically understood in legal, economic, religious, familial, or other terms (Bourdieu 1977). This understanding of institutions as routinized social practices represents a much broader definition than many interpretations that appear in the literature. In terms of the three understandings of power mentioned above, institutionally based power corresponds roughly to the political economic perspective, which focuses on the social structural relationships that shape modes of production in a given context. However, while eminently useful as an explanatory frame, the political economy lens presents two types of biases. First, it emphasizes the domains of the market and the state to the exclusion of other institutions such as religion and family. Second, political economy typically presents purely materialist interpretations that ignore the symbolic facet of institutions. Friedland and Alford's (1985, 1991) writings overcome these biases by offering a broader view of the institutional realm.

In theorizing society as an interinstitutional system, Friedland and Alford (1991, 232) conceptualize institutions as "supra-organizational patterns of activity through which humans conduct their material life in time and space, and symbolic systems through which they categorize that activity and infuse it with meaning."[3] In "concrete" or instrumental terms, this understanding of institutions reinforces the dualism of social structures advanced by Giddens (1984) and Sewell (1992). In one sense, it means that social actors construct the institutions that govern human behavior in a given setting and that they intentionally change them over time. In another sense, however, it suggests that social actors do not completely replace one set of institutions with another but instead refashion rules, norms, and procedures using existing institutional repertoires (Steinmo et al. 1992). In the broadest sense, institutions represent a "mediating concept" or "bridge" that situates human action in society (Friedland and Alford 1991). This is important because the types of possible political interactions including strategies and instruments of power and authority vary institutionally as well as temporally and spatially.

As symbolic systems, each institutional order in a given society features a central logic or set of organizing principles that inform social practices. Friedland and Alford (1991, 248–49) note that "these institutional logics are symbolically grounded, organizationally structured, politically defended, and technically and materially constrained, and hence have specific historical limits." By way of example, they offer that the central logic of capitalism surrounds accumulation and commodification. Given these organizing principles, capitalist enterprises use commodification to attach monetary prices to both material and nonmaterial things. They are unable to enact exchanges in the absence of pricing.

To the extent that the institutions of society are multiple, overlapping, and contradictory, they present potential sources of conflict. "Some of the most important struggles between groups, organizations, and classes are over the appropriate relationships between institutions, and by which institutional logic different activities should be regulated and to which categories persons apply" (Friedland and Alford 1991, 256). Perennial debates over joining conservation and development in rural communities provide an excellent example of contravening institutional logics. Differing opinions regarding the extent to which biodiversity conservation programs should incorporate democratic governance and links to markets in addition to conventional state-led protectionism each present legitimacy claims based in the moral primacy of nature protection relative to social justice. The institutional terrain of conservation and development interventions features nested orders of the rules, norms, and practices that guide social action. At one level are the scientific practices associated with such disciplines as biology and ecology that define the global biodiversity crisis as well as many of the strategies for its alleviation. On another level one finds the formal legal codes of nation-states that classify criminal acts such as poaching as well as the legal-rational bureaucracies that implement programs and enforce laws in the state's name. Rational-legal definitions of property rights may contravene customary law at the local level, however, causing conflicts over the legitimacy of resource access and use claims. Indeed, resource-use rights may be rooted simultaneously in practices governed by the state, market, family, and religion. At yet another level, one might explore the tensions produced by introducing elements of a market economy for "sustainable development" in areas characterized primarily by local bartering, gift exchange, and subsistence production (Chase Smith 1995).

Brechin's examination (chapter 4) of political tensions surrounding protected areas management in South Sumatra, Indonesia suggests how contravening customary and rational-legal social, economic, and political institutions impact decision making regarding conservation and sustainable development. At one level, contemporary struggles over access and use of natural resources between local villagers and the state reflected the progressive dismantling of the clan-based political structure (or *marga*) first under Dutch colonial rule and later by state bureaucracies following Indonesia's formal independence in 1949. Before the colonial regime, the *marga* system provided a widely accepted set of customary social rules and norms that governed forest access and the use of both timber and non-timber forest products. Over time, however, modern rational-legal bureaucracies gained power over forests and imposed vastly different sets of rules that restricted villagers' access to and use of forest resources. Despite the state's formal authority to manage forests, local people viewed restrictions on resource use as illegitimate since they ignored customary practices and constrained their livelihoods. As a result, villagers resorted to "illegal" practices such as cutting trees, removing fuelwood, and extracting other products such as honey from state forests in order to maintain both their cultural identities and rural livelihoods.

As the South Sumatra case suggests, the boundaries of legitimate social practice in large part are defined institutionally. Whereas extractive activities were labeled as forest crimes under the institutional logic of state-run forest management, they were legitimate foraging practices within the customary rules of the *marga* system. To further examine how contradictory institutional practices lead to conflict, it will be necessary to look more deeply at the conceptual logics or narrative understandings that constitute ideas, theories, methodologies, and strategies for action.

POWER-DISCOURSE: WHERE THE CULTURAL MEETS THE POLITICAL

The cultural domain of power refers specifically to those symbolic practices associated predominantly with language use that shape our understandings (Wuthnow 1987). Power in this sense refers to the combined potential as well as the inherent boundaries present in discursive practices. Similar to the enactment of social practices in the institutional characterization of power above, acts of signification (the process of assigning meaning) create more or less complex webs of power relationships. Using Alford and Friedland's (1985) terms, if the institutional realm of power constitutes the "rules of the game," the cultural realm would be the game itself. In this sense, critical reflection of "the game" suggests turning attention to those practices that are simultaneously filled with and generative of meaning. One perspective that explores domains of discourse is loosely labeled "post-structuralism" since it critically analyzes the symbolic realm by historicizing and contextualizing knowledge constructs. Exploration along these lines uncovers the merging of knowledge and power.

The turn to post-structuralism in political ecology is most closely associated with the work of Peet and Watts (1996) and Escobar (1995, 1996), who draw on Michel Foucault's theories regarding discourse. These authors adopt Barnes and Duncan's (1992, 8) definition of discourses as "frameworks that embrace particular combinations of narratives, concepts, ideologies and signifying practices, each relevant to a particular realm of social action."[4] Post-structuralism's emphasis on the use of language centers on discursive practices of representation. Following this perspective, the everyday manner in which social actors articulate their interpretations, and thus generate knowledge, produce power effects since by attaching meaning to events, they categorize and relate people and things artificially (Foucault 1980). This implies that explanations, understandings, and ways of thinking do not emerge from a universally shared order but are constructed over time and space. In this sense, truths are intersubjectively shared interpretations rather than simple reflections of a universal external reality.

According to Foucault (1972), discourses present boundaries that correspond to modes of thought, logics, explanations, or methodologies that can be analyzed as discrete "formations." Like institutional logics, discursive formations feature internal and external contradictions that can produce conflict. More often however, they represent unquestioned explanations and ways of thinking that maintain social continuity. Indeed, discursive formations originate in and reflect institutional settings while institutional logics emerge within specific explanatory frameworks and modes of thinking constructed through discursive practices. Discursive formations, as dynamic entities in time and space, are always contested on some level, either with respect to their internal structures or in relation to competing formations. Thus, even those discursive formations that are so pervasive as to be nominally regarded as "hegemonic" feature internal and external contradictions such that resistance or alternative conceptualization is always possible.

In promoting a post-structural political ecology, Peet, Watts, and Escobar are most concerned with how discursive formations produce patterns of domination by favoring one set of understandings and suppressing others. Following trends in critical studies of modernity and the imposition of Western reason through colonialism, these authors point to the discourse of international development as shaping "societal practices, meanings, and cultural contents" in line with modernist narratives regarding order and progress (Escobar 1995; Ferguson 1990; Peet and Watts 1996, 17). This process is closely associated with the spread of institutions such as capitalism and the rational-legal bureaucracies of the state. Thus, at the same time as it emphasizes one set of understandings, a discursive formation "disallows certain themes, is marked by absences, silences, repressions, [and] marginalized statements" (Peet and Watts 1996, 16).

Sundberg's (1999) study of dominant explanations of deforestation in Guatemala's Petén region suggests how problem definition (through discursive practices) shaped power relations in the Maya Biosphere Reserve by emphasizing land clearing from peasant swidden agriculture and ignoring the impacts of government colonization programs and the logging industry. As a result, numerous international conservation interventions in the reserve dedicated vast resources to curbing slash and burn agriculture without attending to larger forces such as the growth of cattle ranching and illegal logging, which were politically more difficult to address. Indeed, by turning attention away from larger political economic factors that may have been directly and indirectly driving environmental change, Sundberg argues that dominant conservation discourse depoliticized discussions and responses aimed at nature protection.

The most extensive treatment of post-structuralist political ecology to date appears in the writings of Arturo Escobar (1999, 1996). In particular, he presents a conceptual framework for an "anti-essentialist political ecology" that identifies three "regimes of nature."[5] In probing the human-nature interface, this approach historically analyzes concepts of "nature" and "society" that have been left unquestioned. In his own terms he focuses on the "manifold articulations of biology and history and the cultural mediations through which such articulations are necessarily established" (Escobar 1999, 5). In this sense, Escobar seeks to uncover the multiple social constructions of "nature" that result from human interaction with "biophysical reality" over time.

Post-structural perspectives critically analyze the narratives that guide human action, encompassing constructs and modes of reasoning that are typically taken for granted. As with any field of social interaction, conservation and development features numerous causal narratives associated with "protected areas," "conservation," "sustainable development," "local people," "buffer zones," and—as Escobar's discussion uncovers—"nature" that are embedded in wider discursive frames. Discursive practices produce and reproduce unequal power relationships by ordering and shaping human understandings of social interactions vis-à-vis the biophysical realm. They can also ultimately represent a source of conflict when contravening understandings of self, others, rights, resources, etc. interface in the same field of practice. To the extent that post-structural analysis focuses on the symbolic or discursive realm, it de-emphasizes human agency, the presumed basis of politics. Yet, scholars have applied post-structuralist perspectives in terms of "cultural politics" by focusing on struggles over the meanings tied to identity, social practices, and the process by which these meanings are articulated (Jordon and Weedon 1995; Laclau and Mouffe 1985).[6] In the context of a large biodiversity conservation project in Colombia's Pacific coastal region, for example, Afro-Colombian and indigenous groups linked to a broad-based social movement worked to reframe concepts and methodologies associated with territory, nature, and culture (chapter 5).

Underlying the struggles over meaning emphasized in much of the literature on cultural politics, however, are the political cultures that, at a certain level, constitute power relationships. In line with (and in part informing) Escobar's (1999) anti-essentialist approach, Laclau and Mouffe's (1985) post-structural perspective focuses on the political dimension of identity formation. They argue that identity, or the subjective understanding of self, is a relational and historical process that emerges from a recognition of difference relative to other actors. The tensions or antagonisms resulting from the experience of difference are constitutive of social life. As a result, identities are not fixed or given but are constantly being negotiated and rearticulated based on subjective experiences of difference. Congruous with related strains in cultural analysis, post-structural political analysis thus "de-centers" the subject by suggesting that identity formation results from historical discursive practices beyond the bounds of any one individual. In drawing on Foucault's understandings of discourse to problematize conventional notions of identity, Laclau and Mouffe further underscore the ways in which acts of signification simultaneously reflect and constitute power relationships. Foucault (1979) referred to the normalization of such power relationships manifested in obedient subjects as disciplinary power.

CONCLUSION: CARTOGRAPHIES OF POWER AND DOMINATION

In constructing a broad theoretical synthesis on power in practice, I have attempted to contribute to a more explicit statement of the multiple dimensions of power related to biodiversity conservation. In this sense, I do not intend to propose one grand, universal theory but rather a continuing, open dialogue that explores how diverse strands of social theory can inform political ecology's central problematic—an understanding of material and symbolic dimensions of social and political processes tied to environmental change. Throughout this chapter, I have only indirectly touched on the role of nature except to implicitly recognize it as a biophysical resource and constraint. With Escobar's (1999) presentation of an anti-essentialist view of nature, culturally constitutive and historically contingent understandings of nature also come to the fore. Indeed, political and cultural analyses of social processes associated with environmental change often elicit queries along the lines of, "where is the 'ecology' in political ecology?" Although this question is important, I have chosen not to engage it centrally in this discussion (for debates on directions in political ecology see Vayda and Walters 1999 and responses to Escobar 1999 in a special issue of *Current Anthropology*). Instead, I have elected to pursue an equally important line of inquiry that asks, "Where are the 'politics' in political ecology?"

Since action-centered explanations of power have been widely discussed in the literature, I have focused on the structural realm of politics in an attempt to map out some of the less obvious modes of power and domination. Although tightly interwoven with the concept of agency, I separate out two broad constructs of structure—institutions and discourse—because in combination they present historical trajectories or legacies that can be analyzed as heuristic devices independently from human action. When viewed as symbolic systems, these two components of social structures present multiple degrees or "depths" of schema that emerge out of institutional logics and discursive formations.

Viewed in this way, we can characterize power in practice as a combination of "everyday" routine activities and concerted bargaining that takes place within matrices of power relationships constituted by schemata and resources. In other words, power relationships are continuously enacted and transformed within the symbolic and material limits of a given set of institutional and discursive practices. This understanding of politics does not erase the importance of impositional understandings of power like the one advanced by Weber (1978 [1968]), but it does embrace a much wider domain of social interaction, more akin to his broader focus on the role of modern institutions and patterns of domination via a constellation of interests. In addition to favoring the material realm of human experience, agency-centered interpretations of power are episodic in that they emphasize only those instances when actors intentionally impose their will upon others despite resistance (Clegg 1989). Drawing primarily on the work of Foucault (1980), power dynamics comprise a much broader web of social interaction, including those everyday cultural practices often ignored in political analysis.

As the chapters in this section of the book illustrate, conservation interventions are deeply political. This becomes especially clear when we consider that conservation programs dedicate proportionately large amounts of financial and other resources in often remote rural areas in "developing" countries that may only partially participate in the principal institutions and discursive practices of the modern era: the rational-legal state and the liberal "free" market. As a result, the potential for strong resistance and conflict is higher compared to other political arenas because of the sharp contradictions in institutional and discursive logics that emerge. The social and political complexities that I describe in this chapter help to explain why conservation programs produce resistance and conflict. Assuming that nonintervention is not an option given the accelerated loss of biological diversity globally, the main question that surfaces in response is, How can conservation interventions minimize conflict and negative social impacts and maximize social justice? The chapters in the second half of this volume explore this question.

NOTES

A more detailed exposition of the theoretical discussion found in this chapter can be found in Wilshusen (2003). Thanks to Pat West, Peggy Somers, Jill Belsky, Tom Rudel, Crystal Fortwangler, Michael Hathaway, and Nora Haenn for their comments.

1. Post-structuralism covers critical debates and discussions that have emerged in response to structuralism and semiotics. For a discussion pertaining to the literature on power see Clegg (1989).

2. Weber (1978 [1968], 946) writes, "[W]e shall use the term domination exclusively in that narrower sense which excludes from its scope those situations in which

power has its source in a formally free interplay of interested parties such as occurs especially in the market. . . . [I]n our terminology *domination* shall be identical with *authoritarian power of command*" (emphasis in the original). For a discussion of "domination proper" see Guenther Roth's introduction to *Economy and Society* (LXXXVIII–XC).

3. The authors' further discussion adds nicely to this definition (232): "The central institutions of contemporary Western societies—capitalism, family, bureaucratic state, democracy, and Christianity—are simultaneously symbolic systems and material practices. Thus institutions are symbolic systems which have nonobservable, absolute, transrational referents and observable social relations which concretize them. Through these concrete social relations, individuals and organizations strive to achieve their ends, but they also make life meaningful and reproduce those symbolic systems. Social relations always have both instrumental and ritual content."

4. As Escobar (1996, 46) notes, "The post-structural analysis of discourse is not only a linguistic theory; it is a social theory, a theory of the production of social reality which includes the analysis of representations as social facts inseparable from what is commonly thought of as 'material reality.' Post-structuralism focuses on the role of language in the construction of social reality it treats language not as a reflection of 'reality' but as constitutive of it."

5. Escobar (1999, 5) describes the construct *regime of nature* in the following terms: "The nature regimes can be seen as constituting a structured social totality made up of multiple and irreducible relations, without a center or origin, that is, a field of articulations. The identity of each regime is the result of discursive articulations—with biological, social, and cultural couplings—that take place in an over field of discursivity wider than any particular regime."

6. Alvarez et al. (1998, 7) note, "[c]ultural politics [is] the process enacted when sets of social actors shaped by, and embodying, different cultural meanings and practices come into conflict with each other. Culture is political because meanings are constitutive of processes that, implicitly or explicitly, seek to redefine social power. [It unfolds when actors] deploy alternative conceptions of woman, nature, race, economy, democracy, or citizenship that unsettle dominant cultural meanings."

Chapter Four

Wandering Boundaries and Illegal Residents

The Political Ecology of Protected Area Deforestation in South Sumatra Indonesia from 1979 to 1992

STEVEN R. BRECHIN

In this chapter, I use a political ecology approach to explore political barriers to effective protected area management in Indonesia. Political ecology attempts to capture multiple layers of complexity in explaining environmental degradation and the politics of resource access and control. This is accomplished by focusing on several scales or levels of analysis simultaneously, including historical events and institutional relationships that shape ecological outcomes (chapter 3). I tie together local, national, and international events and structures to better understand the complex web of interactions that resulted in increased deforestation of protected forests in the Lahat District of South Sumatra Province, Indonesia, throughout the 1980s. Forest management politics generated a number of severe, unintended consequences for both local people and forests.

The management challenges for the protected forests of Lahat District can be summarized by briefly reviewing the following five points. Deforestation of these forest areas increased rapidly in the early 1980s when (1) the central government started replacing traditional local authorities with bureaucrats

of the modern state. This change in governmental administration diminished enforcement potential of the protected areas in South Sumatra. (2)
This institutional change might have mattered little in the forest management efforts had the price of coffee not reached new highs due to two consecutive years of frost in Brazil, half a world away. Further complications
arose in the local management effort when (3) national government planners unilaterally pursued "rational" actions from their comfortable air-con-
ditioned offices in the capital city, miles away. With a stroke of a pen, they
greatly expanded the country's protected areas. Communities that were at
one moment living legally outside of the protected areas suddenly found
themselves residing illegally within them. (4) Institutionally, all people
residing within or otherwise cultivating protected forests areas were viewed
as illegal residents that had to be removed by the government. However, not
all local people were victims of boundary expansions. A large number intentionally entered the protected forests to achieve greater wealth through illegal coffee production. Still others entered the forest because they had
nowhere else to go to provide for their families. And finally, (5) corruption
by low-level local officials in a few places complicated matters further by
directly and indirectly encouraging deforestation.

     This case study features three kinds of "illegal" residents: (1) victims of
the dramatic change in national forest boundaries; (2) local opportunists, with
their nonlocal allies, attempting to create wealth from coffee production in the
short term; and (3) those landless people, searching for a means of subsistence.
In this context, the following questions arise. Should each type of illegal farmers have been treated the same? How should the government have responded
given the complexity and uncertainty of the situation? What would have been
the most just and fair action to take? What would have been the most appropriate outcome given high population densities, scarce arable lands, and limited financial and administrative capacities of the government? And finally,
what institutional arrangements would have been the most effective in managing the protected forests? As we shall see, there have been some dramatic
political changes in Indonesia since this case study took place that may address
these questions.

REVIEW OF THE REGION AND STUDY SITE

The archipelago nation of Indonesia straddles the equator separating the
Pacific from the Indian Ocean. The country stretches from the Malaysian
Peninsula in the west to the Australian continent in the east. It is three thousand miles long consisting of more than seventeen thousand islands with hundreds of languages and cultures. Indonesia is the fourth most populated country in the world with some 204 million citizens in 1998 (World Bank 2000).

Until the Asian economic and financial crises that began in the late 1990s, Indonesia, like many of the other Asian countries, was experiencing a booming economy with high rates of growth and rapid economic development. Per capita annual income in 1991, was US$592. By 1993, just two years later, this figure had jumped to US$740 (WRI 1996). As in other rapidly developing regions, the pace of growth and change was much slower in outlying rural areas. However, by the mid-1980s, an important new economic opportunity arose in South Sumatra.

South Sumatra is a vast province on the large outer island of Sumatra in western Indonesia. It possesses abundant natural resources including timber, oil, coal, and rich agricultural lands. South Sumatra's geography consists mostly of lowlands and coastal wetlands. The exception is the Bukit Barisan mountain range that runs northwest-southeast along Sumatra's western edge. Within this range sits Mount Dempo, a dormant volcano that marks the province's highest point at 3,159 meters (10,425 feet) (Brechin et al. 1993). Nestled among these mountains with their thick semitropical forests and rich volcanic soils, Lahat District is a center of South Sumatra's famous coffee growing region. Because of its high mountains and frequent heavy rains, Lahat contains many protected forests and important watersheds. The headwaters of the Musi, South Sumatra's largest river, are found here. This commercially important waterway connects the provincial capital, Palembang, with ocean shipping routes.

In spite of its environmental importance and the existing land protection system, by the early 1990s Lahat District was suffering from significant deforestation of its protected areas due to illegal farming. This created a number of environmental and social problems locally such as floods, landslides, and drought, as well as downstream threats to the commercial viability of the Musi River. By 1990, about 18 percent of Lahat's protected forests had been deforested by an estimated 29,000 illegal farmers growing coffee (Brechin et al. 1993; Heydir 1993). However, illegal farming of any significance was a recent phenomenon, the result of the configuration of a number of factors. To more fully understand the political ecology of protected area deforestation we need to review briefly the institutional history of forest management in Lahat.

THE HISTORY OF FOREST MANAGEMENT PRACTICES
AND PROBLEMS IN SOUTH SUMATRA

Traditionally, the people of South Sumatra, like residents in many other parts of Indonesia's outer islands, lived in communes known as *margas*. Clan-based, *margas* served for centuries as the local administrative units in rural areas, occupying and protecting customary *(adat)* territories and following *adat* rules and customs. The *marga's* affairs were typically overseen by a group of elders or governing council headed by a chief, called the *pasirah*. Following *adat* traditions, normally only members of the *marga* were allowed to make use of territorial lands and resources as regulated by the governing council and *pasirah*.

Forests within *marga* territories *(riba marga)* provided community resources such as fuelwood and other timber and non-timber products such as honey. They were carefully protected from outsiders (Heydir 1993, 37). *Adat* rules also facilitated resource preservation. For example, in the Marga Mulak Ulu, *adat* rules included a ban on farming land near natural springs *(ulu tulung)* or within 100 meters of streambeds (Heydir 1993, 38). Because of the strong legitimacy of the *marga* system and its leaders, it was an extremely effective means of political governance with tight social cohesion and social control within their *adat* lands.

When Dutch colonialists arrived in South Sumatra in 1859, they made use of the existing *marga* political structure and the legitimacy of the *pasirah* to maintain control over the vast territory and the many ethnic groups (Heydir 1993). Over the ensuing decades of colonial rule, however, the power of the *pasirah* and *margas* were slowly reduced in favor of colonial administrators. This included their control over forest management. By 1916, the Dutch had formally incorporated the *marga* forests along with the larger unclaimed forest lands as registered forests *(Bosch Wesen)* that were managed from the colonial administration's office in the provincial capital, Palembang. All forest areas were registered, their boundaries clearly marked and patrolled by armed colonial guards. No one was allowed entry into the registered forests without written permission from the colonial forestry office. Violators were considered criminals and those discovered could be shot on sight (Brechin et al. 1993; Heydir 1993). All *pasirahs* were expected to keep a close watch over the registered forests within their *marga* territories and report all illegal activity to the colonial forestry officials. Failure to do so could result in dismissal from leadership. Under Dutch administration, the concept of illegal forest use became more broadly and deeply institutionalized and bureaucratic (Peluso 1992; Wallenberg and Kartodihardjo 2000).

With political independence recognized in 1949, the fledgling Indonesian government at first continued the basic institutional arrangements established by the Dutch. With far fewer governmental resources, less intensive oversight by fewer and more distant and poorly trained Indonesian officials, the traditional *margas* and their leaders were able to regain much of their powers, including protection and management of forests within their territories. However, the forests not under the control of the *margas* were less effectively managed and limited deforestation began in these areas (Brechin et al. 1990; Heydir 1993). Not unexpectedly, the *marga* resurgence was short-lived. Over the ensuing decades, the central and provincial governments chipped away at the ability of the *margas* and their *pasirahs* to independently manage their own affairs. Finally, in 1983, the provincial governor of South Sumatra, acting in accordance with national law (act number 5 of 1979), formally dismantled the *marga* as a functioning political unit. The *pasirah* and *marga* council were stripped of all their formal authority. The well-established, traditional and semiautonomous system of local governance was replaced by the very hierarchical Javanese system of *desa* or village rule of the modern state. This change in governance system was orchestrated by the Javanese ruling elite at the national level, based in the nation's capital, Jakarta, as a way to standardize governmental control throughout Indonesia. Non-Javanese rural folks, such as those of the *margas* of South Sumatra, deeply resented this change in political rule. To them, their ethnic identities and ways of life were eclipsed in favor of the dominant Javanese culture and political system of the central government (Brechin et al. 1990; Heydir 1993).

A national hierarchical system of forest management, first introduced by the Dutch, was re-emphasized. Forestry management flowed downward from national to provincial to district levels. No local authority below district level was given any management control over the forests within their political unit. This weakened the ability of local governments to effectively protect forest boundaries. With the *margas* no longer functioning and the Javanese bureaucratic apparatus that replaced it weak, inexperienced, poorly funded, and viewed as illegitimate by many local people, a serious vacuum in both institutional control and administrative capability emerged. The boundaries of the forest protected areas became unenforceable (Brechin et al. 1990; Heydir 1993). In fact, forest management polices were enforced only sporadically as a result of police actions at the provincial and federal levels (Brechin et al. 1993; Heydir 1993; see Fay et al. 2000 for similar events in nearby Lampung Province). This set of circumstances allowed farmers to enter the forests illegally in pursuit of substantial profits from coffee cultivation with little fear of sanctions. In effect, the forests of Lahat became an open access commons.

ILLEGAL COFFEE FARMING, COFFEE PRICES, AND PROTECTED AREA DEFORESTATION

By the 1980s, local population densities were already relatively high given the local ecology and the established system of land use. Most available agricultural lands within Lahat District were already in production (Brechin et al. 1993). Consequently, the only source of new agricultural lands was protected forests. However, just as the provincial government was dismantling the traditional authority structure, coffee prices reached unprecedented heights. In the late 1970s, two consecutive years of severe frost in Brazil's major coffee growing regions reduced world supplies. With the relatively inelastic consumer demand for coffee, world market prices skyrocketed in the early 1980s (Brechin et al. 1993). Encouraged by the extraordinarily high prices and dreams of great wealth, local farmers and some outsiders swarmed into the district's protected forests to grow coffee as quickly as they could. And because the central and provincial governments had dismantled the traditional *marga* authority structure and replaced it with a weak and relatively ineffective national system, there was no longer a viable administrative authority to stop farmers from illegally entering many of the protected forests.

By the end of the 1980s, the government estimated that nearly thirty thousand farmers were growing coffee illegally in Lahat's protected forests alone. Using an aggressive variety of coffee plants that no longer required a canopy for shade, farmers vigorously removed forest cover to plant coffee. Government officials estimated that by 1990 more than 29,000 hectares, or about 18 percent of the original protected forests of Lahat, had been deforested. Local farmers caused most of the deforestation in Lahat as they added new plots in the forests while continuing to cultivate their existing plots back in their villages. These farmers typically hired "sharecroppers"—usually individuals from outside the region—to attend to and protect their investments from others (Brechin et al. 1993; Heydir 1993). Groups of unmarried local men were another common type of illegal farmer. Staying together for a sense of community and to protect themselves and their crops from theft, these young men would farm coffee until they had earned enough to start a business or purchase land of their own. In effect, illegal coffee farming provided unprecedented opportunities for economic and social advancement otherwise scarce in rural South Sumatra (Heydir 1993).

Another reason illegal farming flourished in Lahat's protected forests was the petty corruption and complicity of local governmental officials. These officials lacked the means necessary to halt illegal farming. With low pay, relative isolation, and little supervision or discipline, some local officials found the temptation of bribes too enticing to ignore. Most of these officials received bags of coffee from the farmers so they would not be recorded as illegal (Heydir 1993). Some officials even changed boundary markers for a price to allow farmers to grow coffee in the forests under the guise of legal production. In an isolated incident, a relatively high local official issued false land ownership documents to farmers seeking land to grow coffee (Brechin et al. 1993; Heydir 1993). The complicity of some local officials thus contributed to the invasion.

News of the rampant, illegal farming in Lahat's and in other districts' protected forests incensed provincial officials. In spite of a public decree by the provincial military governor calling for all illegal use of the forests to cease, few if any farmers abandoned their coffee plots. As a result, the provincial governor ordered a series of military raids with the use of helicopters in the summer of 1990 to forcibly remove farmers from the protected forests. The most dramatic event was known as *Operasi Lestari* (sustainable operation). Authorities attacked a number of sites, burned huts, destroyed coffee trees, and arrested a number of farmers along with a local official who was deeply involved in the illegal activities (Brechin et al. 1993; Heydir 1993). This operation sufficiently frightened the other illegal farmers from the forests, at least for a while. But as time passed, patrolling of the protected forests remained as infrequent as before and farming activities slowly returned. Although the coffee price shock of the early 1980s had long since waned, the lure of extra income and economic opportunities from illegal coffee farming remained relatively strong. By the mid-1990s the situation had fallen into an uneasy truce. At the same time, however, there was another type of illegal farmer that requires our attention.

CHANGES IN THE CRITERIA FOR
ESTABLISHING NATIONAL FOREST AREAS

Since Indonesia's recognized independence in 1949, the protected areas of South Sumatra have undergone three expansions: in 1971, 1975, and 1982. A fourth change took place in 1986 when the state reorganized the classification of existing protected areas (Brechin et al. 1993). The most significant change occurred in 1982 when a new forest policy—*Tata Guna Hutan Kesepakatan* (TGHK—Consensus Forest Land-use)—was instituted (Heydir 1993; Fay et al. 2000). Under this policy change, the government's planning office in Jakarta changed the criteria used for classifying and delimiting protected areas. TGHK divided the national forests into two major categories: permanent and production forests. Permanent forests were for conservation purposes only and included a number of subcategories such as national parks, wildlife reserves, and protection forests (Heydir 1993). Production forests contained categories reserved more for commercial use such as harvesting and included forest designations for conversion to other land uses.

The most significant change, however, concerned the formula used for determining forest designation. The original criteria for designating permanent forests consisted simply of forests with elevations greater than seven hundred meters and a slope of 45 percent or greater. The new criterion for determining designation more generally was a formula that took into account a more complicated set of variables including slope, soil type, and rainfall, each multiplied by a weighted factor for a total summary score (Brechin et al. 1993; Heydir 1993; Fay et al. 2000). The range of scores determined the designation type.

The immediate local result of implementing this new formula, devised by forestry experts from the central government in Jakarta, was to increase the percentage of land under government ownership in South Sumatra by nearly three and one-half times, from 1,562,783 to 5,214,700 hectares (Brechin et al. 1993). In Lahat District, the amount of land affected was more modest. Government-designated forests there rose from around 165,000 to 290,000 hectares, or about 75 percent. Most of these forests, about 80 percent of the increase, were in protection status, off limits to any kind of development or use (Heydir 1993). With the expansion, around 42 percent of the total land area of Lahat District fell under protection status (Brechin et al. 1993; Surapaty et al. 1991). To complicate the implementation of the new TGHK forest policy, funds were not made available to install new forest border signs. Still, it was clear that a number of established communities now fell within the expanded forest boundaries.

INSTITUTIONAL IMPACTS AT THE LOCAL LEVEL: THE CASE OF SEMIDANG ALAS

Government reports concerning the study area indicate that five villages in the Lahat District alone became illegal overnight with the expansion of protected forests. One such village was Semidang Alas, located in the Pagar Alam sub-district. The village was legally established in the late 1950s in a rugged, iso-lated area by a group of Mannas settlers, an ethnic group from southern Bengkula Province, just west of South Sumatra. Prior to the protected area expansion, Semidang Alas rested at the edge of the original protected forests, Bosh Wesen, as the Dutch colonialists called it (Heydir 1993).

Compared to other rural villages in the early 1990s, Semidang Alas was a prosperous community of about 1,200 people, with a number of fine sturdy houses, a mosque, public elementary school, and five coffee processing machines (Heydir 1993). The community also owned five four-wheel drive jeeps used to transport their coffee to the market town, Pagar Alam, in the val-ley below. Relatively speaking, growing coffee provided for an affluent life for the citizens of Semidang Alas and for many rural folks throughout the region.

In 1984, the Lahat District government informed the citizens of Semi-dang Alas of their illegal status and the plans for their forced relocation out of the forest to a new area. This was the beginning of a long and trying series of events, including intimidation by the military, that made life both difficult and uncertain for the community. In 1986, the military required the villagers to participate in a three-month reforestation project, ABRI *Manunggal Reboisasi* (Military's Program of Reforestation) (Heydir 1993). This conscription was a calculated effort to accomplish several objectives, including reforesting the existing agricultural lands, asserting the government's will, and weakening the community's resolve in resisting the relocation plans. Government officials also used thinly veiled threats to label the community residents as members or sympathizers of the outlawed PKI, or Indonesian Communist Party, if they refused to relocate.

The government wanted the residents of Semidang Alas to move farther down the mountain to what was left of unsettled, government-owned land, an area called Padang Muara Dua, in an adjacent subdistrict, Pulau Pinang, near the existing village of Rinduhati. The quality of the land had not been conclusively studied by the planning office, but the fact that it was mostly grassy meadows and scrub brush suggested the soil was not as fertile as in Semidang Alas. For relocation, each village family would be given the same package as most transmigrants: three hectares of land and cash, equivalent of about fifty U.S. dollars, but with no assistance in building their new homes. To make matters more difficult, the nearest source of running water was about one kilometer away (Heydir 1993).

The psychological trauma of relocating coupled with the low fifty dollar subsidy created strong disincentives against relocation. During the late 1980s, coffee farmers of the area typically earned between US$360 and US$915 each year (Heydir 1993). In addition, it would have taken three or four years after planting before the trees would have born fruit, either compounding the sacrifice, or further complicating the relocation by requiring families to attend to both their old and new coffee fields at the same time. Again, it was uncertain as to how well the soils at Padang Muara Dua would have supported coffee production, if at all. Therefore, relocation might have required villagers to take up risky new agricultural activities with which they had little knowledge or experience. Consequently, the villagers were caught between a rock and a hard place—suffering from the threat of government persecution for not relocating or considerable economic sacrifice and community dislocation if they did.

By Spring 1992, only twenty villagers had relocated to Padang Muara Dua. By that fall, all of them had returned to Semidang Alas, greatly angering district government officials. Officials subsequently resettled landless illegal farmers in Padang Murara Dua (Heydir 1993).

THREE TYPES OF ILLEGAL RESIDENTS

This research uncovered three types of illegal farmers. The first were local farmers who purposefully entered protected forests to cash in on the lucrative coffee market. Accompanying this type were outsiders, poor individuals mostly from other districts, who were hired by the locals to watch their illegal investments. A second type were landless families in need of viable land to cultivate. The second type unknowingly entered protected forest areas because of the lack of day-to-day enforcement and the uncertainty as to the exact location of forest boundaries. The third type of illegal farmers, such as the residents of Semidang Alas, were the victims of a change in government forest policy.

In the early 1990s, the government made little distinction among these three types of illegal farmers. Like the Dutch Colonial regime, the Indonesian government labeled anyone occupying government forest land as illegal. In

Lahat District, however, at least most, if not all, suitable agricultural land was already in production. This, in conjunction with the recent increase in the amount of government ownership of land that resulted from the forest expansion, left very little land available for relocation purposes. Available land was of inferior quality, making the law relatively hollow. This provided government officials with very few viable options to pursue in order to resolve the protected forest management problems.

CONCLUSION

This case study demonstrates how a political ecological perspective can help to unravel the complex events and interactions responsible for causing local deforestation of protected areas in Lahat District. Some explanations are found locally, others nationally, and some internationally. There are also important historical processes that explain local decision making. Environmental conditions also contributed to the mix, including the climate, terrain, and soil characteristics of the Lahat District that made it ideal for growing coffee. Severe frost in Brazil was instrumental in raising the price of coffee on the world market, providing the motivation for farmers in Lahat to increase their own production. With existing agricultural lands already heavily used, the only place farmers could find "available" land to cultivate was in the government's protected forests. Entering the forests was relatively easy due to the changes in traditional governing institutions. The *marga* institutions were dismantled and replaced with a legal-rational institutional system of the modern state. While the former were effective in managing local land uses, the latter was not, being administratively weak and viewed as illegitimate by most of the rural villagers. In short, there were no viable institutions or structures in place to stop farmers from illegally entering the forests. The modern state had essentially lost institutional control of the area's forests, creating serious boundary enforcement problems and generating a series of environmental problems.

The existence of three types of illegal farmers complicated matters with respect to social justice. But this problem too is directly related to the institutional changes made by the state regarding the establishment of a new formula for calculating the area of protected forests. This change most likely resulted both from an attempt to improve scientific forest management and increase natural resource-based income (Fay et al. 2000).

Still, it is unclear how to resolve the the problem of "illegal farmers," especially the residents of Semidang Alas. What should the government have done with these farmers? Should they have forced them to relocate? Should the government have treated each type of illegal occupant the same? Or should it have made certain exceptions? Finally, how should the central government have managed its vast regions of protected areas, especially given its limited financial resources and even more limited bureaucratic effectiveness in the rural areas? How might the government have addressed the social and economic needs of the rural communities?

Regarding the management of protected forest areas, a better balance was required in the national-local governmental relationship. Clearer lines of communication between local and national authorities were needed to provide supervision and accountability to reduce opportunities for corruption. It might have made more sense to have forestry officials in subdistrict (township) offices in heavily forested areas as opposed to only at the district level. Decentralization might have provided for greater supervision of the protected forests, but would not have fully accounted for the government's serious lack of resources or the critical issue of local legitimacy. It might have made more sense for the government to maintain the integrity of the traditional *marga* system to carry out local management and enforcement. But this assumes that the *marga* system could function as in years past, unaffected by modern events and needs. It also suggests that the traditional system would not be as easily corrupted by powerful local-regional systems of economic interests that encourage timber harvesting wherever suitable timber exists, including protected areas. Researchers elsewhere in Sumatra have found domination by local government authorities to be a serious challenge to the environmental effectiveness of local citizen rule (McCarthy 2000).

Still, there must be a way to combine greater local management with more social justice while creating even greater legitimacy for the modern state. Potential solutions would require the central government to rethink its institutional arrangements for forest management. In considering this case study, one is left wondering what harm would have come if responsible community members, such as those of Semidang Alas, were simply allowed to live in the forests and maintain their existing agricultural practices and ways of life. Their illegal status was obtained by no fault of their own. Given that the forests in this particular incident were under complete protection, the government gained little economic, social, or political advantage by physically relocating the community. But perhaps this would have been too nuanced a response for the government given the economic gains found elsewhere from forest expansion. Interestingly through, recent political changes may have opened the door to potential solutions to many of these issues of forest management and social justice.

EPILOGUE: NEW FORESTRY POLICIES
AND GOVERNANCE DEVOLUTION

With the fall of the Suharto regime in the late 1990s and the subsequent change in government, Indonesia has adopted new forestry management policies. Through an act of the Indonesian People's Consultative Assembly, the

Basic Forest Law of May 1967 (UU NO. 5/1967) was substantially altered on September 30, 1999 (Wollenberg and Kartiodihardjo 2000). Although it is too early to determine how successful this new legislation has been, it potentially offers a striking change in forest policy, possibly reversing many of the problems presented above (Campbell 1999). The new law sets in motion opportunities to devolve forest management responsibilities to the local level. Most critically, the new forestry law does not simply devolve control of the forests from the national and provincial governments to lower levels within the national administrative authority, but rather turns management over to rural communities.

According to the new law, forestry management is to be directed through two possible institutions: (1) *masyarakat hukum adat* (customary or traditional communities, such as the margas), or (2) community-based cooperatives (Campbell 1999; Wollenberg and Kartodihardjo 2000). Among traditional communities, the new forestry laws create *hutan adat*, or traditional forests, essentially recognizing the *marga* forests of old. As Wollenberg and Kartodihardjo (2000) note, this is the first time the state has reversed its long history of local domination and sought to actually transfer rights to traditional communities. Although the state technically maintains strategic control of the traditional forests, the new legislation would allow the *adat* communities greater rights and access, distribution of forest-related resources, and regulation and management of the forests themselves (Campbell 1999). These communities would be able to make use of the forests as long as they are not contrary to the overarching government laws and policies. For example, logging would still be illegal in protection forests held by *adat* communities, as would to permanently farm them. At the same time, however, it would be lawful for community members to enter their *adat* forests and make use of non-timber forest products found there. Compared to the former forest management arrangements described earlier, this is an extraordinary change.

The idea of using cooperatives is an interesting one, although some reviewers are somewhat critical about their viability and purpose (Campbell 1999). Under this provision, traditional and nontraditional communities within production forests would be allowed to form community cooperatives and make arrangements with the government to harvest specific production forests in *adat* and non-*adat* forest lands. Unfortunately, there seems to be no history of encouraging forestry cooperatives in Indonesia and few if any cooperatives presently exist (Wollenberg and Kartodihardjo 2000). Consequently, they would need both governmental and nongovernmental support. Although cooperatives can be formed by any group, such as logging companies, they also appear to provide an avenue for local communities that were not historically part of a *marga* system, such as Semidang Alas, to make use of nearby forest resources if not claimed by other groups. Still, the future of Semidang Alas is uncertain. The community is located in strictly protected forests, making the cooperative idea irrelevant. But perhaps the notion of local communities exist-ing in forest areas may become a more acceptable norm, perhaps giving the people of Semidang Alas a greater sense of security and justice.

Wollenberg and Kartodihardjo (2000) believe that for devolution to be successful in Indonesia, there needs to be a greater foundation of civil society tradition, practice, and organizational capacity, among the local communities and support organizations as well as among government agencies. Devolution by itself will not be a panacea. If not carefully administered, the macro-level issues of social justice that exist between the political elite and the masses could be replaced by more local-level distributive equity issues along status, ethnic, gender, or religious lines. Moreover, local-regional economic interests could capture excessive power and generate significant environmental change (McCarthy 2000).

Still, changes in forestry policy and the greater democratization of Indonesia more generally could represent a major leap forward, resulting in more fully protecting the nation's forest resources while helping to provide for the welfare of its people. Studies performed in North Sumatra illustrate an upsurge in progressive politics that at times challenged powerful illegal timber harvesting networks (McCarthy 2000). In Indonesia, as elsewhere, promise and reality often end up miles apart. We will have to wait and watch, but these first steps open the door for significant change for Indonesia's rural people and the forests.

NOTE

I would like to thank Charles Benjamin, Crystal Fortwangler, Brian Magu-ranyanga, Peter Wilshusen, and the reviewers for SUNY Press for very constructive suggestions in revising this chapter. I also must acknowledge the assistance of the larger Indonesia research team: Surya Chandra Surapaty, Laurel Heydir, and Eddy Roflin as well as others at Sriwijaya University, Palembang, South Sumatra, Indonesia.

Chapter Five

TERRITORY, NATURE, AND CULTURE

Negotiating the Boundaries of Biodiversity Conservation
in Colombia's Pacific Coastal Region

PETER R. WILSHUSEN

Colombia is among the small group of countries that have tropical regions
considered to be "megadiversity" areas. The Chocó biogeographic region,
which comprises the country's Pacific coastal plain, falls under this category as
one of the world's most biologically diverse zones. It features no fewer than
3,500 plant species (as many as 10,000 may grow there) and one of the world's
highest indices of continental endemism. Estimates suggest that 20 to 25 percent of the region's plant species are found nowhere else on the planet (Wilson 1992). The Pacific Coastal region extends from southern Panama to
northern Ecuador along a heavily forested band bounded by the Pacific Ocean
to the west and the Andean foothills to the east. The region is dominated by
extensive river systems and, while a majority of its estimated 900,000 residents
live in urban areas, about 40 percent remain dispersed among small riverine
communities (Escobar 1997). Black and indigenous communities represent
the vast majority of inhabitants, featuring a rich diversity of cultural practices
(Escobar and Pedrosa 1996; Leyva 1993).[1]

Starting in 1992, Colombia's environmental protection agency received
US$ 9 million from the Global Environment Facility (GEF) and the Gov-
ernment of Switzerland to finance three years of an ongoing environmental

program for the Pacific Coastal Region. The overarching goal of the first phase of the program, known locally as the *Proyecto Biopacífico*, was to consolidate a new strategy for biodiversity conservation and sustainable development for the region with the full participation of local communities. The project focused on four problem areas, including a lack of baseline information (both biophysical and socioeconomic), a lack of planning based on sustainable use of natural resources by local communities, weak institutional structure (number of agencies involved, lack of resources, low capacity), and a lack of effective community participation in the development process. In response, *Biopacífico*'s technical team structured its activities around four thematic areas: science and knowledge *(Conocer)*, socioeconomic valuation *(Valorar)*, political mobilization *(Movilizar)*, and policy and resource allocation *(Formular-Asignar)*. The project's national coordinator, administrative and technical staff were based in Bogotá with area coordinators in each of four regional offices (Wilshusen 1996).

In addition to being one of the first projects undertaken by the GEF during its pilot phase, *Biopacífico* emerged during a period of enormous institutional changes within the Colombian state. Most important among these changes was the promulgation of a new national constitution in 1991, the passage of a new law *(Ley 70)* in 1993 that guarantees tenurial, cultural, and political rights for Afro-Colombian communities, and the restructuring of the environmental sector, also in 1993. In part as a result of this institutional instability, the project lasted almost six years instead of three and featured several internal planning exercises as a means of adapting to rapid change. The *Biopacífico* project generated some important new scientific and socioeconomic studies but did not produce a comprehensive regional conservation and development strategy as originally planned (Ríos and Wilshusen 1999). Whereas it was perhaps less successful at consolidating conventional conservation measures such as protected areas, the project experienced an unusual process of negotiation or *concertación*[2] among technical staff and black and indigenous organizations that exemplifies the "deep" politics of conservation in "developing" areas. How did this complex story of *concertación* unfold in Colombia and what does it tell us about the power dynamics inherent in projects that incorporate local participation?

This chapter uses the *Biopacífico* case to focus on three points of analysis that build on the conceptual discussion of power in chapter 3. First, it examines the politics of local participation within a rapidly changing social and political environment. Questions of local participation produced unforeseen outcomes wherein *Biopacífico* became the stage for negotiation among diverse groups that ended up rearticulating the project's approach. Second, the chapter sets out to explore how material and symbolic aspects of power merge in practice. In this sense, it focuses on the intersection of ethnicity (identity-culture) and nature (territory). The process of negotiation surrounding local participation in *Biopacífico* illustrates the complex ways in which different players frame and counterframe their explanations of the relationship between humans and nature. In this context, notions of "biodiversity" became a conceptual contested ground where definitions of terms produced material advantages for those who counted as participants but also created key alternative understandings of ideas such as territory, culture, and development and their relation to nature. Third, the analysis looks at how conservation interventions are embedded within multiple political arenas. Participants at each level interpreted the project's content in terms of their own political activity and redirected their understandings and available resources to advance their objectives. Although the *Biopacífico* project ultimately failed to complete a comprehensive biodiversity conservation strategy for the Pacific Coastal region, I argue that the midterm reformulation of the project's operative plan was a necessary precursor to successfully pursuing such a goal.

CONSTRUCTING "LOCAL PARTICIPATION" WITHIN THE BIOPACÍFICO PROJECT

In many respects the political trajectory of the *Biopacífico* project between 1992 and 1998 is reflected most clearly in the different approaches that participants pursued with respect to local participation. Despite the project's stated goal of developing a regional biodiversity strategy based in local participation, it was not until mid-1995 that representatives of black and indigenous communities had a significant role in decision making. A dramatic shift occurred at that time wherein a combination of institutional changes, outside pressures, and internal project reform opened political space for dialogue between project staff and those grassroots actors who strongly criticized the way in which the project was being implemented. The result was the formation of a working group or task force called the *equipo ampliado* (expanded team). The working group represented much more than a forum for airing grievances. Over the course of approximately eight months, the *equipo ampliado* met on numerous occasions to negotiate the reformulation of *Biopacífico*'s focus and approach, turning what many considered to be a failed project into a qualified success story.[3] This part of the chapter recounts how this process of negotiation (or *concertación*) played out, placing events within the context of the important political changes that occurred in Colombia during the first half of the 1990s.

Like any conservation and development initiative, *Biopacífico* responded to and was constrained by regional and national political processes. The most important of these was the rapid growth and maturation of a broad-based social movement among black and indigenous groups seeking to consolidate and redefine their citizenship rights within the context of Colombia's 1991 constitutional reforms. Like Ecuador, Colombia's National Constituent Assembly set out to remold the nation as a pluriethnic society, overturning the previous constitution's emphasis on "ethnic homogenization." Black communities did not have any representatives in the constituent assembly because they were not initially considered a separate ethnic group (Escobar 1997). In an interesting turn of events, indigenous representatives were instrumental in passing a transitory article *(Artículo Transitorio 55)*, which called for the development of a law recognizing black communities as an ethnic group . This law *(Ley 70)* was instituted in July 1993 and vastly increased black communities' legal rights to collective territory, ethnic identity, and cultural practices.[4]

Whereas indigenous peoples had developed strong political organizations prior to the 1991 constitutional reforms, black political organizations consolidated between 1991 and 1993 through activities surrounding the development of *Ley 70*. Black political organizations throughout the region represent vibrant and creative collective efforts to make political gains along material (i.e., demarcation of collective territories) and symbolic lines (i.e., alternative conceptualizations of "territory" as cultural living space). Framed as an "organizational process" *(Proceso de Comunidades Negras* or PCN), these organizations emerged as strong actors in the region but by 1998 were still working to define how they intended to participate in Colombia's complex political and economic arena (Asher 1998; Escobar 1997; Grueso et al. 1998; Wade 1995).

A second component of institutional change that emerged out of the 1991 constitutional reforms was the reorganization of the country's environmental management sector. The 1993 Law of the Environment *(Ley 99)* dismantled the longstanding Institute for the Development of the Environment and Renewable Natural Resources (INDERENA) and set up the Ministry of the Environment in its place. In addition, *Ley 99* created the National Environmental Network or SINA *(Sistema Nacional del Ambiente)*, which decentralized management by incorporating existing state-run regional development corporations (based, in part, on the Tennessee Valley Authority [TVA] model) and shifting their mandate from economic development to environmental protection. The law further laid the legal groundwork for establishing several regional research institutes including the *Instituto de Investigaciones Ambientales del Pacífico* (IIAP) (Asher 2000). Among other responsibilities, the IIAP was charged with carrying forward the objectives of the *Biopacífico* project.

Colombia's economic opening or *apertura* represents a third area of institutional change that accompanied the process of constitutional reform. In line with trends across Latin America in the late 1980s, Colombia instituted economic policy reforms aimed at gaining greater participation in emerging global markets. For the Pacific Coastal region, this translated into linking the rest of the country with the economies of the Asia-Pacific rim. In this context, the Inter-American Development Bank (IDB) in conjunction with the

National Planning Department (DNP) allocated $250 million beginning in 1992 for an ambitious infrastructure development program known as *Plan Pacífico*. Although *Plan Pacífico* nominally promoted "sustainable development," it focused on conventional modernization interventions such as the improvement of ports, highways, and telecommunications (Asher 2000; Escobar 1997).

The *Biopacífico* project was launched in September 1992 in the midst of these massive political changes. Initially, it was unclear whether the National Planning Department or INDERENA (which became the Ministry of the Environment in 1993) would exercise institutional control over the project. After a great deal of political maneuvering and a near complete turnover in technical staff, *Biopacífico* began operating within the Environment Ministry/INDERENA in March, 1993. Since the new personnel did not participate directly in the project's design, the first several months of work focused on internal planning and the development of an operational plan covering the period from 1993 to 1997. During this initial phase of activities, all decision making took place in the capital city, Bogotá. A National Steering Committee comprised of the project coordinator and representatives of the United Nations Development Programme (UNDP), the National Planning Department (DNP) and the Environment Ministry controlled project administration. The initial design of the *Biopacífico* project called for the formation of a national advisory committee including representatives of NGOs, universities, and black and indigenous communities, among others. The national advisory committee never formed presumably because UNDP and government bureaucracies avoided the added logistical burden that such a body would have represented.

Although *Biopacífico* faced great uncertainty, particularly regarding the changing structure of the country's environmental sector, it was able to achieve a significant level of decision-making autonomy with respect to day-to-day operations. This freedom allowed the project coordinator to establish an office separate from the ministry and pursue internal planning independently. Throughout 1993 the project had a minimal presence in the Pacific Coastal region, focusing activities mainly in the department of Chocó. Upon completing the initial draft of the first operative plan, technical staff sent copies to approximately 150 representatives of NGOs, universities, public agencies, and communities requesting comments. While this limited process of consultation generated some important observations that were incorporated into the final draft of the operative plan, it also raised expectations across sectors that *Biopacífico* would provide financial support for interested parties.

With the passage of *Ley 70* in July 1993, black political organizations *(Proceso de Comunidades Negras)* refocused their attention from lobbying legislators and drafting proposals in Bogotá to increasing awareness among black communities of the new rights that the law afforded. As a result, black political activists organized regional meetings and made visits to riverine communities to promote, in particular, the legalization of communal territorial claims (Grueso et al. 1998). Starting in early 1994, *Biopacífico* technical staff carried out numerous informational workshops with black and indigenous communities, NGOs, universities, municipal governments, and public agencies to promote the project's operative plan and solicit proposals for subcontracts. During this period, *Biopacífico* favored regional-level projects—particularly scientific research—and thus tended to approve subcontracts with universities and NGOs. This approach generated significant political tensions since, in addition to channeling a majority of resources to NGO and academic activities, both black and indigenous organizations felt that the project's local-level contact with small groups and individuals subverted their work by fragmenting community organization.

In an attempt to adapt to the institutional changes surrounding the 1991 constitutional reforms and the concomitant growth of black and indigenous organizing, *Biopacífico* technical staff formulated a second operative plan that was to cover the period 1995–1996. This second plan was intended to increase participation by emergent black and indigenous organizations and decentralize project administration by creating four regional offices. In effect, the project was slowly trying to build a presence in the Pacific Coastal region by developing stronger relationships with black and indigenous political organizations. Despite these efforts, most of these organizations openly criticized *Biopacífico* by the end of 1994 because community representatives were not directly involved in negotiating project activities as its overarching goal stated. Increasing criticism of the project both from within (National Planning Department representatives, for example, called for much greater community participation) and from grassroots political organizations led the National Steering Committee to organize an independent midterm evaluation in January 1995. The evaluation initiated a process that would lead to the restructuring of *Biopacífico* such that the second operative plan was never implemented (the regional offices were created, however).

The midterm evaluation team included four consultants contracted on behalf of UNDP, the Swiss government, the Environment Ministry, and the National Planning Department. The appraisal produced changes in the project that in one sense disrupted *Biopacífico*'s internal operations but in another sense opened a political forum for direct dialogue between the project staff and black and indigenous organizations. Interviews with groups that were directly involved with the project through subcontracts led the evaluation team to conclude that there were strong complaints against *Biopacífico* by grassroots groups. As a result, the consultants decided to organize open meetings where all interested parties could express their views regarding the project (Hernández C. et al. 1996). The meetings produced heated discussions focusing on the lack of participation by representatives of black and indigenous communities in project planning and implementation. How could it be possible, critics argued, that a project whose stated goal was to develop a regional strategy for conservation and sustainable use of biodiversity through a negotiated process with communities was in fact administered almost entirely from Bogotá with little or no local involvement?

The midterm evaluation report, which was not completed until May 1995, produced immediate results. During a tripartite review held in June, representatives from GEF-UNDP headquarters in New York, and the Swiss and Colombian governments approved a proposal to create a special task force or working group (the so-called *equipo ampliado*) to revise the project's operative plan with full participation by black and indigenous representatives (Navajas 1995). It was the first time that black and indigenous representatives sat in on high-level project meetings as observers. The *equipo ampliado* brought together members of the technical team, regional coordinators (who in most cases were also black activists), representatives from each regional affiliate of the black political movement, and members of the region's main indigenous political organizations. The team worked intensively during the second half of 1995 starting with a large meeting at Piangua Grande, Buenaventura, which brought together activist groups claiming to represent 684 community organizations (discussed in detail below). Based on initial accords reached at Piangua Grande, the *Biopacífico* working group met several times and, after a process of arduous negotiation, produced a new operative plan in February 1996.[5]

The *equipo ampliado* continued to meet throughout 1996, but was less active once the main task of drafting the operative plan was completed. After this shift in focus from planning to implementation, the working group concentrated mostly on questions of resource allocation. A special committee comprised of project technical staff and representatives of the Environment Ministry and the National Planning Department dealt specifically with the approval of subcontracts. By late 1996, two members of the *equipo ampliado* resigned over sharp disagreements that emerged regarding proposals submitted by their organizations that were rejected as well as the standards for project approval. Despite the gradual closing of the working group's activities, the sustained dialogue surrounding the third (and final) operative plan established an important precedent adopted in large part by subsequent environmental projects in the region.

REARTICULATING BIODIVERSITY
CONSERVATION AT PIANGUA GRANDE

The meetings that took place from August 28 to September 1, 1995, at Piangua Grande, Buenaventura, represent a turning point in the *Biopacífico* project. The encounter brought together representatives from diverse black and indigenous organizations that together make up a broad-based social movement. Two sets of discussions took place including formal dialogue among black and indigenous groups to consolidate their position with respect to the project and, subsequently, a meeting of the *Biopacífico* working group *(equipo ampliado)* to develop an initial proposal regarding the project's future. It is instructive to consider in detail several of the points that came out of these meetings because they encapsulate the central arguments and understandings of the different participants involved in negotiating the project's content and methodology. I present four main themes that emerged in the black and indigenous groups' proposal for reformulating *Biopacífico* and also look at how these ideas were integrated into the working group's initial accord to carry forward the restructuring process. These themes include biodiversity, territory and tenure, scientific research, and participation. By using numerous excerpts from the Piangua Grande proposals, I attempt to give voice to those who crafted the narrative.

Biodiversity

The term *biodiversity* most often carries little meaning for those who do not work directly in the international conservation arena. As the text that follows illustrates, different understandings of biodiversity created strong conceptual contradictions that produced perceptions of the *Biopacífico* project as something entirely foreign and of little relevance to communities. The process of negotiation that took place within the working group did not fully resolve the contradictions but did generate a dialogue that reinforced and promoted cultural links to nature that did not appear in the project's initial formulation. Regarding biodiversity, the black and indigenous groups' proposal for reformulating *Biopacífico* states,

> For indigenous communities, to speak of biodiversity is to make mention of the ethnic, cultural and social diversity of a people that is tied to both nature and man. As such, the environment is also a space where an ethnic group manifests its cosmovision of knowledge. That is to say, the place where a shaman or herbalist *(Jaiban·, Yerbatero, Tonguero, Nele)* guard their powers as well as the places of work, the lagoon, the river, or simply the territory and its contents. For the black community, as for the indigenous communities, the concept of biodiversity comes from outside; the people do not use this concept. The black community has used the word "bush" *(monte)* in more or less the same manner in which the word Biodiversity is applied since one finds diverse forms of life in the bush. The relationship between Nature (Territory), culture and everyday life is equal to biodiversity. The concept of nature is wide and humans are immersed in this.[6]

In contrast to these definitions, the 1992 Convention on Biological Diversity establishes that "for the purposes of this Convention,"

"Biological diversity" means the variability among living organisms from all sources including, *inter alia*, terrestrial, marine and other aquatic ecosystems and the ecological complexes of which they are part; this includes diversity within species, between species and of ecosystems. "Biological resources" includes genetic resources, organisms or parts thereof, populations, or any other biotic component of ecosystems with actual or potential use of value for humanity. "Ecosystem" means a dynamic complex of plant, animal and micro-organism communities and their non-living environment interacting as a functioning unit.[7]

While the *Biopacífico* working group did not focus on definitions of bio-diversity, participants did adopt the notion of "territory" presented in the black and indigenous groups' proposal, recognizing the link between "biodiversity" and "culture." The idea that biodiversity or *"monte"* underlies cultural practices and identity is absent from the Convention's definition. Rather, according to the Convention, biological diversity's only link to humans is as a resource featuring actual or potential value for use. It is also interesting to note how black and indigenous groups framed their cultural practices as favorable to maintaining biologically diverse landscapes. One of their principal claims underlying the definition of biodiversity as the relationship between Nature (territory), culture, and everyday life states, "The human-nature relationship reflected in the traditional and ancestral practices of social organization and production among black and indigenous communities that inhabit the Colombian Pacific Coastal region establishes a usage of biodiversity that has guaranteed its conservation."[8]

Territory and Tenure

A second basic concept that goes hand in hand with biodiversity focuses on "territory."

For black and indigenous communities, the Colombian Pacific Coastal region constitutes a sociocultural category and not commercial real estate. Territory is the space that embraces life in the communities in an integral way, the space in which cultural practices are recreated and strengthened and the environment that provides a material basis for the reproduction of life.

As noted in the discussion on biodiversity above, territory and Nature coincide as living space. The points highlighted by black and indigenous representatives at Piangua Grande make a deliberate conceptual move away from economistic understandings of territory as a commodity by calling it a "socio-cultural category" that underlies the production and reproduction of cultural practices. In addition to presenting alternative understandings, however, participants also focused on questions of legal tenure rights and territorial zoning *(ordenamiento territorial)*, a central component of the 1993 *Ley 70*.

> The subject [of territorial zoning] is fundamental for black and indigenous peoples of the Pacific Coastal region. We understand it as the possibility to define territoriality based in the legal recognition of our territory. . . . Thus, the definition of property and uses of the territory are the consensus of black and indigenous social and political expression. It means technically defining the limits of our territories [including population and conservation areas].

In both their formulation of territory as cultural living space and insistence on tenure security, black and indigenous activists called attention to the perception that their ways of life were completely ignored within dominant neoliberal economic planning models. According to this view, neoliberal approaches—manifested in state development programs such as *Plan Pacífico*—promoted macroeconomic efficiency through private property and land commodification. Black and indigenous representatives pointed out that these strategies stood in direct opposition to their long-standing communal land management practices. In this sense, they argued that territory and tenure were fundamentally linked to their collective survival.

Scientific Research

In the context of the *Biopacífico* project, questions of how to manage scientific research produced strong tensions among academics and black and indigenous activists regarding methods, application of results, and intellectual property. As a result, the Piangua Grande talks dedicated a significant amount of time to this topic. Their proposal for restructuring the project notes,

> An obstacle that we see for developing any type of research in our communities are the precarious relations that the national and international scientific community has established with us, which, in its search to modernize our society has forgotten our culture and our interests. Thus, we wonder what interests lead them to want to contribute to regional development? How do they understand our cultures and how do they think to establish relationships with them? In the response to these inquiries is the key for establishing serious, honest, transparent, supportive and tolerant relationships with our communities, cultures and interests.

While they recognized the importance of generating new knowledge through research, black and indigenous representatives highlighted the negative aspects of science as data extraction. In this sense activists responded both to their experiences with individual researchers who "collected" data from "knowledgeable informants" and their understanding of the commodification of local knowledge or "bioprospecting" by pharmaceutical companies and other interested parties. In this context, they made clear their position regarding intellectual property.

> Traditional wisdom and knowledge are fundamental to the life of black and indigenous ethnic groups in the Colombian Pacific Coastal region . . . and are essential elements of their identity. As such, they represent their cultural heritage *(patrimonio cultural)* and should be recognized as part of biological diversity and respected in all its forms at national and international levels in accord with the Convention on Biological Diversity.

In line with this perspective on the role of research, the Piangua Grande document proposes a number of conditions for carrying out studies in black and indigenous territories including prior review/consent by both communities and political organizations and recognition of black/indigenous intellectual property rights.

Participation

The Global Environmental Facility's (GEF) operational strategy for programming establishes that, "GEF projects will provide for consultation with and participation, as appropriate, of the beneficiaries and affected groups of people" (GEF 1996).[9] The vast conceptual distance between this limited definition of participation and the desires and expectations of local and regional actors becomes clear when compared to the demands recorded at Piangua Grande. On one level, the *Biopacífico* project itself was framed, in part, in terms of sustainable use of biodiversity for the benefit of local communities. Ample participation in the project by these communities was seen as fundamental to its success although mechanisms for involvement were not defined. On another level, Afro-Colombian and indigenous organizations had grown significantly as political interlocutors for communities by 1995 and, under *Ley 70*, claimed the right to participate in programs that affected them. Given these circumstances, black and indigenous political groups felt they had a right (both legal and moral) to insist that the project be reformulated to more directly benefit local communities. *Biopacífico* presented a key political opening as well as a sizeable risk for the emergent political organizations because it was a first crossover from critiquing a government project to potentially working to reconstruct it. In this context their discussion states,

> The participation of black and indigenous communities should be considered as the only means of taking on the challenge of maintaining the ethnic,

cultural and biological diversity of the regions that we inhabit and have a future as peoples and communities. A participatory process in regions like the Colombian Pacific Coast should begin by recognizing the ethnic and cultural diversity of the region as well as the organizational types and levels. Arenas like the *equipo ampliado* ["expanded team"] of the *Biopacífico* project should serve to reach the aspirations of our communities, offering elements that allow for the consolidation of development strategies based in our diversity.

As such participation in this process should not just serve for the construction of an operative plan but above all it should permit us to clearly define the levels of planning, management, co-management, implementation, monitoring, accounting, evaluation and decision making within the *Biopacífico* project. We, the community representatives who are in the *equipo ampliado*, should be complete equals in terms of decision making with respect to the rest of the people who make up the team. As such we require the means and guarantees of information and resources as well as time to be able to move forward on the necessary consultations for decision making. We are representatives of organizational processes, of peoples who have their future in play and that need to weave a dignified present based in respect for our cultures and territories, as an essential foundation for well-being.

Whereas the *equipo ampliado* itself became the main mechanism of black and indigenous participation in *Biopacífico*, the initial agreements established by the working group made clear that communities were to be the project's main beneficiaries. In effect, this move largely transformed *Biopacífico* into a small grants program during its last two years by funding diverse community-level projects.[10]

The activities of the project have a primary beneficiary, which is distinct from talking about beneficiaries in general. Efforts must be focused in order to have real benefits in the collective territories. In this sense, black and indigenous communities are understood to be the project's primary beneficiaries.

UNRAVELING THE POLITICS OF PARTICIPATION

In terms of "action-centered" politics—actors seeking to advance their interests through the use of resources—the process of negotiation or *concertación* produced important advancements for both black/indigenous organizations and the *Biopacífico* project. The initial agreements of the *equipo ampliado* at Piangua Grande defined several points that would shape how the project's operative plan would be reformulated and implemented, including decision making in planning, definition of beneficiaries, the role of black and indigenous political organizations, and focus of research.

In addition, if one examines *Biopacífico* as a political arena embedded within a wider institutional setting, two sets of observations stand out. First, both professionals associated with the project and activists in the region used *Biopacífico* to increase their legitimacy vis-à-vis their respective constituents. For black political activists, the project became a platform to consolidate the position of the black communities movement, arguing, for example, that black political organizations should participate fully in all aspects of project decision making and that they should provide consent for research projects in addition to communities. The project also became a source of needed resources for reaching the often remote riverine communities. The *equipo ampliado* itself contributed to the consolidation of the black and indigenous organizational process by permitting successful negotiation among separate factions of the black communities movement as well as between black and indigenous groups.[11] For project staff, negotiation and restructuring allowed access to communities but also vindicated *Biopacífico*'s image among peers and superiors in Bogotá and New York (UNDP headquarters).

A second set of observations focuses on the impacts of institutional change on project politics. The 1991 constitutional reforms precipitated new laws that restructured the environmental sector and granted important legal rights to black communities. Within the scope of the *Biopacífico* project, these legal changes altered power dynamics significantly since, for example, black and indigenous groups could claim the legal and moral right to participate and project staff had the flexibility to experiment with unconventional approaches such as the working group. Conversely, Colombia's economic *apertura* produced larger order indirect effects on project politics. In this sense, it transformed national development policy by framing the Pacific Coastal region as the economic portal to the markets of the Pacific Rim. The IDB-financed project known locally as *Plan Pacífico* came to embody this logic of progress based on infrastructure, large-scale production, and growth. *Biopacífico* became an important arena in which black and indigenous activists could present alternative understandings of development.

Beyond considerations of conventional politics, the *Biopacífico* case illustrates how the material and symbolic aspects of power merge in practice. The issues of territory and intellectual property offer excellent examples of this process. On one hand, black and indigenous political organizations manifested instrumentalist arguments focused on legal recognition of collective territory and property rights over traditional knowledge of medicinal plants among other things. Both are considered elements of biodiversity that make up real and potential local economic production. At the same time, according to the arguments recorded at Piangua Grande, territory and knowledge underlie black and indigenous cultural practices, each influencing, in part, community identity and organization. Black and indigenous activists worked to rearticulate understandings of biodiversity, territory, participation, and research to counter dominant approaches that jeopardized communities in the region both culturally and economically.

Finally, the *Biopacífico* case shows clearly how the power dynamics associated with conservation projects are embedded in wider political arenas. In this sense, political actors operating at multiple levels—locally, regionally, nationally, internationally—interpret events and make decisions within the sphere of interaction that most directly affects their perceived interests. The most obvious manifestation of this process was the issue of territorial control. Within the context of *Biopacífico*, members of black and indigenous political organizations argued forcefully that the formal zoning process *(ordenamiento territorial)* was fundamental to biodiversity conservation since providing tenure security for communities meant securing nondestructive land use patterns. While the project was not expected to focus on resolving land tenure problems, it did support the titling process and provided small grants for community sustainable use projects. At the national level, project staff faced numerous challenges to their relative autonomy from within the Environment Ministry and the National Planning Department in the context of the legal reforms that restructured the country's environmental sector.

For some observers, the Colombian experience with *Biopacífico* illustrated exactly those processes linked to community-based management and sustainable use that dilute concerted action aimed at biodiversity conservation. While the GEF phase of the project did not generate a comprehensive biodiversity conservation strategy as originally intended, it did (in spite of itself some might say) establish a strong basis for consolidating such a program by constructing a process of dialogue *(concertación)*. In the face of deep institutional changes and the emergence of a broad-based black and indigenous social movement, *Biopacífico* followed a path that allowed it to build legitimacy. Had the project continued to pursue a strategy dominated by scientific research, it most likely would have faltered in the face of local resistance. While *Biopacífico* featured numerous shortcomings between 1992 and 1998, all parties involved succeeded in creating an innovative organizational structure (the *equipo ampliado*) and in sustaining a dialogue *(concertación)* that generated important new ideas about regional biodiversity conservation. Most importantly, this dialogue began constructing new boundaries of authority (legitimate power) that brought black and indigenous actors and ideas into the conservation arena for the first time. It remains to be seen if Colombian government agencies and grassroots actors can continue building on this process in the context of other initiatives.

NOTES

Fieldwork for this study was carried out in June 1996 under the auspices of a UNDP-GEF financed review of six GEF projects (INT/96/683) and in October 1998 while performing as a member of the *Biopacífico* project's final evaluation team

(COL/92/G31). The ideas and opinions expressed in this chapter are those of the author and do not represent the views of the United Nations Development Programme (UNDP) or the Global Environment Facility (GEF). I would like to thank Fernando Casas, Robin Hissong, Luz Marina Rincón, Libia Grueso, Carlos Rosero, Victor Guevara, René Grössman, Manuel Ríos, Edgar Cortés, Dr. Jorge Hernández, Julio Tresierra, Yellen Aguilar, Jairo Miguel Guerra, Alfredo Vanin, Juan Manuel Navarrete, Mirta Bosoni, Elias Córdoba, Enrique Sánchez, Claudia Leal, Jairo Hernando, Fernando Gast, Xavier Malo, Sally Timpson, Javier Amaya, and Nancy Colmenares. Arturo Escobar and Kiran Asher provided thoughtful conversation and unpublished work that proved very useful. Thanks to Eric Keys and Crystal Fortwangler for helpful comments on earlier drafts.

1. In this chapter I primarily use the term *black* to describe the people of African descent living in the region rather than other terms such as *Afro-Colombian* in deference to the widely prevalent use of *negro* by these people to describe themselves.

2. The word *concertación* in Spanish does not have an adequate translation in English. While it refers to a process of negotiation as well as a negotiated agreement, it also carries connotations of reconciliation and harmonization that are not necessarily communicated by the English word *negotiation*.

3. The project's midterm evaluation made strong criticisms regarding *Biopacífico*'s nonparticipatory approach. See Hernandez et al. 1995. The GEF Secretariat noted the success of the "project management" or working group in a bulletin published by their monitoring and evaluation division. GEF, "Building Partnerships with Communities," *Lessons Notes*, No. 1 (March) (Washington, DC: GEF Secretariat, 1998). Available at *www.gefweb.org* (as of May 2000).

4. Escobar (1999) explains that *Ley 70* recognizes black communities' collective territorial rights as well as their status as a separate ethnic group with rights to their identity and culturally appropriate education. It requires the state to develop social and economic policies in accordance with black culture and establishes that development strategies for black riverine communities must respond to black culture and community aspirations and the preservation of ecosystems.

5. Source: Proyecto *Biopacífico*, Acta del Equipo Ampliado, February 10, 1996. This operative plan covered the period 1995–1997 and focused on producing a negotiated strategy for conservation and sustainable use of biodiversity in the Pacific Coastal region.

6. Propuesta de Reformulación del PBP presentada por los Procesos Organizativos de Comunidades Negras e Indígenas, Documento marco, Buenaventura, Agosto 29 de 1995, 2. All translations are mine.

7. Convention on Biological Diversity, June 1992, Article 2, "Use of Terms." For the full text of the convention see the website: www.biodiv.org. It is interesting to note that the 1991 draft of the convention included human cultural diversity in its definition of biodiversity: "Human cultural diversity is manifested by diversity in languages, religious belief, land management practices, art, music, social structure, crop selection, diet, and any number of other attributes of human society" (WRI, IUCN, and UNEP 1992).

8. Propuesta de Reformulación, op cit, 3.

9. See chapter 1 of the GEF's Operational Strategy, Ten Operational Principles for Development and Implementation of the GEF's Work Program. Available at *www.gefweb.org* as of May 2000.

10. By the end of 1997, *Biopacífico* had dedicated approximately 40 percent of its total budget on community-level projects. Following completion of the negotiated operative plan, the project pursued subcontracts almost exclusively with community-level groups (Ríos and Wilshusen 1999).

11. The initial agreement of the *equipo ampliado* at Piangua Grande offered two guiding principles that touch on the importance of mutual respect among black and indigenous peoples: "As black and indigenous peoples, we jointly assume the defense of our ancestral territories of the Pacific Coastal region built upon mutual respect and tolerance as a foundation for living together and strengthening the unity of action." In addition, the statement proclaims, "We affirm the right to recognize and respect our differences, among ourselves and with the rest of Colombian society. Among the ethnic groups of the Pacific Coastal region are black communities, in their diversity, and distinct indigenous peoples: Tules, Katios, Woaunan, Eperara-Siapidara, Chami, Awa, Zenues and Emberas."

Chapter Six

Unmasking the "Local"

Gender, Community, and the Politics of Community-Based Rural Ecotourism in Belize

JILL M. BELSKY

Community-based conservation has emerged over the last decade in response to critiques that strategies for environmental protection have been developed at the expense of concern for people, especially historically marginalized peoples or the "dispossessed." The rationale for envisioning local communities as partners in conservation rather than as in the past as passive recipients of the latters' design, builds on the assumptions of integrated conservation and development programs (ICDPs). The goal of ICDPs is to increase the economic opportunities of resource-dependent rural communities as a means of increasing nature protection without the social problems caused by strictly protectionist approaches. Within the umbrella of ICDPs, community-based conservation attempts to locate design of local development strategies and management within the community in collaboration with other government and nongovernmental actors. The rationales for community conservation include: that local or resident groups have a strong, vested interest in the sustainable use of natural resources upon which their livelihood or cultural survival rests, that they have experiential knowledge that can assist in the identification and design of environmental management strategies, and that they are more capable of managing local resources than distant state or corporate managers

(Rao and Geisler 1990; West and Brechin 1991; Western and Wright 1994). Case studies of long-term community management of forests in Asia (Poffenberger 1990) and in Latin America (Alcorn 1993) have been instrumental in documenting the value of local communities and local knowledge in natural resource management.

To date, evaluations of ICDPs have yielded mixed results, especially in reaching significant environmental protection goals (Brandon and Wells 1992). The failure to successfully achieve environmental protection goals has led observers to suggest returning to a more strictly environmental protectionist paradigm (Kramer 1997; Hackel 1999; Robinson 1993). But supporters of integrated conservation and development projects in general, and those that promote community-based and collaborative approaches in particular, claim it is too early to discard them. They strongly caution about returning to what they refer to as a "new protectionist paradigm" and the social injustices as well as practical pitfalls associated with these approaches (Wilshusen et al. 2002). Instead, what they argue as critically needed are deeper and more comprehensive understandings of international biodiversity conservation approaches themselves as social and political process (Zerner 2000; Brechin et al. 2002).

Social science scholars and practitioners as well as conservation biologists have been raising important insights into the opportunities and constraints of integrated conservation and development approaches including community-based efforts. In an insightful article, Brosius et al. (1998) brought attention to the fact that despite similar labels and claims, community-based conservation and natural resource management programs are constituted differently and defended by claims and concepts that are often ill defined and not empirically well grounded. Furthermore, they highlight the problems encountered when advocates and practitioners, while deeply committed to the goals of devolution and community conservation, are unwilling or unable to approach resource management efforts with a nuanced understanding of resource conflicts in their areas. Adams and Hulme (2001) also argue that community conservation is not one thing but many, and is evolving both conceptually and practically. Importantly, these authors conclude that the key questions about community conservation are who sets the objectives on the ground and how trade-offs between the diverse objectives are negotiated. Li (1996) also warns that community conservation efforts are too frequently based on generic models that are neither sufficiently attuned to particular historical contexts and political struggles, nor critical of the multiple meanings and strategic deployment of concepts that guide such efforts. Agrawal and Gibson (1999) in another highly significant work caution that the image of community in conservation historically has vacillated between that of two extremes: either the cooperative and ecologically knowledgeable "enchanted" community or the tradition-bound and ecologically destructive "disenchanted" community. In the former archetype, the one commonly evoked in community conservation efforts, the rural community is represented as a socially homogenous and conflict-less entity, despite the historic reality of intracommunity divisions, struggles, and conflicts (Agrawal 1997; DuPuis and Vandergeest 1996). Another assumption that is rarely acknowledged or explored in community-level efforts is whether communities can participate and operate successfully in resource management efforts in light of inequities and disincentives for conservation that persist at broader political, economic, and institutional scales (Little 1994).

In this chapter, I revisit a study that I have written about elsewhere (Belsky 1999, 2000). It explores a community-based rural ecotourism project begun in the early 1990s in Gales Point Manatee, Belize, that I, along with groups of American and Belizean students, examined over the course of six years. My writings on this project have been critical of an undifferentiated and apolitical understanding of this small, Creole community, including who/what constitutes the "local." They have also been critical of reserving analytical and management attention solely to the local or community level of social action without acknowledging the important and instrumental ways that the "local" is shaped by extralocal social and political forces. In the case of Gales Point Manatee, Belize, these extralocal forces include: the history of British colonialism, state formation in British Honduras, now known as Belize, development aid and debt restructuring, institutionalized racism, tourism, and the contested discourses of the causes and presumed solutions to environmental degradation, including the role of community-based rural ecotourism itself (Belsky 1999, 2000). My objective here is to discuss the variable ways men and women from Gales Point participated in a community-based rural ecotourism project, and the reasons why this effort was only partially successful at integrating conservation and local economic development. I particularly want to highlight gender and its politics in this volume because there has been insufficient and uncritical attention to these forces in analyses of biodiversity conservation efforts on the ground. In contributing to this discussion, I will discuss the ways that local politics including gender relations are intricately linked to inequities operating within and extending beyond the local community, which I submit lie at the root of problems with integrated conservation and development programs including community conservation. My position is that the obstacles facing ICDPs often have less to do with problems inherent in the model per se, but in the social and political systems in which they are embedded, which continue to deny the poorest and most vulnerable peoples access and control over resources to secure their livelihood and craft their own futures.

GENDER, COMMUNITY, AND BIODIVERSITY CONSERVATION

Few assessments of community-based conservation have explicitly taken up the question of who specifically within a community has benefited from these efforts and what effect it has had on natural resource management. In particular, there has been limited attention to how gender influences these efforts. Indeed, some feminist scholars have questioned whether womens' interests are enhanced or submerged with a community-based approach to conservation (Leach 1992; Li 1996). Biodiversity conservation, especially as practiced in North American–influenced models, has largely been based on the environmental understandings and activist strategies of middle-class white males (Taylor 1997). Some suggest that when gender has been considered in international environmental management broadly defined, the design of interventions has largely been based on popular and partial understandings of womens' interests and activities, with unfortunate results (Leach 1992). This is despite the fact that development institutions and park managers have been urged to recognize rural women's multifaceted and crucial roles in resource extraction and environmental management (Agarwal 1986, 1989; Dankelman and Davidson 1988; Shiva 1989). Women are still largely depicted as victims of environmental degradation or uncritically assumed to benefit uniformly by "environmental" programs (Leach 1992). Few studies emphasize the differences among rural women and how they creatively think and reshape development and conservation programs to meet their own strategic goals and agendas (Johnson 1997, 1998; Momsen 1993).

The assertion of a biological connection between women and nature has also been controversial and contested. Some ecofeminists suggest an inherent or essentialist "woman/nature relationship" involving harmony among women as well with nature (Mies and Shiva 1993; Warren 1990). Others focus on a feminist critique of development emphasizing the perils of modern technology, Western development, and patriarchy for women (Shiva 1989; Harcourt 1994). Another group of feminist social scientists are highly skeptical of essentialist and universal arguments, preferring instead to understand women's relationship to each other, to men, and to the physical environment as socially and historically constructed (Jackson 1993; Leach et al. 1995; Rocheleau 1995). Their position argues the need to disaggregate the category of "women" and start from real-life situations and problems of resident people within concrete social and historical contexts. The answers to such questions as how does gender influence biodiversity conservation/protected area management including community conservation efforts and how is nature understood, used, and managed by men and women and for whose benefit, are largely contingent and need be answered through a context-specific, historically grounded approach. Whether and how particular groups of men and women and environmental interests are complementary or not cannot be theorized a priori, but must be examined empirically for a particular people, place, and time. To do so demands individual and micropolitical analysis, but also how these are linked to broader political, economic, and ideological projects.

COMMUNITY-BASED RURAL ECOTOURISM
IN GALES POINT MANATEE, BELIZE

The community of Gales Point Manatee, Belize, is located on a narrow peninsula extending into the Southern Lagoon, a four-hour boat ride from Belize
City, the nation's largest city. Since the early 1990s, American wildlife biologists and other long-term visitors to Gales Point worked to designate approximately 175,000 acres including the community of Gales Point Manatee as a
biodiversity reserve known as the Manatee Special Development Area
(MSDA). The MSDA has since been recognized by the Belize state and
entails a comprehensive plan for protecting endangered species, particularly
the manatee and sea turtle. Informed by their earlier work in the Community
Baboon Sanctuary, the planners sought to foster conservation in the MSDA
through an ICDP approach built around rural ecotourism, community management, and close collaboration between the private and public sectors (Horwich and Lyon 1998). Working with the support of Belizean government officials and the Belize Audubon Society, they organized residents into five
associations based on the major ecotourism activities: a bed and breakfast
(herein B&B) association; a tour operators and guides association; a farmers'
association; and a craft association. These associations were managed through
an umbrella cooperative known as the Gales Point Progressive Cooperative
comprised of the chairs of each of the associations along with local village
council leaders. The planners organized a Manatee Advisory Team to provide
technical and logistical support during the first few years (Horwich and Lyons
1998). The project leaders (whose training was largely in the biological sciences) acknowledged the presence of complex social and political dynamics
(Horwich, pers. comm. 1996; Greenlee, pers.comm. 1996).

  In the early 1990s when the rural ecotourism project was being formed,
Gales Point Manatee consisted of approximately 350 individuals living in sev-
enty-seven permanent households, in addition to vacation cottages owned by
wealthy residents of Belize City. The community was largely a mixture of
older and young people, with many people in their middle years absent for
months or years at a time seeking employment in the United States or Belize
City (GPPC 1992). While many households farmed, fished, and hunted in
the nearby karst mountains, forests, savannas, rivers, lagoons, and ocean, these
activities provided supplementary food and income. The vast majority of
households obtained their staple food of beans, rice, and vegetables through
purchase from markets in Belize City. In telling stories about rural and environmental change in the area, residents emphasized the links between declines
in local natural resources and commercial fishing, logging, and hunting by
nonresidents. Residents' accounts differed strongly from those of local and
foreign environmental groups who explained resource scarcities solely as the
result of the nonsustainable local livelihood activities and the "maladapted"

values of Gales Point residents. The majority of households in Gales Point earned food and income from hunting and selling bush meat and fishing. A smaller minority found employment in government service, nearby citrus farms, and tourist lodges, and wove baskets from local vines and prepared snacks for sale to tourists for supplementary income. Most families relied on remittances from employed children in Belize City or the United States for their income.

Given the sparse economic opportunities available in Gales Point and awareness of the income being generated in the Community Baboon Sanctuary, many Gales Point residents welcomed the efforts of outsiders to assist them with developing ecotourism. In exchange, those participating in the ecotourism associations agreed to limit hunting of threatened wildlife species, to cooperate with boating regulations to protect manatee habitat, and to provide labor on a limited basis to scientific studies conducted in the area.

As reported in more detail elsewhere (Belsky 1999), B&B operators increased their income considerably in the first few years of the ecotourism project (1992–1994). Of particular economic importance were student groups (such as ours) who stayed in a large number of B&Bs for longer than a few days. However, after 1994 the number of tourists visiting Gales Point declined, as did state funding. Additionally, the support of outside organizers became more sporadic, and the project "floundered" for a number of years.

Nonetheless, the rural ecotourism project generated important links between conservation and development among a handful of Gales Point households, but it also exacerbated rivalries and divisions across the community. I argue that the limited benefits as well as associated conflicts cannot be traced to singular causes, but rather to a complex intersection of gender, age, class, family allegiance, and political party affiliation that predated but were intensified as a result of the ecotourism effort. Within this matrix, the social construction of gender was pivotal though not sufficient to explain what happened.

GENDER, CLASS, AND FAMILY INTERESTS
IN ECOTOURISM ASSOCIATIONS

Not surprisingly, gender influenced the composition of rural ecotourism activities and membership in the various associations in important ways. The socialization of women as the major caretakers of home and domestic activities underlies their control over B&B enterprises and in the craft association, as both home care and weaving baskets were historically taught to and expected from females. In contrast, males were more likely to fish, hunt, and be hired by commercial firms such as loggers. Hence, their knowledge of boating and the surrounding marine and forest environments led males to dominate the boat operators and nature tour guide associations (there was only one female member in the tour boat association). Moreover, the potential for intra-household conflict, which could have arisen with womens' increased income as a result of B&B enterprises was mitigated by the opportunity for males to earn income through complementary activities as nature and boat tour guides. Indeed, it was women and men of the same handful of households who had the material resources and interpersonal networks to enable them to take advantage of new opportunities.

Females welcomed the opportunity to operate B&Bs because there were few other economic opportunities in the community and this enterprise complemented their homemaking skills and responsibilities. One young woman explained that she began the B&B "because it can be done while I keep the house, cook, and watch the little ones, and don't put out my man." An older woman with three teenagers said she joined "because it based on skills I know and it's a way to make a dollar where I say where to put it . . . to help the children go to school in Belize City and [husband] don't always agree to it being spent that way." They enjoyed the fact that their domestic skills were honored and financially rewarded.

But gendered knowledge of housekeeping and cooking or of nature and boat touring were not sufficient to permit all women and men to operate B&Bs, become nature/boat guides, or to participate in management associations. There were important economic entry costs to operating B&Bs and serving as a nature and boat guide that excluded poor women and men. To operate a B&B, there had to be an extra bedroom or the ability to temporarily displace family members from their bedrooms. According to standards set by the project, guest bedrooms had to have walls and standard furniture such as beds with sheets, mosquito nets, and fans. Cooking and bathroom facilities also had to meet basic sanitation standards. Wallpaper and cheerful decorations were also desirable. To be a boat operator/nature guide required access to a boat, engine, life jackets, and fuel. Clearly, women and men who had access to these material resources were not from the lowest economic stratum.

In addition to economic prerequisites for entry, the ability to gain access to clients and wield power within the ecotourist association and community at large was also influenced by one's family ties. It is common among women's groups in Belize for social and material barriers to impede some women's membership (McClaurin 1995/1996). In Gales Point, the Welch clan extended their historic leadership to the new ecotourism trade. Hortense Welch chaired the B&B association for its first five years of operation. Her long-time partner, Moses Andrewin, was the lead boat operator and nature tour guide. Their son, Kevin, was the boat operators' association chair, and their relatives Ivan Welch, Osmond Welch, and Gibert Welch comprised a large share of the association itself. Hortense was also a long-term member of the Gales Point village council. Not surprisingly, Walter Goff, who chaired the GPPC, the umbrella ecotourist cooperative, also was the village council chair.

To provide a mechanism for promoting equal access to ecotourist guests, one of the planners organized the use of a rotation schedule. A sign was located at the entry to the village (via the road) instructing tourists to locate ecotourist association leaders for B&B and boat operating/tour guiding assignments. The leaders assigned tourists to particular providers *in turn*, following a list. Initially, many B&B providers commended the rotation schedule. They appreciated the assistance of project planners who made reservations and arranged for prepayment so B&B hostesses could purchase food before the arrival of guests. But especially when the number of student groups and ecotourists declined and the assistance of project planners decreased, the use of the rotation schedule became hotly debated. A major complaint was that formal procedures were not followed and that the B&B association chair, Hortense Welch, was unfair in her assignment of ecotourist guests. "Hortense always favor her relatives, and herself, and anyway the real decision are made by Hortense's family members outside of the association's meeting." Hortense countered that many B&B operators were not home to receive guests when they were assigned, do not publicly share their concerns at association meetings, and do not appreciate her work burden as association chair and the insufficient measures the project provided as compensation. She said she had "tired" of the other women complaining and "not telling their troubles in front of all but only behind my back." According to Hortense, the planners told her she could "take an extra guest here and there" as payment for her services as association chair. Hortense said,

> The trouble with the rotation system is that when tourists enter the village they don't always get to me first. Sometimes someone else invites them to stay at their house. Or when I figure out whose turn it is, that person is in Belize City or not prepared to have a guest for that night—either they don't have enough food, or are too tired from doing some other works and don't want to cook and clean for a guest that night. So I keep going down the list. But the members don't remember this and complain I don't do it fair.

After three years as association chair, she said she was "burnt out" and admitted:

> I don't like to call meetings anymore because not even half of the members come, the others are either out of the village or too busy with other activities. I'm tired of making all the decisions and being criticized later when someone doesn't like them. I was told in the beginning I could take a few extra guests because of the planning work I do, but the members don't like this.

As the project progressed, many of the B&B providers found employment in nearby tourist lodges that were also developing to take advantage of the tourism trade. But combining regular employment, their domestic duties, and maintaining a B&B created tensions and difficult choices for B&B operators and their families. Those with access to female extended support transferred B&B hosting duties to daughters, sisters, or mothers. A young daughter in such a home communicated to us her strong dismay over her increased workload, though the burden was mitigated somewhat by the opportunity to interact with American students. Another strategy taken by a B&B operator with an outside job was to leave a cold, bag lunch on the table for guests rather than provide the customary hot cooked lunch of rice, beans, and meat (traditionally bush meat or fish). This coping practice raised contradictions between the advertised "authentic" Creole experience of rural ecotourism and the reality of being served a sandwich made from imported Spam and mayonnaise. Inauthenticity arose also over the implications of hunting prohibitions that foreclosed serving traditional cuisine based on local wild game (Belsky 2000).

GENDER, RURAL ECOTOURISM, AND NATIONAL PARTY POLITICS

Peoples' participation in the community ecotourism project was skewed not only as a result of gender and class, but also by connections to national politics. Historically, Gales Point has been known for its support of the PUP national party (Peoples United Party), rather than for the other major party known as the UDP (United Democratic Party). Their close connection to the PUP and to the minister of the environment at the time was widely understood as a reason for strong, initial PUP governmental support for the project (Belsky 1999). Most of the men and women who assumed key roles in the ecotourism associations were strong supporters of the PUP. Those with party affiliation to the UDP claimed that their party ties restricted their ability to participate in the rural ecotourism efforts, despite the fact that community associations were technically opened to any local resident. A female UDP supporter explained:

> I know I can't work with Hortense and the other women. I have to go it
> alone if I want to run a B&B. But that's okay with me because I know I have
> the ability, and (her partner) knows many people through his work as a boat
> operator. We don't need the community nor the PUP to get tourists.

In 1994, the UDP regained political power (only to lose it again to the PUP in 1998). Starting in 1994 political and financial governmental support for the MSDA and ecotourism project declined (though it rekindled at the end of the decade to some degree because of resumed PUP patronage). The withdrawal of governmental backing in 1994, coupled with the sporadic presence of project advisors (who turned the project over to the community), took its toll on the ecotourism project and community. Management of both the local village council and the Gales Point Progressive Cooperative faltered. In 1997, PUP backer Walter Goff resigned his positions as chair of the village council and the Gales Point Progressive Cooperative (GPPC). Not knowing the PUP would regain power so soon, both Hortense Welch and her son, Kevin Andrewin, switched political party affiliation to back the UDP. Kevin was elected chair of the GPPC in 1997, only to lose the seat the following year. Participation in community-managed associations continued to slide: few people attended meetings, paid dues, were willing to provide regular water transportation to and from Belize City, or take responsibility for producing and distributing brochures to market Gales Point as an ecotourist destination (Belsky 1999).

Indeed these intra-community conflicts produced further backlashes and resistance. Non-association members refused to carry phone messages and reservation requests for ecotourist providers. Some also refused to pay their share of the community electricity bill claiming that ecotourist homes with refrigerators and fans used more power. In addition, someone torched the craft center. Men and women not benefiting from ecotourism were particularly resentful that they were expected to abide by restrictions on hunting, fishing, and farming while other community members received some albeit small compensation through tourism. A particular source of anger and resentment was the presence of state and state-backed commercial entrepreneurs who flouted environmental regulations and logged, dredged, and purchased threatened wildlife in the Manatee Special Development Area. They were also greatly angered over state backing for development of commercial agriculture by foreigners in the area over assisting local farmers. A few stories circulating in the community at that time attested to these strong feelings. One story involved government officials who visited Gales Point to purchase threatened and prohibited sea turtle meat. Another entailed government officials who suggested that, in exchange for supporting the community ecotourism project, residents would receive legal access to farmland made available by the construction of the new Manatee road linking Gales Point to two major highways. But by 1999 no land titles had materialized for residents and, in fact, one Gales Point farmer with mature perennial crops, but no formal title, lost his land when the government sold it to a wealthy Jamaican farmer eager to establish a citrus plantation. The lessons were obvious: this poor rural community had little political voice, whether male or female, PUP or UDP:

> We all vying to be close to the government. But it don't matter PUP or UDP either one going to sell that land to make big money. But without land to farm we in Gales Point never be able to get ahead. Food is expensive and now the government don't want us to hunt anymore. What are our kids going to eat? Why should we respect the government and its rules for hunting when they are cutting in the reserve? They don't care what happens to us.

Given this situation, one can understand why gender must be viewed in connection with national position, class, and race. As a woman in Gales Point summed it up for me,

> It hard being a woman here. But it harder being poor and from this place where no one really care what happening to us. We hoped that the tourists make others see that we here. But it just the same, the same as always it hard to get by.

IMPLICATIONS FOR GENDER, JUSTICE, AND INTERNATIONAL BIODIVERSITY CONSERVATION

The case study of Gales Point Manatee, Belize, raises a number of issues that are germane to current debates in international biodiversity conservation and especially to the opportunities and constraints of ICDPs and community-based conservation. Above all, this example reinforces the fact that biodiversity conservation/protected area management is not a neutral but a highly social and political process. Every approach to conservation is constructed on a particular understanding of the forces selected as significantly shaping rural and environmental change in a particular area. In Gales Point and in many other cases, different accounts emerged that were hotly contested. The accounts given by poor, rural residents (and especially by poor, rural women) did not inform the objectives or procedures of biodiversity conservation policies and programs. Had they been given consideration in Gales Point, the project would have included the following: protection of threatened wildlife and habitats from state-supported logging, dredging, commercial fishing, and agricultural development; assistance to local residents to keep control of tourism from nonresident entrepreneurs and cruise ships; attainment of land titles for local farmers; development of markets for local goods and handicrafts; and improvement of basic community infrastructure. They also might have incorporated ways to minimize the economic and political costs that prohibited the most impoverished women and men from participating in and benefiting from the activities that were implemented in the community. Some loans were available but the terms and conditions were highly problematic especially for the least well off (Belsky 1999).

Second, this analysis recognizes and applauds the goals of project planners, Belizean nongovernmental organizations, and their backers in the government to develop a project that assisted Gales Point residents with economic development to support wildlife and habitat conservation. This coalition did try to develop local management capacity and control and assisted with economic activities that included women as well as men. And a handful of families achieved the hoped-for links between local development and conservation, though it was not clear whether these could be sustained. Should we criticize the ICDP/community conservation model for its limited success or should we look to the complex and intersecting forces in that particular place and time that mitigated full community involvement and significant environmental management? Perhaps both. One problem is that development programs—ICDP or otherwise—need to build on existing development practices, especially those that are the most economically valuable. But their economic value also makes them of interest to elites who are usually unwilling to give them over to local residents. In the case of Gales Point, important opportunities for local development were missed by not building on local experience and keen interest to further develop sustainable farming, fishing, hunting, and possibly logging in addition to rural ecotourism.

Another issue regards variability in community governing capacity. While a village council provided local governance in Gales Point, there were no communal or customary natural resource management rules or traditions upon which to build community resource management. Indeed, resource use and management were open access, and strategic opportunism based on individuals and their families characterized the livelihood strategies of residents. The community is also remote, not well connected to transportation and communication infrastructure, and crisscrossed with historic rivalries and tensions. While its ecological conditions suggest the Gales Point area as a biodiversity "hot spot" worthy of conservation attention, it is a socially complex place to develop a community conservation effort. For such an effort to succeed, the community would require additional support and assistance that was not provided during earlier attempts. Indeed there were no special efforts made to understand the history of economic development activities in the area, and especially from the residents' perspectives.

Related to the above, it is likely that the "model" for biodiversity/protected area management implemented in Gales Point Manatee emanated from the minds and representations of its outside planners rather than from ongoing dialogue with members of the Gales Point rural community. A dialogue could have generated a different or modified approach or at least suggested ways to provide the social support and assistance structures noted above. Even so, there are no guarantees. Unanticipated or unintended consequences will always emerge. But no effort can survive, let alone succeed, if the majority of local residents continue to bear the large proportion of the costs of environmental conservation while marginally sharing in its benefits. This seems to be what has largely happened for so many attempted ICDPs, social and community forestry programs, and "participatory-based development efforts" of the past. The ideal model never really gets played out on the ground. Social and political forces operating from within but also from beyond, the local community rarely permit control over valuable resources from sustainable economic development to be controlled or even significantly shared with and across poor, rural communities. While community dynamics, including the intersection of gender with other sociopolitical forces, are critical to understanding the micro-operation of community efforts, it is these larger inequities that seem to represent the real obstacles to ICDPs and to the symptoms we identify and lament in community-based efforts.

Chapter Seven

THE POLITICAL ECONOMY OF ECOTOURISM

Pendjari National Park and Ecotourism Concentration in Northern Benin

PATRICK C. WEST, CRYSTAL L. FORTWANGLER,
VALENTIN AGBO, MICHAEL SIMSIK, NESTOR SOKPON

Ecotourism is believed to be the fastest growing type of tourism (Ecotourism Society 1998).[1] Many have come to view it as a means of reconciling the conflicts between the needs for protected area conservation and the pressing needs of local people. While observers note that ecotourism is no panacea, they continue to argue that it has the potential to contribute to successful conservation and provide benefits to local communities in or near protected areas (Young 1999). Indeed, the United Nations designated 2002 as the International Year of Ecotourism (IYE) and its Commission on Sustainable Development requested that international agencies, governments, and the private sector undertake supportive activities.

Yet despite these attractive arguments, local populations have in many cases received limited benefits, if any, from ecotourism operations and conflict over natural resources has not decreased (Bookbinder et al. 1998; L. M. Campbell 1999; McLaren 1998; Pearl 1994; Young 1999). In some cases, the impact on local people has been negative. Moreover, ecotourism has provided little protection for protected areas (Brandon and Margoulis 1996; Honey 1999). Groups such as the Third World Network recognize these complications, arguing that in its experience "bad policies and practices in ecotourism by far outweigh the good examples" (Third World Network et al. 2000). The Rethinking Tourism Project further argues that many ecotourism projects do not bring the benefits touted, pointing out that projects often increase social, environmental, and other problems in communities (McLaren 2000).

In examining the successes and failures of ecotourism, much of the literature overlooks the political economic forces that shape ecotourism and hinder small-scale, local operations (Weaver 1998; Sherman and Dixon 1997). Some sources, however, provide more nuanced examinations of political economy (Bailey 1991; Honey 1999; Woo 1991; Young 1999). Political economic perspectives highlight the considerable barriers to local participation in and ownership of ecotourism as well as the distribution of economic and other benefits within communities. If political economic forces block the delivery of benefits to local people, then the promise of ecotourism as a means of merging conservation and development can easily fail. Unfortunately, the concentration of ecotourism benefits in the hands of a few powerful actors at the expense of the rural poor is more often the rule than the exception.

In this chapter we examine a case that illustrates strong domination of ecotourism markets by an international hotel chain operating in and around Pendjari National Park, Benin, West Africa. We argue that excessive concentration of ecotourism benefits detracts from both conservation and community development objectives. This case is examined in comparative perspective with other examples from the literature that explore "exception niche theories" in which certain structural situations allow for local benefits to flow to local people in spite of difficult political economic conditions. We conclude with a discussion of why and how local people can benefit from this type of enterprise.

ECOTOURISM AND POLITICAL ECONOMY

Political economic forces play a strong role in shaping the success or failure of ecotourism projects. Exploring such forces helps to understand why many local people cannot capture the benefits purportedly offered by ecotourism and why foreign multinationals, wealthy individuals, and large national operators benefit instead. For example, foreign tourism companies and nonlocals own 90 percent of all coastal development in Belize (Munt 1993), 61 percent of hotels near Royal Chitwan National Park in Nepal (Bookbinder et al. 1998), 80 percent of Costa Rica's beachfront property (Honey 1999), and 100 percent of the safari companies near the Central Kalahari Game Reserve in Botswana (Hitchcock and Brandenburgh 1990). At the same time, in some places the reverse is true: in Dominica more than 62 percent of facilities and 70 percent of units are fully owned by local people (Esprit 1994).

For the purposes of this chapter, the term *political economy* refers to the struggle over power and influence to monopolize benefits from ecotourism (chapter 3). We use the term *power* in a Weberian sense as the ability of powerful actors to impose their will on government policy making in the face of potential resistance (Weber 1978 [1968]; West 1982, 1994). *Influence* is a broader term that refers to the use of social network contacts by actors to create personal relations with government officials to persuade them to make decisions in favor of special interests (Banfield 1961). Influence can be enhanced in situations where government agencies have self-interests that lead them to act in accord with other powerful interest groups.

Ecotourism boosters argue that local people can be stakeholders in natural resources protection when they are given incentives to pursue ecotourism rather than resource extraction. Under this "stakeholders' theory," ecotourism is promoted as a way to protect resources because it provides economic opportunities to "keep trees in place" and gives local people an incentive not to overutilize or degrade resources by providing income from nonextractive activities (Honey 1999). In the case of protected areas, proponents assume that if resource-dependent rural populations receive economic and other benefits through "bottom-up" ecotourism then they will have an incentive to protect resources within and around a protected area (Cater 1994; Western et al. 1994).

Honey (1999, 25) defines ecotourism in the following terms: "travel to fragile, pristine, and usually protected areas that strives to be low impact and (usually) small scale. It helps educate the traveler; provides funds for conservation; directly benefits the economic development and political empowerment of local communities; and fosters respect for different cultures and for human rights." Unfortunately, studies show that the vast majority of tourism income disproportionately benefits a small number of powerful actors, which may be international, national, or local. Some studies suggest that foreign firms from industrialized countries or multinational tourism conglomerates often monopolize tourism benefits, a structural process that is often created, enhanced, and preserved by power and influence relations throughout the tourism sector (Machlis and Burch 1983; Truong 1990). A World Bank study estimated that 55 percent of tourist spending in developing countries eventually leaked back to developed countries because many of the goods and services essential for foreign operators based in the country were imported, while profits were repatriated (Brandon 1993). Other studies suggest that many times the benefits of ecotourism accrue in the hands of only a few wealthy local people (J. Campbell 1999; Hall 1994).

Multinational tourism conglomerates (joined at times by wealthy national tourism operators) often monopolize ecotourism profits, effectively squeezing out local operations and precluding the creation of others (Akama 1999; Young 1999). They succeed in part because they hold a competitive advantage over local and smaller enterprises. For example, in times of depression or during low season, small operators find it difficult to stay in business whereas large-scale operators draw on resources from other tourism or business enterprises, thus ensuring a continuous cash flow. Because of limited capital, local people may be kept out of seasonal tourism entirely or might sell to larger operators for a significant profit. Access to international markets is also an advantage for large-scale operators. They can offer package deals to help ensure that hotel reservations are booked and paid in advance. For example, 54 percent of hotel reservations near Royal Chitwan National Park are made in advance from Kathmandu for large-scale operators (Bookbinder et al. 1998).

Large-scale operators also succeed because they share similar interests with central governments concerning foreign exchange. These operators establish themselves as political players at the regional or national level via personal relations with government officials such that they can persuade officials to make decisions that favor their interests. Such influence is also likely because of the considerable amounts of money the foreign companies invest in the host country.

The financial power and ubiquity of large-scale tourism operators is impressive. For example, British-owned Airtours, the world's largest air-inclusive holiday company, is not only a tour operator but also a travel agent, cruise line, and airline (Pattullo 1996). The company's 1999 fiscal year profits before taxes were about US$255 million. In greater competition with ecotourism operators is Abercrombie & Kent International Inc. (A&K), a tour operator well known for its nature-based adventure safaris. A&K advertises, "African safaris are the mainstay of Abercrombie & Kent. No one does it better—no one has done it longer." The company explains how it maintains quality: "With 33 worldwide offices—we offer a support system virtually unmatched in the industry. Our 'on-site' offices are small enough to offer knowledgeable, personalized service, yet as a company, A&K is large enough to secure the best available guides, transport, accommodations, activities and amenities for our guests. In addition, quality is maintained by designing, managing, controlling—or in some cases, owning—the product line" (Abercrombie and Kent 2000).

The type, number, and interaction of the above factors will vary from case to case but the strong tendency toward concentration of benefits remains constant. In order to explore some of these factors in greater detail we examine the barriers to locally managed ecotourism operations in Tanougou, northern Benin.

POLITICAL ECONOMY OF ECOTOURISM IN NORTHERN BENIN

Tanougou is a small Gourmanche village wedged between Pendjari National Park and the Atacora Mountains. In 1987, approximately five hundred residents of Tanougou were removed to a three-kilometer strip between the park boundary and the Atacora Mountains. A study by Hough (1989) laid the groundwork for assessing the disastrous effects this displacement had on the people of Tanougou. As a result, farm size decreased and some villagers became landless. Because the soils in the region are poor and rainfall is slight, land must be cropped by rotation farming. There is not enough land within the three-kilometer strip to support residents over the long term. Rotation times have diminished from ten to two to three years and soil fertility has declined. In recent years, periods of hunger have occurred, making malnutrition a health concern in the village (Agbo 1992; Agbo et al. 1993; Simsik et al. 1993).

At one time, a state-run hotel monopolized tourism facilities within Pendjari National Park. The facility fell into disuse and ill repair because of low demand. After a few years a British woman, Mrs. "E" received government approval to establish a campground near the old hotel site. While it was not highly profitable, the manager of an international hotel chain operating in Benin believed that Mrs. "E's" operation was successful financially. Anticipating large profits, the international hotel chain manager took action to get Mrs. "E" removed from the park in order to go ahead with plans to renovate the old Pendjari Hotel. Not surprisingly, the Ministry of Tourism would not grant Mrs. "E" a permit to carry on her campground activities the following year—the same year in which the international hotel chain received a permit and began reconstruction work. In the context of our discussion, the fate of Mrs. "E" is less important than the fact that the international hotel chain had her quickly removed. At the same time, the international chain received a permit from the Ministry of Tourism to build Tata huts using modern materials. Traditionally, they are round mud dwellings with grass thatch roofs. It also renovated the hotel despite holding debt with the government of Benin. While Mrs. "E's" campground was not a locally owned enterprise, it was a small-scale operation with little power and influence.

How might we interpret this case in terms of political economy? A small operator is removed so that a larger operator can monopolize the tourism concession in a national park. How did this happen? Was it power-based "political clout" or social network–based influence between the international hotel chain and the Ministry of Tourism? Did the Ministry of Tourism perceive that the international hotel chain could draw in more investment capital, tourists, and foreign exchange and thus advance the state's interests? Was it because the international chain was already in debt to the government of Benin when it entered the Pendjari Park market for about eleven million Central African francs (or US$21,000 in 1993)? Did the government want to guarantee repayment of the debt? In light of these factors, the local manager of the international hotel chain appeared to be in a position to influence decision making within Benin's Ministry of Tourism. The Forest Service's inability to stop the proposed development plans within the park is another indicator of the international hotel chain's influence within the Ministry of Tourism. The Ministry of Rural Development, which houses the Forest Service, is considered one of the country's most powerful organizations because of the centrality of agriculture and rural development in the national economy. But in this case, even though the Forest Service had authority over park management policy and officially objected to the plan, the natural resource management agency backed down.

In spite of the clues and questions that we uncovered, our data does not enable us to argue unequivocally in favor of any of the competing explanations mentioned above. We found evidence of large operators displacing small ones but could not pinpoint the exact influence processes or power relationships in play. Most likely some combination of all of these factors best explains how the international hotel chain came to influence decision making within the Ministry of Tourism. It would seem to be based more on "influence" and the ability of the chain to advance the interests of the government than on coercion. We can conclude that the Ministry of Tourism was in some way influenced to quickly use its permit approval/denial authority in favor of a large "neocolonial" firm at the expense of a small firm. We also know that, while the Pendjari Hotel became profitable (making fifty-six million CFAs or about US$100,000) during their first season in operation (1990–1991), the international hotel chain remained in debt to the national government. This debt helped to bind the Ministry of Tourism to maintaining the chain's dominance of tourism development, thus ensuring both loan repayment and increased foreign exchange.

How did the chain's strong influence within the Ministry of Tourism affect the villagers of Tanougou? Had the villagers developed a small artisan workshop in their village, the international chain most likely would not have objected. However, if local villagers had tried to get a permit to build a second hotel in the park, the chain probably would have felt very threatened and would have moved to block such an effort. It is not likely, however, that the villagers of Tanougou would have gone that far since they did not have the financial capital for that scale of activity.

The conclusion that the international chain might have tried to block village tourism efforts is based on prior research. The chain blocked a hotel proposal for Tata hut construction by a regional tourism firm at Tanougou Falls in the late 1980s. Although the regional firm had permit rights to the falls, the Ministry of Tourism forbade them from constructing anything there. As one interview respondent noted, "All they can do is permit people to camp there with their own tents." The ministry imposed these restrictions because the international chain running the Hotel Pendjari was worried that the regional excursion firm would steal their business. If the international chain and the ministry took this action against a midsized and fairly influential excursion firm, then they could easily have blocked initiatives to help local villagers develop tourist lodging.

THE POLITICAL ECONOMY OF A WATERFALL

We now turn to an analysis of the complex political struggle over who controls the rights to exploit the tourist potential of the Tanougou waterfalls. These falls are located next to the village of Tanougou and generate the majority of ecotourism benefits in the area. While the falls are outside the boundaries of the park, the following analysis is important because it reveals much about key elements of the political economy of ecotourism in the region.

The Tanougou Falls are a beautiful multitiered cascade that flows from the Atacora Mountains. They are the highest and most beautiful falls in Benin, attracting more tourists every year as they become better known. As mentioned above, the regional tourism excursion firm emerged as the winner in a complex struggle for permit rights to the falls, gaining a fifteen-year lease permit from the Ministry of Tourism. Mr. "J," a Frenchman and principal owner of the excursion firm, became the official holder of the lease. He maintained offices in Cotonou and in other neighboring capitals such as Lome (Togo), Onagndougar (Burkino Faso), Bamako (Mali), and Niamey (Niger). With well-established markets, he drew his business mainly from French tourists.

A struggle over access to the falls began in the 1980s as they became better known as a popular tourist site. In 1989, Mr. "A" wanted to operate a campground at the falls and needed a business partner who could help him obtain the necessary permits from the Ministry of Tourism. He approached Mr. "P" who had many connections in the government, which would be helpful in gaining access and influence within the Ministry of Tourism. As a result of this relationship, Mr. "P" succeeded in starting his own operation at the falls during the 1989–1990 season. However, a struggle for control between Mr. "P" and Mr. "A" then ensued with Mr. "A" emerging as the winner in a court battle. Mr. "A" then needed another partner with access and clout within the Ministry of Tourism. He formed a partnership with Mr. "M" and built eighteen small huts to house tourists who wanted to camp at the site. This construction was done without approval of the Ministry of Tourism since building was forbidden at the falls, and as a result, the huts were torn down and the enterprise was terminated.

Mr. "A" required yet another partner to ensure a tourism business at the falls. He turned to the regional excursion firm, which brought tourists to Tanougou Falls and Pendjari National Park. Mr. "J," the president of the firm, agreed to work with Mr. "A" in forming a new partnership. This was the key transition point leading to power struggles over who controlled tourism at Tanougou Falls. Note that Mr. "A" was not a partner in the excursion firm. Instead, Mr. "J" put up the necessary money and used his influence and clout to help Mr. "A" obtain renewed authorization from the Ministry of Tourism to continue using the campsite at the Tanougou waterfalls.

The permit to operate the campsite was in the name of Mr. "J," the principal owner of the excursion firm. Mr. "A" then managed the site for Mr. "J." Just as with Mrs. "E," the Ministry of Tourism turned its favoritism from Mr. "P" and Mr. "M" to Mr. "J" and the regional excursion firm who seemingly had more internal access and clout with the ministry. It was the power of relative personal influence in high places and the stability of that working relationship that won the day.

These two examples reveal the raw edge of tourism in the region and suggest that any attempt to help the Tanougou villagers with independent development efforts would need to account for potential roadblocks imposed by those who possess internal access and clout. While the exact form of domination could not be determined from our data, it would seem that network-based influence was more important than coercion. We suspect that the government's interest in maximizing tourist flows and foreign exchange may have led it to favor the interests of the regional tourism excursion firm. It is clear that political economic forces posed major stumbling blocks in achieving the elusive ends of using ecotourism as a means of integrating conservation and development. It raises in stark relief the question: development for whom? To explore this question, we turn to a comparative analysis of the structural conditions under which rural villagers may benefit from ecotourism. We call these "exception theories."

EXCEPTIONS TO ECOTOURISM CONCENTRATION

Despite the influence of the multinational and national tourism operators, some circumstances make it possible to mitigate against ecotourism concentration. The literature discusses at least five exceptions supporting an argument that it is possible for local people to benefit from ecotourism despite an unfavorable political economy. Each of the following is discussed and critiqued below: (1) prior establishment of cottage industry; (2) absence of the state; (3) niche exceptions; and (4) coalition support providing favorable policies and laws for the small-scale ecotourism sector.

Prior Establishment of Cottage Industry

Kutay proposes that early establishment of small-scale cottage industries (prior to the entry of large-scale operators) can maintain a foothold against the competition and political influence of later large-scale entrants (Kutay 1984). He discusses small-scale ecotourism enterprises in and around Cahuita National Park in Costa Rica. In low profit areas where tourism is marginal or when ecotourism produces a relatively modest profit or small profit margin, cottage industries may survive and large-scale entrants may stay away (L. M.

Campbell 1999). In northern Benin, the debate over this exception is moot because there was no such cottage industry before external capital penetrated and captured the tourism markets. Also, market potential was sufficient to motivate a takeover even if it had existed.

Although existing cottage industries may flourish, large-scale operators may pursue local markets and disrupt locally controlled operations. For example, villagers in Malaysia developed a firefly-viewing ecotour where huge numbers of the insects feed on mangrove trees, creating a spectacle of luminescent flashes. The tours became so popular and profitable that neighboring villages began competing with locals for access to the river and driving the profits down for the people in Kampung Kuantan (Markels 1998). Similar cases from Bolivia and Dominica appear in the literature (Hendrix 1997; Pattullo 1996; Esprit 1994).

Absence of the State

Fortmann (1997) suggests where the state is weakest, such as in remote areas or following civil war, local institutions and knowledge can and do prosper. An article by the Bawa Village Community (1997) in Mozambique highlights how a local ecotourism project has prospered in the absence of strong state penetration. Similarly L. M. Campbell (1999) suggests that the state may avoid becoming involved in local ecotourism operations given the low potential for foreign exchange earnings.

In Benin, this exception is also moot since a state actor has long been involved in the local political economy. Moreover, the possibility exists that as the ecotourism ventures of local people become more profitable, the state will want to absorb a share, possibly decreasing the share for locals. Even if the state does not demand economic participation, it may impose new taxes. For example, after declaring the area near Ostional Wildlife Refuge "non-touristic" in 1980 and playing no role in tourism development, the Costa Rican government eventually found it in its interest to begin collecting taxes from accommodation owners in 1995 (L. M. Campbell 1999).

Niche Exceptions

There are at least three types of "niche" exceptions: (1) when local people have an advantage because of their own unique skills (skill-based), (2) when they can concentrate on activities that complement rather than compete with large tourism operators (symbiotic niches), and (3) special property rights. The first suggests that certain small-scale operators can monopolize key skills or resources in ways that cannot be displaced by large-scale entrants into local tourist markets. Weber (1991) found this to be true for the Sherpa guiding enterprises in Nepal's Sagarmatha National Park. The Sherpas' ability to carry heavy loads in cold, high altitude atmospheric conditions provided a skill base that large-scale capital could not displace. This is also true to some extent for Inuit outfitters in Northern Territory parks in Canada (Lawson 1985). Another example of a skill-based niche is the ability of local people to iden-tify local flora and fauna (and especially the historical and cultural uses). Although outside agencies can gather this information, many ecotourists pre-fer to have a local person guide them.

The second niche exception suggests that small-scale enterprises can be successful if they complement or at least do not interfere with large-scale tourism entities. We call these symbiotic niches. By focusing on enterprises that complement large-scale interests, the latter may see it as in their own interest to allow such an enterprise (West and Brechin 1991). For example, the sale of crafts and presentation of dance performances responds to their tourists' interests in other cultures. Similarly, the production of local foods by local people may reduce food costs for large-scale tour operators as well as add local "cultural color" for their guests. In Benin, the sale of crafts has been pursued and not challenged or hindered by large-scale operators (West et al. in press).

Another type of symbiotic niche is one in which small-scale operators focus on different ecotourists than those sought after by the larger operations. For example, Barkin (2000) explains the potential for rural communities in Mexico to secure ecotourism benefits by focusing on national middle- and working-class tourists. Victurine (2000) argues that in Uganda small-scale entrepreneurs should focus on "yuppy adventurers" and "energetic expats" rather than the "affluent africaphiles."

Although symbiotic niches provide opportunities to co-exist with large-scale tourism and in some cases revive past traditions, negative cultural impacts are possible. A Yagua tribe member living in the Peruvian Amazon writes, "[W]e see how our crafts are exploited to such an extent that in many of our communities our brothers have to spend their whole time on this activ-ity, causing them to abandon the cultivation of land and thus the production of food. Consequently they have to buy food, which has resulted in the dete-rioration of their diet, and that is why they have tuberculosis and, worse still, whole families have turned to alcohol" (Survival International 1991a, 9). The bags and jewelry are made hastily since the producers are paid so little that bag decoration is compromised (Survival International 1991a). Local dancing can also serve as a symbiotic niche; however, it is a mixed blessing. The Basarwa of Botswana have become so tourist oriented that some dance in place and remove clothing when they spot tourist vehicles (Hitchcock and Branden-burgh 1990). In order to keep up with tourist demand, many times local peo-ple have to perform during sacred holidays or when they would not normally do so (Survival International 1991b).

Another variant of niche theory is the category of "special property rights." Occasionally, local people may have special property rights that protect their ability to establish and maintain ecotourism enterprises in the face of ecotourism concentration. In the case of the Annapurna Conservation Area in Nepal for instance, national laws prohibited the foreign ownership of land during the establishment of locally controlled tourist lodges. These laws were later relaxed but by then local control of tourist lodges was firmly entrenched and external tour operators found that the majority of their profits came from packaged tours that used local lodges (Jain 1999). In the case of Benin, local people have "patrimonial" (traditional) ownership of the little land they still control after their removal from Pendjari National Park. Although the authors assured the community of these rights, villagers were still concerned that any effort on their part to establish tourist lodging and food services on their land would be taken away from them. Specific resources needed to better ensure these rights would include access to legal resources in case the tourism interests challenge patrimonial land rights in court. They would also need technical assistance in developing and managing lodging and food enterprises, and in ensuring that all health and safety standards are met to prevent the Ministry of Tourism from shutting them down. Thus, the effective use of the property rights niche in this case would also require the involvement of a coalition of external resources to improve the probability of the satisfaction of those rights.

Securing Favorable Policies

Another exception to multinational dominance is possible when communities, conservationist organizations, development agencies, national and local governments, and ecotourists form coalitions in support of policies that favor socially responsible tourism. A coalition of supporting organizations could be formed to intervene on behalf of and with the participation of local people. Development NGOs, universities, and similar organizations could be drawn into such a constituency. Conservation organizations such as Conservation International (CI), The Nature Conservancy (TNC), World Wildlife Fund (WWF), and the World Conservation Union (IUCN) have supported ecotourism ventures (Honey 1999).

Beyond financial support for ecotourism projects, these conservation organizations could join with others to fight for policies that favor local ecotourism ventures, including the legalization of property rights, the implementation of zoning regulations, and bottom-up rural development. They could help fight large-scale tourism ventures that capture money from locals by infiltrating and exploiting community resources and conservation programs. In addition, such coalitions could help communities form land partnerships to reduce pressure to sell properties to outsiders (Horwich and Lyon 1998).

Another coalition possibility is to establish credit schemes and financing programs to help remove capital constraints for small enterprise, something coalitions could advocate and encourage at the government and international level (Victurine 2000). Like Honey (1999), we suggest that coalitions could also press the World Bank's International Finance Corporation and other funding agencies to provide loans to local, small-scale projects.

In addition, a coalition could help ensure that local, small-scale operators have access to successful marketing techniques. Honey (1999, 83) argues, "[I]neffective or insufficient marketing is probably the primary reason why worthy ecotourism ventures in developing countries fail to attract visitors." And the World Tourism Organization emphasizes that if a destination is not on the Internet, it may be ignored by millions (World Trade Organization Business Council 1999). Many ecotourists know about large-scale ecotourism operators before leaving home since most, if not all, are accessible via the Internet. It may be the case that small-scale or local operators do not want to attract the Internet masses, however, international travelers could be attracted to locally owned and operated ecotourism operations if they had similar access to them as they do the large-scale operators. This is especially important because many large-scale ecotourism operations book both accommodations and activities in advance.

Fortunately, some coalitions have pushed forward and others are beginning to take root. One of the earliest efforts was the WWF's Wildlife and Human Needs Program. In 1985, USAID provided WWF assistance in promoting twenty pilot conservation and development projects in developing countries, one of which was the Annapurna Conservation Area Project in Nepal. The project focused on decreasing the negative environmental effects of trekkers and increasing local income from ecotourism. The project trained seven hundred local people to work in ecotourism lodges, built an education center for visitors, and instituted a US$12 conservation fee per person (Honey 1999). In Mozambique, the Ford Foundation supports the Department of Wildlife to help the Bawa people in the Zambezi Valley fight a foreign safari company that exploited the local resources and hoarded ecotourism profits (Bawa Village Community 1997).

Beyond local level alliances, large-scale coalitions such as the Indigenous Tourism Rights International (RTP) have emerged in support of small-scale tourism. Founded in September 1999, RTP is "an Indigenous Peoples nonprofit organization dedicated to preservation and protection of lands and cultures. Its mission is to (1) develop community education about tourism and (2) develop a global network of Indigenous and non-Indigenous support groups to share information and resources about tourism. RTP examines the pros and cons of tourism and assists in both urgent actions when there is an imminent threat to Indigenous Peoples (i.e. displacement from homelands due to tourism development) and promotes sustainable alternatives that are Indigenous owned, managed, and produced" (Rethinking Tourism Project 2000).

CONCLUSION

While ecotourism supporters remain optimistic, the reality is that, despite genuine efforts by many parties, ecotourism has not yet been entirely successful in providing benefits to local communities or in spreading the benefits throughout a community. Moreover, it has been largely unable to increase local support of protected areas. Despite such shortcomings to date, the exception theories provided in this chapter can help offset the power and influence of large-scale capital interests in order to level the playing field so that less powerful local people can compete. Continued studies of the political economy of ecotourism should be able to provide insights into how local people can own and maintain ecotourism operations in the face of large-scale ecotourism operators. However, local people will no doubt face considerable challenges to keeping ecotourism profits from fleeing offshore or into the hands of wealthy tourism operators.

In each case, different exception theories might be more or less relevant. For the Sherpas in Sagarmartha, "skill-based niches" were most relevant (Weber 1991). In the case of Benin, the combination of a "special property right" niche and a coalition of external support, assurance, provision of legal resources, and technical expertise assistance would be the best way to reverse the marginal participation by local people.

NOTE

1. It is difficult to estimate the percentage of ecotourism from total tourism dollars. See Honey (1999, 6) for details. According to the World Tourism Organization (WTO), 663 million people in 1999 spent at least one night in a foreign country, up 4.1 per cent over the previous year, spending US$453 billion (WTO 2000). By 2020, WTO expects 1.6 billion travelers.

Chapter Eight

PRIVATIZING CONSERVATION

JEFFREY LANGHOLZ

Mounting evidence suggests that current approaches to biodiversity protection are more difficult and less successful than was originally hoped (Kramer et al. 1997; Brandon et al. 1998; Terborgh et al. 2002). The struggle for solutions has led to new approaches and conservation partnerships, many of them involving the private sector (Endicott 1993; McNeely 1995; Gustanski and Squires 2000). Although the private sector continues to play an increasingly large role in international biodiversity conservation, there has been little systematic analysis of its characteristics or implications. This chapter examines one of privatization's peculiar yet little studied manifestations—the surge of privately owned protected areas worldwide.

Despite the recent proliferation of private nature reserves, and studies of them, we still know little about them. Coverage of private reserves in the literature has been superficial and sporadic. Given limited public resources available for conservation, and growing interest in private sector initiatives, it is imperative that we begin a systematic examination of this emerging conservation approach. This chapter takes a step in that direction. It has three specific goals: (1) to provide an overview of the private reserve niche; (2) to discuss key strengths and weaknesses of the private reserve model, with special attention to social issues; and (3) to provide three private nature reserve examples that highlight key issues and challenges.

THE PRIVATE NATURE RESERVE NICHE AND ITS ORIGINS

Despite their apparent newness, privately owned parks have a long history. Like agroforestry, mulch-based agriculture, community-based natural resource management, and other popular themes from recent decades, private parks represent a recent incarnation of an old idea. Alderman (1994) comments that establishment of private reserves is not a new development, noting that "their precursors trace back hundred of years to royal hunting preserves." Likewise, Runte (1979) mentions hunting and riding reserves set aside for Assyrian noblemen as far back as 700 B.C., as well as open spaces reserved for the ruling class in Ancient Rome and Medieval Europe. As Geisler and Daneker (2000) note, however, conventional distinctions between public and private property are overly simplistic and often inappropriate. Although early reserves were private in the sense that access was limited to a wealthy elite, one could argue that owners were indistinguishable from the state, and that these reserves thus represented a form of public ownership.

Conservation literature has been slow to acknowledge the privately owned parks' expanding role, and has done little to evaluate their promise and pitfalls. The first and strongest modern reference to privately owned parks was Recommendation #10 from the First World Congress on National Parks. The recommendation noted that many reserves throughout the world are "owned by private individuals, but are nevertheless dedicated in perpetuity to the conservation of wild life and of natural resources." Additionally, it is "desirable to increase the number and diversity of such areas." The recommendation concludes that "such individuals and institutions who have already taken such action are to be commended for their activities and that others are urged to do likewise" (Adams 1962, 379).

Like other conservation themes, considerable ambiguity surrounds privately owned nature reserves. Their diversity allows categorization under numerous conservation trends such as community-based conservation, devolution, decentralization, privatization, participation, and sustainable development. To confuse matters further, private reserves are often self-defined. An area viewed by one landowner as a parcel of unused jungle may be considered a protected natural area by another.

No one knows how many privately owned parks exist. The World Conservation Union (IUCN) is the global organization responsible for tracking protected natural areas, but to date has lacked sufficient resources to identify and analyze private reserves fully. Previously, private reserves appeared in Category IV protected areas (IUCN 1984). The most recent United Nations list of the world's protected areas did not include privately owned parks. It did, however, briefly discuss them, noting:

> Private protected areas are not usually significant in terms of the area they
> cover, but they are important because of the quality of the management and

the protection afforded to them. Private areas include those areas administered by foundations and private enterprise, as well as those established and
run by communities themselves. Excellent examples of private initiatives
which support and complement state systems abound: The Royal Society for
the Protection of Birds in the UK, The Nature Conservancy in North America, the Fundación Moises Bertoni in Paraguay, and the Royal Society for the
Conservation of Nature in Jordan. Private protected areas may increase in
importance, particularly in tropical countries, where state resources are very
limited. (IUCN 1994, xiv)

While it is impossible to say how many reserves exist, anecdotal evidence
suggests that they number in the thousands and that their numbers are growing. Langholz and Lassoie (2001) provide estimates of worldwide coverage,
including several region-specific examples. The sparse data available indicate
that private parks may in fact be evolving into a shadow park system that sup-
plements national conservation strategies. Equally mysterious are the reasons
behind the ongoing proliferation of private parks. Government failure, rising
societal interest in biodiversity, and the ongoing ecotourism explosion top the
list of likely causes, and are detailed in Langholz and Lassoie (2001) and
Langholz (2002).

Like the biological diversity they protect, private nature reserves have
undergone considerable evolutionary branching. Langholz and Lassoie (2001)
describe a proposed typology for private nature reserves worldwide (Table
8.1). It is loosely modeled after the World Conservation Union's category system for publicly owned parks, in which management objectives are an important distinguishing feature (IUCN 1994). Granted, the proposed categories
overlap among themselves and are not mutually exclusive. Also, like the
IUCN category system, they are likely to undergo periodic revision. The following ten subsections provide descriptions of each category, expanding upon
the information presented in Langholz and Lassoie (2001).

Formal Parks (Type I) enjoy legal designation as recognized units in a
nation's protected areas system. This is the most formal form of biodiversity
protection available on private lands. In terms of size and land use, the public equivalent would be the United States National Wildlife Refuge. This
category does not include reserves participating in nongovernmental "networks" of private reserves that are becoming common in the tropics, unless
network membership also implies formal government monitoring and
recognition. Recreational uses such as tourism are common, though not a
prerequisite. An example would be Costa Rica's Private Wildlife Refuge category (Langholz et al. 2000).

Program Participants (Type II) are those reserves formally participating in an
incentive program designed to promote biodiversity conservation on private

TABLE 8.1
Proposed Typology for Private Nature Reserves Worldwide

Type	Category	Management Objective
I	Formal Park	Protect nature, as a formally recognized unit in a national protected area system. Must be legally gazetted through legislation or executive decree. Includes monitoring and evaluation by government.
II	Program Participant	Participate in a formal, voluntary incentive program designed to promote biodiversity conservation on private lands. Program includes restrictions on land use. Not as formal or as lasting as Type I.
III	Ecotourism Reserve	Combine nature conservation with tourism. Tourism is a principal revenue generator, and takes place on part or all of the landholdings.
IV	Biological Station	Combine nature conservation with scientific research. Reserve serves as outdoor laboratory. May incorporate scientific and other forms of tourism, as well as education.
V	Hybrid Reserve	Protect nature as one component of a diverse land use strategy. Often large ranches combining agriculture, forestry, or cattle ranching, with reserve providing watershed protection and other amenities.

(continued on next page)

lands. Landowner commitment to conservation is less formal and possibly more temporary than that required for Type I. An example would be the Republic of South Africa's Natural Heritage Program. Launched in 1984, the program is a cooperative venture between government, the business sector, and private landowners. By 1991, a total of 151 sites had been registered, protecting 216,332 hectares. More than a hundred of these natural areas were owned by private individuals. In each case, landowners voluntarily dedicated some or all of their land to nature conservation, while retaining full ownership of the land (Cohen 1995). Other examples include various set aside programs, conservation contracts, conservation easements, and payments for ecosystem services such as those proposed in Ferraro (2001).

Ecotourism Reserves (Type III) combine conservation with tourism, with tourism revenues being a principal income generator. They range in size and

TABLE 8.1 *(continued)*

Type	Category	Management Objective
VI	Farmer-owned	Safeguard water sources and other locally accrued environmental services, at the individual or family level. Usually informal, small (<20 hectares), and not involved in tourism industry.
VII	Personal Retreat Reserve	Maintain a natural area as a personal haven, at the individual or family level. Frequently owned by urbanites who purchase or inherit land in a rural area, and who are not reliant on the reserve for income generation. Often the site of a second home.
VIII	NGO Reserve	Protect nature under the auspices of a local, national, or international nonprofit conservation organization. Base of support is broader than that of most other reserve types.
IX	Hunting Reserve	Maintain natural area for purpose of sustainable wildlife utilization. Animals are collected for trophies and/or meat production. Includes game ranches and lands owned by hunting clubs.
X	Corporate Reserve	Protect nature as a tool for creating favorable publicity. Often owned by large multinational corporations, especially when their primary activities typically degrade natural resources.

Source: Lassoie and Langholz (2001)

purpose from large resorts with a reserve as an added attraction for guests, to small family-run lodges depending exclusively on tourism revenues. Motives are mixed. In some cases, nature conservation occurs primarily as a vehicle for promoting tourism. In other cases, the opposite is true, and tourism occurs principally as a means to support nature conservation. Conservation "piggybacking" can occur, when tourist revenues finance protection of the entire reserve even though visitors only use a small part of it. Although Ecotourism Reserves can formalize under a government program (Type I or Type II), their strong dependency on ecotourism revenues distinguishes them from other reserve types. An Ecotourism Reserve example is Explorama Inn in the Peruvian Amazon, which relies on ecotourism revenues in order to survive. As Yu et al. (1998) explain, Explorama Inn and other Ecotourism Reserves could get away with doing practically no conservation at all if they so chose. This could be accomplished by a second form of piggybacking in which owners rely on an area's conservation reputation without contributing to it. In effect, owners can get away with protecting only the surprisingly small amount of habitat needed to stage a nature walk, relying on a typical tourist's inability to recognize substantially degraded habitat. For additional details on ecotourism at private reserves see Langholz and Brandon (2001) and Langholz et al. (2000).

Biological Stations (Type IV) combine nature conservation with scientific research. They often benefit from foreign investment of human or financial resources. Although usually owned and operated by nongovernment organizations, they differ from NGO-run Reserves (Type VII) in that their primary mission is research. Biological Stations can host ecotourists as a supplemental revenue generator and frequently conduct environmental education activities in the surrounding area.

The Jatun Sacha Foundation provides an example of this kind of reserve. In July 1989, the government of Ecuador approved establishment of the Jatun Sacha Foundation as a private, nonprofit foundation dedicated to biodiversity research and conservation. The foundation owns and manages the Jatun Sacha ("big forest" in Quichua) biological field station in the Napo Province. By 1993, the station was protecting 1,200 hectares of tropical wet forest, with plans to expand. Research has focused primarily on biological inventories, such as reptiles, amphibians, birds, trees, vascular plants, fungi, butterflies, mammals. Longer term ecological research has emphasized multi-taxonomic monitoring and silvicultural trials. The station has also hosted various field courses on subjects such as ethnopharmacology, dendrology of Amazonian Ecuador, and tropical ecology.

Hybrid Reserve (Type V) is a term coined by Alderman (1994). Hybrids typically occur on large ranches or plantations, although that is not always the case. Protection of water supply needed for cattle or agriculture is often a primary motivator. Hybrid Reserves can be informally protected or be part of a formal government program. Although ecotourism frequently occurs, it is part of a diversification strategy rather than primary revenue source, which distinguishes this category from Type III reserves. The number of Hybrid Reserves in Latin America and Sub-Saharan Africa is estimated to be between 33 percent (Alderman 1994) and 44 percent (Langholz 1996). An example of a Hybrid Reserve is 80,000 hectare Hato Pinero, in Venezuela, which combines nature conservation and tourism with cattle ranching.

Farmer-Owned Forest Patches (Type VI) represent the largest category of reserves in terms of amount of land protected and number of owners. Unfortunately, it is also the category about which the least is known. It is safe to estimate that many thousands, perhaps millions, exist worldwide. This category represents a particularly crucial area for future research. This type of conservation area is usually small (<20 hectares) and owners typically are uninvolved in government protection programs or in the tourism industry. Forest patches in the tropical landscape have begun to receive increased attention by researchers (Schelhas and Greenberg 1996). Research in Costa Rica, for example, showed that a principal motive behind forest patch conservation was watershed protection and that religious affiliation often played a role. Farmers valued forest patches for subsistence products such as timber, fuelwood, vines for basketmaking, and as informal "bank accounts." They also protected them for nonutilitarian reasons such as a desire to provide a home for animals, to protect a legacy for children, and to provide coolness and diversity (Schelhas et al. 1997).

Personal Retreat Reserves (Type VII) serve as natural areas where owners' friends and family members can be surrounded by nature. Owners either live on the premises or use it as a secondary home. In many cases the land has been purchased or inherited by an urban-based family. Formal protection and ecotourism are possible but uncommon. Owners often belong to middle or upper economic classes and rely on their professional careers for livelihood rather than on the reserve. Motives can include not just having a place in the country to relax, but also a sense of duty to nature and to future generations. An industrialized world example comes from the Adirondack State Park. The largest protected natural area in the contiguous United States, roughly 60 percent of Adirondack State Park is in private hands. Many of the lands are held by urbanites who use the area for summer retreats (Comstock 1995). The San Jose–based owner of a reserve in Costa Rica explained it this way: "I've made a little shack there—four poles with a roof. I go there for a few days at a time. I watch wildlife. Bathe in the rivers. Do some maintenance on the road. Look at the vegetation. It's very peaceful there. I spend time thinking about things from my life here in the city—the things of people. It's like a little haven for me" (Langholz 1999).

NGO Reserves (Type VIII) exist primarily to protect nature. They are owned by local, national, or international nongovernment organizations (NGOs) interested in conservation. Unlike numerous organizations that have been given only management authority and/or concessionary rights over public natural areas throughout the world, these foundations, associations, trusts, and other organizations exercise outright ownership of the protected natural areas. In the United States and other industrialized countries, this category would include land trusts, and reserves owned by The Nature Conservancy and similar organizations. While NGO Reserves frequently share qualities with other reserves, such as ecotourism, or combinations of land uses, the distinguishing features are their nonprofit status and broad base of support that extends beyond one individual or family. NGO Reserves can also include a community development component that complements the conservation mission. A well-known example is The Children's Rainforest in Costa Rica, which is larger and better funded than the majority of the country's national parks (Langholz 1999).

Hunting Reserves (Type IX) maintain natural areas for the purpose of sustainable wildlife utilization. Animals are collected for trophies and/or meat production. This category includes game ranches common to eastern and southern Africa, as well as lands owned by hunting clubs worldwide. As Zeide (1998, 16) notes, "[A]lthough it seems paradoxical to combine environmental concerns with hunting, this combination is not unusual." Even Aldo Leopold, one the world's most famous conservationists, was an avid hunter who insisted that "trophy-hunting is the prerogative of youth, racial, or individual, and nothing to apologize for" (Leopold 1966, 268).

Corporate Reserves (Type X) are owned by private for-profit businesses and are often established as part of a company's charitable works. Examples in the industrialized world include natural areas owned by golf courses, schools, paper companies, and others. Examples in the developing world are often owned by large multinational corporations, including the forestry industry. They sometimes are used as a tool for creating favorable publicity, especially when a company's primary activities degrade nature (e.g., a mining company that owns a wildlife preserve). As Barborak (1995, 32) notes, "[L]arge corporations in some countries control hundreds of thousands of hectares of forested land, which many times is better managed than similar areas in government hands."

Corporate reserves can combine with Type III reserves, such as the case of Earth Sanctuaries Ltd. This South Australia holding company has interests in four publicly owned companies, each of which owns at least one wildlife sanctuary in Australia. According to Bennett (1995), the reserves depend on ecotourism revenues and have proven to be profitable ventures. They have been criticized for being too small, too much like a "zoo," and too competitive with parks run by the National Parks and Wildlife Service. The sanctuaries eradicate feral pests, then use electric fences to prevent reinvasion, which makes them islands where endangered species can survive.

Clearly, a wide variety of private reserve types exist representing numerous ownership structures and management objectives. Many reserves could potentially fall into more than one category. An extreme example would be 1,500 hectare Reserva La Marta in Costa Rica, which crosses four categories. It is owned by a nongovernment organization (Type VIII), is home to a research station (Type IV), hosts a regular stream of ecotourists (Type III), and has been legally designated as a formal unit in the nation's park system (Type I). Finally, these reserve types will likely define and expand further as the private reserve niche continues its evolutionary branching.

STRENGTHS AND WEAKNESSES
OF THE PRIVATE RESERVE MODEL

Like every conservation tool or direction, private nature reserves bring not just advantages but also disadvantages. Political conservatives may view private conservation in general as a panacea for the future, heralding them as a holy grail of conservation and development. Meanwhile, skeptics question private reserves' small size, their frequent dependence on ecotourism, and the overall trustworthiness of the private sector. Such sweeping generalizations are unwarranted, given the diversity described in the preceding section.

Langholz and Lassoie (2001) and Langholz (2002) highlight key strengths and weaknesses of the private nature reserve model as a whole, acknowledging its diverse manifestations (Table 8.2). The following section goes beyond these two previous discussions in its emphasis on privately owned parks' social advantages and disadvantages.

Social Strengths

Two important social themes in conservation and development are "participation" and "devolution" with respect to resource control. Private reserves touch upon both of these key themes. In Colombia, for example, the private reserve phenomenon is closely linked to *campesino* empowerment, representing a bold step toward devolution of resource control to the rural poor. Commenting on Colombia's well-organized network of more than one hundred private reserve owners, the World Wildlife Fund notes, "[T]he expansion of private reserves in Colombia provides an alternative to the government's insufficient management of natural lands and resources. The private approach to conservation increases the total area of protected lands, and more importantly, directly involves citizens as stewards of their country's own natural resources for the future" (WWF 1997, 2).

Private reserves could also be considered paragons of participation. Figure 8.1 shows a continuum of participation in protected area management. Private reserves would occur at the far right-hand side of the scale, where participation is greatest. They represent participation taken to the extreme. Their proliferation requires a new way of thinking—one in which locals control decision making instead of merely seeking to participate in it, one in which residents own the table instead of merely being offered a seat at it. As Zube and Busch (1990) note, "local ownership" of a protected area is one of the most important and extreme vehicles for public participation.

Social Weaknesses

The myriad negative social consequences of protected areas in general have long been known (Rao and Geisler 1990, West and Brechin 1991). Privately

FIGURE 8.1
Participation in Protected Area Management—A Continuum

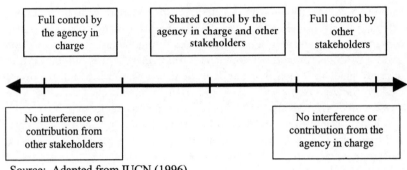

Source: Adapted from IUCN (1996)

owned protected areas should be subject to similar scrutiny. Two major social disadvantages seem obvious. First, private reserves can become islands of elites—places where wealthy landowners host wealthy tourists. Ecotourism has emerged as the fastest growing segment of what is generally regarded to be the world's largest industry (Weaver 2001). Various authors in this book and beyond have discussed its uneasy alliance with biodiversity conservation (Boo 1990; Wells 1997; Honey 1999). Brandon (1996) offers an especially detailed analysis of ecotourism's relationship with conservation, noting that one of ecotourism's key benefits has been its stimulation of private conservation efforts. Alderman (1994) and Langholz (1996), for example, documented private reserves' overwhelming dependence on ecotourism revenues in Latin America and Sub-Saharan Africa. They showed private reserves to depend on ecotourism revenues more than any other source and that this dependency was rising. Even when done well, ecotourism causes several negative social consequences in local communities, among them resentment (i.e., community members feeling that the area has been developed for foreigners only), and discontent (residents must keep working while tourists enjoy a holiday), and alterations to cultural norms and behaviors (Wearing 2001). It is crucial, therefore, that private reserves embody cultural sensitivity and develop meaningful links to surrounding communities, such as those described in Alderman (1994), Langholz (1996), and Mesquita (1999).

A second social pitfall of private reserves is their contribution to land concentration. Access to land by the rural poor has been and continues to be a persistent issue throughout the developing world. Incentives programs supporting private reserves can unwittingly help large landowners maintain their holdings. Brinkate (1996), for example, documented a case in which wealthy white South African landowners were declaring their lands as conservation

areas in order to avoid government land redistribution schemes. Conservation was serving as a haven for the rich.

This sentiment has been echoed by landowners elsewhere. Costa Rica,
for example, enjoys a reputation as a society of middle-class yeoman farmers,
yet has suffered from land distribution inequalities that have plagued much
of Latin American. As noted earlier (Table 8.1), the government currently
provides incentives to landowners seeking official designation as formal Private Wildlife Refuges. By Costa Rican standards, refuge owners were large
landholders, ranking among the 8 percent of landholders who control 67 percent of all private lands. In protecting them from squatter invasions by the
country's poorest people, the national government could be supporting the
elite. A reserve owner in the study's control group (nonparticipants)
explained it this way: "The Private Wildlife Refuge Program is a shelter for
the rich. Wealthy landowners can protect themselves, and access government
help" (Langholz 1999, 112). Clearly, private reserves represent a flashpoint
where two broadly supported goals—social justice and biodiversity conservation—can be placed at odds.

A final social disadvantage lies with foreign ownership of private reserves.
Alderman (1994) found 33 percent of reserves in Africa to be exclusively for-
eign-owned, with an additional 7 percent jointly owned by nationals and foreigners. She also found 23 percent of private reserves in Latin America to be
completely owned by foreigners and another 25 percent to be owned by partnerships involving foreigners. While the majority of private reserves in these
two regions were owned exclusively by nationals, the large foreign presence
may be disturbing to those who consider it a form of neocolonialism.

All three disadvantages—land concentration, resentment against the
wealthy, and anti-foreign sentiment—converged into a single frenetic land
grab in Zimbabwe during much of 2000 and 2001 when wealthy white ranch
owners lost entire estates to groups of angry nonwhite citizens. Many of these
lands were private nature reserves protecting threatened species, owned by
long-time citizens of Zimbabwe. President Robert Mugabe supported this
spontaneous land redistribution, fanning fires of xenophobia and class war-
fare. Mugabe's motives likely had more to do with drawing attention away
from the country's economic hardships and corruption than with genuine
concern for the masses. Nevertheless, the events poignantly reveal the precar-
ious position of wealthy "outsiders" and the strength of pent-up resentment
against them.

EXAMPLES FROM COSTA RICA.

The following three cases provide real world examples of the topics discussed
above. While the examples showcase private reserves in a single country

TABLE 8. 2
Strengths and Weaknesses of the Private Reserve Model

Strengths	Weaknesses
Ecology	
• Protect biodiversity, especially compared to likely alternative land uses • Provide many of same values as public parks (e.g., purification of air and water, climate regulation, water production, and recreation) • Can serve as temporary "way station," protecting valuable habitat until it can be declared a park by the government	• Often small in size, which limits abilty to support biodiversity, especially megafauna • Informal status may lead to temporary or tenuous protection for some reserves • Little, if any, monitoring and evaluation by higher authorities (i.e., governments)
Economic	
• Often profitable, allowing owner to earn a livelihood while protecting resources • Represent a substantial savings for governments who would otherwise have to purchase land and pay for its protection as a park	• Dependency on ecotourism revenues may be a vulnerability for some • The need for financial self-sufficiency can lead to activities that place economics over ecology
Social	
• Can be example of "devolution" of control over natural resources • Can be example of "participation" in resource decision making	• Reserves can be islands of elites, owned and visited only by the wealthy • Can cause social displacement, and support land concentration by wealthy elites • Foreign ownership may be viewed as new form of neocolonialism, causing considerable resentment

Source: Langholz (2002)

(Costa Rica), the underlying issues are generalizable across much of the developing world. The profiles are designed to give readers a sense of who private reserve owners are, what they do, why they do it, challenges they face, and the social issues surrounding their actions. The section is based on face to face interviews conducted with reserve owners in 1997 and 1998. Readers are referred to Langholz and Lassoie (2002) for in-depth analysis and full description of research methods.

Durika Biological Reserve: Community-based Conservation in Action

Durika Biological Reserve is an example of a private reserve owned and operated by a nonprofit, community-based organization. It demonstrates the intense conservation motivations that a community group can have, as well as the biodiversity benefit of layering private protection on top of public protected area designations.

The forest reserve sits high in the Talamanca Mountain Range, where it commands a panoramic view of the vast Valley of the General. Perched on the western flank of Costa Rica's highest mountain range, it is one of the most remote and inaccessible locations in the country. The forest reserve itself consists of 792 hectares, roughly 70 percent of which is primary rainforest. Biological inventories have recently begun to reveal its incredibly rich biodiversity and samples of numerous newly discovered species have been shared with the National Biodiversity Institute.

Approximately forty people, mostly Costa Ricans, call Durika home. The community was established simultaneously with the forest reserve, with all residents originally arriving as transplants. Many traded professional jobs in the city for a largely agrarian lifestyle in the mountains. The community strives to live in a self-sufficient and sustainable manner. They grow their own organic vegetables and raise livestock to meet their dietary needs. Homemade bread and fudge are sold throughout the country to facilitate purchase of items that cannot be grown or made on site. Legally, the group has organized into the not for profit "Association for the Conservation of Durika Biological Reserve," which exercises legal ownership over the land and serves as a conduit for fundraising.

Since the reserve's founding in 1991, the residents have strived to create a community in harmony with itself and with the natural world around it. As one community member put it: "Generally, people believe that nature is something they own. They don't see themselves as part of nature. They think they can come and harvest nature's offerings until it's all gone. We're striving for a life that's more harmonious with nature, more of an exchange."

One of the most revealing aspects of Durika is not just the owners' strong commitment to conservation or the remarkable biodiversity contained within the forest reserve, but rather what exists around the forest reserve. The reserve

is surrounded on three sides by a moonscape of extremely denuded lands—
vast hillsides so eroded and lifeless from repeated burnings that hardly any
vegetation grows, let alone sufficient grass to make cattle grazing worthwhile.
A casual observer might not realize that the moonscape is actually a park with
two levels of formal protection by one of the world's most revered National
Park Services. As part of the Amistad Biosphere Reserve and the Cabagra /
Ujarras Indigenous Reserve, one would expect something other than a biological desert. The border with Durika is easy to see, however, for Durika is
covered in forest. The contrast between these barren lands with two levels of
protection and neighboring forested lands with a third level of protection—
private nature reserve—is impossible to miss.

Now that Durika Biological Reserve is secure, the community wants to
expand the forest reserve until it links with nearby Amistad National Park.
Garcia describes the need for a corridor, saying,

> [L]ooking at it from a scientific ecological viewpoint, the area is too small.
> If all we had were our eight hundred hectares, species such as the puma,
> jaguar, and harpy eagle could survive for a while, but not forever. Without
> protection of adjacent areas, these species would disappear. If we can flesh
> out the seven kilometer corridor to the Amistad National Park, I believe we
> would have enough area protected for these species to survive. Species like
> the tapir and harpy eagle need lots of room. On an organizational level, we
> have demonstrated over the first seven years that we are quite capable of
> administering a protected area. And so far we've done it all on our own, with
> practically no outside assistance. Just our own efforts.

The community is slowly making their corridor plans a reality. It now
hosts a small number of ecotourists, who pay between $25 and $35 per night
to stay in the community (including meals) in rustic but comfortable cabins.
This tourism, however, is clearly motivated by conservation rather than profit,
with earnings going into a special fund for buying and reforesting more land
in the corridor area.

Hacienda Baru: A Squatter Invasion and Eviction

Land tenure laws in much of the developing world have long promoted forest clearing as a path to ownership. Landowners who keep parcels forested
run the risk of losing their forest to squatters who would develop this "idle"
land. The case of Hacienda Baru offers a vivid glimpse into how a squatter
invasion can happen, who is behind the invasion, why they do it, and how it
can be resolved.

The forest consists of roughly 300 hectares and is located on the central
Pacific coast. It contains a variety of habitats, including 110 hectares of primary forest, 40 hectares of rainforest that were selectively logged two decades

ago then left alone, 15 hectares of former pasture that is regenerating into forest, and 16 hectares of mangroves and estuarine habitat spread along a three
kilometer beachfront. Ecotourism is the primary revenue generator for the
reserve but there are also fruit orchards and hardwood plantations. Jack and
Diane Ewing bought the land in 1970, when it was reachable only by horse-
back. They were recently joined in ownership by fellow North American Steve
Stroud. All quotes are based on a lengthy interview with Jack Ewing unless
otherwise noted.

The Ewings knew that an invasion was coming. Many beachfront properties nearby had been invaded as well and they had been hearing rumors that
Hacienda Baru was the next target. Then, on July 22, 1995, a group of thirty
people showed up on the premises. "They came in cars, motorcycles, trucks.
The next day another thirty showed up. They came in and divided the beach
up into 104 lots." Squatters quickly built assorted dwellings in the reserve
ranging from simple plastic sheets stapled to wooden frames to a two-story
wooden house. Most dwellings were tents or single-story wooden shacks. The
total number of squatters eventually reached one hundred and ten.

Who exactly were the squatters? Opinions vary. The Ewings and many
other landowners in Costa Rica insist that they are organized thieves. According to Jack Ewing, "The squatters these days are not poor peasants who need
land. They're people that want to do a real estate business." Ewing's wife
Diane echoed this belief, commenting, "Squatting today in Costa Rica is
strictly a capital gain venture. And it's organized. Crooks organize it. It's kind
of a low grade mafia. It was not poor people. They wanted to sell to foreigners to make a capital gain." The Ewings and other landowners report that
many of the squatters are indeed poor and have been hired by wealthy backers who keep them supplied with provisions. According to Diane, "They hired
poor people. Supplied them with construction materials. Brought them food
and water on a regular basis." Apparently, the poor people, numbering roughly
three-fourths of the squatters, were simply pawns being used by wealthier
backers. According to Ewing, most of the backers were businessmen in the
nearby city of San Isidro:

> The day after the invasion they opened a real estate office in San Isidro
> and started selling lots. We figure that the leaders made about twenty-five
> million Colones [$100,000] from the sale of lots. They sold lots without any
> receipt and without any documents whatsoever. The buyers . . . were oppor-
> tunists, who knew exactly what was going on, and had been convinced that
> the squatters were going to win. The buyers knew there was no receipt and
> no guarantee, but that if the squatters won, they would have purchased five
> million Colone lots [$20,000] for only half a million [$2,000]. I mean, this
> guy and his lawyer raked in big money.
> The months during the occupation were tension filled and dangerous.
> There were a number of death threats, and at least one murder contract put

out on me. They had hired an assassin and paid him one million colones [$4,000]. They tried to attack this house several times but we had armed guards. At night they would come with a large group of them. But the guards would fire and chase them away. We figured they were trying to burn the house down. They started harassing my employees. Whenever my car went to town, whoever was driving it they'd follow him around and take pictures of him and the car. And tell him he'd better quit because something bad might happen to him if he didn't.

Squatters also reportedly intimidated children associated with the refuge, such as the daughters of an employee: "His two little girls were riding their bicycles to school, and a group of squatters pulled up beside them and waved guns at them. And so we started giving them a ride to school all the time."

Because the invasion occurred shortly before the reserve was formally declared a Private Wildlife Refuge by the Costa Rican government, primary responsibility for the eviction rested with the local municipal government rather than with the national environmental ministry (MINAE). MINAE, nevertheless, played a role. "MINAE backed us a hundred percent," said Ewing. "But the day the municipality evicted the squatters then MINAE took over responsibility. So if they had reinvaded, MINAE would have been responsible" (because it was now a refuge). After months of legal wranglings, a judge ordered municipal government leaders to do the eviction or risk criminal prosecution themselves. "They [the squatters] found out that legally they have no place else to turn. They've been to the Supreme Court three times to make their case, and have been rejected every time."

The eviction took place on January 16, 1996. "We had fifty policemen. All of them armed with M-16 machine guns." The captain of the police informed the squatters that they were going to be evicted, and that anyone who wanted to dismantle his own building so as to save the materials should do so immediately. Twenty-six squatters accepted this offer. The remaining structures were demolished with chainsaw and tractor. "They tried everything in the world to stop it," says Ewing. "Some guy drove up in a taxi and said it's been called off, that there's a counter order against the eviction. The minister has rescinded the order. They're going to hear our case." This stopped the eviction until phone calls could be made to the proper authorities, who confirmed that it was a lie. "Then one of the corrupt politicians in Quepos called up the police chief in San Isidro, identifying himself as a lawyer for the municipality, and told them that the eviction was to be stopped, that the municipality no longer wanted to do the eviction." The police chief in San Isidro refused to halt the eviction based only on a phone call, insisting that he would only stop it if he were to receive a fax with the signature of the minister of public security.

The squatters left peacefully and in the same mode of transportation in which they had arrived months earlier. "All of them had cars. Most of them had later model, more expensive cars than mine. We used the tractor to haul away the material, taking it to a central location where it was later burned. It took us a month to clean up. We cleaned up everything. We destroyed every plant they had planted. They planted coconut palm and everything so they could come back five years from now and reinvade, saying, 'Well, I planted this five years ago.' We made sure there was nothing left they could come back and say, 'I did that.' Plantains. Ornamental plants. One of them had built a sidewalk of stones all the way out to the beach. We tore that all up and threw the rocks on the beach where he got them."

One week after the eviction, the squatters attempted to reinvade. "We figured out where they were likely to try the invasion, and hid all these rural guardsmen [police officers] in the forest. Just before they got to our fence, thirty rural guardsmen and six private guards stepped out of the jungle with their guns ready. It was a complete surprise for them. They just turned around and ran. It was like a stampede. And then, after that, nobody wanted to come back."

In the aftermath, the police captain filed formal charges against the squatters in Quepos. "They've pretty well given up. Eleven of them have been indicted on criminal charges and will have to go to trial for the invasion. Two of the squatter leaders will almost certainly go to prison." The judge also ordered an investigation into the ringleaders to see what other illegal activities they've been involved with, including previous squatter invasions. The squatters' own lawyer sued them for $15,200 in legal fees and arranged for their bank accounts to be frozen and businesses embargoed until the fee is paid.

While the worst of the nightmare appears to be over, the Ewings still do not rest easy. "I never go anywhere without a gun. I have a Smith and Wesson nine millimeter automatic. Holds fifteen shots. Diane never goes anywhere without a gun, either. We have come to accept that the Costa Rica of peace and tranquility no longer exists. And it never will exist again. Costa Rica has come into the modern world; it's just as dangerous as L.A. or New York, or anyplace else in the world. We intend to stay. We intend to build a reputation for having very good security at our hotel." When asked if he had any advice for other forest reserve owners based on this ordeal, Ewing commented, "Register your property with MINAE in some program that gives squatter protection, and build your credibility with MINAE. Work with them. Work with them and show through your actions that you're sincere about conservation."

Copano: Forest Slayers and Stewards

Copano National Wildlife Refuge portrays an ethical dilemma relating to forest conservation on private lands. The dilemma pits a family's dependence on an environmentally destructive business (operation of a sawmill) against their desire to protect a forest reserve. Remote and reputedly dangerous, the Osa

Peninsula is often called the "Wild West" of Costa Rica. It is a place where loggers, gold miners, cattle barons, and more recently conservationists, battle for control of vast resources, occasionally taking the law into their own hands. The Costa Rican Bellanero family came to this region three generations ago. They own the 839 hectare Copano National Wildlife Refuge, as well as an additional 2,500 hectares of mostly mangroves, forests, and pastures. All but fifty hectares of the refuge is covered in primary rainforest. In the 1960s, a U.S. Peace Corps volunteer suggested that instead of continually converting their land into cattle pasture, perhaps the family would be interested in forestry. One thing led to another and now the family operates a commercial sawmill in Puerto Jimenez where they have been processing logs for nearly a generation. They also have portable sawing equipment, which is used for working within forests. The family has prospered by exploiting the Osa's stands of valuable hardwoods. They process logs not just from their own holdings but also from other ranches. All told, the family and their sawmill have undoubtedly played an important facilitating role in the ongoing reduction of the Osa's once vast forests.

A dilemma arises, however, when one realizes that the Bellanero family is simultaneously making a considerable contribution to conservation. Their refuge, Copano, is more than four times larger than the median POPF in Costa Rica. The refuge also contains a much higher percentage of intact primary forest than most reserves. Finally, the family is in the process of declaring an additional 855 hectares of forest as legally designated Private Wildlife Refuge. Obviously, a family that runs a sawmill on one hand and a large and expanding forest refuge on the other presents an ethical dilemma with respect to environmental stewardship. Are they environmental slayers or stewards? The answer is that they are both. While their situation may seem unique, on a broader level it is similar to that of many private reserve owners whose activities are a combination of protection and production.

CONCLUSION

Conservation, like other pursuits, occasionally lurches from one buzzword to the next. New directions or tools take on a life of their own, attracting funding and rising to magic bullet status. Like ecosystem management, adaptive management, and an eco-regional approach, private reserves risk following this standard course. They will likely continue growing in stature and importance, receiving increased attention from the conservation community. Within a few years or decades, however, key shortcomings will emerge. As criticisms mount and new buzzwords spring to life, the private nature reserve bandwagon will slow, then eventually halt. In the end, the private nature reserve model will assume its rightful place as yet another conservation tool—an approach with both strengths and weaknesses to be used under certain conditions. I have attempted to preempt this boom and bust buzzword cycle by mentioning key advantages and disadvantages at the outset, with an emphasis on social implications. Hopefully, such analysis will better serve people and parks in the long run than discussions based on preconceptions and ideology.

Meanwhile, privately owned parks continue to burgeon. Without a doubt, their potential contribution is huge, given government failure to protect nature, society's increased interest in biodiversity, and ongoing ecotourism expansion. The potential looms even larger when one considers the vast amount of biodiversity occurring on private lands worldwide, the financial indebtedness of many developing nations, and the reduction of state expenditures for public park establishment and operation.

The academic community should play a much more active role in evaluating this key conservation trend. To date, far more questions exist than answers. For example, how many private parks exist? Where are they? What are they protecting? Who owns them? What are the owners' motivations? Which incentive programs work best? Why are private parks practically absent from Southeast Asia? How have they performed economically and biologically? Which strategies best incorporate local residents into private protected areas and address the social issues? Eventually, our state of knowledge will evolve beyond these descriptive studies and into more sophisticated hypothesis testing about private reserves. Kramer et al. (2002) provide a roadmap for such studies, emphasizing the need to test specific assumptions and develop general yet nontrivial guiding principles for private sector conservation. Such a research agenda would enhance our understanding of this little understood but potentially important conservation tool.

Privately owned parks should not and will not be a replacement for government protected areas. Nevertheless, they can be a substantial complement to them. The private park niche continues to expand regardless of what the conservation community thinks or does. The challenge for researchers and practitioners is to engage this trend and help channel its growth in a way that safeguards both biological integrity and human dignity over the long term.

NOTE

This research was funded by a National Science Foundation grant on "Ecological and Social Challenges in Conservation" (BIR-9113293, DBI-9602244) and by the Central America Committee of the Cornell International Institute for Food, Agriculture, and Development. Special thanks go to Marta Marin and Amos Bien of Costa Rica's Network of Private Reserve Owners and to numerous colleagues at Cornell who provided input. Most of all, I thank private reserve owners worldwide who have been so generous with their time and information, and so dedicated in their pursuit of development in harmony with conservation.

Chapter Nine

THE POLITICAL ECOLOGY OF BIOPROSPECTING IN AMAZONIAN ECUADOR

History, Political Economy, and Knowledge

MICHAEL K. DORSEY

Bioprospecting—the attempt to identify and eventually commercialize potentially valuable genetic and biochemical resources—is not a new activity.[1] Transnational, commercial flows of medicinal plants date back to the sixteenth century (Ortiz Crespo 1995). What is new about the present transnational resurgence[2] in bioprospecting is that it is driven primarily by four interlocking factors:[3] (1) global, market-based economic rationales; (2) rapid and broad technological changes, especially in the biotechnology industry; (3) a growing interest by pharmaceutical actors[4] to link their bioprospecting profits with environmental conservation;[5] and (4) efforts to harmonize and standardize global discourses on biodiversity and intellectual property rights regimes. Beyond these factors practitioners and theorists often claim that bioprospecting is a "win-win" scenario for local communities, the institutions and firms that engage in it and the nation-states where prospecting occurs (Ten Kate and Laird 2000; Reid et al. 1995). Since those that control the factors that define contemporary bioprospecting—hereafter *pharmaceutical actors*—wield enormously disproportionate access to resources, information, technology, and capital, preliminary data indicates that the benefits of bioprospecting overwhelmingly accrue to them and not to nation-states, nor to communities where prospecting takes place. Evidence from the field, as we shall see, under-scores this point—*particularly* for Ecuador.

This chapter on Ecuador explores why bioprospecting is never a win-win scenario for those involved. Many recent analyses of bioprospecting take a normative, ahistorical, and apolitical outlook on bioprospecting. Ten Kate and Laird (2000, 12), for example, note in *The Commercial Use of Biodiversity*, that "the book does not set out to judge what is fair and equitable" vis-à-vis biopiracy or "companies' methods of acquiring genetic resources." For these policy makers and shapers, bioprospecting happens "in the ever present now," devoid of a historical, political-economic context and legacies of past exploita-tion of the prospected materials in question. Scholars such as Jim Miller, head of the Missouri Botanical Garden's Applied Research Department, echo this perspective. He noted in a published debate with the author, "[W]e really need to be careful about looking back retrospectively too far at what's gone on in the past because of the entire legal structure for regulating . . . [bio-prospecting] . . . has changed tremendously . . ." (Miller 1999, 2).

This chapter examines a tale of three pharmaceutical actors' bioprospect-ing in Ecuador. One of these individual actors, Loren Miller, exercised his claims to Western intellectual property rights over a sacred species—*ayahuasca* or *yage (Banisteriopsis caapi)*. In 1999, more than a decade and a half after Miller obtained his patent from the U.S. Patent and Trademark Office (USPTO) an international coalition began procedures to revoke the patent. Miller's bioprospecting efforts underscore how Western (in this case U.S.) patent laws are especially biased against indigenous communities who might contest them and predominantly benefit the bioprospector. Secondly, I look briefly at the case and promises of the U.S.-based Shaman Pharmaceuticals and their exploits in the Ecuadorian *Oriente*. The firm was arguably one of the most socially progressive bioprospectors in the *Oriente*. They maintained a policy of both pre- and post-profit revenue sharing with local communities. In areas where they operated they actively allocated upward of 15 percent of expedition costs to fund projects or programs that are based on the expressed needs of the communities with whom they work. In spite of these noteworthy efforts, community members in myriad communities deep in the Ecuadorian *Oriente* express ambivalent and even antagonistic reactions to Shaman. Rather than underscore how "bad" Shaman is, these reactions help us understand the insurmountable political-economic realities the firm faces in its operations, and how anomalous its singular efforts are with respect to the broader phar-maceutical industry engaged in bioprospecting. Lastly, we will examine a "case in progress" surrounding the mysterious efforts and controversial publication track record of a group of scholar-venture capitalists operating in southern Ecuador. This last case highlights the ends to which some "scientists" will go to gain access to potentially valuable genetic materials, sometimes by any means necessary. The point of this final case is to show how the lack of any real regulatory agency, infrastructure, or initiative enables such activities, potentially to the detriment of all involved.

Beyond the specific cases, I briefly trace how and why certain Ecuadorian civil society coalitions, composed primarily of nongovernmental organizations and affected communities, have formed creative, transnational *anti-biopirateria* (i.e., anti-biopiracy) campaigns against the likes of Loren Miller, Shaman Pharmaceuticals (now ShamanBotanicals.com), and a host of other bioprospectors. The overarching goal is to place the practice of bioprospecting into a broader historical and political-economic context—specifically, a capitalist, neoliberal one. Historicizing and elaborating the broader context in which bioprospecting takes place enables one to situate the legacy of exploitation out of which current prospecting emerges and upon which it is essentially dependent. Elaborating this legacy demonstrates how fundamentally difficult—perhaps even impossible—it is to facilitate any form of equitable benefit sharing and access to biogenetic resources. Such a historicization is needed as many of the leading scholars on bioprospecting focus narrowly on its potential as a process to yield "powerful" new drugs to fight myriad diseases and ailments and provide financial wellsprings for conservation schemes (Balick 1994; Cohen and Tokheim 1994; Cox and Balick 1994; Gentry 1993; King 1994; McChesney 1993; Miller 1999; Reid et al. 1993; Sittenfeld and Gamez 1993). In so doing, they fail to present bioprospecting as a process whereby wholly incommensurable actors, institutions, and ideologies vie for control over precious genetic materials and often-scarce financial resources. These scholars simply "present information and analysis . . . to serve as a 'bridge' between the different languages and experiences of business, conservation and development" (Ten Kate and Laird 2000, 12).

Elaborating the broader historical and political-economic context within which prospecting occurs also enables one to better trace how powerful actors and institutions shape bioprospecting. We may better understand their effects on the conservation and protection of biological and cultural diversity, as well as the promotion of particular intellectual property rights (IPR) regimes. Instead of serving and building bridges between "business" and an ill-defined, dehumanized, and unspecified "conservation and development," we may learn where, why, and how specific capitalists conduct bioprospecting; what and why certain communities and organizations are both participating in and protesting against such prospecting; and what are the larger implications for ecosystems and intellectual property rights regimes.

THE LEGACY OF BIOPROSPECTING IN ECUADOR

The legacy of plant hunting and commercialization is extensive in Ecuador in part because in proportion to its area, the country is one of, if not the most species-rich country in all of South America and arguably the world. One factor that contributes to high endemic levels of biodiversity is that the Andes mountains rise from sea level to more than six thousand meters, thereby splitting Ecuador into three major biomes: coastal, high Sierran, and lowland rainforest. The combination of altitudinal effects and latitudinal position give rise to high levels of speciation through time (Stevens 1989). Ecuador's high levels of biodiversity conditions have drawn a large variety of explorers, naturalists, and others in search of plants and their byproducts (e.g., Bates 1863 [1989]).

The search for plants in Ecuador predates the creation of the nation as well as the arrival of the Spanish colonists (Ortiz Crespo 1995). Indigenous healers, shamans, or *yachacs* as they are more commonly known in Quechua communities in Ecuador, Bolivia, and Peru have long made use of the thera-peutic aspects of much of the region's flora and fauna well before the arrival of Europeans. Moreover, indigenous markets commonly contained myriad medicinal plants for sale and barter. For example, knowledge of the *cinchona* bark's *(Cinchona oficialis)* ability to treat the so-called fiebres—what is now known as malaria—was widely held by many Amazonian indigenous peoples (A. de la Calancha 1638 in Ortiz-Crespo 1995). The Spaniards learned of the properties of this plant and applied it effectively as an antimalarial rem-edy in the mid-1500s.

Scientific collecting efforts prior to the eighteenth century are not well documented, in part because the Linnean method had yet to come into use. A flourish of immaculately detailed codices and travelogues that describe numerous colonial quests for plants marks this period (Steele 1964). What is noteworthy, however, is that most of the early efforts were driven by commer-cial aspirations.

Indeed the accidental "discovery" of the Amazon River by the Spanish conquistadors Gonzalo Pizzaro and Francisco de Orellana was prompted by colonial interest in exploiting and exporting *canelo*—wild cinnamon *(Endlicheria sp.)*. *Canelo* from the region was first considered as a potential means to eliminate European dependence on African and Far Eastern cinna-mon *(Cinnamomum zeylanicum* and *Cinnamomum verum)*. Pizzaro and Orel-lana never found the anticipated, vast groves of *canelo*. Indeed, they got lost searching deep in what they called *Tierra del Canelo* ("Cinnamon Land"), what is now Ecuador's upper Amazon basin. More than a year and half after their journey began, when they were long considered dead, they emerged at the mouth of the Amazon River on the Atlantic Ocean. From the Piz-zaro/Orellana expedition diaries we learn that every one of the more than four thousand Indian "helpers" were lost by the end of the journey (Henry E. Huntington Library and Art Gallery 1925).

Despite the fact that the Pizzaro-Orellana expedition into *Tierra del Canelo* was largely a failure, it marked the genesis of subsequent efforts to commercialize and exploit flora and fauna in the region. Unfortunately, this moment was premised and reliant upon the exploitation and devastation of local culture, which included loss of life. Even though thousands may not perish today as a direct consequence of the quest for specific plants, many maintain that there is a continued disregard by those who hunt for plants for differential cultural uses and practices of local people.

During the last five hundred years, much has changed yet many things strikingly resemble the past. The legacy of colonial exploitation morphed into the gain and gaffe of Northern capital/industrially rich states, at the expense of their Southern, biodiversity rich states. This exploitation continued against a backdrop where biodiversity was understood as the "common heritage of humanity" and not the sovereign property of any one nation. For centuries plants, subsequently dubbed "plant genetic resources," and now "biodiversity," were nothing more than a raw material (overly abundant in the South) for input into myriad Northern commercial, industrial, and scientific practices. In 1992, in the face of considerable opposition from Northern interests, the Convention on Biological Diversity (CBD) came into force and recognized states' sovereign rights over their natural and biological resources. Although apparently beneficial and championed by many Southern activists and scholars, christening plants as property underneath the jurisdiction of the state was a mixed blessing. Member nations were formally given what was arguably already theirs and simultaneously obligated to erect sufficient regulatory infrastructure to protect these resources from continued exploitation and expropriation.

In the last decade of the twentieth century, Ecuador established many political structures and processes to better regulate what is increasingly called "access and benefit sharing" (ABS) of its plant genetic resources. Ecuador's *Grupo Nacional de Trabajo sobre Biodiversidad* (the National Biodiversity Working Group, or *GNTB*) reports directly to the Ministry of Environment and is largely responsible for policy development regarding ABS issues. The GNTB is composed of six key subgroups that include biosafety and security; legal mechanisms; economic development; access to genetic resources; ecosystems; and indigenous rights and knowledge. In addition, the government attempts to monitor and regulate both commercial and scientific plant collection efforts by national and foreign entities. Foreign collectors must work with a national counterpart and are required to leave at least one identical version of the sample(s) they intend to remove from the country in the holdings of the National Herbarium *(Herbario Nacional)*, or other relevant scientific institution.[6] This procedure is often overlooked or ignored, especially in the face of few or no government enforcement mechanisms. As a result of enforcement gaps, many ostensibly dubious bioprospecting efforts to remove plant genetic resources from Ecuador for commercial purposes have become the cause celebre for many NGOs and indigenous coalitions. Groups such as *Acción Ecológica* (also

Friends of the Earth Ecuador) and the *Coordinadora de Organizaciones Indíge-nas de la Cuenca Amazonica* (COICA or the Coordinator of Indigenous Orga-nizations of the Amazon Basin) have run large campaigns against various bio-prospectors and even against proposals for bioprospecting.[7] Campaign results have been mixed, but they have nevertheless managed to heighten public awareness over the importance and value of Ecuador's plant genetic resources.

A TALE OF THREE PROSPECTORS

One Man Party: Loren Miller, the Ayahuasca, and Plant Patent Rights

In 1984, Loren Miller, working on behalf of the California-based firm Inter-national Plant Medicine Corporation, obtained a sample of *Banisteriopsis caapi*, commonly known in the region as *ayahuasca* or *yage*. The *ayahuasca* sample, according to Miller, came from an undisclosed Ecuadorian Amazon community's "domestic garden."[8] In a series of events shrouded by rumors and what some claim Miller's "arrogance and ignorance," he claimed he "discov-ered" a "unique" variety *B. caapi* and then filed for a U.S. patent that was granted on June 17, 1986 (Hammond 2000; United States Patent Office 1986). Miller patented the "new" *caapi* variety, dubbed "Da Vine," presumably because of its medicinal value in cancer treatment, psychotherapy, post-encephalitic Parkinsonism, as well as its ornamental value as "an attractive house plant which occasionally blooms" (USPTO 1986). The central question that emerges is: how could the U.S. Patent Office (USPTO) accept the "new variety" as "new" if it had been cultivated for centuries by indigenous people throughout the upper Amazon basin who knew and utilized the plant for both medicinal and spiritual purposes? To gain some insight into this decision we need to examine the nature and the inherent biases in the patent system, espe-cially as it concerns living organisms.

In order to the put the USPTO decision to patent "Da Vine" into proper perspective we must trace the ultimately successful campaign to overturn the patent. The campaign harnessed the collaborative efforts of an international coalition of lawyers, indigenous, environmental, and human rights activists, and concerned scholars. The successful challenge of the USPTO marks the first time that indigenous people from developing countries challenged a U.S. patent based on materials and knowledge acquired from them (Center for International Environmental Law 1999).

In 1996 at the Fifth Congress of the *Coordinadora de Organizaciones Indí-genas de la Cuenca Amazonica* (COICA), more than one hundred delegates from Brazil, Ecuador, Venezuela, Surinam, Bolivia, Peru, The Guyanas, and Colombia denounced the patenting of *ayahuasca*. The congress unanimously labeled Miller's patent as "an offense against all the Amazon indigenous peoples and an affront that can not be tolerated" (Jacanamijoy 1996). Beyond denouncing the patent, COICA declared Miller "an enemy of the people" and deemed his safety uncertain within its territories.

In response to COICA's actions, the Inter-American Foundation (IAF), a U.S. government–supported development organization, stated that the resolution was "excessive, abusive and completely inappropriate" and requested a retraction. If a retraction was not forthcoming, the IAF threatened to cease funding the organization (IAF 1998). The IAF tempered their statement by noting,

> [T]he Inter-American Foundation "does not represent the private interests of Mr. Miller related to his US patent to develop and commercialize [sic] the plant Ayahuasca. However, as we also explained, the Inter-American Foundation believes that the resolution of COICA with relation to Mr. Miller is abusive and reprehensible, constituting a threat against the security and well-being of Mr. Miller as well as the officials of his company. (IAF 1998)

Antonio Jacanamijoy, the General Coordinator of the COICA, responded in a letter to the IAF, stating,

> [T]o let it be clarified, COICA does not retract nor will it retract the resolution adopted through mature and sovereign means by more than 80 delegates representing 400 groups of indigenous peoples from nine Amazonian countries. (COICA 1998)

He continued,

> It concerns [the COICA] that the Inter-American Foundation, an organization with which we have established an impartial, transparent and horizontal relationship of cooperation throughout many years, today demonstrates absolute partiality in defending the interests of a particular person in spite of what others think, such as in this case, that does not consider the opinion of the victims in this plundering. (COICA 1998) (author's translation)

More than thirty nongovernmental organizations (NGOs) responded to the threats by the IAF to suspend its support of COICA. The U.S.-based Sierra Club, the Environmental Defense Fund (now called Environmental Defense), the Brazilian *Instituto Socioambiental,* and a host of NGOs throughout Ecuador wrote letters protesting the IAF's actions. Most notable was a letter from Shaman Pharmaceuticals, Inc. (now Shamanbotanicals.com) supporting COICA's position regarding intellectual property rights.[9]

The crux of the dispute centers around the nature of how Western intellectual property rights (IPR) regimes favor corporate and financial rights over the collective and cultural rights of indigenous people, and not so much in the acerbic back-and-forth between the COICA and the IAF (Hammond 2000). Acutely aware of the bias inherent in Western IPR law, COICA representatives, in coalition with the U.S.-based Amazon Coalition, called on the assistance of the Washington, D.C., Center for International Environmental Law (CIEL) to challenge the patent. Before the international exchanges with IAF got into full swing, representatives from COICA staked out their position directly to Loren Miller. In a letter to Miller in June 1996, COICA representatives informed him, "[W]e will initiate all actions that may be necessary in order to revoke the patent."[10] Less than one month later, Miller aggressively replied to Piyahuaje, noting, "I do not have a patent on *ayahuasca*. The plant I am working with does not belong to you. It did not originate in your land."[11]

Following up on COICA's petition, CIEL asked Miller to dedicate and return his patent to the public domain in June 1998, thereby relinquishing his private property claims over the plant (CIEL 1998). CIEL's involvement marked the start of a full-scale, legal campaign that eventually led to the revocation of Miller's patent on *Banisteriopsis caapi* in November 1999. Rather quixotically the patent office reversed its rejection, reinstating the patent in January 2001.

In 1998, U.S. patent official Doug Robinson told the *Multinational Monitor* that one reason why Patent #5,751 may have been granted was because of the lack of scientific literature on *Banisteriopsis caapi* (Knight 1998). *B. caapi*, however, was not an unknown plant. Hence, why CIEL argues "The PTO 'got it right,' the first time when it rejected Miller's 'DaVine' patent claim. The rambling, conclusory, and often circular reasoning of the examiner's statement restoring the patent does not reveal whether Miller prevailed on the basis of his arguments or simply by wearing the examiner down" (Wisner 2001). The scientific literature is fairly clear that the characteristics Miller notes as novel were fairly well known—or part of "prior art" in the parlance of IPR law (CIEL 1999). COICA also cites several scholarly references regarding the use and cultivation of the plant.[12] Hence, in many ways the USPTO failed to sufficiently research Miller's claims of *caapi*'s "novel" medicinal qualities.[13]

Beyond the failures of the USPTO, Patent #5,751 exemplifies the problems that can arise when the Western patent system encounters a radically different system for creating, managing, and protecting knowledge that has accumulated in other cultures (CIEL 1999). Western IPR regimes accord primacy to private interests and private property. Accordingly, they can simultaneously threaten nonprivate interests and conservation efforts. Indeed, U.S. plant patent laws, promulgated in the 1930s, were designed to encourage the private sector to increase plant-breeding programs and develop better yielding agricultural crops.

The USPTO's decision to patent *B. caapi* not only favors private property rights, but it does so beyond collective rights. As Hammond has noted, "That the patent claim procedure enabled Miller to gain a patent on a plant that is widely cultivated throughout the Amazon, proves that the patent process needs to be revised to protect the intellectual property rights of indigenous peoples." (Knight 1998) By favoring a system of private rights that enables certain economic expansion activities (i.e., potential drug development and financial capital development) the Western IPR system jeopardizes rights that favor the protection of cultural and conservation practices. The system does so by giving primacy to economic values and refusing to recognize traditions and religious values that have served to reinforce ecological conservation. As Jacanamijoy noted, Miller's patent was a desecration of a "sacred symbol" and demonstrated a lack of respect for indigenous culture and customs (COICA 1998). Critics argue that there is no clear link between the collective rights indigenous people have claimed for *B. caapi* and conservation practices. It is, however, well documented that the use of *ayahuasca* is premised upon both a spiritual and cultural connection to the environment as well as a particular conservation ethic (Furst 1976). Hence, both the symbolic and real expropriation of *ayahuasca*—by one individual and the IPR system—threaten to compromise biological and cultural diversity in Ecuador.

Dreams of a Shaman: The Case of Shaman Pharmaceuticals

In 1989 Lisa Conte and a group of venture capitalists set out to do the impossible. They formed Shaman Pharmaceuticals with the goal of developing pharmaceutical products with the direct assistance of shamans and local healers around the world. Shortly after its formation, the company added to its ambitious agenda by creating the Healing Forest Conservancy. The Conservancy's mandate was to funnel unspecified percentages of profits back into the communities that assisted with Shaman's drug development. By the spring of 1999, approximately one decade after its founding, Shaman Pharmaceuticals was busy filing for bankruptcy. More than half the staff was suspended in the rapid downsizing. Although Shaman Pharmaceuticals continued to exist, it became the "parent" company of "Shamanbotanicals.com"—presumably with the hope of sharing in the stock market "dot.com" fever.[14] Shamanbotanicals.com was born almost overnight but most of the dreams of Shaman, the original company, remained unfulfilled. In retrospect, it seems as if science, political economy and the vagaries of development work "beat the Shaman."

Shaman Pharmaceuticals was self-portrayed and idolized as the "most progressive" biodiversity prospecting firm because of its efforts to provide compensation packages for the indigenous and traditional communities with whom they worked (Dorsey 2001). From the beginning Shaman was also a target of those critical of the company's progressive promises. Numerous scholars, activists and policy makers attacked the idea that the firm could engage in "multi-stage benefit sharing with governments and traditional cultures" and simultaneously participate in "investing in the sustainable management practices of plant resources as a part of long-term drug development" (King 1994; Meza 1999). Cultural Survival Canada and the Rural Advancement Foundation International (RAFI) dubbed Shaman's many patents on various compounds from *Croton lechleri,* commonly know in the upper Amazon basin of Ecuador and Peru as *sangre de drago or sangre de grado,* "an affront to the indigenous peoples of the Amazon." (RAFI and Cultural Survival Canada 1997). In Ecuador, Acción Ecológica, one of the most well known and respected environmental organizations in the country, has labeled Shaman a biopirate. Shaman's potential was not lost on the arbiters of the market. The comments of the financial services firm Smith Barney are notable:

> [W]hile Shaman's activities may appeal to certain pools of capital dedicated to socially responsible investment activity, and while Shaman does appear to be an ideal model for environmental and corporate behavior . . . *we have allotted no value to Shaman's enterprise beyond that which we believe to ultimately realizable in monetary terms.* (Cohen and Tokheim 1992, 8; italics in original)

Shaman officially began its work in Ecuador in 1991. Early that year they were granted permission to export thirty kg of dry plant samples from various plant families (Ministerio de Agricultura y Ganaderia 1991). During this same period, in late 1990, they registered their first patent (U.S. Patent #596–893) on a material labeled SP-303. This patent was based on their work with species in the genus *Croton* and *Calophyllum.* The registered patent for the SP-303 was abandoned and filed as U.S. Patent #5,211,944 in July 29, 1991, which was subsequently granted on May 18, 1993 (USPTO 1993). This is notable inasmuch as it confirms that the Shaman's work on derivatives from *Croton* (and *Calophyllum*), pre-date its work in Ecuador with indigenous communities there.[15] For the next six years Shaman sponsored and conducted a variety of studies on *C. lechleri, sangre de drago.* They sponsored studies on how best to manage, propagate, and harvest *sangre de drago* (Revelo 1994a; Revelo 1994b); on the nature of its local markets (Jordan and Associates 1996); and conducted internal tests on how to synthesize the chemically active compounds within the plant—presumably in order to avoid permanent dependence on local supply. During this time period Shaman representatives boasted in numerous publications, meetings, and presentations about the amount of money they returned to native communities (King 1994; King et al. 1996). Shaman representatives have put forward the figure that 15 percent of "its drug discovery expedition costs fund projects and or programs . . . are based on the expressed needs of (traditional) communities" (King et al. 2000). In the six years the company researched *sangre de drago* (1991–1996) in the Ecuadorian Oriente approximately 19 percent (about $33,100) of its reported "technological exchanges" and "benefits received by various groups" ostensibly went to indigenous groups (Shaman Pharmaceuticals 1999). When this number is balanced against actual company expenses during this time, the overall contribution to indigenous peoples falls below a fraction of a percent. Furthermore, there was no return on profits to any community since Shaman made no profits during this period. Also, approximately half of the $33,100 ($16,000) seems to dovetail precisely with both the needs of the company and the community, making it difficult to distinguish who requested what.[16] This correspondence matches Svarstad's (2000) findings for Shaman projects elsewhere. She has noted, however, that the area of "community reciprocity" is "a more problematic aspect of the Shaman's strategy" since "the company (really) decides both its 'short-term' and 'long-term' reciprocity" usually in its own interest and not necessarily in line with conversation needs, nor community desires (Svarstad 2000).

Shaman's activities in the Ecuadorian Oriente have prompted a widespread shift in local agricultural practices with unmeasured effects on regional conservation. In early to mid-1998, shortly before Shaman entered economic hard times and was forced to radically restructure itself and more or less abandon its Ecuador operations, it obtained *Cartas de Compromiso* ("Promise Letters") from at least eleven community leaders, representing more than 178 families to "provide latex from *Croton lechleri*" (Shaman Pharmaceuticals 1998). Many of the communities' members, anticipating just market compensation, no longer in the form of "reciprocity," eagerly began dedicating their lands to *sangre de drago* production. Shaman understood that it would take the company two to four years before they could offer some communities any return for producing latex (Jatun Sacha 1997). Hence, a Shaman representative in Quito implied in an interview in 2000 that the Shaman restructuring probably adversely affected some community members (Shaman representative 2000). While Shaman pursued its "sustainable development and management of *sangre de drago*" field scheme, it also actively tried to synthesize the active compounds in *sangre de drago* to cut its dependency of its local suppliers.

In 1999, the U.S. Food and Drug Administration (FDA) forced Shaman to conduct a new series of clinical trials on a drug largely based on chemicals found in *sangre de drago*. The FDA decision was a major setback for Shaman and sent its publicly traded shares plummeting, causing the restructuring noted above. Almost overnight, in an effort to sidestep the regulators, Shaman morphed from a pharmaceutical firm into a "dietary supplement company." Complicating matters, efforts to synthesize the active compounds in *sangre de drago* have proved largely unsuccessful.

In just one decade, the Shaman sustainable development and conservation model, premised on "multi-stage benefit sharing with governments and traditional cultures" and "investing in the sustainable management practices of plant resources as a part of long-term drug development" has proved largely bankrupt. It is notable that just months after the restructuring, world

renowned ethnobotanist and former bioprospecting advocate Dr. Mark
Plotkin publicly severed his ties with the company. According to the *New York
Times*, he also had the company remove every reference to his name from its
Web site (Christensen 1999). Plotkin renounced bioprospecting "because it
had become too controversial in South America, where indigenous tribes had
complained that bioprospectors were stealing their secrets and getting rich
from them" (Christensen 1999). A close analysis of Shaman's activities in
Ecuador reveals that its collaborations with traditional communities represent
only a fraction of its "reciprocity efforts" in the country. Third-party consulting firms and nonindigenous communities recouped a great deal of Shaman's
"reciprocal benefits."[17] It appears that the consultants apparently benefited the
most in terms of resources gained and shared (at least financial and technical
ones) from the company. Moreover, the conservation of biological diversity
has been compromised in many areas in untold ways where the presence and
interests of Shaman has proved an incentive for planting agroforestry plantations of *Croton lechleri*. Biodiversity conservation and conservation in general,
although extolled as necessary and appropriate by the company, were apparently only secondary goals to having a steady supply stream of the product, in
this case the latex from *sangre de drago*. In spite of protests and active global
and local advocacy against the company, Shaman demonstrated an inability to
deliver comprehensive "reciprocity" to the myriad local communities. Further,
the company provided inadequate returns to its venture capital supporters.
Lastly, it failed to produce conservation results, beyond a few showcase projects, on scales comparable to the extent of its operations. Its overall failure is
symbolic, as it underscores the conclusion that local-level sustainable development and conservation efforts cannot and do not flow from globally oriented, market-based schemes. Indeed, such schemes, be they development
projects or the work of transnational firms and/or their subsidiaries, have, at
best, caused uneven development and, in the worst cases, encouraged under-
development of local communities. As far as conservation efforts are concerned these schemes jeopardize and even undermine local conservation. The
results of Shaman's work in the Ecuadorian Oriente, in the eyes and opinions
of many on the ground there, bring home these points.

Low Down in Loja: The Case of the University of California at San Diego

In May 1996 a small, inconspicuous, two-day meeting titled "Genetic Prospecting and the Protection of Biodiversity: The Vilcabamba Project," was held at the
Stanford Law School. The meeting's purpose was twofold. First, it set out to
"describe a new ethno-botany [sic] project in a region of Southern Ecuador
known for extraordinary plant diversity and the active practice of traditional
medicine." The project would take place in Loja Province, in the vicinity of
Podocarpus National Park (PNP), an area known for its high degree of species

endemism and biodiversity. Secondly, the conference sought to provide a round-table discussion to explore three key questions related to the project: (1) How realistic is genetic prospecting? (2) If genetic prospecting is a realistic means through which to seek valuable new substances is there an existing legal framework to support such work? and (3) What advantages and disadvantages does the ethno-botany perspective add compared to other types of genetic prospecting? (Francis 1996). The conference announcement notes that the Vilcabamba Project, is directed by Dr. Douglas Sharon, an anthropologist and director of the Museum of Man in San Diego, Dr. Ezra Bejar, a pharmacologist with extensive experience studying medicinal plants, Dr. Raineer [sic] Bussmann, a plant ecologist at Bayreuth University in Germany, and Ivan Gayler, a biomedical developer in San Diego (and chair of the Museum of Man board).

The working paper for the meeting was titled: "Ecuadorian Medicinal Plant Lore." It was distributed with a cover letter from Marc Miller, who at the time was a visiting professor from Emory attached to the Law School, and Don Kennedy, Bing Professor of Environmental Science at Stanford and former head of the FDA during the Carter Administration. An interview with Miller revealed that he was the principal author of the "Ecuadorian Medicinal Plant Lore" (Miller 2000).

By most accounts, the Stanford meeting was yet another gathering of would-be bioprospectors; from another perspective, it was a meeting of biopirates. The meeting conveners gathered a combination of faculty and authoritative experts. Some of those present were in support of the project, while others were opposed. Still others were simply fascinated by the habits of this group of "Indiana Joneses" combing distant jungles ostensibly in search of plants to save humanity.[18]

I received the "Ecuadorian Medicinal Plant Lore" paper in the mail almost a year after the meeting at Stanford, just after I attended the forty-ninth *Congreso Internacional de Americanistas* that July in Quito. The International Congress of Americanists is perhaps the largest gathering of scholars that work in the Americas. More than seven thousand scholars from almost every conceivable discipline attend panel discussions, workshops, and cocktail parties for a two-week span. During the *Congreso* I attended a workshop on "Medicinal plants of Vilcabamba" *(Plantas Medicinales de Vilcabamba)* where Dr. Douglas Sharon and other colleagues distributed a paper of the same title (Congreso de Americanistas 1997).

Interestingly, the Stanford paper was an expanded version of Sharon's conference offering *"Plantas Medicinales de Vilcabamba."* When I compared the two papers I realized that they were different in a rather peculiar and alarming way. The Spanish version, *"Plantas Medicinales de Vilcabamba,"* publicly presented in Ecuador, elaborated a scientific research project. Whereas the English version, "Ecuadorian Medicinal Plant Lore," outlined what can only be characterized as a venture-capital backed, bioprospecting development project where the researchers in question had done considerable preparatory work, including purchasing large tracts of land, in order to achieve their objectives—which went unmentioned in the Spanish version.

It may be argued that during the course of one year, plans for "Ecuadorian Medicinal Plant Lore" may have changed in the minds of the researchers in response to the comments received at the Stanford workshop. Indeed, this is what the English version's "ghost author" Miller suggests (Miller 2000). Two major problems, however, remain. First, critical data discoveries and project accomplishments were removed from the Spanish version presented in Ecuador. Various glaring examples stand out. In English we learn that the "researchers traveled to Southern Ecuador on a project funded by Mr. Ivan Gayler, a San Diego bio-medical developer and president of the Museum of Man (Ecuadorian Medicinal Plant Lore 1996)." While in Spanish we are told, "The investigators traveled to the South of Ecuador, specifically to the city of Loja, capital of the province of the same name" (Bejar et al. 1997).[19] In the Spanish version all references to the venture capitalist and "bio-medical developer" Ivan Gayler, are removed. More worrisome is the deletion of the following from the Spanish version:

> Mr. Gayler preceded the team to establish links with the University of Loja as well as a non-profit conservation foundation Colinas Verdes (Green Hills), which is currently engaged in collaborative research with the Museum of Man. He also began negotiations for the purchase of a tract of tropical rainforest, the transactions for which were concluded in late 1995. At this time, Mr. Gayler is contracting for the construction of a research station, Estación Científica San Francisco, on the purchased land and consortium agreements for student training, conservation and research with San Diego State University and DFG (Germany) are being drawn up.[20]

In the Spanish version there is no mention that researchers have made extensive purchases of land with venture-capital support. Indeed, in the Spanish version there is no mention that the researchers intended to build the research station from which they currently operate.[21]

Beyond the deletions and omissions between the Spanish and English versions of otherwise verbatim translations, the English publication records of the researchers hints at their continued interest in commercialization of potential botanical findings. Bejar et al. (1998) note,

> Two databases of medicinal plants—one in English, one in Spanish—have been created. These databases contain information—from fieldwork and computerized literature search [sic]—about medicinal plants from the Vilcabamba area. The purpose of the databases is to create a book in Spanish for local dissemination as well as to allow scholars to sort plants in accord with a variety of parameters.

Presumably since this sentence is a fragment from the Stanford conference paper, the undescribed parameters are "a variety of anthropological, ethnobotanical and phytochemical parameters." Given such parameters, which correspond to Natural Products Alert File (NAPRALERT) research precedents (Bejar 1998), it is not far-fetched to anticipate that the databases will be used to track extracts submitted for pharmacological testing, in other words, bioprospecting.[22]

During this period, several NGOs asked the Ecuadorian government to intervene and investigate the activities of the aforementioned researchers, including ongoing research at the *Estación Scientífica de San Francisco*. Correspondences from as early as May 1996 through June 1997 took place between the Loja, Ecuador-based *Fundación Ecológica Arcoiris* (The Rainbow Ecology Foundation), the Quito-based *Acción Ecológica*, and the *Instituto Ecuatoriano Forestal de Areas Naturales y Vida Silvestre (INEFAN)*, the government agency responsible for forestry, protected areas, and wildlife; replaced by a new Environment Ministry, *El Ministerio de Medio Ambiente*) (Arcoisris 1996; Acción Ecológica 1996). Two environmental NGOs, *Arcoiris* and *Acción Ecológica*, raised issues over whether or not researchers and staff at the *Estación Scientífica de San Francisco* were conducting their research illegally, engaging in undisclosed bioprospecting and removing plant varieties from the Vilcabamba area without proper government permits.

The researchers mentioned above have not officially responded to the extent to which the aforementioned claims are valid. The officially stated objectives of the *Estación Scientífica de San Francisco* do not mention any aspects of commercialization of biological materials, bioprospecting, or even more general aims of the development of medicinal plant lore.[23] Arguably, the researchers are using the station's officially designated institutional objectives to obscure their real "research interests." In a June 1997 communication to *Acción Ecológica* former INEFAN Executive Director Mario Cárdenas notes, "[I]n the research permits requested by the Station they have not mentioned bioprospecting" (Cárdenas 1997). By this time the researchers had already held the Stanford Conference and were on the eve of giving their presentation at the *Congreso de Americanistas*.[24] The Ecuadorian *Ministerio de Agricultura y Ganaderia* (*MAG*, the Ministry of Agriculture and Livestock) was unable to confirm if researchers at the station had or had not removed plant species collected in the region from Ecuador.

CONCLUSIONS AND NEW BEGINNINGS

Ecuadorians are on the verge of something spectacular with respect to the conservation of biodiversity. On one hand, the Convention on Biological Diversity (CBD) has finally established that biodiversity, which include plant genetic resources, is the property of nations. This decision reversed centuries of thinking that deemed biodiversity everywhere as part and parcel of the "common good." It created opportunities for two-thirds of the world's nations from the so-called South. In light of the guidelines included in the Convention, the *JUNAC* (the *Junta del Acuerdo de Cartagena ahora Comunidad Andina de Naciones,* or Andean Pact) promulgated a variety of laws demarcating and legislating the nature of access and benefit sharing of genetic materials. Ecuador has yet to ratify the JUNAC laws, but as this intervention goes to press, a draft of the *Reglamento de Acceso a Recursos Geneticos* (Regulation of Access to Genetic Resources) is being reviewed by various government Ministries and is expected to become law by summer 2001. The previously mentioned *Grupo Nacional de Trabajo sobre Biodiversidad* (the National Biodiversity Working Group, or *GNTB*) is leading the charge to mold and shape the JUNAC decisions and resolutions to Ecuadorian reality.

On the other hand, however, the promise of bioprospecting as a potential "win-win" scenario for all involved: the state, the leading institutions and individuals (whether they are corporations, universities, botanical gardens, museums, individual scientists, or venture capitalists), communities, not to mention biodiversity and humanity, looms large. Bioprospecting so framed is the late twentieth century's Holy Grail, *El Dorado,* and fountain of youth all in one. Yet, if left, unmonitored, the promise of bioprospecting is not only empty but also deleterious for conservation, local communities, the state, and even, on occasion, for the institutions that propose and perpetuate it. This fact has a great deal to do with the historical, political-economic legacy from which bioprospecting emerges. It is not always easy for institutions that have been conducting themselves in a certain hierarchical, exploitative way for centuries (e.g., the Royal Botanic Gardens) or those others (e.g., the University of California Museum of Man) that may look to them or their counterparts (e.g., the Missouri or New York Botanical Gardens) for leadership and know-how to suddenly make a sea change when a new global accord comes along. They may try, earnestly and sincerely, but failure is just as likely as success, given the stakes—millions, if not billions of dollars; prestige and fame (if a magic cure is ever found).

Thus, biodiversity prospecting potentially represents both disaster and opportunity for everyone involved. Banning access to genetic resources is as impossible as comprehensive effective enforcement. The challenge lies in a balance—somewhere between disaster and opportunity. Would-be bioprospectors must be better regulated, while existing community capacity such as intellectual property rights protection regimes must be better understood, respected, upheld, and enforced. Yet these meager recommendations have their shortcomings. Accordingly, they mark modest beginnings, to be verified and modified with research and experiences from the field. Without balance, as Mooney notes "there is no 'bioprospecting'. There is only biopiracy." (Mooney 2000). In a vacuum of international standards and norms, where practical and credible regulatory, monitoring, and enforcement mechanisms are nonexistent, the theft of local knowledge and the adverse consequences for conservation will only accelerate in the years ahead.

NOTES

1. See Reid et al. (1993, 1) for definition of bioprospecting.

2. Scientists argue that between 20–50 percent of current pharmaceutical products have their origins in natural products. Although high profile cases of bioprospecting (e.g., Merck's work in Costa Rica) have not had publicly recorded successes, natural products research (NPR) commands between 1–5 percent of pharmaceutical research and development expenditure. For more detailed discussion on this point see the volume: Grifo and Rosenthal, eds., *Biodiversity and Human Health* (Washington, DC: Island Press, 1997).

3. Not all bioprospecting efforts are defined by this quartet. Many actors only care about profit. Herein, however, I will pay special attention to those influenced by the four factors.

4. I use the term *pharmaceutical actors* to highlight the fact that myriad entities have a commercial interest in global biodiversity. Thus, "actors" include, at least: independent individuals, often contracted by larger firms; university researchers from myriad departments (e.g., anthropology, botany, biology, zoology, etc.); botanical garden employees; in addition to transnational corporations (TNCs) of various sizes.

5. See J. Rosenthal, "Integrating Drug Discovery, Biodiversity, Conservation, and Economic Development: Early lesson from the International Cooperative Biodiversity Group (ICBG)," in *Biodiversity and Human Health*, ed. Grifo and Rosenthal (Washington, DC: Island Press, 1997).

6. INEFAN Decision 019 is the *"Instructivo que regula la investigación, colección y exportación de flora y fauna silvestre,"* or the "Directive that regulates research, collection and exportation of wild flora and fauna."

7. Pfizer Pharmaceutical's desire to establish a bioprospecting project that would mirror one established by Merck Pharmaceuticals in Costa Rica was abandoned by the government as a result of the criticisms of a coalition of indigenous organizations and NGOs.

8. It is very likely that Mr. Miller removed his samples of *Banisteriopsis caapi* from Ecuador illegally. To date (January 30, 2001) there is no record that he applied for the required Ecuadorian permits to remove the plant.

9. The Shaman letter is notable, as some Ecuadorian based environmentalists have accused Shaman of bioprospecting.

10. Organización Indigenas Secoyas del Ecuador, Prov. Sucumbios. 14 June 1996. Correspondence to Loren Miller, from Elias Piyahuaje. (Original in Spanish; translation Dorsey). Piyahuaje's message comes since earlier in 1996 Miller noted that the community where he "discovered" ayahuasca was in Secoya territory.

154 MICHAEL K. DORSEY

11. Loren Miller. 3 July 1996. Fax Correspondence to Elias Piyahuaje from Loren Miller. Of course, two years prior the USPTO issued Miller, as inventor, patent #5751 on *Banisteriopsis caapi*, i.e., ayahuasca.

12. The letter from COICA (COICA, March 3, 1998, op. cit.) notes: "These are some contemporary books to which you can refer to verify our statements: 'One River,' Wade Davis, 1996. 'The Jivaro: People of the Sacred Waterfalls,' Michael J. Harner, 1972. 'Hallucinogens and Shamanism,' edited by Michael J. Harner, 1973. 'Von Roraima zum Orinoco,' by the German student Koch-Grunberg, 1917–1928, and a hundred years of categorical ethnobotanical writings from the Englishman Richard Spruce (that recognized the first samples of *Banisteriopsis caapi* in 1851), until Richard Evans Schultes of Harvard University in the decade of the 1970´s."

13. In order for inventors to receive a patent, they are required to demonstrate their invention's novelty, utility, and non-obviousness. See Wisner 2001.

14. This sharing might have been characterized as overly ambitious, since by the time Shamanbotanicals.com was created Shaman stock (SHMN) was trading at an all time low. Additionally, there was no initial public offering windfall for shamanbotanicals.com.

15. It seems the bulk of Shaman's work on SP-303 was done with collaborators in Mexico, Peru, and Colombia and *not* in Ecuador (See Jatun Sacha, *Posibilidades de Manejo de Sangre de Drago en la Parte Alta de la Via Hollin-Loreto* (Quito: Proyecto Gran Sumaco, 1997). Indeed, the double blind experimental drug tests using SP-303 where conducted in nine Mexican clinics. (See Shaman Pharmaceuticals, *Informe Clinico Al Final del Estudio, Protocolo SP-303T-A-02, Estudio Doble Ciego Con Control Placebo Para Evaluar la Eficacia y Tolerancia Clinica de Vivernd(para el Tratamiento de Infecciones Recidivantes por el Virus del Herpes Simplex (VHS) en Sujetos con el Sindrome del Inmunodeficiencia Adquirida (SIDA)* (South San Francisco: Shaman Pharmaceuticals, 1996).

16. Shaman paid $10,000 "extra" to "extend a runway" in a community that owned no plane, but nevertheless was where Shaman was seeking the consultation of the local healer and removing samples of local flora. Furthermore, the company gave $6,000 to support community knowledge building workshops on medicinal plant identification, presumably at least in order to help community members help Shaman representatives identify plants in the field.

17. Approximately 70 percent of its expedition costs in the six years between 1991–1996 went to such consultants, not all of whom were Ecuadorian.

18. The meeting was categorized as such by the former director of the Stanford Environmental Justice Law Clinic, who was invited (See Don Kennedy and Marc Miller, Correspondence/Invitation to Professor Veronica Eady, February 23, 1996) and attended.

19. The exact lines in Spanish are: "Los investigadores viajaron al sur de Ecuador, específicamente a la ciudad de Loja, capital de la provincia del mismo nombre" (Dorsey translation).

20. Marc Miller notes in his telephone interview (op. cit.) that Ivan Gayler is still heavily involved "in the background" on the Vilcabamba project. According to Fun-

dación Arcoiris Gayler acquired 450 ha of land north of Podocarpus Nacional Park (See Fundación Arcoiris, Correspondence to Angel Paucar, Direccion de Areas Naturales, 7 Marzo, 1997, Of. No 036-FAI-97.).

21. For information on Estación Científica San Francisco visit: *http://132.180.60. 32/lehrstuhl/sfstation.htm.*

22. The NAPRALERT File (NAtural PRoducts ALERT) contains bibliographic and factual data on natural products, including information on the pharmacology, biological activity, taxonomic distribution, ethno-medicine, and chemistry of plant, microbial, and animal (including marine) extracts. In addition, the file contains data on the chemistry and pharmacology of secondary metabolites that are derived from natural sources and that have known structure.

23. The five listed objectives can be found at: *http://132.180.60.32/lehrstuhl/sfstation.htm*

24. The paper presented at the Congreso de Americanistas, *Plantas Medicinales de Vilcabamba,* was already written by this point as *"Copyright © 1996"* is emblazoned on the bottom margin of the first page (italics in original).

Part II

Institutions, Organizations, and Participatory Processes

Conceptual Tools for Constructing Biodiversity Conservation with Social Justice

Chapter Ten

CRAFTING CONSERVATION
GLOBALLY AND LOCALLY

Complex Organizations and Governance Regimes

STEVEN R. BRECHIN, PETER R. WILSHUSEN,
CHARLES E. BENJAMIN

The array of organizations and institutions typically engaged in promoting biodiversity conservation make concerted action a highly complex undertaking. A brief list would include international conservation nongovernmental organizations (NGOs) such as the World Wildlife Fund (WWF), The Nature Conservancy (TNC), Conservation International (CI), and the World Conservation Union (IUCN). Development agencies linked to the United Nations system such as the United Nations Development Programme (UNDP), the United Nations Environment Programme (UNEP), the United Nations Educational, Scientific, and Cultural Organization (UNESCO), the Food and Agricultural Organization (FAO), and the Global Environment Facility (GEF) are typically key players. Bilateral development organizations like the United States Agency for International Development (USAID), the Canadian International Development Agency (CIDA), and Germany's *Geselleschaft für Technische Zusammenarbeit* (GTZ), among others, offer programming and financial support in many developing countries. Multilateral lending organizations such as the World Bank, regional development banks (e.g., the Inter-American Development Bank [IDB]) also play an important role in structuring conservation-development initiatives at the transnational level. Global institutions such as the Convention on Biological Diversity or the United Nations Framework Convention on Climate Change guide government action on problems that defy national boundaries. These international organizations and institutions have national, regional, and local counterparts including NGOs, state agencies, rural producer cooperatives, private associations, commercial businesses, village councils, and social movements.

While each of these organizations has singular approaches, competencies, capacities, and shortcomings, the remarkable point is that each likely will need to interact and collaborate with counterparts in order to achieve effective collective action. Yet the conservation and development literature frequently cites examples of organizational failings at all levels. Governmental natural resource management agencies tend to have limited political power and are often poorly funded (Poffenberger 1990b; Terborgh et al. 2002). In addition to inadequate resources, many of these agencies maintain structures and "cultures" that protect agency interests first or follow objectives that do little to serve natural resource management. Local communities tend to distrust these agencies and their personnel, viewing them as harsh and unsympathetic to their needs and concerns (West and Brechin 1991). Multilateral organizations such as the World Bank also have been sources of environmental degradation as well as solutions (Brechin 1997; Rich 1994). Even the once idealized NGOs are showing signs of organizational limitations and even "pathologies" (Edwards and Hulme 1996; Fisher 1997). To date, conservation planners have underutilized organizational studies and have thus missed important opportunities to strengthen biodiversity policy. Not all organizations are equally effective. Nor will any organizational arrangements do. It does matter which organizations are involved and who does what. There are different kinds of organizations operating at very different levels, with distinct mandates, world views, and financial and human capacities (Brechin 1997, 2000).

In this chapter we explore these organizational issues and related institutional arrangements in terms of crafting governance structures. The first part of the chapter centers on complex formal organizations, with an eye toward understanding how they commonly fail and uncovering alternatives for improving performance. We suggest that, given the high complexity and uncertainty inherent to conservation and development interventions, organizations will most successfully manage the diverse tasks involved by adopting flexible structures, instilling a "generative, learning culture," and establishing strong collaborative arrangements. The second part of the chapter considers institutional design principles drawing on international relations and common property theory. We focus on crafting rule-based norms for collaboration that can effectively bring together diverse organizational actors to create "governance regimes" that can stabilize competing expectations with respect to a limited, shared resource base. We present two examples—the Convention on

Biological Diversity (CBD) and community-based forest management in Mali—to illustrate the structure and dynamics of long-term cooperation at the global and local levels. The chapter concludes with a discussion of how organizational and institutional crafting merge with the growing body of literature on social capital, suggesting that socially just biodiversity conservation depends upon establishing and maintaining vibrant and stable arenas for concerted negotiation and collaborative implementation.

UNDERSTANDING COMPLEX ORGANIZATIONS

Along with social movements, formal organizations represent the principal conduit for human collective action. In this book's context, organizations such as governmental resource management agencies, international development agencies, NGOs, and community associations are the main entities that enact conservation initiatives. Paradoxically, organizations can simultaneously advance and impede the formal objectives of conservation and social justice in the course of pursuing their goals and interests. In order to build stronger organizational arrangements for international biodiversity conservation, it is essential to understand the nature and behavior of organizations and how they fit into broader social structures. Although definitions of what constitutes a formal organization differ, analysts generally accept five broad components or elements, including goals, structure, participants, core technology, and environment. Other important concepts include organizational culture and power dynamics.

To the extent that organizations work for a specific purpose, they formulate and pursue formal goals. In this sense an organization's goals give it direction, allowing members to identify and choose alternative courses of action (Simon 1964). Organizational goals can also serve to motivate members and foster organizational identity. At the same time, however, not all goals are formally stated. Frequently, organizations often pursue informal goals that, despite serving the organization in some way, can compromise its formal, stated goals (Burch 1971; Selznick 1949). For example, an organization may work to expand or maintain its own power base or authority or to serve powerful constituency interests first, even if these actions undermine its stated goals of protecting natural resources (e.g., Clark 1997).

Structure reflects the physical qualities of the organization as well as the professional and personal relationships within it. The *formal structure* represents the more normative aspects of the organization, as typically reflected in an organizational chart. This includes the chain of authority and relationships among organizational units and individuals. *Informal structure* refers to the unplanned interactions, personal relationships, and unofficial power dynamics among the organization's units and participants. Structures present a spectrum ranging from a complex, centralized hierarchy with rigidly defined rules and top-down authority to more decentralized, less formal, "organic" forms. These qualities impact both the organization's nature and its ability to perform in different settings.

Participants are the organization's employees. Organizations must hire, train, and retain staff to carry out and manage their activities and functions. In order for an organization to be effective, it must have appropriately skilled, dedicated, and loyal participants. Many of the problems associated with natural resource management stem, in part, from the small number of poorly trained and paid employees.

Perhaps the least understood aspect of an organization is its *core technology*. Every organization transforms inputs, such as materials, energy, labor, creativity, and information into some kind of good or service (Thompson 1967). How the organization structures its activities to create these outputs fundamentally affects its nature. It influences the organization's form, types of employees hired, how work is organized, and even how the employees view the world, providing a collective sense of identity. Organizations tend to establish specialized core competencies. This process of specialization creates boundaries of organizational capacity that are both a strength and a limitation. For example, a park management agency that defines itself mainly around enforcement activities likely will have difficulty providing community-based outreach activities if it lacks the capacity, as well as culture, to offer those types of services.

All organizations are embedded in a complex matrix of social, political, and physical relationships known as *organizational environments*. They can be characterized in many ways such as being stable or turbulent, simple or complex, institutional or technical, supportive or unsupportive (Scott 1998). Technical environments refer mainly to competitive marketplace settings where organizations compete to varying degree for customers and revenues. Institutional environments signify the political, legal, and other normative settings where organizations exist.

Although not a standard organizational element, *culture* is a key feature of any organization. In this context, culture encompasses the symbolic and material practices related to an organization's mission as well as its ability to perform work. To a certain extent, these practices are constitutive of participants' identity and also inform how members should act within the organization. At the same time, practices ranging from routines, ceremonies, and specialized language and symbols serve to constitute the organization. Scott (1998) notes that organizations work to strengthen their cultures in order to better achieve their goals. However, an organization's culture can also constrain its ability to innovate (Schiff 1966) and interact with other organizations (Clark 1997; Hough 1994).

An organization's formal structure and its technology define *power relationships* for that entity but also constitute the types of power resources that it has at its disposal to pursue its objectives. Power resources are materials and capacities such as land, capital, information, and technical knowledge (Weber 1978 [1968]). An organization such as the World Bank possesses an enormous array of financial, political, and intellectual power compared to a community NGO. Yet in the context of conservation and development projects these two groups may interact and become dependent upon one another if they both value performance objectives. At the same time, organizations themselves become contested terrain as internal and external constituencies struggle over their resources and the outputs that they provide. These struggles profoundly shape the organization, its vision, mission, nature of outputs, and relationships with other organizations and groups (Burch 1971; Selznick 1949, 1957). Given the uneven power dynamics among organizational actors in conservation arenas, care must be taken by the players that all stakeholders are fairly represented and engaged in the conservation process to foster successful outcomes (chapter 3, this volume, Hough 1994).

ORGANIZATIONAL FAILURES AND PATHOLOGIES

Organizations can generate unanticipated consequences from their purposeful actions as well (Coleman 1974; Merton 1936). In his insightful essay on the American environment, Burch (1971) showed how a number of U.S. natural resource management agencies in the mid-1900s not only failed to protect the natural resources under their charge, but actually helped to further their degradation. The agencies were often more beholden to constituency interests and to politics than to achieving their specific conservation objectives. Likewise, private NGOs, although widely hailed as effective structures for change, have limitations and pathologies of their own, including overpowering local organizations, or favoring external values and perspectives over local ones (Edwards and Hulme 1996; Fisher 1997; Sundberg 1999). Consequently, a key to making organizations more effective is recognizing and addressing their pathological tendencies. While all organizations experience periods of inefficiency or internal conflict, pathologies represent more "built-in" or recurrent failings (Vaughn 1999).

Referring first to structural inefficiencies, one can identify at least three common problems associated with "tall," hierarchical organizations, "flat," decentralized organizations, and detached units. For example, large, centralized organizations tend to be less capable of responding effectively to complex, rapidly changing situations. In order to deal with such conditions, organizations often choose to decentralize their operations and give greater decision-making power and resources to their subunits. While this restructuring can offer the organization greater flexibility to attend to on-the-ground conditions, it can easily produce inefficiency, often by making direct coordination among organizational units more difficult. Such a tradeoff between local responsive-ness and overall coordination can place decision makers in a "limbo" that results in organizational mistakes and bungling (Perrow 1984).

A third general type of structural inefficiency, more commonly found among public agencies than private organizations, is the separation of struc-ture from action. This type differs from the other two because of its political nature. In these cases, new structures or practices are created more to appease public expectations or meet legal requirements than to achieve effective implementation. In doing so, officials often separate the new structure from the organization's core activities. Decision makers typically create these "detached structures" when the organization faces stiff criticism from higher authorities or society at large and thus represents a strategic move to gain legitimacy and protect operations (Vaughn 1999). Since these types of orga-nizational structures are created more for show than operation, they tend to produce negative outcomes in the long term since they raise constituency expectations but typically lack the capacity to perform effectively in practice. Lee Clarke's 1999 book on emergency action plans as fantasy documents pro-vide an illustration of structural inefficiency.

Building on the points above, some organizational failures can result from a combination of inefficient structures and political practices. Political and/or cultural reasons can generate a high degree of collective inertia that prevents goal attainment. Consequently, organizational performance depends upon both structural capacity and commitment to goals. Whereas *capacity* comes as a result of establishing and maintaining appropriate structures, technologies, financial and human resources, *commitment* refers to the personnel's degree of dedication to its stated objectives (see Lester 1990).

Hough (1994) discusses organizational constraints that hindered early attempts at integrating conservation and development at Madagascar's Amber Mountain National Park. The example nicely illustrates how intra- and interorganizational politics linked to goals, structure, culture, and commitment can combine to limit or even undermine a project's conservation and develop-ment objectives. Regarding organizational goals, the unstated objectives of the Worldwide Fund for Nature (WWF) and the Malagasy environmental protec-tion agency (SPN) led each to act in ways that hampered a full integration of the stated conservation and development objectives. On one level, the formal goals of both organizations centered on conservation and thus the strategies they adopted focused exclusively on protected area management. This narrow focus on conservation objectives caused an important organizational partner, the local Diocesan Development Committee (DDC), to withdraw from the project because it no longer emphasized participatory community development as originally planned. The DDC also lacked independent power to successfully promote the development piece. As a result it became marginalized by the two lead conservation organizations as they strove to pursue their own objectives.

On a second level, the Malagasy environmental protection agency, SPN, pursued an informal "agenda" where it used project funding to build offices and houses for staff and rationalized the action as capacity building. Certainly government agencies need to establish an adequate infrastructure to operate effectively, but in this case, SPN's actions served to isolate the organization from other potential collaborators including local communities and other government agencies. On a third level, the informal goals of donor organizations influenced how project staff structured the Amber Mountain project. In this case, the United States Agency for International Development (USAID) channeled funds for the project through WWF. Amber Mountain was the first donor-funded integrated conservation and development project in Madagascar. As a result, WWF and SPN felt pressure to produce fast results. Project personnel designed activities around protected area management and tree planting so that they could easily implement them in the short term, but diverted further attention and resources away from the long-term objectives of integrating conservation and development.

Organizational cultures and core technologies also had a strong impact on the Amber Mountain Project. For example, Hough (1994) showed that in designing project activities, WWF and SPN fell back on what they knew best, core technologies designed around a top-down approach to protected area boundary demarcation, tourism development, law enforcement, and forestry. In part, the social development agenda was neglected because the two organizations had no experience with or capacity in that domain. SPN personnel in particular also rigidly maintained their perceived roles as law enforcers, typically adopting an authoritarian attitude with local communities. As a result, the agency's authoritarian approach, in combination with the informal goals and competitive behavior mentioned above, served to isolate the lead organizations from other potential collaborators. In the end, the project took on a narrow set of conservationist goals rather than a broader integration of conservation and development activities. In chapter 11, Lisa Gezon explores the organizational lessons learned from Amber Mountain, ten years after its original development. She also outlines current organizational and management challenges in in Madagascar concerning conservation management at the landscape scale.

Second-order organizational failures are commonly called "pathologies" due to their chronic persistence. In their classic monograph, Blau and Meyer (1987) present two pathologies typical of bureaucracies (i.e., organizational forms that tend to be hierarchical, rule-bound, and fragmented), including excessive rigidity and resistance to innovation. With respect to excessive rigidity, bureaucracies become predominantly oriented toward internal rules rather than performance goals. While rules and regulations can help to increase an organization's operational efficiency, they can also become ends in themselves, sometimes replacing the original mission of the organization. Rules may also limit the capacity of workers to "think outside of the box," thus reducing creativity and broader effectiveness. This process is often called "trained incapacity" (Morgan 1997). Under these circumstances, efficiency may become synonymous with job conformity where individuals with the greatest knowledge of the rules become those most highly respected and rewarded. Crozier (1964) noted that excessively rigid bureaucracies do not learn well. Due to poor feedback loops from fragmentation of work and responsibility, they tend not to learn from their mistakes. When criticized, participants often rally around the written rules and become even more rigid (Vaughn 1999).

A second common pathology of bureaucracies is resistance to innovation. New ideas, arrangements, or practices may be seen as threats to many members of an organization and resistance can be fostered through internal or external relationships. Given that most public bureaucracies are staffed by civil servants, or career employees, from middle management on down, politically appointed, often short-term administrators may have difficulties implementing new ideas. Career civil servants sometimes alter or even ignore new directives, especially if they conflict with existing rules. Indeed, innovations may threaten established procedures and relationships of authority. Consequently, civil servants often conduct their work in a manner that best reflect their views, self-interests, existing power structures, and cultural beliefs. For example, Schiff's (1966) research showed how U.S. natural resource management agencies actively resisted the scientifically innovative notions of ecological dynamics and the constructive use of fire in resource management programs because they conflicted with standard operating procedures and cultural beliefs.

Clark's (1997) analysis of a long-term recovery program for the endangered black-footed ferret (BFF) *(Mustela nigripes)* in Wyoming, USA further illustrates organizational pathologies. With the sensational news that the BFF, once thought extinct, still existed came the attention of many organizational actors willing to help with the recovery effort. Although all the interested organizations could agree on the overarching goal—saving the species from extinction—there was little agreement on the best ways to achieve it. This created a politically charged and operationally confusing setting in which the Wyoming Game and Fish, (WGF), the U.S. Fish and Wildlife Service, and associated NGOs had to operate. Instead of engaging in dialogue with the other organizations and developing a protocol of collaboration and coordination, WGF's response was to withdraw from the debate and work instead to maintain decision-making control over the recovery project.

This was a pathological response by WGF given that the state agency had very limited working experience and organizational capacity for dealing with endangered species. As a wildlife management agency, its core technology and culture revolved around managing sport species in the wild, not endangered species requiring specialized captive breeding interventions. Because of its growing suspicion of the other organizational actors, it framed all negative responses and information as unfounded criticism. This framing of information occurred even when WGF received accurate intelligence on a dramatic drop in population numbers by an on-site conservation NGO that WGF itself had hired. WGF simply ignored the reports for months. WGF's delayed response nearly led to complete mortality of the on-site population. When it finally acted, WGF attempted its own captive-breeding program and due to inexperience placed in jeopardy the few remaining ferrets. Although the breeding program was eventually successful, it can be easily argued that WGF was more lucky than effective, and due to its pathological behavior had actually placed the BFF at greater risk, not less.

OVERCOMING ORGANIZATIONAL PATHOLOGIES: PRINCIPLES OF DESIGN AND PERFORMANCE

Organizational scholars view performance in relative terms. Performance for whom? is a question that is commonly asked. In spite of the subjective nature of effectiveness, it is possible to evaluate organizations based upon stated goals, such as those concerned with the linkage of biodiversity conservation with social justice. In this context, we consider four general points including structural design, physical location, organizational learning, and generative organizational cultures. We then end with a brief introduction to "bureaucratic reorientation."

Structural Design

The complex and dynamic nature of conservation programs demands special organizational arrangements. Management situations on the ground tend to be unpredictable and decision making results from unique contextual conditions. What works in one place likely will not work in another. At the same time, conditions are ever changing. What works today may not work tomorrow. How can one design organizational arrangements that allow for effective collective action under such difficult conditions? Within organizational studies, "contingency theory" posits that there is no universally accepted best way to organize. Rather, how an organization should be designed depends upon the environmental conditions that it faces (Lawrence and Lorch 1967; Perrow 1967).

Under conditions of complexity and uncertainty, flatter (i.e., decentralized, nonhierarchical), more organic (less fragmented and formal, more informal, holistic, and responsive) structural forms that carry flexible core technologies will most likely support organizational effectiveness. Organic forms tend to rely on informal personal interactions in contrast to formal, authoritarian-based hierarchies (Burns and Stalker 1961). These types of organizational arrangements consist of skilled employees who work "on site" and possess sufficient decision-making power and resources to respond to changing conditions. Flexible and organic organizations can make decisions and implement actions when and where they are needed. In contrast, with taller, more bureaucratic forms, information from the field flows up the chain of authority to superiors who then send decisions back to the field. Under this type of arrangement, information frequently becomes distorted, decisions delayed, and responses out of touch with local needs and situations. Consequently, in more complex and turbulent environments, the operational advantages of flatter, organic structures are enormous. However, this leaves the coordination problem from decentralization mentioned above with respect to structural inefficiencies. Although there are no simple answers, the potential mistakes and other failures can be addressed partially through the quality of the relationships between field site units and centralized headquarters offices.

Headquarters Versus Field Offices

Not all organizations face the same type of environmental pressures. Although it is likely that most conservation organizations need to be flexible, learning organizations to some degree, one should make a key distinction between field offices and headquarters. The flat and flexible organizational structures described above are more likely appropriate for field site activities, whenever immediate, context-specific decisions and actions are required. Headquarters have important functions to carry out, including oversight activities, coordination among units, quality control, a source of technical and financial resources, and more routine administrative functions. To promote performance-oriented organizational structures, decision makers at headquarters need to ensure that the decentralized units have clear frameworks to follow as well as the resources required to do their job while focusing on the overall quality control without interfering in the day-to-day operations of field staff. Tendler (1975, 12) described this relationship as: "decentralized professionals working out problems themselves with easy access to superiors." Today many conservation programs create decentralized "high performance teams" that employ the characteristics described above. Tim Clark (1997) recommends high performance teams as a key means of increasing the efficiency of endangered species recovery efforts. For an example of a successful team effort see chapter 5.

Organizational Learning

By definition, effective, high-performance organizations learn from their mistakes, detect changes in their environment, and respond thoughtfully and proactively to those new conditions. Full learning, however, is more than simply monitoring the organization's efforts. Data collection that assesses progress toward reaching organizational goals is known as "single-loop" or incremental learning (Levitt and March 1988). While timely and accurate information is critical for understanding organizational performance, true *organizational* learning takes place through a process experts call "double-loop" learning (Argyris and Schön 1987). In this case, the information gathered is compared to a broader set of organizational goals, objectives, and norms. In contrast to conventional, single-loop monitoring, double-loop learning assesses whether the organization's overarching goals remain appropriate given changing conditions. Double-loop learning prods participants to ask demanding questions, such as whether the organization should approach conservation in a radically different way. When learning is only practiced by a few at the top, creativity becomes stifled and responses muted. Only by fully engaging the organization's participants and drawing upon their external networks can learning flourish.[1]

Generative Organizational Cultures

Although the concept of double-loop learning is straightforward, it is often difficult to implement well. One way to promote both effective single and double-loop learning is to institutionalize learning within an organization's routines and practices, a process that Westrum (1994) refers to as creating a "generative" organizational culture. Westrum contrasts generative organizations with two other types, "bureaucratic" and "pathological." Bureaucratic organizations are rule-bound organizations that are indifferent to learning and change, in essence run on "automatic pilot." Pathological organizations, however, are those that actively fight against learning and change. They hide information, messengers are "shot," responsibilities are shirked, bridging is discouraged, failures are covered up, and new ideas are crushed.

In stark contrast, generative organizations value performance over other goals and actively seek out performance-related information and welcome new ideas and change. Participants in generative organizations value teamwork and the sharing of responsibility to the degree where failure is openly discussed and corrected. Learning becomes an integral part of the organization's cultural fabric, woven by leaders but operationalized by all through enacting the use of accurate and free-flowing information (Yanow 2000).

Bureaucratic Reorientation. Most bureaucratic organizations lack the learning capabilities noted above. Yet change is most critical in these types of organizations, often requiring a complete overhaul of their goals, structure, technical capacity, and culture. This is particularly true of many natural resource management agencies that have maintained top-down, authoritarian approaches to conservation. One strategy for instilling the organizational design principles described above is through bureaucratic reorientation, which involves reforming an agency from the bottom up, through field-based action research with full support from top administrators (Korten and Uphoff 1981; Korten and Siy 1989; Poffenberger 1990a). The key elements of bureaucratic reorientation include engaging internal and external change agents, forming small working groups, learning from the field, developing a reform package, initiating pilot projects, and disseminating the tested reform package throughout the organization. This approach has been used throughout South and Southeast Asia (see Poffenberger 1990b), including the State Forestry Corporation of Java (see Peluso et al. 1990 for case study).

EMBRACING COMPLEXITY THROUGH
INTERORGANIZATIONAL COLLABORATION

Because of their complexity, most conservation and development efforts require more capacity than any single organization can provide given the broad spectrum of technical competencies necessary to accomplish all tasks. As a result, organizational collaboration has become commonplace, creating mutual benefits and challenges for all parties (Conley and Moote 2001; Huxham 1996; John 1994; Westley 1995). Gray (1989, 912) defines collaboration as: "(1) the pooling of appreciations and/or tangible resources, e.g., information, money, labor, etc., (2) by two or more stakeholders, (3) to solve a set of problems which neither can solve individually." Brechin (1997) extends this notion by arguing for constructing a "niche arrangement," bringing together different organizational types to cover the full requirements of task implementation. No matter the model, interorganizational collaboration creates significant challenges. These include perceptions of higher transaction costs, loss of autonomy over policy and budget decisions, loss of organizational integrity and lack of resource control and other environmental constraints, including constituent expectations, legislative or legal obligations (Alexander 1995; Weiss 1987). Given the inevitable trade-offs, most successful collaborations tend to be voluntary, where different parties come together in recognition of potential mutual benefits. Acknowledging interdependence, sharing common values and goals, and perceiving that collaboration can produce beneficial outcomes above transaction costs are among a number of conditions critical to creating the willingness to engage in joint action (Gray 1989; Weber 1998). Mandated collaborations tend to have low success rates, particularly if there are inadequate incentives to motivate different organizations to join forces (Alexander 1995; Thomas 1997).

There are two potential types of collaborative efforts, one that focuses on planning and decision making and a second that produces some level of structural integration in order to implement collective policies. Collaborative decision making typically involves stakeholder input to a government agency or other organization as a means of improving management and policy decisions.

Given this outside advice, the lead agency carries out the decision. Examples of this approach include ecosystem management in the western United States (Dombeck et al. 1997; Kohm and Franklin 1997; Wondolleck and Yaffee 2000) and development of environmental policies such as the Clean Air Act, also in the United States (Scheberle 1997; Weber 1998).

In the second approach, structural integration, implementation as well as decision making is carried out by a group of organizational actors. This type of collaboration is increasingly taking place in the United States where natural resource management needs cross jurisdictional boundaries and political sub-divisions (Kohm and Franklin 1997; Westley and Vredenburg 1997; Wondolleck and Yaffee 2000). This approach to conservation typically takes place through discussion and consensus among the affected stakeholders. This may include organizations and interest groups from the local, national, regional, and international levels incorporating a broad spectrum of interest perspectives comprising conservation organizations, indigenous peoples, human rights groups, local communities, government agencies, and development groups among others. A variant of this second model is sometimes called a "project team approach" (noted above) where a semiautonomous implementing unit is created that comprises members of the various stakeholders. The idea here is to create a "flatter," more responsive implementing organization than a collection of formal stakeholder organizations could ever provide. Both models emphasize the difference between collaborative decision making and organizational implementation.

Collaboration broadens the potential base of support for any given group through networked global contacts made possible by increased ease of world travel and advances in communication technologies, including international cellular phone systems, electronic mail, and the Internet. These networks can form horizontally, that is, among similar groups at a similar scale and levels of power, such as among community associations or international conservation NGOs. Networks can also form social bonds vertically with different groups operating at different scales and power levels, such as international conservation NGOs connecting with local community groups. At all these scales, networks connect groups and organizations with one another sharing sources of knowledge, skills, finances, and wider social and political audiences .

CRAFTING GOVERNANCE INSTITUTIONS
FOR CONSERVATION

Although the terms *institution* and *organization* are often used interchangeably, they represent different concepts. Whereas complex formal organizations represent physical structures with participants that pursue specific objectives, institutions extend beyond the domain of organizations to encompass the formal and informal rules and procedures that structure the behavior of social actors (Scott 1998).

In this section we present general concepts regarding governance institutions in terms of their structural, procedural, and operational aspects. We illustrate how each of these components functions at the global level by citing the example of the Convention on Biological Diversity (CBD), an international treaty that emerged from the 1992 United Nations Conference on Environment and Development (UNCED) . At the local level, we explore the community-based institutions that have formed around the management of common pool resources in Mali's Kelka Forest.

Institutional theory as we apply it here centers on crafting mutually agreeable rules and norms of interaction that stabilize expectations of all involved parties and thus increase the probability that participants will receive benefits from collaboration. This notion of crafting institutions for collaboration is often discussed in terms of "regimes." Young (1989, 12–13) defines regimes as "social institutions governing the actions of those involved in specifiable actions. . . . They may be more or less formally articulated and may or may not be accompanied by explicit organizations." This broad definition refers to the proactive construction of rules and norms to regulate and regularize collective action in relation to a given objective.

Regime structure stems from the rights and rules that establish relationships among social actors as well as the opportunities available to each. Along with rights comes a set of responsibilities incumbent upon regime participants. Typically, participants who do not follow the rules or fulfill their responsibilities regarding resource use face some type of sanction. The procedural aspects of regime analysis center on collective decision-making processes pertaining in particular to the allocation of labor and other factors related to production as well as the distribution of benefits that result from cooperative efforts. Decision-making procedures also establish the modes of dialogue among participants and thus can serve to reduce polarization of ideas and intergroup conflict when interests diverge. Finally, the operational component of regimes deals specifically with collectively authorized compliance mechanisms that promote conformance with either the regime's substantive component or the outcomes of its decision-making procedures (Young 1989).

One of the most advanced applications of regime theory to collective natural resource management challenges appears in the literature on common property. Local people everywhere have depended upon communally owned resources such as forests, pastures, fisheries, and water systems and have developed rules to govern their use (McCay and Acheson 1987). Because many people in rural areas throughout the world depend upon their immediate natural environment for their livelihoods, international and national biodiversity conservation programs are increasingly acknowledging the customary regimes that they have established for resource use and protection. Common-pool resources are generally characterized along two axes—the nature of consumption and the nature of exclusion (Bromley 1992; Ostrom 1990; Thomson 1992). By its nature, consumption of common-pool resources is "rivalrous" since that which is consumed by one person cannot be consumed by another. They are therefore vulnerable to depletion. Ostrom (1990) distinguishes between a resource "stock" and a "flow of resource units." Examples of resource flows include forest and range biomass production, groundwater discharge, fishery production, and canal irrigation water supplies. If the off-take rate of resource units exceeds the production rate, the stock is eventually exhausted. Sustainable use is achieved when off-take rates are maintained below the production rate and the stock is preserved. Because of the generally dispersed nature of common-pool resources, the exclusion of "unauthorized" users is generally problematic.

Given the particular dilemmas associated with collective reliance on common-pool resources, user communities have frequently developed regimes, such as tenure systems, that govern the use of shared resources. These institutions specify rights and duties among resource users, creating incentives that shape individual behavior and in some cases encourage resource conservation (Hanna et al. 1996; Ostrom 1990). Collectively, they define the local systems of governance that have facilitated the persistence of sustainable natural resource management in subsistence economies. Three types of rules are particularly important in these local governance systems: operational, collective choice, and constitutional (Thomson 1992). *Operational rules* define such day-to-day matters of resource use as who has rights to what resources, how much of the resource they can harvest, when they can exercise their rights, and where they may harvest. Operational rules also set policies for the monitoring and enforcement of rules and for the resolution of conflicts among resource users (Ostrom 1999). Rule monitoring and enforcement in common-property regimes is carried out in some cases by resource users themselves and in others by individuals designated by user groups. *Collective choice rules* define the procedures by which new operational rules can be made or existing ones changed, which is often necessary under changing environmental or socioeconomic conditions. *Constitutional rules* define how collective choice rules are made or changed. Decision making in common-pool resource management ranges from situations in which a single person determines the rules to situations where all members of a community must reach consensus (Becker and Ostrom 1995). Therefore, we cannot necessarily assume that all community-level regimes are egalitarian in terms of process or outcome.[2]

Considerable attention has been paid to the "crafting" of institutions that simultaneously maintain local livelihoods, conserve natural resources, and respond to the legal-administrative realities of modern state systems (Berkes and Folkes 1998; Ostrom 1998).[3] This is premised on an assumption that appropriate local governance systems can be designed and draws attention to the role of outside agencies in the process. Conservation and development initiatives that seek to reconcile the conservation of biodiversity with the maintenance of local livelihoods must deal with local institutions on two fronts. On the one hand, efforts must take into consideration and ideally build upon pre-existing, "traditional" institutions. On the other hand, they often must work with local people to develop new regimes, particularly when local institutions are engaged in a broader state legal system. Community-based natural resource management (CBNRM) projects, often implemented by outside NGOs, generally seek to promote community participation, to incorporate local ecological knowledge and to build upon community institutions. However, they must also confront local politics and structural inequalities that skew access to natural resources.

To illustrate the role of governance regimes in shaping biodiversity conservation, we turn to two examples, one international and the other local. First, we present the Convention on Biological Diversity (CBD) and discuss how it has helped augment global responses to species and habitat loss. Second, we turn to the system of rules that have emerged in Mali where local communities—in conjunction with the state and NGOs—are cooperatively managing common-pool resource use in the Kelka forest.

GLOBAL REGIMES: THE CONVENTION ON BIOLOGICAL DIVERSITY

The Convention on Biological Diversity (CBD) provides an institutional framework that guides the actions of a wide-ranging number of actors, at various scales, working more or less collaboratively in the nature conservation arena. By 1999, more than 175 countries had ratified the agreement (CBD 2000). These nations form the Conference of the Parties (CoP), the CBD's ultimate political authority. The CBD's administrative duties are performed by a secretariat located in Montreal, Canada. In conjunction with other organizational partners, the secretariat organizes technical and financial assistance for the implementation of national biodiversity conservation strategies and action plans at the national level.

Structurally, the CBD presents three main goals: (1) the conservation of biological diversity, (2) the sustainable use of the components of biodiversity, and (3) the fair and equitable sharing of the benefits from the use of genetic resources (CBD 2000). In particular the treaty emphasizes the importance of conserving biological diversity while nations continue their economic development, arguing that the two—conservation and economic development—are intricately linked. The CBD covers all genetic resources, species and ecosystems. A good portion of the agreement defines appropriate use of genetic resources by biotechnology and pharmaceutical firms along with their local sources (CBD 2000, see also chapter 9). In all, the CBD contains forty-two articles, which outline its mission and provide guidance to its members. One of the convention's core components concerns member nations' commitment to establishing a system of parks and other protected areas as part of their overall strategy (Article 8). In the process of developing protected areas, member governments are expected to involve local communities, which includes respecting, preserving, and maintaining the traditional knowledge, resource use practices, and governance structures of indigenous peoples. In this sense, the CBD establishes explicit norms regarding public involvement, democratic processes, and indigenous rights surrounding conservation practices. Among other responsibilities, the CBD also requires member nations to survey and continually monitor their biological riches (Article 7), create strategies that identify and protect threatened species and populations (Article 8k/ Article 9c), and rehabilitate degraded ecosystems (Article 8f).

The procedures governing the CBD's decision-making activities are typical of most international agreements. The ultimate decision-making authority rests with the Conference of the Parties (CoP), a body that relies on democratic principles. Each member has one vote or they may be part of regional economic organizations (such as the European Union) that carry the same number of votes as the number of nations in the organization. In addition to providing a general forum to share ideas, lessons learned, and policy suggestions among members, the CoP often forms ad hoc committees and working groups to explore various topics of interest in greater depth. For example, current working committees include the "Working Group on Access and Benefit Sharing" and the "Working Group on Article 8(j)," which is exploring traditional knowledge and use of biological resources by indigenous and local communities (CBD 2000). The work of these committees is ongoing and seeks to implement mechanisms protecting the rights and knowledge of traditional people while working with multinational pharmaceutical and biotechnology firms in search of useable chemicals.

Operationally, the CBD identifies common problems, sets broad goals, policies, and obligations. The overall responsibility for carrying out the CBD's mandate, however, rests largely with the individual member nations themselves. Member nations are expected to develop national biodiversity strategies and action plans (Article 6). As such, the CBD provides a broad regulatory framework that each country transforms into binding domestic rules or standards. Environmental cooperation in this context depends upon the degree to which the implementation process relies upon and is shaped by existing domestic institutions and political structures (Raustiala 1997). In short, the greater the governmental capacity and commitment, the more likely the terms of the agreement will be fully implemented.

Implementation of CBD agreements is accomplished through various sector-planning activities in agriculture, energy, fisheries, forestry, transportation, and other areas that might affect a nation's biological resources. These efforts are also reflected in government policies, the rules and regulations that guide not only the government's use of the nation's natural riches but also those of other users such as private corporations and local communities (CBD 2000). Prior to developing a national biodiversity strategy and action plan, member nations are expected to carry out a country study or survey of the nation's biological resources. Beyond specific actions on protecting biodiversity, the national strategy should provide for monitoring of resource use, rehabilitation of degraded ecosystems, and reporting on advances toward meeting established protection goals.

To a large extent, compliance depends on national public opinion, "peer" pressure from other member nations, and persuasion by the convention's secretariat. For most of the world's developing nations, the CBD's adoption was predicated upon the willingness of wealthier countries to provide the technical and financial assistance necessary to fulfill the biodiversity protection agenda. As a result, bilateral, multilateral, and NGO support has coalesced around this agenda. Since 1992, the Global Environment Facility (GEF) has been the financial mechanism for implementing the treaty's action programs. Organizationally, the GEF operates through three co-administrating agencies: the World Bank, the United Nations Development Programme (UNDP), and the United Nations Environment Programme (UNEP). The GEF was created in late 1990 as a pilot program to address global threats such as climate change, biodiversity loss, ozone depletion, and degradation of international waters. The GEF trust fund channels financial resources from developed countries to their lesser-developed counterparts through projects covering diverse geographic scales. By 1999, the GEF had financed nearly US$1 billion in biodiversity projects in more than 120 countries (CBD 2000). For an overview of one GEF biodiversity conservation project in Colombia, see chapter 5.

LOCAL REGIMES: COMMUNITY-BASED
COMMON-POOL RESOURCE MANAGEMENT IN MALI

The political decentralization movement in Sahelian West Africa provides many illustrations of the potentials and pitfalls associated with reliance on community-based institutions in the management of natural resources (Deme 1998; Ribot 1996; Winter 1997). Decades of centralized control of forest resources, initiated under French colonial rule and intensified after independence, progressively divested local peoples of managerial authority. Successive forest policies undermined the knowledge, institutions, and incentives that previously allowed communities to manage these resources in a manner consistent with local ecological and social realities (Thomson 1983,

1995; Thomson et al. 1997). In the early 1990s, a number of NGOs began working with Sahelian communities and government officials to build local forest management institutions (Winter 1997). One such project was the *Walde Kelka*, which grew out of institutional changes precipitated by the 1991 Malian revolution.

The Kelka forest is a savanna woodland covering approximately 106,000 hectares in the Mopti region of Mali, an area that contains fifteen villages and supports approximately 6,600 people of mixed ethnic background. A system of parkland agroforestry combines aspects of cereal crop cultivation, small-scale gardening, animal husbandry, and maintenance of utilitarian trees under complex tenure arrangements. The local population also commercially harvests deadwood from the forest to meet regional household energy needs. Within the Kelka forest, each village has developed a unique set of rules that governs land and tree tenure and access to forest products. However, these customary arrangements often run counter to the recently revised national forest code. Permission must be obtained from the forest service to harvest forest resources for all but immediate subsistence uses, and the harvesting of certain species is also restricted. Because they are often contradictory, customary law and national forest policy have coexisted uneasily, frequently resulting in conflict (Lawry 1989).

Demand for Kelka fuelwood increased significantly in 1984 following the completion of a paved road connecting the Kelka forest to the urban center of Mopti, 150 kilometers away. At that time, under Mali's forest code, the forest service issued harvesting permits for a quantity of wood that could be harvested in the Kelka without specifying precisely where it should be harvested. These permits were issued on a fee basis, regardless of where the applicant lived. While communities continued to apply customary rules locally, Kelka villagers had no legal authority to control access to their forest resources by outsiders. In addition, several major transhumance routes traverse the Kelka forest and have brought sedentary and nomadic populations together annually for generations. These relationships have become strained, as land scarcity and relaxing cultural sanctions encourage agriculturists to farm directly on the transhumance routes, complicating the passage of livestock without damaging crops.

In 1991, the Near East Foundation (NEF), an American NGO, embarked on a project to organize forest users in the Kelka region into a legally constituted association that would provide them with the legal status, authority, and operational capacity to enter into a co-management arrangement with the national forest service. After a series of consultative meetings with local communities, NEF worked with the traditional village leadership to facilitate the creation of a multitiered forest management association, a process that included technical assistance, institutional development, and organizational capacity building. A representative supra-village organization, the *Walde Kelka*,[4] brings together fifteen semiautonomous village-based forest user associations. Each village-level association has its own constitution, membership, and statutes and draws heavily upon traditional, noncodified institutions. These associations are made up of a general assembly, a managerial committee, and a surveillance committee, which work together through consensus to establish and enforce rules and procedures for using forest resources (Deme 1998; Mortimer 2001). The supra-village organization, whose structure mirrors that of the village associations, is a representative coordinating body, dispute mediator, and interlocutor with the state (Deme 1998; Mortimer 2001).

Although it is still a young organization, the *Walde Kelka* has already improved forest management in many ways. In collaboration with the forest service, village associations issue wood harvesting permits and monitor forest use.[5] The association does not have formal authority to sanction outsiders and must rely upon the forest service for this. However, outsiders caught harvesting wood illegally often prefer the less severe fines imposed within the village-based systems to those imposed by the forestry service (Deme 1998). Because the territorial rights of villages overlap geographically in some cases and because the exact boundaries are sometimes unclear, the supra-village association also plays an important role in dispute resolution among local forest users and among constituent villages (Deme 1998; Mortimer 2001). The *Walde Kelka* has successfully mediated several major disputes of this type (Winter 1997).

The Kelka forest example further illustrates the importance of understanding local institutions in their broader social and political context. First, increased pressure on the Kelka woodstock and changes in local institutional effectiveness has to be understood not only in terms of villager use but also in terms of urban market penetration. Second, the constitution of a legally recognized association was necessary for the local population to engage in forest management within the Malian administrative system, illustrating the importance of local conformity to national laws governing collective action and natural resource use. The 1993 decentralization law (Loi no. 93-008) attributes no autonomous administrative authority to the village level and the national forest service retains authority over forest resources under the new forestry code (Loi no. 95-004). The case also underscores the importance of an enabling policy framework. To this end, several NGOs in the Mopti Region together have formed a horizontal network, the Réseau de gestion décentralisée des ressources naturelles dans la cinquième région (GDRN5), both to share experience in decentralized natural resource management and to lobby government for a more hospitable policy environment. Finally, NEF's work with the villages of the *Walde Kelka* began before 1991 and has continued to the present. This type of long-term engagement between organizations is critical in building robust and viable local institutions.

ORGANIZATIONAL DEVELOPMENT
AS SOCIAL CAPITAL FORMATION

Throughout this chapter we have argued that nature conservation is a process of human organization. It has been about crafting the organizational and institutional capacity necessary for pursuing socially just biodiversity conservation. Socially just conservation can only be obtained through the human capacity to negotiate agreements of understanding and responsibilities among all affected parties. The capacity to fully act upon those agreements depends in large part on the organizational and institutional structures we create and maintain. Yet, both complex organizations and governance regimes represent only the essential framework or arenas for the formation of social capital.

The concept of social capital has a long history associated with the classical sociological works of Karl Marx and Emile Durkheim. In recent years the term has experienced a strong resurgence in popularity although its broad application in numerous contexts has been accompanied by a loss of definition. For our purposes here, we distinguish between social capital as a source of power for individuals and groups and social capital *formation* as a deliberate process of organizational capacity building. Following Portes (1998), we discuss the sources of social capital as well as associated effects, pointing out key conceptual elements that can give the term greater definition.

Contemporary scholars define social capital as the ability of social actors to secure "actual or potential resources" as a result of participating in "a durable network of more or less institutionalized relationships of mutual acquaintance or recognition" (Bourdieu 1985, 248; Portes 1990). In this sense, social capital is not a tangible power resource. It manifests itself as the structure of the relationships among the "possessor" of social capital and other individuals and groups (Bourdieu 1985; Coleman 1988). Thus, the social ties that form a network and the resources that actors gain as a result of social interaction are separate but closely related aspects of social capital. Given this key distinction between social ties (source) and resources (outcome), it is important to define the boundaries of the social network for a given context. In this regard Coleman (1988) suggests that networks achieve "closure" when a sufficient density of social ties exists to guarantee or institutionalize the observance of behavioral norms.

Bourdieu's (1985) definition of social capital recalls the discussion of structurally based power in chapter 3, which suggests that the combination of formal and informal rules, norms, and cultural practices shape power relationships among actors. Referring specifically a set of social ties based on trust and reciprocity, social capital represents a kind of institution since it relies on mutually understood and recognized rules or norms. Portes (1998) specifies four interrelated types of rules and norms that represent the sources of social capital including (1) internalized norms, (2) norms of reciprocity, (3) bounded solidarity, and (4) enforceable trust. The notion of internalized norms refers to rule-following behavior that is largely taken for granted and is done out of a sense of obligation. Coleman (1988) offers the example of cultural norms that inhibit crime (but are also reinforced by sanctions) and allow community members to walk the streets at night. Norms of reciprocity represent a second source of social capital in which individuals or groups provide access to resources to others with the expectation that their generosity will be fully repaid in the future.

The third source of social capital, bounded solidarity, holds that individuals and groups develop ties because they share a common fate. For example, many indigenous peoples have created extensive networks to assist each other in overcoming commonly shared problems such as environmental degradation, social disruption from unwanted development projects, and government oppression (e.g., Broad and Cavanaugh 1993; Keck and Sikkink 1998). Finally, the idea of enforceable trust suggests that the community or social network provides sufficient power to reward and sanction participants and thus guarantees exchanges between "donors" and "beneficiaries." In this sense, the donor garners returns from the community or network (e.g., prestige) not from the recipient, and both parties act in accord with the norms of exchange given strong social sanctioning practices (e.g., ostracism).

Paralleling the four sources discussed above, Portes (1998) finds that social capital can produce two broad outcomes that are relevant to our discussion on socially just nature conservation: norm observance (social control) and network-mediated benefits. In the first case, institutionalized norms represent collective understandings regarding the boundaries of appropriate behavior. These rules and associated sanctions (such as shame) become internalized by group members, providing self-imposed controls on deviant behavior. We would expect to find, therefore, that the need for externally imposed social control (enforcement) will diminish proportionately with increases in the strength of network ties among individuals and groups that are based in mutual trust and reciprocity built around the objectives of socially just conservation.

In the second case, individuals and groups garner benefits as a result of their ties to other individuals and groups. These network-mediated benefits are typically cited to explain social mobility (e.g., employment promotion) and social stratification. In terms of protected areas and the dispossessed, we might explain differential impacts of an integrated conservation and development project (ICDP) among communities in a buffer zone area in terms of this second form of social capital. For example, one community may feature stronger kinship-based network ties to merchants in a large city in the region compared to other villages and thus have greater opportunities to sell artisan goods produced as part of the ICDP.

In light of the potential beneficial effects of social capital, numerous actors involved with policy challenges such as conservation and development have applied the term to refer to the enhancement of a group's collab-orative capacity toward advancing common interests (Montgomery and Inkeles 2000). Indeed, as Portes (1998, 3) suggests, "social networks are not a natural given and must be constructed through investment strategies ori-ented to the institutionalization of group relations, useable as a reliable sources of other benefits." In this regard, we can distinguish social capital *formation* as the proactive development of social networks with the intent of institutionalizing collective human organizational skills and capacity to reach a desired goal.

The assumption is that individuals' and groups' collective ability to reach their desired goals is directly proportional to increases in the quantity (or "density") and quality of social ties. This proposition extends beyond the idea of "strength in numbers" (quantity) to capture aspects of commitment, coor-dination, and interdependence (quality) that the norms of participation (sources of social capital) imply. The definition that we propose also suggests that the ultimate goal of social capital formation is the creation of durable net-works bound by deeply embedded or "institutionalized" norms of interaction and exchange. In other words, social capital is more than just the network. It is the enactment of norms of reciprocity, producing outcomes such as social control or network-mediated benefits.

There are no predefined pathways of social capital formation, however those actors with relatively greater power compared to other members can play key roles in developing strong networks. Numerous examples suggest that both nongovernmental and governmental actors can form strong bonds that increase collective human organizational capacity (Fisher 1998; Tendler 1997). Fox (1996) is somewhat more cautious in his discussion of emergent elements of civil society in Mexico, noting that agents of change within state agencies can effectively encourage social capital formation but that reactionary currents in the same organizations can also dismantle these efforts. In this sense, it is important to remember that social capital formation is typically a highly politicized undertaking.

By viewing international biodiversity conservation management in large part as a problem of human organization, it can be approached as a continu-ous process of experimentation, adaptation, and learning (see Buck et al. 2001). In this sense, the biodiversity conservation policy and management *processes* parallel understandings of ecosystem dynamics. Ecologists no longer view natural succession as a linear progression that culminates in a "climax steady state" such as an old-growth forest but rather as a dynamic process of disturbance, adaptation, and change. In like fashion, the conservation policy process is one of endlessly assessing new information and conditions, con-structing dialogue with participants, and adapting organizational and institu-tional arrangements to respond to constantly changing circumstances. Because nature protection is socially, politically, and ecologically complex, its success will ultimately depend upon the formation of sufficient social, organizational, and institutional decision-making capacity to support and enhance the management process.

As Rudel (2000) points out, sustainable development involves conflicts and trade-offs given the tensions among conservation, use, and social justice objectives, and organizations are required to mediate these conflicts and to implement and enforce resulting agreements. "[O]rganizations play an important procedural role because they create 'civic' arenas for crafting plans for sustainable development" (Rudel 2000, 78). By bringing together groups of people with different interests with respect to natural resources, civil arenas provide occasions for negotiating the trade-offs that permit sustainable development in a region. This process can create enduring social relationships of trust and reciprocity (social capital) that form the foundation of biodiversity conservation with social justice.

NOTES

1. Along with collaboration, discussed below, learning organizations have become a critical feature of modern conservation activities. Adaptive management processes within the broader concept of ecosystem management require organizations to experiment, learn, and adjust their activities to complex and dynamic ecosystem responses (see Buck et al. 2001).

2. Locally devised institutions tend to be more effective in management efforts than externally imposed ones for several reasons. One is that rules devised by local communities are likely to draw upon ecological knowledge that has been refined over generations of intimate contact (Berkes 1999). Rules are more likely to be aligned with the nuances of ecological complexity. Similarly, local people are able to adjust rules in accordance with changing social and environmental conditions, often in the face of ecological stachasticity. Institutional flexibility permits responsiveness to variation in the flow of resource units (Turner 1999). Furthermore, mutual monitoring can foster strong social norms of rule compliance.

3. Institutional theorists increasingly argue that, while institutions do matter, they must be understood in terms of their broader social and ecological contexts (Gibson et al. 2000; Ostrom 1998; Thomson 1992).

4. *Walde* is the Fulani word for association; *Kelka* is the name that refers to the area culturally and geographically.

5. Under an agreement signed between *Walde Kelka* and the forest service, the association has exclusive rights to purchase harvesting permits at full price. It then adds a marginal surcharge to the permits when it resells them, and the profit remains with the association.

Chapter Eleven

THE REGIONAL APPROACH
IN NORTHERN MADAGASCAR

Moving Beyond Integrated
Conservation and Development

LISA L. GEZON

The year 1997 marked the beginning of the second five-year phase of Madagascar's environmental plan. Along with a new funding cycle came new policies, practices, and philosophies of conservation and development. The government of Madagascar, along with the international donor community, embraced new structural arrangements meant to address similar conservation and development goals as the first phase, but in more sustainable and comprehensive ways. The shift in approach has been driven intellectually by an eco-regional, or a landscape ecology approach (what I will refer to as a regional approach) that places conservation and development issues at a regional scale instead of at the localized scale of individual protected areas and their surrounding buffer zones. One of the most significant changes in practice has been a move away from Integrated Conservation and Development Projects (ICDPs) in favor of an approach that organizationally separates the mandates of conservation and development.[1] Instead, it encourages collaboration and partnerships among organizations specializing either in conservation or development. Part of the logic of this shift was to broaden the scope of conservation and development activities from buffer zones, the traditional setting for ICDPs, to other areas experiencing environmental pressures. Another practical change has been an increased recognition of the importance of the role of both the Malagasy national parks service (ANGAP) and the Malagasy Ministry of Water and Forests (MEF) in meeting the overall conservation goals of the country.

A central goal of this chapter is to evaluate the implications and consequences of these policy shifts for local communities—both those in the buffer zones of protected areas and those within the larger economic and ecological region. I argue that while it was vital to give managerial authority over protected areas to ANGAP, the park service model of protected area management may lead to a decreased emphasis on integrating local-level development into conservation goals. This could have the effect of reversing the progress made in the approaches to conservation in the 1980s and 1990s recognizing the need to involve local populations in the management of their resources (McNeely and Pitt 1985; McNeely et al. 1990; West and Brechin 1991; Lewis and Carter 1993; Western et al. 1994; Furze et al. 1996). In addition, organizational restructuring and alternative funding priorities appropriately meet some goals (such as the need to recognize that it is not only protected areas that need protecting) but not others. What has not been addressed in the changes of the second phase is the need proactively to incorporate local people fully in all phases of program design, implementation, and evaluation, following the recommendations made by professionals such as Little (1994) and Wright (1994). Finally, the conclusion warns against discarding the principle of integrated conservation and development projects. It advocates incorporating an integrated approach that focuses on resource users within the regional perspective.

CONSERVATION IN NORTHERN MADAGASCAR

The regional approach of the second phase emphasizes the need to situate conservation activities beyond the peripheral zones of protected areas. This is done in order to meet the needs of a broader target population and to address the importance of ecosystemic dynamics that extend beyond the boundaries of the protected islands. According to the United States Agency for International Development (USAID), the landscape ecology approach "links activities in priority conservation zones to threats, opportunities and development needs in a more extensive landscape (USAID 1997a, 4)." While this shift in conservation thinking has emerged in other global settings (Brandon et al. 1998), several factors within Madagascar have led policy makers to adopt this guiding philosophy. First, a series of donor-funded meetings in the capital of Madagascar with the international scholarly community in 1995 concluded that a regional perspective needed to be taken both with regard to ecological and socioeconomic factors (Hannah et al. 1998). First, they pointed out that corridors between protected areas are critical for the maintenance of biodiversity. Second, they pointed to the need for explicitly addressing rural-urban linkages and the regional political economy of resource use and marketability.

In addition to a move *toward* a regional approach, this shift also explicitly signals a move *away from* funding integrated projects in buffer zones. Before and during the first environmental phase in Madagascar (EP1), USAID focused their funding for conservation projects on ICDPs, dedicating millions of dollars from 1989 to 1997. USAID's Strategic Objective Agreement, which formally signals the agency's support of Madagascar's second environmental phase (EP2), evaluates the lessons learned from EP1. It states that "the ICDPs are not a sustainable answer [to the alleviation of poverty which exacerbates the spiral of environmental degradation] as they are *too costly for the limited population reached*" (USAID 1997a, 3; emphasis added). The document does support the need for development activities. It states that ICDPs "demonstrated the importance of the linkage between conservation and development," but future efforts must be "expanded within a larger landscape to effectively address the pressures on the natural resource base."

The move away from ICDPs was a political decision as much as it was an economic and ecological one. First of all, donors recognized the need to turn more real authority over to the Malagasy government and professionals. One reason for this is that ICDPs tended to become paralyzed due to conflicts of authority between the Malagasy Project directors and the expatriate technical assistants, each of whose signatures were often needed before staff members could take practical action (Gezon 1997a; Hough 1994). The ICDPs were almost entirely funded by international donors. In the case of several prominent ICDPs in Madagascar, USAID funded nongovernmental organizations, such as the World Wildlife Fund (WWF), to execute the management of the protected areas. In the case of the Amber Mountain Project, WWF hired a technical assistant to co-manage the project with a Malagasy director and staff. The international donor community tended to hold the expatriate technical assistants ultimately responsible for the success or failure of the projects, even though the Malagasy director had final authority on paper. This unclear separation of authority became a problem for the Amber Mountain Project, which saw the coming and going of four technical assistants between 1991 (the beginning of the environmental phase one—EP1) and 1997 (when ANGAP took over). At least three of them left as a result of this tension. In reflecting on the ICDP phase, one staff member, who had been with the office since its inception in 1989, remarked that under the authority of each technical assistant, critical project activities were often halted because one of the two leaders refused to condone certain initiatives.

In place of the ICDP, the EP2 has turned sole managerial authority over protected areas to the Malagasy national park service (ANGAP), established with heavy donor support during the EP1. In accordance with a national move toward decentralization, ANGAP has established semiautonomous offices for each protected area. In the north, individual ANGAP offices have replaced the central project office that was in charge of managing four separate protected areas. A regional office, which oversees the activities of most of the protected areas in the province of Antsiranana, remains in the city of Antsiranana. Despite the transition to a new organizational structure, many of the Malagasy personnel from the ICDP phase remain with ANGAP. In the case of WWF, instead of technical assistants in charge of each ICDP, three technical assistants have remained in the entire country, covering the north, the south, and the central headquarters regions in Antananarivo. They focus not on the management of general operations, but on their own area of expertise—be it ecological monitoring or ecotourism. Staff of the office in the north have commented that this arrangement has eliminated the most serious personnel problems of the ICDP phase. Both the technical assistant and the project staff in the central ANGAP office seemed to have a higher level of job satisfaction in 1999 than did people in those same positions during the ICDP phase.

Turning authority over to the national park service has weakened organizational commitment to integrating conservation and development, although it has not eliminated it altogether. ANGAP's priority, according to its mission statement, is "to establish, conserve and manage in a sustainable manner a network of National Parks and Reserves" (USAID 1997b, 25). The statement goes on to say that managing protected areas should "contribute to the development of peripheral zone communities and to regional and national economies." Funding for development, however, is minimal compared to the ICDP phase. ANGAP has continued a policy developed in the ICDP phase of giving 50 percent of tourist permit revenues over to local communities (although villagers reported in 1999 that ANGAP has not yet actually given them any of this money). For any specific projects that ANGAP wants to initiate, they must solicit funds from outside donors such as the World Bank, WWF, and Conservation International.

In addition to creating contests of power between expatriate and Malagasy managers, the placement of ICDPs in the buffer zones of protected areas created tension with the Malagasy Ministry of Water and Forests (MEF) (Gezon 1997a). One of the problems of the EP1 was an overlap in jurisdiction between the MEF and the ICDPs together with ANGAP (at the time, a quasi-governmental agency coordinating the activities in the protected areas). Buffer zone land and forests were officially under the jurisdiction of the MEF and conflict arose over the right to work in these areas and sanction infractions. Interviews with a variety of officials in Antananarivo in 1995 revealed a general sentiment that the MEF had been neglected during EP1.[2] The disparity in salary and other physical amenities between ANGAP and MEF made it difficult for the two entities to work together productively.[3]

Broadening the geographic scope of EP2 has made the projects in and around protected areas just one component of a multifaceted conservation strategy. Now, classified forests and other lands managed by the MEF have become equally important targets of donor time and money. Although German aid money has been contributing to issues of conservation and development since at least the late 1980s in northern Madagascar, their projects outside of the protected areas seem to have gained a new strength and vitality in EP2. One, called POLFOR *(Politique Forestiere)*,[4] is working directly with the DIREF *(Direction Inter-Régional des Eaux et Fôrets*, the regional office of the national forest service) and has contributed material support to the functioning of the office (a computer and a vehicle for monitoring infractions). GREENMAD has focused on energy and tree-planting.[5]

IMPLICATIONS OF ADOPTING A
REGIONAL APPROACH TO CONSERVATION

What are the implications of the EP2's move away from the integrated conservation and development project (ICDP) in favor of a regional approach to conservation? The following section will examine the effectiveness of incorporating a regional model into the actual activities of EP2, the effects of the organizational separation of conservation and development goals, and the role of community involvement in the ultimate success of conservation goals.

The Regional Model

As an intellectual construct, the regional model has considerable merit for both biological and socioeconomic reasons. An effective conservation strategy cannot focus only on the islands of protected areas. A region of Madagascar that illustrates the need for a regional approach is the eastern rainforest in the province of Fianarantsoa. This region contains extremely high levels of biodiversity (Wright 1997), and many species of flora and fauna would arguably suffer if only isolated protected forests remained. Since this forest also meets subsistence, religious, and medical needs of many people (Harper 2002), its loss would be devastating on a human as well as an ecological level. A regional approach is also important for recognizing that people are affected by resource degradation at many levels, including local, regional, national, and international. A conservation strategy that recognizes the regional dynamics (including the rural-urban and regional-national political economic links) of ecological relationships and resource use is necessary.

To put these observations into effect, conservation and/or development organizations have developed different approaches. The German-funded GREENMAD, for example, has attempted to establish coordination between all NGOs with offices in the northern city of Antsiranana by holding periodic meetings to discuss approaches to common concerns through an effort they refer to as AIDEN. USAID has embraced a regionalized planning and decision-making approach called AGERAS *(Appui à la Gestion Regionalisé et à l'Approche Spatiale)*. The goal of AGERAS is to "seek a collective understanding of the management and conservation challenges facing a given resource . . . in the context of the resources' broader bio-physical and socio-economic landscape" (USAID 1997a, 6). It is presently too early to evaluate the effectiveness of EP2 in meeting these goals, since much of the infrastructure is still being established. In the north, for example, the AGERAS process is in the planning stages. In other regions (such as Tulear and Fianarantsoa), however, USAID-funded teams have begun the AGERAS process of fostering discussion between representatives of multiple levels of spatial analysis (village-level, regional, national).

What seems valuable about this approach is that it is pressure driven, seeking responses to specific human needs and environmental pressures. It gets away from the common fallacy of ICDPs that use general economic development in buffer zones as a way to reduce environmental pressure. Hough and Sherpa (1989) identify this as a "basic needs" approach to conservation where the logic is that a project must compensate for that which resident people lose by being excluded from a protected area. In the basic needs approach, a project will work toward meeting general health, education, and economic development needs of people in the buffer zones with the goal of encouraging people to stop using protected area resources. A problem with this approach is that it often becomes an unsustainable quid pro quo that does not generally address specific environmental pressures, and which sometimes exacerbates them. General economic development in buffer zones can have the unintended effect of serving as a catalyst for migration into the region. This in turn may result in putting even more pressure on local resources (Wells and Brandon 1992). Furthermore, the basic needs approach often equates development with modernization instead of taking it as a process for facilitating specific goals, conservation or other (Furze et al. 1996).

In contrast with this basic needs approach, the AGERAS process attempts to identify specific pressures and human resource–related needs. It then seeks solutions through discussions with people affected by these issues at local, regional, and national levels. A potential drawback of this process, however, is that it seems to remain in Hough and Sherpa's (1989) category of "top-down" approaches, which are "centralized, often highly capitalized programs where investments and profits are externally controlled" (Brechin et al. 1991, 14). Although the goal of AGERAS is to generate broad participation, the attempt to forge discussion between individuals from a wide variety of sociocultural contexts could prove uncomfortable for representatives from less powerful and non–Western educated sectors of the population. Rural dwellers would seem least likely to be able to participate fully in such a setting. Even if some may be comfortable participating in these types of meetings, such a format may not be designed for discovering the needs of the more marginalized members of communities—often the women, the newcomers, and the non–Western educated.

The regionalized planning and decision-making processes could potentially be an important part of addressing conservation and related development issues at a broad geographic scale. Without having read documents advocating the regional perspective in Madagascar (USAID 1997a; Hannah et al.1998), however, an observer of changes in northern Madagascar would have a difficult time knowing this was a priority. The everyday situation is that the EP2 seems to have been more about the institutional dissolution of the integrated conservation and development approach than about the extension of these ideals to a regional scale of application. Since USAID's AGERAS process has not become operational and the German-sponsored AIDEN forum is not well known even by some of the other conservation and development agencies, the changes of EP2 seem merely like shifts in funding priorities (segregating conservation and development, extending emphasis beyond buffer zones).

*Organizational Separation of Conservation
and Development in Buffer Zone Management*

Policy shifts of the second phase meet Hough's (1994) recommendation to encourage collaboration among organizations dedicated to conservation and those dedicated to development. It is not yet clear, though, whether or not this change will make integrated conservation and development efforts more effective in the organizational context of EP2. It must be remembered that Hough made this recommendation for the ICDP managerial context, where both conservation and development components were actively involved in monitoring pressures and designing responses in buffer zones. In EP2, however, it is the conservation agency (ANGAP) that must solicit help for interventions in conjunction with buffer zone management. According to the organizational design, development agencies are not involved from the beginning in identifying the relevant issues in protected areas. Hough's recommendation has therefore only been partially fulfilled.

Despite the rhetoric that continues to emphasize the importance of development, a report (final USAID-funded KEPEM project report) published in the middle of the EP2 (Wordsworth 2000) critiqued a lack of attention to sustainable development, poverty reduction, and national economic development plans. Integrating conservation and development is more difficult than either conservation or development by itself, in large part because of the history in the West of compartmentalizing these needs both educationally and organizationally. The danger in separating the conservation and development mandates is that development goals may be further marginalized if people working in the organizations become discouraged by the challenges of working together in a task that may have few immediate returns and may take much time and effort to organize. A related danger is that economic development projects have often bypassed both the needs of local people and biodiversity protection. Indeed, sustainable development has often been criticized as an oxymoron (Sachs 1993; Hornsborg 2001)—a critique that demands close consideration if it is being considered as a pillar for future environmental protection strategies.

Despite the organizational separation of conservation and development efforts, the personnel at ANGAP in Antsiranana were trained in the ICDP phase and many remain committed to the principle of joining the two objectives. Since ANGAP has very little money for such activities, however, its staff must dedicate valuable time and energy on collaborating with funding organizations in order to finance development activities. People in several communities in the buffer zones of protected areas have already expressed feeling as if less emphasis has been placed on development and participation at the community level since ANGAP took over. Only time will tell if ANGAP personnel are able to maintain even the level of commitment to development that they had in the summer of 1999.

Participation and the Role of Local Populations

Not even the most appropriate organizational restructuring will be sufficient to increase effectiveness in meeting conservation and development goals. Even development organizations have a poor record of incorporating local people as full actors in all phases of project design, implementation, and evaluation (Kottak 1991). A positive aspect of EP2 is that agencies are on some level aware of the value of responding to the stated needs of local communities. In their policy of returning half of protected area tourist entry fees to communities, ANGAP embraces the notion that communities should be allowed to identify their own problems. In terms of the projects they initiate, the personnel at ANGAP claim that they base their development interventions on the stated needs of community members. It seems that they are indeed working on meeting a fair number of these demands, although many local people remain unaware even of the possibility of making their needs known to ANGAP. In addition to the issues of equity and the distribution of local power, a fundamental problem with this approach is that a given pressure on the protected area may never be addressed if the people do not identify it as a problem. Without a concerted effort to target development interventions at specific environmental pressure points, the development component becomes a "basic needs" approach aimed at general economic development and not specifically at conservation.

A process that actively takes local communities as *partners* in an explicit resource management process will arguably yield the most appropriate resource-related development projects and the most effective conservation. Conservation and development planning must move away from the notion, inherent in the "basic needs" approach, that resource management and other forms of community development go along two separate trajectories. Little (1994) notes that success in conservation programs correlates with the extent to which local populations participate in the identification of resource-related problems. One of the reasons for this, as Kottak (1991) points out, is that people are much more likely to adopt a new practice if it corresponds with problems and issues that they have identified.

Building partnerships with local people must include a social and natural science research component. These must be designed to obtain well-informed histories of resource use. Fairhead and Leach (1998) have pointed out, for example, that relying on untested received knowledge or assumptions about environmental problems can lead to the inaccurate—and ultimately unfair—targeting of local people as perpetrators of forest degradation. Also, understanding cultural patterns of resource use and management provides a critical foundation for productive working relations, which reduces the occurrence of miscommunication (Leff 1985; Gezon 1997b; Gezon 1999, 2000). Social science research—particularly in-depth ethnographic research—is particularly important, according to Furze et al., (1996, 36) since "[p]rotected area management, while obviously concerned with managing ecosystems, is fundamentally about the management of people, their aspirations, and their relationship with nature."

Implementing a strategy of local participation, however, is not straightforward. First, effective participation depends on the extent to which local people are given rights to make binding decisions. Constraints occur on the levels of both policy and bureaucratic procedure. According to Little (1994, 355), "Empowering local communities to manage their own resources without outside interference, sanction resource offenders, and decide upon conservation and development goals has not been a primary objective of most local conservation programs." The 1996 Malagasy law promoting local tenure security (called *gélose*—see endnote 4) could yet prove to be an important exception to this tendency. It will be several years, however, before evaluations of even the first attempts at implementation can be made. In addition to lack of political voice, demands for excessive bureaucratic documentation can inhibit local participation. International donor agencies, such as USAID, often demand periodic work plans that identify the activities that will take place. This makes executing organizations hesitant to consider suggestions from local people because doing this may entail deviating from their original work plan (Gezon 1997a).

A related issue is that local communities are not homogeneous and efforts at participation must problematize internal complexities. People are differentiated socially according to many factors, including gender, age, level of income, and land of origin (Gezon 2000, 2002). Including any subset of people in a decision-making process will simultaneously empower some groups while excluding others. In recognizing the delicacy of this situation, Agrawal and Gibson (1999) recommend a decision-making approach that considers multiple actors with various ways of negotiating rights and access to resources. Wright (1994) and DeCosse (2001) point to the importance of working with local leaders, including indigenous and religious leaders as well as people holding local political offices (Gezon 1997b, 1999). Wright (1994) also mentions the importance of identifying the pressures on the protected area and making sure that those responsible (i.e., hunters or producers of charcoal) are included in the decision-making process. Also important is building the confidence of marginalized groups—such as women or landless people—which will enable them to be a part of the participatory process.

At least since the mid-1980s, conservation planners have been pointing to the need for local community involvement in the management of their resources. This thought is what originally led to the creation of ICDPs. Although the regional approach appropriately broadens the scope of analysis, preliminary research in northern Madagascar suggests that its focus on resource users at multiple levels has diluted an emphasis on participation at the local level—though this dilution of participation is by no means inevitable in a regional approach. Ideally, the regional approach should incorporate the principles of the ICDP phase and apply them to wider scales. The goal of identifying more effective ways of working with local people in managing their resources must become a cornerstone of all conservation attempts—no matter what the institutional framework.

A PRESSURE-DRIVEN REGIONAL APPROACH— BEYOND THE RHETORIC

An important goal of EP2 is to adapt the integrated conservation and development model to a regional scale. During EP1, the ICDP approach was applied solely to the buffer zones of protected areas. Now, the philosophy of the integrated conservation and development approach must extend to non-protected (or minimally protected) ecological zones as well as to broad economic and political networks of people who benefit from the environmental resources. A pressure-driven approach may guide this process, as planners identify pressures on both resources and people that result from conservation measures.

Currently in northern Madagascar, for example, pressures on resources include charcoal production, the cutting of trees for construction wood, and the destruction of forests for agricultural production (including cash crops such as pineapples and the drug *qat*). Addressing these issues must involve at least two steps: (1) research into the nature of the problem at multiple levels of analysis, and (2) collaborative attempts between conservation and development organizations to find solutions that put minimal pressure on those who currently benefit from the degradation (stakeholders). As for the first step, research must be *interdisciplinary*, including both natural and social science perspectives (see Furze et al. 1996 for a discussion of social science concepts and methods, as they are relevant to conservation issues). It should also *include multiple levels of geographic analysis*. In addition to the traditional local use studies (for example, the Social Impact Assessment studies advocated by Hough 1991), methodologies must be developed for studying rural-urban economic, political, and social links. A commodity chain approach, for example, which could trace resource use from production to eventual consumption, holds much promise for this kind of research (Bernstein 1996; Ribot 1998).

Kottak and Colson's (1994) linkages approach also provides a way of applying traditional ethnographic methods to the understanding of urban and regional settings. It emphasizes the importance of longitudinal studies, as well as ones that recognize the links between local settings (however that may be defined: a rural village or an urban neighborhood) and wider systems. Such an approach could provide the means for learning about the dynamics of charcoal production (for example) within the villages where it is practiced. It also provides a framework for understanding the destination of the finished product (i.e., the resource use patterns of urban dwellers) and the national and externally imposed policies that either encourage or discourage such production.

A regionally based research design can then provide a framework for practically addressing problems of resource degradation. Knowledge of complex socioeconomic and political systems, for example, can be the basis for encouraging participation at many local levels: at the site of production, at the site of utilization, and at the site of policy making. Instead of diluting the role of local people, the regional model should expand it to an understanding of the ways in which networks of people and locations are linked with one another.

EP2 is the important middle phase of the fifteen-year, three-phase environmental plan in Madagascar. The challenge of the first phase was to develop a model for integrating conservation and development in the buffer zones of protected areas (met with varying degrees of success—see Gezon 1995; Gezon and Freed 1999). The goal of the second phase has been to broaden the scope of attention and funding to consider environmental and social needs at a regional level. The challenge of the third phase will perhaps be to combine the most positive aspects of the first two phases, creating a synthesis that is greater than the sum of its parts.

NOTES

Funding for the most recent phase of research was provided by a Faculty Research Enhancement Award, given by the Sponsored Operations office of the State University of West Georgia. I would also like to thank a few of the many people who gave me valuable insight into the current state of conservation and development efforts: Lyn Robinson, Moustafa, Mr. Raymond of the DIREF, the personnel at GREENMAD, and Pascal Lopez.

1. Gezon has been working in Madagascar since 1990. In 1991, she and a team of researchers worked with Hough and the personnel of the Amber Mountain Complex Integrated Conservation and Development Project in studying remotely sensed images in the context of the environmental pressures and socioeconomic dynamics on the ground. She lived in a village on the western side of the Ankarana Special Reserve (one of the projects in the ICDP) in 1992–1993 and has made brief follow-up visits in 1995 and 1999.

2. In the EP2, Conservation International has been working closely with the MEF in a focus on forest management, regional plans, and decentralization strategies (DeCosse 2001).

3. See references to the SPN in Hough (1994). The SPN was, in the early 1990s, the equivalent of what is now called the Direction Inter-Régional des Eaux et Fôret (DIREF). The DIREF is the regional office of the MEF. In conjunction with the national efforts at decentralization, the DIREF has more autonomy financially and in terms of decision making than did the SPN. The DIREF nevertheless retains many of the characteristics of the SPN elucidated by Hough (1994).

4. POLFOR is helping with the implementation of a 1996 law on the *gestion locale securisée (gélose)*. This law takes managerial control of forests and water resources out of the hands of the DIREF and places it in the hands of local communities. The process is for the DIREF to make contracts with local communities for the sustainable management of resources. To date, only a few of these contracts has been made. Some are hopeful that this initiative will eliminate some of the problems of land tenure, especially in cases where outsiders take over local lands (such as in the region of the *Mt. Des Français* in the north). Others fear that local communities may not internalize the need for long-term conservation of biodiversity. In any case this national support of local tenure rights will provide an important testing ground for the recommendations of community-based conservation (Western et al. 1994).

5. See Gezon and Freed 1999 for a more extensive discussion of the history of agroforestry and other types of tree planting in northern Madagascar.

Chapter Twelve

Scaling Up from the Grassroots

NGO Networks and the Challenges of Organizational Maintenance in Mexico's Yucatán Peninsula

PETER R. WILSHUSEN, RAÚL E. MURGUÍA

Most discussions of community-based conservation emphasize the importance of providing incentives for ecologically beneficial local development but tend to overlook the importance of strong organizational arrangements in sustaining these activities over the long term. Effective organizing for conservation and development can be particularly challenging in contexts characterized by authoritarian rule within both rural agrarian communities and the ranks of state agencies. Mexico, which is the focus of this chapter, presents a rural political environment that has been largely inhospitable to grassroots organizing. Despite its history of agrarian reform, peasant organizing, and, more recently, community management of forests, the country presents an institutional legacy of state control of resources, domination by local and regional bosses *(caciques)*, and community dependence on state subsidies. Within the context of Mexico's economic *apertura* beginning in the mid-1980s, the number of large-scale, state-run rural development programs decreased. As a result new opportunities emerged for actors operating outside the state's domain to pursue initiatives focused on community development, environmental protection, and, in some cases, political opposition (Fox and Hernández 1992).

This chapter explores an ongoing initiative to build and maintain an organizational network for conservation and sustainable development in Mexico's Yucatán Peninsula. Unlike many programs that attempt to join conservation and development, participants in the Yucatán experience have explicitly accounted for organizational arrangements and decision-making processes that promote grassroots democracy. This effort was legally constituted in February 1997 when representatives of twelve small and medium-sized nongovernmental organizations (NGOS) operating in the region formed the Sustainable Development Network or ROSDESAC (as it is known in Mexico by its Spanish acronym).[1] The network seeks to scale up efforts aimed at strengthening community-level organizations, generating alternative economic income opportunities, promoting environmental protection, and encouraging rapidly disappearing cultural practices, particularly among Mayan communities. ROSDESAC emerged out of a small grants program administered by the United Nations Development Programme (UNDP) with funds from the Global Environment Facility (GEF)[2] and has grown from an informal support group of five NGOs to an independent network of fifteen NGOs working across the Yucatán Peninsula.

The ROSDESAC case is important for three reasons. First, it suggests that a wide spectrum of participants can "scale up" or expand community-based conservation and development efforts to the regional level by crafting organizational arrangements and consensual decision-making processes (Brown and Ashman 1998; Fox 1996; Uvin 1995; Uvin et al. 2000). Second, the case presents evidence that international conservation and development organizations such as the GEF and UNDP can play an important role in this scaling-up process through small-grants programs. Third, ROSDESAC's experience to date illustrates several challenges that proponents of conservation and social justice face in maintaining such a network within a largely unsupportive political and economic environment. In order to expand on each of these points, this chapter proceeds along three lines of discussion. First, it recounts how ROSDESAC formed, placing special emphasis on key institutional changes that favored increased participation by local NGOs in rural development. The second part of the chapter analyzes ROSDESAC's institutional structure, considering in particular the role of power sharing as a means of counteracting conventional relationships of domination between rural and coastal producer organizations on one side and NGOs, international donor organizations, and state agencies on the other. The chapter's final section presents a discussion of some of the factors that underlie the network's qualified success at generating democratic structures and social process. It also explores several organizational challenges that participants have faced in maintaining the network by presenting an initial appraisal of organizational efficiency, stability, commitment and community representation of several member groups.

EXPANDING POLITICAL SPACE FOR CIVIL SOCIETY:
THE EMERGENCE OF ROSDESAC

ROSDESAC appeared in the mid-1990s in the midst of key social, political, and economic reforms in Mexico. Under President Carlos Salinas de Gotari (1988–1994), Mexico experienced a shift away from state-led development toward neoliberal economic policies that stressed reduced government involvement, privatization, and free trade. The country's entry into the General Agreement on Tariffs and Trade (GATT) in 1986 and the North American Free Trade Agreement (NAFTA) in 1994 were accompanied by a large-scale reorganization of many government agencies and their programs. For example, the reforms included revisions to Article 27 of the national constitution that announced the end of agrarian reform. This change replaced the agrarian reform ministry, which historically had intervened in most aspects of rural communities' economic and political development, with what amounted to a land-titling program. By the early 1990s, the organizational and political landscape in rural Mexico had been completely transformed (Corneling and Myhre 1998). Many community-level organizations such as producer cooperatives and associations, which had been created by state agencies, were left without financial and other resources to fuel operations. These broad changes in state-sponsored development were accompanied by a rapid increase in the number of nongovernmental organizations working in rural Mexico (Fox and Hernández 1992). For the Yucatán Peninsula, one estimate identified some 1,320 community-based and regional NGOs as of 1993 (Murguía 1998).

In combination, these factors had two important effects. First, the redefinition of state programs created a resource void for many community-level organizations, in particular those cooperatives and associations that had been created for the express purpose of receiving government funding. Second, the diminished presence of state actors and the increase in activities by nongovernmental actors changed the political landscape in many rural areas. In one sense, community organizations were less beholden to government agents and thus freer to seek assistance from other sources. In another sense, however, community-level organizations were left with few options, many existing in name only.

While these two broad processes of change—the reorganization of the state and the rise of organizations of civil society—favored increased interrelationships between NGOs and community-level organizations, external support from an international small grants program provided sufficient resources to enable and sustain the interaction. The United Nations Development Programme (UNDP) initiated its Small Grants Programme to Non-Governmental Organizations (SGP/NGO) in 1992 in response to the growing importance of NGOs on a global scale. The program funds community-based activities carried out by grassroots NGOs or local groups that combine community development and environmental protection and respond to the GEF's priority areas of biodiversity conservation, protection of international waters, and mitigation of global climate change. As of September 2000, UNDP supported small grants programs in forty-six countries around the world.[3] UNDP initiated its Mexico Small Grants Programme in March 1994, adopting a regional focus on the Yucatán Peninsula. The program developed more rapidly than in other countries given a strong, pre-existing base of community-level and NGO activities centered on grassroots conservation and development (Murguía 1990). By January 2001, the Mexico Small Grants Programme had financed a total of 102 projects for a total of US$1,791,151, of which small and medium-sized NGOs associated with the network had carried out forty-nine and community-based organizations (CBOs) had administered fifty-three.

Although the original proposal for the Mexico Small Grants Programme did not include the creation of an NGO network, it did allow the program's coordinator to dedicate a significant amount of resources to organizational capacity building. One of these projects helped to create a technical support group for community-based organizations (known by its Spanish acronym GATOB)[4] and another that provided group members with Internet and e-mail access. The GATOB initially comprised four professionals who worked in different subregions around the peninsula assisting community organizations to design and establish small projects using participatory planning methodologies. Based on this experience, five NGOs adopted the approach and soon came to call themselves "hub" organizations *(organizaciones pivotes)*. In addition to coordinating activities for a given subregion, the GatoB, and later the hub NGOs, served as "translators" by helping community groups to transform their ideas into projects that fit with GEF and Mexico-SGP criteria. Eventually, four more organizations became hub NGOs once the small grants program expanded to a total of nine micro-regions in 1997. The hub-NGO concept eventually led participants to pursue the idea of creating an NGO network with an independent legal status. Initially, the Mexico Small Grants Programme approved a US$25,000 grant that permitted members of the hub-NGOs to meet on a regular basis, thus allowing technical interchange among members working on like projects. In October 1994, twelve affiliate organizations met in Ciudad del Carmen, Campeche, to consider the direction of the Mexico SGP after its first five months in operation. The meeting set the stage for the creation of a legally constituted network of organizations.

Participants at the meeting decided that the network should be a collegial body, independent of any state or international agency. The member organizations worked informally together for two years and legally constituted the sustainable development network ROSDESAC in February 1997. By January 2001, ROSDESAC was composed of fifteen nongovernmental organizations including regional NGOs and other legally constituted groups working in connection with the UNDP/GEF Small Grants Programme. In all, ROS-

DESAC has a core membership of approximately fifty professionals. The network maintains a small office in Mérida and has cultivated ties with other regional cooperatives, artisan federations, and nongovernmental networks.

COMPOSING A SUSTAINABLE DEVELOPMENT NETWORK

ROSDESAC's experience to date can be examined on at least two levels that may be instructive for similar efforts in other contexts. In terms of organizational structure and process, the network has established explicit rule-based norms for membership, collective decision making and, to a lesser extent, compliance that stabilize the expectations of diverse participants around a set of common objectives. In this sense, the rules established for participation in the network create boundaries of legitimate governance (Young 1989, see Table 12.1).

The network's bylaws recognize two types of members: active and cooperating. Of these two, only active members may participate in ROSDESAC's general assembly. Active members include the twelve founding members and any additional organizations the network's general assembly unanimously allows to join. Each active member has one vote in the general assembly. In general, active membership is predicated upon full acceptance and implementation of the mission and approach of the sustainable development program. Cooperating members, in turn, may provide financial and/or technical support and work in conjunction with the network. Cooperating members do not enjoy voting rights within the general assembly. Like active members, their participation is contingent upon unanimous approval of the network's general assembly.

Regarding collective decision making, the members of ROSDESAC have established that major decisions will go into effect only when and if all representatives reach full consensus. Major decisions are those that require obligatory action on the part of member organizations. Ordinary decisions require a simple majority to pass. Unlike many decision-making bodies that require a simple majority or two-thirds vote in order for a major resolution to pass, ROSDESAC has elected to pursue a more challenging and more time-consuming approach. Another important procedural rule makes collective decision making even more difficult. For those collective decisions that might impact member organizations individually, consensus first must be reached within each organization based on its own internal procedures. Once each member organization reaches agreement on a resolution of this kind, the network as a whole must arrive at a consensus before it becomes a policy. Members of the network suggest that, while arduous, consensual decision making is fairest to all members. And although resolutions take significant amounts of time to pass, once decided upon they tend to endure.

Perhaps the greatest oversight in ROSDESAC's bylaws regards compliance. Although they outline who may participate and how decisions will be made, the network's bylaws do not discuss procedures by which the general assembly might discipline or even remove a member organization that does not follow the rules. By September 2000, members of the network had developed a draft resolution that considered compliance since some expressed concern that certain organizations were operating in ways incongruent with the network's grassroots sustainable development approach (discussed below).

ON THE RISE: ROSDESAC'S INITIAL ACHIEVEMENTS

ROSDESAC has made important advances that have allowed it to grow beyond the scope of the GEF Small Grants Programme. At the same time, the network's NGO members continue to face internal and external organizational challenges. The network has worked diligently to establish autonomy from external partners such as state agencies and international donor organizations. To that end, the network has signed formal agreements with different

TABLE 12.1
Structural Character of Yucatán Peninsula
Sustainable Development Network (ROSDESAC)

Component	Structure	Procedure
Participation	Active members	• Selection based on unanimous approval • Requires full commitment to mission and goals • Requires full participation
	Cooperating members	• Provide technical and/or financial support
Collective Decision Making	Major decisions	• Require full consensus of active members • Require prior internal vote/approval of each member organization
	Ordinary decisions	• Require simple majority of active members
Compliance	*None* (draft resolution Sept. 2000)	• No formal rules or guidance currently exist for sanctioning or deconstituting members

parties to establish boundaries for cooperative relationships. In addition, the network has created a regional fund to channel low-interest credit to community-based organizations.

Collective Progress

In its first progress report released in March 1998, ROSDESAC outlined a wide variety of services that it had offered to communities including economic development, basic social services, and Mayan cultural support (ROSDESAC 1998). Regarding economic development, member organizations assisted communities with production and marketing of honey, chicle (chewing gum resin), timber, captive breeding of wild animals for bush meat, fisheries, embroidery and other handicrafts, organic agriculture, and ecotourism. The network achieved greatest advances in honey production. ROSDESAC worked with seven producers groups across the Yucatán peninsula including more than 1,180 producers (80 percent Yucatec Maya). The network provided technical assistance, low-interest loans, and marketing support. Together, the communities and supporting organizations set up three collection centers, a breeding facility (for queen bees), as well as production facilities for organic honey. As of 1998, annual honey production was estimated at 738 tons, worth approximately US$700,000.

With respect to basic social services, ROSDESAC provided health, education, and legal services. Health services centered on traditional medicine and sanitation. For example, the network helped establish four small botanical gardens with the participation of approximately fifty people, including traditional healers. An additional forty people produced traditional medicines for some six thousand users. Twelve traditional physicians received support to increase awareness of their practices among community members. Educational services, in turn, centered primarily on child care, early development, and youth activities in primary schools. Regarding legal support, ROSDESAC helped raise awareness of womens' and youths' rights through twelve workshops in four subregions.

Finally, network members undertook numerous activities to strengthen and recover Mayan cultural practices. These ranged from modes of production to cultural identity and included agricultural methods such as complex mixed cropping, traditional honey production using the *melipona* bee *(Mellipona bechii)*, home gardens, theater and dance, community museums, youth workshops, and publications in Yucatec Maya.

Agreements with External Partners

From the outset, the members of ROSDESAC have confronted the paternalistic legacy of state-run rural development in Mexico. Under this model, local or regional bosses *(caciques)* linked to the PRI, the country's historically dominant political party, monopolized control of financial, legal, and other resources. These powerful actors or groups directly and indirectly dominated local communities by providing financial subsidies, equipment, legal support, and other resources in exchange for political support. To maximize its autonomy, ROSDESAC pursued two main strategies including explicit agreements with donors and establishment of a regional fund. In the first case, the network signed agreements with each of the national and international donor organizations from which it received financial and other support. The accords clearly established the respective roles and responsibilities of each party, helping to stabilize expectations on both sides. The network's aim in signing such agreements was to establish diverse partnerships and avoid dependency on any one source. In addition to the GEF, ROSDESAC has received support from UNDP-Mexico, the National Solidarity Institute (INSOL), the National Social Enterprise Fund (FONAES), the United Nations Womens' Fund (UNIFEM), the W.K. Kellogg Foundation, Fondo Mexicano para la Conservación de la Naturaleza (FMCN), and the Fondo Indigenista Latinoamericano (FILA).

Creation of a Regional Fund

The program's second strategy focuses on financial autonomy. Historically, the state controlled access to grants and loans for rural development. In an attempt to open access to grants and credit, ROSDESAC established a peninsular fund. The goal of the fund was to provide working capital and technical assistance as well as promote savings for the production and marketing of environmentally sustainable and socially just products. Unlike the Small Grants Programme, the peninsular fund operated as a trust, offering low interest credit to community-based organizations. Whereas the Small Grants Programme responded to the GEF's programming criteria, loans made through the peninsular fund were not contingent on these guidelines. At the same time, the goals of the fund directly complemented the GEF's. As of January 2001, the fund had approximately US$575,000 in available capital. Of that total, US$200,000 represented targeted funds from the United Nations Women's Fund (UNIFEM). The National Social Enterprise Fund (FONAES) provided another US$375,000. In each case, the financial relationship between the donors and ROSDESAC was mutually beneficial. The network recovered the interest on loans to community-based organizations and the donor organizations could claim that they had mobilized the funds.

THE CHALLENGES OF GRASSROOTS
ORGANIZATIONAL PERFORMANCE AND MAINTENANCE

In spite of the network's significant advances in developing a regional community-based conservation and development initiative, ROSDESAC faces key organizational challenges that have limited its overall impact. To illustrate these challenges, we present a preliminary appraisal of nine NGO members of the sustainable development network based on their participation in the UNDP/GEF Mexico Small Grants Programme.[5] As of July 1999, when the assessment was conducted, the NGOs had received twenty-one grants and had facilitated another thirty-two awards on behalf of communities. The organization that had participated the most had received two grants and had facilitated eleven community projects for a total of US$273,075. The newest participating organization had only received one grant and facilitated one community project for a total of US$30,875 (Table 12.2).

The appraisal considered a combination of quantitative and qualitative indicators in four areas: project implementation efficiency, organizational stability, goal commitment, and community representation. Analysis of the information grouped into these four areas focused on the degree to which each organization advanced with respect to the network's three broad goals of promoting conservation, sustainable development, and grassroots democracy. While some organizations showed progress along these lines, others performed less effectively and at least one operated in ways that detracted from the network's goal of promoting grassroots democracy. In general, findings suggest that, even though significant financial resources for community-based projects may be available, grassroots NGOs must carefully monitor and adapt organizational strategies given variation in each group's efficiency in project implementation, ability to sustain its activities, commitment to the network's goals, and level of community representation. In what follows, we present the parameters and results of the organizational assessment and discuss in greater detail how questions of organizational performance and maintenance affected the impact of the sustainable development network.

Project Implementation Efficiency

In mid-1999 the National Steering Committee that oversees the Mexico Small Grants Programme requested a performance review of nine organizations serving to coordinate activities in each of the micro-regions around the Yucatán Peninsula.[7] As a result, the program's national coordinator developed a performance efficiency index that incorporated five quantitative indicators: benefit transfer, local participation, technical assistance, project completion, and overhead (Table 12.3). While these indicators were not intended as a comprehensive assessment, they did suggest important trends that the committee could begin to account for in individual agreements with each organization. The results of the assessment suggested three groupings, including three organizations with a high efficiency rating, three in the category of medium efficiency, and three others that presented low efficiency scores

TABLE 12.2
NGO Participation in the Mexico Small Grants Program*

Organization	Projects[1] #	Project Amount ($)	Projects Facilitated[2] #	Projects Completed[3] #	Project Amount ($)	Technical Assistance[4] ($)	(% total)
Marea Azul, A.C.	5	$53,497.45	0	0	$0.00	$0.00	0
Pro Selva, A.C.	2	$14,306.00	7	3	$129,921.39	$39,483.37	30.39
EDUCE, A.C.	2	$16,969.45	1	1	$5,540.26	$0.00	0
IEPA, A.C.	3	$61,377.46	7	6	$89,873.44	$0.00	0
MOCUP, A.C.	2	$38,647.22	0	0	$0.00	$0.00	0
CIRN, A.C.	2	$21,929.01	11	3	$251,145.85	$42,938.42	17.10
Misioneros, A.C.	3	$22,207.83	3	3	$14,674.79	$0.00	0
Yum Balam, A.C.	1	$46,431.52	2	2	$35,481.91	$5,789.48	16.32
Yaxché, A.C.	1	$1,270.00	1	1	$29,604.50	$0.00	0
TOTALS	21	$276,635.94	32	19	$556,242.14	$88,211.27	63.81
"Ideal," A.C.**	1	$100.00	10	10	$1,000.00	$200.00	20.00

Source: UNDP/GEF Mexico Small Grants Programme.

* Figures through July 1999.
** Ideal, A.C. represents a hypothetical NGO to establish baseline performance using criteria established by the Mexico Small Grants Programme's National Steering Committee (endnote 6).

1. Number of SGP Grants to the NGO.
2. Number of SGP grants to community-based organizations (CBOs) channeled through the NGO.
3. Number of CBO projects that successfully completed 75 percent of their proposed objectives.
4. Amount of CBO projects paid to NGO for technical assistance.

(From Table 12.3—high efficiency: [above 0.0150]; medium efficiency [0.0100–0.0149]; and low efficiency [0.0050–0.0099]).

Those organizations that produced the lowest efficiency ratings—Marea Azul and MOCUP,A.C.—presented similar trends since they both featured absolute minimum scores (-100.00) in terms of benefit transfer and channeled no community-level projects. At the same time, both organizations had significant overhead costs. These low ratings take on clearer meaning when we consider questions of goal commitment and organizational stability below. EDUCE's relatively low efficiency rating was due largely to the organization's programming approach. The NGO initially solicited small grants support (two projects for $16,969) to consolidate a micro-regional strategy, identify local partners, and leverage additional funding. As a result it had facilitated only one community level project as of July 1999.

Participating NGOs with mid-range efficiency scores—CIRN,A.C., Misioneros, and Yum Balam—also pursued development strategies similar to EDUCE but transferred greater benefits to the community level. Even though all three achieved higher efficiency ratings, EDUCE performed better overall when other indicators such as organizational stability and community representation were considered. CIRN,A.C., Misioneros, and Yum Balam successfully coordinated community-level projects (a total of eight completed grant projects). Yum Balam, in particular, administered three grants (US$46,432) along the way to developing a micro-regional strategy with community groups. At the same time, the NGO became dependent on the Small Grants Programmme grants to cover its operating costs (see discussion below). Interestingly, CIRN,A.C. coordinated the largest number of community projects (11), and thus had the highest benefit transfer score (68.22), but only three of these had successfully completed 75 percent of their objectives.

The two organizations with the highest efficiency ratings—IEPA,A.C. and ProSelva—offer some interesting contrasts. IEPA,A.C. was the program's most efficient organization. As of July 1999, it had solicited three of its own projects and facilitated seven others in conjunction with community-level groups (six of these were successfully completed). The NGO subsidized its technical services with funds from other sources (and thus zero technical assistance costs). Three of the more than twenty community-based groups that IEPA,A.C. supported eventually operated as independent organizations within ROSDESAC. ProSelva also channeled a high number of community projects (seven) and received two small grants (US$14,306). It featured the second-highest benefit transfer score. Compared to IEPA,A.C., ProSelva was less successful at encouraging community organizations. Of the seven projects it initiated with communities, only three were successfully completed. Indeed, four of the organizations it helped to create no longer existed by July 1999 and complaints emerged about the high cost and low quality of its technical support

TABLE 12.3
Efficiency Indicators for Members of the
Yucatán Peninsula Sustainable Development Network (ROSDESAC)

Organization	Benefit Transfer[1]	Local Participation[2]	Technical Assistance[3]	Project Completion[4]	Overhead[5]	Efficiency Rating[6]
Marea Azul, A.C.	-100.00	0.00	0.00	0.0	4.59	0.0052
ProSelva, A.C.	52.79	9.46	30.39	42.86	4.61	0.0169
EDUCE, A.C.	-50.77	1.35	0.00	100.00	1.46	0.0086
IEPA, A.C.	18.84	9.46	0.00	85.71	5.27	0.0195
MOCUP, A.C.	-100.00	0.00	0.00	0.00	3.32	0.0052
CIRN, A.C.	68.22	14.86	17.10	27.27	5.56	0.0137
Misioneros, A.C.	-20.42	4.05	0.00	100.00	1.91	0.0116
Yum Balam, A.C.	-13.37	2.70	16.32	100.00	3.98	0.0129
Yaxché, A.C.	91.77	1.35	0.00	100.00	0.11	0.0282
"Ideal", A.C.	63.64	9.09	20.00	100.00	2.73	α

(continued on next page)

TABLE 12.3 *(continued)*

Source: UNDP/GEF Mexico Small Grants Programme (July 1999).

1. *Benefit Transfer:* Percentage of total projects financed in the micro-region divided by the "cost" of the hub organization. Hub organization cost is derived as the difference between total dollar amount of projects facilitated and total dollar amount of NGO projects/technical assistance funds.

2. *Local Participation:* Percentage of all projects in the program that were channeled to community-based organizations in the micro-region.

3. *Technical Assistance:* Percentage of all projects financed in the micro-region paid to hub organizations in technical assistance.

4. *Project Completion:* Percentage of projects administered that achieved 75 percent of their proposed objectives.

5. *Overhead:* Percentage of total project monies received by each hub organization.

6. *Efficiency Rating:* Index rating representing the inverse of the distance between the organization in question and a hypothetical "ideal" organization, which establishes a performance baseline (endnote 6). High efficiency: (above 0.0150); Medium efficiency (0.0100–0.0149); and Low efficiency (0.0050–0.0099).

(see discussion below). Finally, it is important to note that Yaxché featured an anomalously high efficiency rating (0.0282) because it worked with only one community-based organization as compared to other participating NGOs that worked with fifteen or more.

Organizational Stability

In order to assess each organization's stability, we made a qualitative projection of the degree to which the NGOs would be able to sustain their activities over the following five years given existing personnel and other resources. We assumed that the scope of each organization's activities would remain constant. The following questions were posed in order to appraise organizational stability: Does the NGO currently have (or will it likely have) sufficient financial resources to carry out its proposed activities over the next five years? Can the NGO likely maintain a core group of professionals over the same period? Does the NGO have access to sufficient material and nonmaterial resources such as vehicles and technical information to continue activities? To answer these questions, we drew information from an evaluation of Mexico Small Grants Programme projects, interviews with NGO personnel, and project site visits. Each organization was rated as having high, medium, or low stability.

Results of this part of the assessment showed that five of the nine NGOs had high (3) or medium (2) organizational stability. The two organizations with medium stability—Marea Azul and CIRN,A.C.—both had strong core personnel and resources such as office space, technical skills, information, etc. However, neither of these two organizations had secured sufficient financial resources to sustain its activities. The four organizations with low stability ratings—Yum Balam, MOCUP,A.C., Misioneros, and Yaxché—had difficulties maintaining their activities due to a lack of resources. While MOCUP,A.C.'s weak performance was reflected in all four assessment areas, Yum Balam's case suggested that low organizational stability hampered an otherwise promising program (see discussion below). Similar to Yum Balam, the group Misioneros had not garnered significant financial support but possessed other resources given links to the progressive wing of the Catholic Church (ecclesiastical base communities). At the time the evaluation was performed, Yaxché was an incipient organization that showed few signs of stability except access to technical information.

Goal Commitment

This qualitative indicator refers to the degree of dedication that each organization demonstrated in promoting ROSDESAC's goals of environmental conservation, sustainable community development, and grassroots democracy. We assessed goal commitment by reviewing the organizations' individual missions and overall activities. For each of ROSDESAC's three broad mission goals we asked the following general questions: First, do the NGO's mission, training, and experience reflect the network's mission? Second, do the NGO's overall activities positively reflect ROSDESAC's three mission goals? As with the assessment of organizational stability, information was derived from an SGP evaluation, interviews, and site visits. Each NGO was given a rating of high, medium, or low goal commitment. Like organizational stability, goal commitment is an important indicator because it helps to explain, for example, why certain NGOs with low project implementation efficiency continue to play important roles in the network.

In general, two-thirds of the NGOs demonstrated strong goal commitment (six organizations), while three showed low levels of dedication (see Table 12.4). Of those organizations that received high goal commitment ratings, Marea Azul stood out for its relatively lower scores in the other three indicator areas: efficiency, stability, and representation. Marea Azul was founded mainly as an activist group to protest environmental degradation and social injustices precipitated by Mexico's state-owned oil company PEMEX. The members' dedication to ROSDESAC's goals made it a key player in the network, although evaluations raised questions as to whether the organization would be able to effectively carry out projects with communities. By January 2001, Marea Azul's project implementation efficiency had improved significantly. Similarly, the three NGOs that received low goal commitment scores—ProSelva, MOCUP,A.C., and Yaxché—presented mission goals and actions that were not in accord with ROSDESAC's stated goals. MOCUP,A.C.'s operational goals emphasized legal and political support for rural and urban workers rather than community-based conservation and development. Thus, both its goal orientation and experience were not fully in line with ROSDESAC's mission (the organization became inactive in 1999). Both ProSelva and Yaxché favored economic development goals at the expense of environmental protection and grassroots democracy. While it was unclear at the time of this assessment whether or not Yaxché would bring its strategy and programs more in line with the goals of ROSDESAC, the actions of ProSelva suggested that its work with communities tended to rely on authoritarian practices (see discussion below).

Community Representation

This last indicator was used to assess each organization's relationship with the communities they represented. To a certain extent, elements of NGO representation emerge in the efficiency indicators such as "benefit transfer" and "local participation" summarized in Table 12.3. Similarly, representation is suggested by an organization's commitment to ROSDESAC's goals as discussed above. In addition, we chose to more directly appraise how each NGO performed in advancing partner communities' social, political, and economic interests. Three questions were considered in order to assess levels of community representation. First, does the NGO undertake activities that advance communities' social and political interests? Second, does the NGO undertake activities that advance communities' economic interests? Finally, have communities been able to hold NGOs accountable for their commitments (or alternatively, are there formal or informal mechanisms in place by which the NGO can be held accountable to communities)? We based this assessment on interviews with NGO representatives and site visits.

Compared to the other three assessment areas—efficiency, stability, and goal commitment—appraisal of community representation produced the highest number of low ratings (six). The remaining three NGOs received high ratings. Those NGOs with low scores tended to advance community interests in one area (either economic or social/political) but not the other. In all cases, these NGOs were not accountable to their community partners (a total of six NGOs fell into this category). In some cases, such as with Marea Azul, a lack of resources accounted for the low level of community representation. In other cases, such as with ProSelva, the NGO tended to work with communities as clients rather than partners and thus was less responsive in terms of social/political interests and accountability. The lack of accountability among NGOs and partner communities suggested a need for strengthened grassroots democratic process in project development and implementation at the community level.

Two examples of NGOs that became inactive in the Mexico Small Grants Programme after 1999—Yum Balam and ProSelva—illustrate quite different trajectories that produced low organizational effectiveness. Yum Balam's case suggests how low organizational stability can truncate promising activities that are moderately to highly successful in terms of efficiency, community representation, and goal commitment. ProSelva's performance indicates the exact opposite: that highly stable and efficient organizations can be unsuccessful at sustaining interventions when goal commitment and community representation are weak.

In terms of goal commitment and community representation, few of the network's member organizations were as dedicated to local conservation and development as Yum Balam. During 1995 and 1996, the organization worked closely with communities, cooperatives, and regional organizations to carry out participatory rural appraisals of environmental and social problems. Through a combination of mapping and planning exercises, communities developed a sense of their own needs and produced project proposals accordingly. One of the organization's main achievements involved facilitating the creation of a locally managed protected area. While Yum Balam successfully encouraged community development, however, the organization generated very few resources to sustain itself.

Yum Balam helped to produce a regional community development and environmental protection strategy and encouraged some forty community-based

TABLE 12.4

Performance Evaluation for Members of the Yucatán Peninsula
Sustainable Development Network (ROSDESAC)*

Organization	Efficiency[1]	Stability[2]	Commitment[3]	Representation[4]	Status[5]
Marea Azul, A.C.	Low	Medium	High	Low	Active
ProSelva, A.C.	High	High	Low	Low	Inactive
EDUCE, A.C.	Low	High	High	High	Active
IEPA, A.C.	High	High	High	High	Active
MOCUP, A.C.	Low	Low	Low	Low	Inactive
CIRN, A.C.	Medium	Medium	High	Low	Active
Misioneros, A.C.	Medium	Low	High	Low	Active
Yum Balam, A.C.	Medium	Low	High	High	Inactive
Yaxché, A.C.	High	Low	Low	Low	Active

*Status as of July 1999.

1. *Efficiency:* Quantitative measure based on five variables: benefit transfer, local participation, technical assistance, project completion, and overhead (Table 12.3).
2. *Stability:* Qualitative measure of organization's sustainability including budget, personnel, and resources.
3. *Commitment:* Qualitative measure of goal commitment.
4. *Representation:* Qualitative measure of level of community representation.
5. *Status:* Whether or not organization continues to participate in the UNDP/GEF Small Grants Programme.

organizations, of which fourteen were still in existence as of mid-1999. Despite these early successes, the organization began to wither in 1997. Of an original nucleus of eight professionals, only two remained at the end of 1999. In large part, attrition occurred because the organization had minimal sources of income such that its members could not sustain themselves or their families. Unlike some other members of the network, Yum Balam did not collect fees for services rendered or secure external grant support. In addition, one of the organization's founding members spent two years working as the (unsalaried) president of ROSDESAC. Yum Balam became inactive in 2000 although individual members continued to work on some of the community-based activities it helped to initiate.

Unlike Yum Balam, the organization ProSelva, based in Escarcega, Campeche, grew rapidly during the three-year period following its creation in 1995. ProSelva operated as a forestry and rural development consulting firm, offering technical assistance to agrarian communities *(ejidos)*. The NGO generated sufficient income to maintain salaried technicians and all operations. Despite initial successes, however, client communities accused ProSelva of domineering and even corrupt tactics. In addition, the NGO participated minimally in the activities of the sustainable development network. Because of its alleged authoritarian style of interaction with communities and its lack of participation in the network, several members of ROSDESAC's general assembly questioned ProSelva's dedication to grassroots sustainable development.

ProSelva offered technical services to communities ranging from forest management, chicle (chewing gum) production, and beekeeping, among others. Unlike Yum Balam, it collected fees from communities for their services and representation. In this sense, ProSelva's approach was to serve as an intermediary, identifying and recommending community projects for small grants. In addition, ProSelva established its own rural development trust fund to encourage chicle and honey production. At the same time, however, control over these resources allowed ProSelva to impose a top-down decision-making structure that reproduced paternalistic relationships of dependence between the NGO and its client communities. Thus, while ProSelva initially generated the greatest profits and production levels of any of the other NGOs, its authoritarian management style precipitated strong resistance at the community level, causing most of its projects to stagnate. In 2000, the Mexico Small Grants Programme national steering committee decided to revoke ProSelva's status as coordinating NGO for central Campeche.

Two factors help to explain why ProSelva's otherwise successful technical interventions spawned criticism both locally and from within ROSDESAC. Most likely, the group's low commitment to the goal of grassroots democracy and low level of community representation were the result of limited professional training and competition from another local organization. First, unlike

Yum Balam, the members of ProSelva had relatively little experience in managing the complexities of participatory project development. Each of ProSelva's eleven core members were highly qualified foresters, agronomists, and biologists but had had limited success at sustaining strong relationships of mutual trust and respect with communities. Second, ProSelva and another local provider of technical services occupied very similar economic niches and thus competed for many of the same community clients. In an attempt to control as much of the sector as possible, ProSelva pursued a domineering approach wherein the NGO rigidly controlled community access to financial resources and technical support.

CONCLUSION: CRAFTING COMPLIANCE AT ALL LEVELS

Between 1997 and 2000, the Yucatán Peninsula Sustainable Development Network—ROSDESAC—successfully established a regional organizational structure that included a deliberative decision-making process. During that period, it navigated important organizational maintenance challenges linked to project implementation efficiency, stability, goal commitment, and community representation. In terms of scaling up or expanding the reach of individual NGO programs, ROSDESAC presents an important example of how organizational networks can perform as governance institutions that stabilize participant expectations through the establishment of clear rules and responsibilities. The network also presents opportunities for creative synergy among member organizations, establishes a marketing front for handicrafts, organic agricultural products, and other specialty commercial goods, and allows for increased leveraging of funds and coordination of small-scale lending. Although ROSDESAC's general assembly strongly encourages collegial decision making, its initial lack of formal compliance mechanisms make it difficult for the network to respond to member organizations that fail to adhere to its goals.

Although the bulk of this chapter has focused on organizational performance and maintenance, the ROSDESAC case points to the possibility of scaling up community level interventions to the regional level given consistent, long-term financial and programming support (in this case the Global Environment Facility's [GEF] Small Grants Programme [SGP]) and adequate organizational arrangements. While community-based activities in this study favored ecologically friendly development, the cumulative outcomes from small grants projects appeared to positively support biodiversity conservation. With respect to habitat protection, in particular, the Small Grants Programme strengthened community *(ejido)* participation in a World Bank/GEF initiative to establish three biological corridors that link diverse protected areas across the Yucatán Peninsula. Further, despite weak performances by some member organizations, ROSDESAC and the Mexico Small Grants Programme successfully established an effective *social process* including organizational consolidation and adaptation, regional strategy development, and strong links with communities.

Despite ROSDESAC's significant advances, our analysis of organizational performance of network members points to the need for continuous appraisal and accountability at all levels. While overall performance was strong for most of the organizations, the assessment uncovered important trends that threatened ROSDESAC's long-term effectiveness. Individual examples of these trends include low efficiency especially in terms of benefit transfer to communities (e.g., MOCUP,A.C.), low organizational stability (e.g., Yum Balam), weak goal commitment, and authoritarian relationships with communities (e.g., ProSelva). In an attempt to reverse these trends, the Mexico Small Grants Programme national steering committee developed written contracts with the nine "hub" organizations in 2000 that identified specific actions that each needed to take in order to continue receiving grant support. While three NGOs became inactive in the Small Grants Programme during 1999–2000 (Yum Balam, ProSelva, and MOCUP,A.C.), all but one (MOCUP,A.C.) continued to participate in ROSDESAC in late 2000.

On one hand, the scope of the network's mission and activities is broader than the Small Grants Programme. As such, the criteria for strong participation extend beyond project implementation efficiency. On the other hand, however, ROSDESAC does not have an independent review council comparable to the Small Grants Programme's national coordinating committee with the authority to oversee the network's activities. As such, ROSDESAC remains a highly promising but still incomplete conservation and development regime. As the network continues to develop, members will need to focus attention on crafting rules and responsibilities for compliance at all levels: community, NGO, and network.

NOTES

An earlier version of this chapter was presented at the XXI International Congress of the Latin American Studies Association, September 24–26, 1998 in Chicago. Peter Wilshusen carried out fieldwork for this study in July 1996, July 1998, and sporadically during 1999–2000. The authors wish to thank Sally Timpson, Carmen Tavera, Guillermo Alonso, Paco Remolina, Javier Hirose, Lourdes Rodriguez, and Xavier Moya. The ideas and opinions expressed in this chapter are those of the authors and do not represent the views of the United Nations Development Programme (UNDP) or the Global Environment Facility (GEF).

1. The name of the network in Spanish is: *Red de Organizaciones del Sureste para el Desarrollo Sustentable A.C.* or RODESAC.

2. The GEF is a multilateral financial mechanism for the environment that was created as part of negotiations surrounding the 1992 Earth Summit in Rio de Janeiro, Brazil. It is administered jointly by the United Nations Development Programme (UNDP), the United Nations Environment Programme (UNEP) and the World Bank.

3. During the four-year pilot phase (1992–1996), the UNDP/GEF Small Grants Programme received US$18.2 million and was subsequently allotted US$24 million for the first two years of the first operational phase (July 1996–June 1998). Of the latter sum, US$17.95 million (75 percent) went to grant expenditures. Average grant sizes for the two-year operational phase were US$22,500. Approximately 75 percent of grants were directed toward biodiversity conservation (Wells et al. 1998). See *http://www.undp.org/sgp/* (current as of May 2002).

4. *Grupo de Apoyo Técnico a Organizaciones de Base* (GatoB).

5. While the observations we present appear to be representative of each organization's overall performance, it is important to remember that they all carry out activities beyond the scope of the small grants program.

6. For the purposes of assessing implementation efficiency, the Mexico Small Grants Programme National Steering Committee set a comparative baseline in terms of an "ideal" participating organization. This hypothetical "ideal" organization administered one project for a total of $100.00. It facilitated ten projects for a total of $1,000 and all of these have achieved 75 percent of their proposed objectives. Community-based groups paid 20 percent of this latter total for technical assistance.

7. In line with UNDP/GEF guidelines, each country program sets up a National Steering Committee. The Mexico SGP National Steering Committee is composed of ten conservation and development experts who work on a voluntary basis, and is responsible for project review/approval and program oversight.

Chapter Thirteen

YOUR PARK, MY POVERTY

Using Impact Assessment to Counter the Displacement Effects of Environmental Greenlining

CHARLES GEISLER

It is axiomatic that protected areas come with social benefits and social costs. Social impact assessment (SIA), a now familiar way of cross-referencing these benefits and costs in hopes of better public policy,[1] is particularly relevant when costs include involuntary human displacement. Hard as it is for some to imagine protected areas as anything but benign, their expansion should be no more immune to SIA than other large infrastructure projects and public works that activate social and environmental impact reviews (Rao and Geisler 1990; Geisler 1993).

SIA applied to protected areas benefits society in several ways. It incorporates stakeholder perspectives—including local residents—into the public record in the critical "upstream" or pre-implementation phase. It provides a comparison of alternative "development" scenarios and, importantly, includes the status quo ante among them. This gives local residents needed legitimacy and reduces the likelihood that they will be wantonly expelled from protected areas. And, though not a guarantee of mitigation, social impact assessment is a logical step toward such action. In the absence of laws guaranteeing the right of humans to reside in protected zones, SIA is a form of "due process" which buffers residents against highly uncertain futures and displacement processes.

What occasions the present chapter, however, are not the strengths of social impact assessment, but its weaknesses. Most projects that trigger SIA—such as new technologies, new infrastructure applications, or new public policy—have predictable life cycles. They are expected and even planned to last a finite number of years. Protected areas, on the other hand, have no such constraints. Their architects look to the indefinite future. Their vision is multigenerational. And here is the sticking point: SIA cannot predict the unpredictable. Predictability is inversely related to project longevity and declines as project scale and time frame amplify. Precisely because protected area planning increasingly reflects the bigger-is-better and longer-is-safer philosophy of ecosystem and eco-regional planning, SIA is dwarfed by the task at hand.

It would be misguided, however, to abandon SIA when the opportunity exists to refashion it. My intention here is to elaborate on one such opportunity, which, if implemented, would help SIA overcome the challenges inherent in the long-term planning horizons of protected area management. At the heart of this rethinking is adaptive environmental co-management, about which more will be said below. My core concern is the impact of exclusionary conservation on those who use and inhabit protected areas. I will refer to such people as "conservation refugees." They are a variant of environmental refugees—the victims of multiple forms of environmental insecurity—but, interestingly, this insecurity arises from the creation of large-scale conservation enclosures. Their displacement is not an "act of God."

To illustrate my point, I offer a case study from a national park in the Dominican Republic that has grown eightfold in recent years and displaced thousands of local residents. My intent, I should note, could be easily misunderstood. What follows is not a case against conservation or protected area expansion, but a case for instituting improved social assessment procedures when human dislocation is a likely policy option. SIA will perform best, I argue, when it is both adaptive and collaborative.

THE EVOLVING MEANING OF "REFUGEE"

As noted elsewhere (Geisler and de Sousa 2001), the typology of world refugees is evolving. A 1967 protocol released by the United Nations High Commission on Refugees defines "refugee" as "[a]ny person who is outside the country of his [sic] nationality . . . because he has or had well-founded fear of persecution by reason of his race, religion, nationality, membership of a particular social group or political opinion and is unable or, because of such fear, is unwilling to avail himself of the protection of the government of the country of his nationality" (Goodwin-Gill 1983, 5–6). Today, many dispute this arbitrary "cross-boundary" definition, and refugee status is expanding to include economic and humanitarian asylum seekers. Those favoring a more inclusive definition assert that refugee homelessness can be long or short term; displacement can result from direct or indirect violence; and asylum may or may not be across an international boundary. Increasingly, "refugee" is coming to mean "someone compelled to leave home" (Zolberg et al. 1989).

In 1985, the United Nations Environmental Program proposed that a broad range of environmental disasters can generate refugees even if international boundaries are not involved (Westing 1992). Such refugees are the victims of long-term mismanagement of nature by humans (soil erosion, greenhouse gases, toxification of air, water, soil or food chain, deforestation, and desertification), of massive public works intended to control nature (dams, highways, power plants, urban renewal), or of unforeseen "acts of God." This recognition of environmental refugees has prompted calls for greater environmental security in many parts of the world (Kreimer and Munasinghe 1991; Gadgil and Guha 1995; Leiderman 1995; Renner 1996), a summons that is blurring the lines between conservation and refugee organizations.

As refugee categories multiply, refugee numbers have tended to climb. According to the 1967 UNHCR definition, 14.5 million people were political refugees in 2000 (World Almanac 2001). This is up from most refugee estimates at midcentury (Table 13.1) but down from UNHCR counts earlier this decade. A more inclusive definition embracing environmental refugees tells quite another story. Authors such as Hinnawi (1985), Jacobson (1988), Suhrke (1993), Myers (1993), and Hugo (1995) all suggest that environmental disasters are dislocating people well in excess of UNHCR refugee counts.[2] A report completed late in 1998 by the Worldwatch Institute and the insurance industry found that three hundred million people had been displaced from their homes that year, or more than the combined populations of Canada and the United States (Trenberth 1999). Though 1998 was a disaster-prone year, trend data for recent decades suggest that displacement that year was not a freak occurrence (Table 13.1).

This research describes another category of environmental refugee, one omitted in the above inventory of storms, floods, droughts, fires, and El Niño effects. These "conservation refugees" are the victims of what Albert (1994, 46) has termed "ecological expropriation" and are often generated by governments and conservation organizations that with compelling reasons seek to increase environmental security. They are people displaced by the creation of national parks and protected areas without prior impact assessment or subsequent mitigation. As with people displaced by natural or unnatural disasters, civil wars, and ethnic cleansings, these refugees are involuntarily removed from their homelands. Following an overview of conservation refugees in global terms and a case study well known to the author, I offer the following conclusion: social impact assessment can, with the benefit of conscious adaptive and collaborative components, potentially mitigate the conservation refugee problem.

TABLE 13.1
Global Refugee Growth

Year	Refugee Estimate	Source
1917	3.5–5 million (excluding war refugees free to return home)	Brookings 1942
1926	9.5 million (reflects post-Bolshevik Revolution)	Zolberg et al.1989
1960	15.0 million	UNHCR 1967
1983	10.4 million	World Almanac 1985
1991	18.5 million	U.S. State Dept. 1992
1994	16.3 million	World Almanac 1995
1998	13.8 million	U.S. Committee for Refugees 1999
2000	14.5 million	World Almanac 2001

WHY THE OER PROBLEM MATTERS

Policies intent on conserving nature can be every bit as disruptive to resident populations as unplanned hurricanes, floods, oil spills, or toxic accidents. Zolberg et al. (1989) note that violent disruption is common to all refugees, but that some violence is indirect ("passive") and may follow from seemingly benign government policy. In creating or expanding protected areas, governments have unusual authority. Their right to assemble land and to assign it conservation status off limits to everyone except scientists, conservation managers, and tourists is rarely contested. Their laws may require them to compensate, rehabilitate, and resettle protected area refugees. These mitigation strategies are apt to be token, however, if disconnected from impact assessment that is both comprehensive and widely accessible to the populations targeted for removal at the planning stage.

Although the conservation refugee phenomenon is not new (Geisler 2003), its salience has increased with the intensified campaign by international environmental networks for more and larger national parks and ecosystem/eco-regional designations (Western et al. 1994; Brandon et al. 1998; Inamdar et al. 1999). These gains for the environment were consolidated in the 1992 UN Convention on Biological Diversity. They had then and still have multiple motivations, including ecotourism revenues, prestige, international funding, and genuine interest in protecting nature's patrimony. As a conceptual matter, there is a bias in most ecosystem/eco-regional planning for increased scale ("bigger is better") based on theory (island biogeography), empirical evidence that many at-risk biota exist outside current parks and refuges, and cogent arguments by conservation biologists about the dynamic, ever-shifting nature of ecosystems (Geisler and Bedford 1998; Soule 1999).

So, the conservation refugee phenomenon matters for many reasons. Planners and demographers ask where the substitute housing and infrastructure for those dislocated by conservation will come from. Environmentalists and conservation biologists debate whether such refugees are enemies or allies of conservation and what the consequences are of removing them from protected landscapes. Property rights groups are suspicious of the IUCN and of the international conventions that propel them. Human rights groups worry that conservation refugees are being deprived of legal and moral rights. Even where protected areas are economically marginal with low human densities, there is displacement potential. In poor countries with high population densities, marginal lands are often settled by economic and ethnic minorities— those least equipped to recover from the expanding footprint of global conservation efforts. In other instances marginalized populations lacking title or even credible squatter rights rely on protected zones for all or part of their livelihood. Losing use rights to resource-rich places is an important part of environmental insecurity for sedintary (Saberwal, Rangarajan, and Kothari 2001; Momberg, Puri, and Jessup 2000) and mobile peoples alike (Chatty and Colchester 2002).

THE CASE OF PROTECTED AREA REFUGEES
IN THE DOMINICAN REPUBLIC

In Latin America and the Caribbean, ten countries now protect over 10 percent of their national territories (Table 13.2). Much of this protection is relatively new. Its protected area refugee effects are routinely overlooked in standard summaries of refugees throughout the region (and of protected area net benefits calculations). The majority of protected areas shown in Table 13.2 appeared in the past decade. Here, we focus on a small but environmentally active country in the Caribbean, the Dominican Republic, for further protected area refugee insights. IUCN records show 31.5 percent of the Dominican Republic in protected status in 1997. More conservation refugees may have originated in a single Dominican national park in the past decade than did all the conventional refugees for the entire Caribbean in the same period.[3] It is this park to which we now turn.

Hispañola's refugee history has many episodes. During World War II, Dominican dictator Rafael Trujillo welcomed Europe's political refugees as part of his campaign to "Europeanize" a country having significant African heritage (Brookings Institute 1942). Later, the Dominican Republic witnessed repeated influxes of Haitian refugees fleeing their own dictator and, like Salvadorans entering Honduras prior to the infamous Soccer War of 1969, fleeing Haiti's environmental desolation. In the 1980s, Dominican sugar plantations *(bateyes)* gained notoriety for enslaving Haitian workers

TABLE 13.2
Protected Areas in Selected Latin America Countries

Country (1997)	#	Area (1,000 ha)	% of National Areas Protected
Belize	18	478	20.9
Bolivia	31	15,602	14.4
Chile	72	14,134	18.9
Costa Rica	35	707	13.7
Cuba	65	1,907	17.4
Dominican Republic	26	1,523	31.5
Ecuador	20	11,927	43.1
Guatemala	30	1,820	16.8
Panama	21	1,421	19.1
Venezuela	124	31,976	36.3

Source: WRI/UNEP/UNEP (1998)

who, upon experiencing the hardships of the *bateyes*, sought refuge elsewhere in the country. Today, the Dominican Republic (like many other countries) generates large numbers of unnoticed, internal refugees through infrastructural projects (dams, highways, urban renewal, resort spas), as well as through its parks and protected area initiatives.

National parks in the Dominican Republic have expanded noticeably in recent decades. Despite the country's small size, its life zones and biodiversity are significant; it has the highest elevation in the Antilles (3,175 meters) as well as the lowest (40 meters below sea level), yielding a flora of 5,600 species, 36 percent of which are endemic. This information led one author to conclude: "These ecological values have to be protected from human interference in the Dominican Republic like in most parts of the world" (Hoppe 1989, 13). With the assistance of the World Wildlife Fund, The Nature Conservancy, the Spanish Agency for International Conservation, the Global Environmental Facility, and a spectrum of domestic environmental organizations, Dominican national parks have grown from roughly 10 percent of the country in the late 1980s to just over 30 percent today. In 1989 a research team from Cornell University selected Los Haitises National Park (LHNP) on the country's north central coast as a long-term site for studying interactions between ecosystems and human systems.

Like many Third World parks, LHNP is a refuge for people as well as flora and fauna. Its geography is tortuous yet alluring, a deeply eroded karst plateau, with pitted valleys and "haystack" (overhanging) mountains lush with neotropical vegetation. Its relative inaccessibility makes it a safe haven for bereft Haitian and Dominican farmers who maintain families in the small villages around the park and survive on slash-and-burn cultivation within. Infrastructure consists of narrow footpaths and little more. Despite the park status of its core area, the region is rarely patrolled and has suffered incursions in the past by railroad interests seeking timber for ties, cattle interests (domestic and international) seeking free pasture, Haitians seeking deliverance from nearby *bateyes,* and innumerable Dominicans whose lands elsewhere in the country were confiscated between 1930 and 1960 by Rafael Trujillo or devastated by hurricanes of the past half-century.[4]

The hardship of slash-and-burn survival in the forbidding interior of LHNP is offset by the presence of a highly lucrative root crop, *Xanthosoma sagittifolium (yautía),* which is sold locally as well as exported. *Yautía* plots occur throughout the park. In the early years of Cornell's field research, such plots were even eligible for loans by the country's Agricultural Bank. This attracted still more small farmers to the region. It gradually became widely known that, in good times, marginal farmers could make annual income well above the Dominican national average by planting and harvesting *yautía* in LHNP. Subsidized bank credit, a modicum of indigenous knowledge, and open access to the park's interior only increased this likelihood.

LHNP expanded dramatically in the 1990s and with it the country's protected area conservation refugee problem. On the eve of the 1992 Earth Summit in Rio, the Dominican Armed Forces received a presidential order to remove humans and twenty thousand head of cattle from the park. A military census of the region that year put human population between five thousand and twenty thousand (Stycos and Duarte 1993), the uncertainty stemming from unclear park boundaries and the meaning of "permanent resident" (see Geisler et al. 1997). Complicating matters further, in the following year another presidential decree (No. 83–93) quadrupled the park size from 208 to 920 sq. km.; in 1996, still another decree (No. 233–96) pushed the park size to nearly 1,600 sq. km., or more than seven times its original size. Residency within the park was declared illegal, new boundaries were mapped, and the Dominican Army renewed its periodic maneuvers along the park perimeter to intimidate any lingering residents. As the park has expanded in size, its boundaries have overtaken numerous villages that formerly encircled the smaller park (for a similar case see chapter 4).

The expansion of LHNP makes much sense from a conservation standpoint. The park sits atop the country's largest aquifer; its endemism is significant; its geographic location on Samana Bay, at the mouth of which humpback whales from the North Atlantic spend several months each spring, is unmistakably beautiful. Increasing the park from a small preserve to an entire ecosystem—it now encompasses most of the karst platform adjoining the bay—makes its boundary more distinguishable. Its heavy rainfall helps the region recover quickly from slash-and-burn cultivation. When the World

Bank/United Nation's Global Environmental Facility awarded the country research funds to protect coastal zone ecosystems in 1995, there was no hesitation in including LHNP. Nor was there a shortage of interest over including LHNP as a core area in a pending United Nations Biosphere Reserve designation for the region.

Yet LHNP's growth has had unambiguous refugee consequences. In 1996, Cornell and collaborating Dominican researchers interviewed nearly six hundred household heads from the park region, some living in land reform projects, others in urban slums or in squatter settlements near the park. High percentages of these identified military presence in the region since 1992 as the cause of their move (73 percent among those destined for land reform projects and 94 percent of others).[5] The research also explored their degree of victimization, a refugee criterion suggested by Zolberg et al. (1989). Those sampled were asked the extent of suffering their families experienced as a consequence of the 1992 removal and what their families lost in economic terms. More than 90 percent assigned their suffering to the worst category we presented, and even those in land reform projects reported maximum suffering 89 percent of the time.

Respondent assessments of economic loss were also pronounced. Once again, levels of estimated loss averaged 90 percent or more and conformed with what researchers observed first hand; most respondents had lost their *yautía* plots and other income sources, their proximity to friends (farm work in the Dominican Republic is frequently performed through *convite* or reciprocal labor exchanges), and "community" in its many meanings. When we asked respondents to compare their life now with life in the park prior to 1992, only 10 percent of those receiving land reform and housing plots reported better current circumstances. A control group consisting of respondents from communities not forced to move reported high dissatisfaction as well, being cut off from subsistence activities in the park as well as from emergency government rations distributed for several years after the 1992 military census and removal.

Eviction and poorly planned relocation of resident populations from protected areas in the Dominican Republic is not fundamentally different from conservation refugee experiences in many other countries—Indonesia, Brazil, India, Thailand, Guatemala, Mexico, the U.S. Virgin Islands, and many countries in Africa and the Middle East (Colchester 1994; Geisler and de Sousa 2000; Chatty and Colchester 2000) among them. Costa Rica, a model of conservation planning in the Western Hemisphere, has high rates of rural poverty and landlessness. It is rife with squatter settlements that include people dislodged from expanding protected areas throughout the country. The 1997 attack on Guatemala's San Pedro Biological Research Station came from sixty evicted squatters from a national park in a country where the poor are buffeted about by a combination of civil war and large-scale conservation planning (Meyerson 1998). "Conservation," according to the World Wildlife Fund draft discussion paper on eco-regional-level planning, "is about tempering the impact of deleterious human activities on the environment—a goal that puts WWF in opposition to a wide variety of economic actors and interest groups within an ecoregion. . . . Tenure restrictions may have particularly high social costs on politically vulnerable populations" (Freudenberger and Larson 1997, 3).

ADAPTIVE IMPACT ASSESSMENT

Adaptive management has aroused considerable discussion in reference to ecosystem management (Holling 1978; Walters 1986, 1993; Lee 1996, 2001). At its core, it takes an experimental approach to public policy (e.g., protected area management) and performs "replications" based on "experimental" field results, successful or otherwise. It has been applied to fisheries ecosystems in the Columbia River Basin (Volkman and McConnaha 1993) and Tasmania (Peterman and Peters 1998), to forest ecosystems (FEMAT 1993), to river ecosystems (Barinaga 1996), to nature reserves (Fisher 1999) and other protected areas (Buck et al. 2001), and additional settings compiled by Lee (2001) (see also Gunderson et al. 1995). Both social and environmental impact assessment are enhanced by segmenting protected area management into discrete units and episodes which, given this experimental approach, become learning opportunities facilitating subsequent "mid-course management corrections."

There is little doubt, if one accepts that forced migration from homelands ranks high among human traumas, that protected areas built on ecological expropriation should be subject to social impact assessment. SIA is routinely employed in the siting and construction of dams, roads, pipelines, airports, new communities, and other macro-level land use changes. There are precedents as well for using SIA to anticipate the social effects of protected areas (Geisler 1993). Yet SIA practitioners must be realistic in confronting the temporal and spatial challenges of ever larger and "longer" protected areas (Ellis 1989). The multiphased self-correcting logic of adaptive management offers a way to perform and later update SIA.

Such an approach is certainly more valid and valuable than *ex ante* SIA that struggles (with difficulty) to see beyond the horizon and anticipate erratic state policy, migration fluxes, changes in tenure law and park boundaries, new permit agreements, volatile land markets, and ever-changing human values. Crosscutting these vagaries is the conservation refugee phenomenon, a socialcultural impact which may occur in the early stages of protected area implementation (e.g., South Africa's Kruger National Park, Costa Rica's Cahuita National Park, and St. John's National Park in the U.S. Virgin Islands) or much later in the life of the facility (Yosemite National Park, Los Haitises National Park, or India's Greater Himalayan National Park). SIA simply cannot foresee all the eventualities that occasion the eviction of local owners and users from a protected zone. For example, parks and biosphere reserves that commence as integrated conservation and development projects (ICDPs) may convert to people-free protected areas should they fail as ICDPs.

How can adaptive impact assessment improve the situation? The problem is indirectly addressed by Kai Lee in his 1993 book, *Compass and Gyroscope*. Here, "compass" refers to adaptive environmental management. Conservation policy, consistent with the logic of adaptive management, is viewed as an experiment with no right or wrong result. Instead, the commitment is to ever more accurate and useable information that might improve the management objective. "Gyroscope" refers to the steadying influence of democratic public input in the design and execution of the experiment. The combined effect of democratic experimentation in large-scale conservation policy is likely to be that human removal, if it happens at all, will result from negotiations rather than top-down decrees, be performed in stages rather than in one catastrophic event, and include multilevel monitoring and mitigation. Elsewhere, Lee (1996, 337) refines the meaning of "gyroscope," seeing cooperative management of policy experiments as indispensable. He offers as a partial success story the multiparty negotiations over habitat conservation of the Endangered Species Act.[6]

From Lee's perspective, adaptive impact assessment done collaboratively with residents and significant local users has conservation refugee–reducing potential. In a recent appraisal of adaptive management, Lee (2001) stresses that adaptive management will not please those who favor command-and-control approaches to protected areas, but may appeal to those concerned with the ethical dimensions of conservation. Referring in his own way to conservation refugees, he states (2001, 7):

> Those who operate the human infrastructure of harvest—farmers, ranchers, dam operators, loggers, fishers—are usually those who know most, in a day to day sense, about the condition of the ecosystem. Their reports contain information that can be obtained at a reasonable cost. Harvesters also see themselves as stewards of the resources upon which they rely, a claim that frequently turns out to be well-founded.

Lee goes on to emphasize that iterative, "in-stream" impact assessments in the absence of collaboration isn't enough. It leads to the moral dilemma of banishing local people from biologically diverse habitats targeted for conservation. The local human infrastructure, as he calls it, must be encouraged to join with its nonlocal counterparts if the ethical dilemma of involuntary displacement is to be avoided. In simple terms, Lee is willing to accept compromise in the quality of ecosystem management in exchange for environmental justice toward local interests.

Lee's position is not an argument against ecosystem management or protected areas as a means of achieving it. Powerful conservation coalitions, public and private, have marshaled impressive resources to the world's protected areas and change the geography of the world, but only a subset routinely use some form of social impact assessment with "compass and gyroscope" components to distribute benefits widely and mitigate costs. And an even smaller subset considers consultation, robust devolution, and co-management as their ethical responsibility.[7]

The Dominican Republic's approach to protected area creation and growth falls somewhere in between the extremes. Its government met the ethical dilemma with several forms of conservation refugee mitigation but with neither adaptive nor collaborative impact assessment preceding it. The government, responding to protests by local residents, religious groups, and former organizations, spread the eviction of its protected area refugees over several years (which allowed many micro adjustments at the community and household level), provided food rations for asset-deprived families, permitted selected harvesting of LHNP crops, resettled between two and three thousand families on new land reform settlements, and developed alternative buffer zone and overall management models for the region. The hardships for former inhabitants of the park have been undeniably acute, but the deprivation would have been patently worse without these intermediate measures. Conservation biologists and environmental activists in the Dominican Republic are confronting the conservation refugee issue. While not always agreeing on solutions, there is an increasing sense that such refugees should neither go unrecognized nor unaided.

CONCLUSION

Various observers have forecast that by 2050 protected areas, overrun by human settlement and its extensions, may no longer exist. Others worry that "socialized conservation"—partnerships with local residents and users to protect nature—will result in compromises that doom endangered species, habitats, and environmental services. Both views are simplistic in underestimating the ability of humans of many descriptions to learn from deliberative experience. A more likely scenario is that we will both gain and lose protected areas in the future for multiple reasons, that new types of protected areas will continue to emerge with new management strategies, and that the ethical issues surrounding conservation refugees will be increasingly debated. New and existing protected areas will be viable, in the opinion of this author, to the extent that collaborative adaptive management is embedded in the planning, execution, and evaluation components of such projects; or, in contemporary terms, in their upstream, instream, and downstream phases. Other things being equal, however, the total area dedicated to conservation will continue to grow in the future. If we accept the ethical challenge Lee and others pose regarding residents and users of areas targeted for protection, the conservation refugee phenomenon may subside. But there is no room for complacency. Some predict that current food production technologies make it possible to retire up to one-third of the planet's land now in agriculture and expand nature conservation proportionately (Waggoner 1994). The implication is that protected areas could expand onto former agricultural lands without harm to world food supplies. Perhaps, but little thought is given here to who resides on these lands or to their plight if such conversion occurs. It is time to ask how working landscapes could be viewed as experimental sites for combinations of conservation and production subject to adaptive impact assessment rather than as sites in which human displacement is a "necessary" cost of conservation.

NOTES

This research was made possible thanks to funding from the Cornell International Institute for Food, Agriculture and Development (CIIFAD) and the Global Environmental Facility (Project Number DOM/94/G31). I am grateful to Norman Uphoff, Mary Kritz, Barbara Bedford, and Gigi Berardi, the editors and reviewers of this book and of a related work (Geisler and de Sousa 2001) for useful insights.

1. Social impact assessment is the *ex ante* estimation of the social consequences likely to arise from a specific public policy actions, particularly in the context of the U.S. National Environmental Policy Act of 1969 or its overseas equivalents (U.S. Dept. of Commerce 1994).

2. There is continuing interest in how population growth and rising consumption patterns among each new generation contribute to greenhouse gas emissions and global warming, which may affect sea level change and lead to coastal zone evacuation. See Green (1992) for a summary overseas impacts Irish potato famine victims and the "Okies" in Steinbeck's *Grapes of Wrath* were early environmental refugees.

3. *The World Almanac and Book of Facts* (1999, 864), citing the 1998 World Refugee Survey, states that, as of December 31, 1997, for countries estimated to host at least 50,000 refugees, there were 616,000 refugees throughout the Americas and the Caribbean. 491,000 were in the United States, leaving 125,000 in other countries of the hemisphere. At most, a quarter of the remaining refugees lived in the Caribbean islands, a number well below the estimate number of protected area refugees from LHNP (estimates that do not count Haitians sequestered in the park). Readers interested in conservation refugees in Africa should see Geisler and Let-soalo (2000); Geisler and de Souza (2001); Chatty and Colchester (2002); and Brockington (2002).

4. For a recent account of Haitian refugees in the Dominican Republic, see Kirk (1992).

5. Source: IEPD/Cornell Survey: Encuesta sobre Población y Medio Ambiente en el PNLH, March, 1996.

6. Lee is no romantic. His 1996 work suggests that preservation of pristine environments under the adaptive management model may no longer be an option; that is, there may be dire trade-offs if an inclusionary rather than exclusionary approach is taken to resident human populations.

7. Von Benda-Beckmann (1997) explores the complexities of human rights perspectives applied to indigenous people, complexities that multiply when nonindigenous but marginalized groups are included.

Chapter Fourteen

The Challenges and Rewards of Community-Based Coastal Resources Management

San Salvador Island, Philippines

PATRICK CHRISTIE, DELMA BUHAT,
LEN R. GARCES, ALAN T. WHITE

The residents of San Salvador Island, off the coast of Masinloc, Zambales, in the Philippines, face challenges typical of fishing communities in the Philippines. Lack of awareness and poverty have encouraged fishers to use unsound fishing methods such as explosives, sodium cyanide, and fine-mesh nets. Swidden upland agriculture and logging has resulted in the deforestation of much of the nearby Zambales Mountains, which contributes to the siltation of San Salvador's coral reefs. These factors have resulted in declining fish yields from the island's coral reefs beginning in the early 1980s, according to local fishers.

Social conditions common to many small Philippine communities had encouraged San Salvador residents to believe that such a downward trend in environmental quality was irreversible. Inclusion into a demanding and largely unregulated market economy and the influence of unscrupulous local leaders and government officials, who supported destructive fishing methods for their own gain, had created the perception among San Salvador fishers that management of the local coral reef and fishery resources was beyond their control. The financial and organizational limitations of the Philippine government prevented it from addressing these complex resource management problems. Furthermore, numerous case studies have demonstrated that complete reliance on the national government is rarely the most effective strategy in the Philippines (Christie et al. 2002; Christie and White 2000; Ferrer et al. 1996; White et al. 1994). There is a strong consensus among many observers that natural resources cannot be sustainably managed unless those who use the resources perceive it to be in their interest and are deeply involved in the planning and management process (Burkey 1993; Christie and White 1997; Korten 1990; Olsen and Christie 2000; Pollnac et al. 2001; Pomeroy 1995).

The concept of community-based development or resource management is based on the principal that people are capable of understanding and resolving many of their own environmental problems (Burkey 1993; Freire 1993; Korten 1990). Community-based resource management evolved in the Philippines from experiences in community development and community organizing projects (Deguit 1989; Ferrer et al. 1996). The impetus for the community-based development model began in the mid-1940s when the government was implementing top-down infrastructure development projects. This approach was found to be ineffective in terms of creating long-term, holistic development. Consequently, the growing discontent over the socio-economic and political situation and the ineffectiveness of delivery of services from the government sectors led religious organizations and other community sectors to form groups to affect societal change through mass organizations or unions. These organizations were more effective in stimulating collective, long-term mobilizations and the community organizing approach—which includes education, capacity building, and implementation of concrete projects—was popularized and adapted by many Philippine organizations working for community-level economic development and resource management.

In response to largely unsuccessful attempts to sustainably manage marine resources throughout the Philippines, Silliman University initiated a community-based resource management approach on three islands: Apo, Pamilacan, and Balicasag (Cabanban and White 1981; White and Savina 1986). All are highly successful examples of local people benefiting from active involvement in the management of their reef fisheries (Alcala 1998; White 1988), although recent research demonstrates limitations of relying solely on marine protected areas for fisheries management (Christie et al. 2002). The main objectives of this community-based resource management plan are: to empower the community to become active and functional as a self-reliant entity, to equip community members with knowledge and skills for sustainable resource management, and to build the capabilities of community members in establishing links with support groups (Ferrer et al. 1996). The lack of attention to these fundamental practices has contributed to the high rate of marine protected areas failure in the Philippines (White et al. 2002). The Marine Conservation Project for San Salvador (MCPSS) began in 1989 by encouraging the island community to address the problems of resource mismanagement through education, local organizing, and community involvement in the establishment of a municipal marine reserve and sanctuary. Introduced by two community fieldworkers, this approach helped to reverse the decline of the island's coral reef and associated fishery. The island's culturally heterogeneous population, low per capita income, poor coral reef status, conflicts between legal and illegal resident fishers, and easy accessibility by nonresident fishers are typical of many Philippine islands. Therefore, a case study of the process and the results of the MCPSS provides useful information for furthering the tradition of community-based resource management.

PROFILE OF SAN SALVADOR ISLAND

San Salvador Island, with an area of 380 hectares, is approximately two kilometers west of Masinloc, Zambales. The hilly interior is approximately 30 percent secondary growth forest, 60 percent rice fields, and 10 percent mango tree groves. Off the northern, western, and southern coasts are wide reef flats dominated by seagrass *(Enhalus acoroides, Thalassia hemprichii)* and sargassum *(Sargassum oligocystum)* beds. The fringing coral reefs, routinely exposed to intense wave action during the monsoon season (July to October), exhibit deep spur and groove formations dominated by massive and encrusting coral types. Protected areas, with more delicate branching corals *(Acropora spp.)*, were heavily damaged by decades of dynamite and sodium cyanide use prior to the MCPSS.

In 1988, surveys of the substrate cover documented a range of 5–50 percent living coral cover, with an average coverage of 23 percent for the whole island (Christie and White 1994). The average dead standing coral cover was 19 percent. Table 14.1 displays the results of the 1988 substrate surveys in the least damaged area, which was declared a sanctuary, and the surrounding traditional fishing reserve area. These findings are similar to those of Gomez and Yap (1982) where, out of twelve reef sample stations in Zambales, two were in good condition (50–74.9 percent living coral cover), three in fair condition (25–49.9 percent), and seven in poor condition (0–24.9 percent).

Currently, approximately 1,620 people, comprising 284 families, live on San Salvador (Katon et al. 1999). This represents an 8 percent increase from 1989. Four ethnic backgrounds are represented on San Salvador. Sambals comprise approximately 50 percent of the population, Ilocanos and Pangasinenses approximately 20 percent, and Visayans approximately 30 percent

TABLE 14.1
Coral Reef Substrate Cover and Topography for San Salvador Island in 1988

Parameters	Sanctuary (ST mean)		Traditional Fishing Reserve (ST mean)	
	%	(n=20)	%	(n=20)
Sand	8	(13)	13	(16)
Rubble	12	(16)	16	(18)
Blocks	36	(23)	9	(14)
Dead standing coral	9	(14)	29	(22)
Marine plants	9	(14)	13	(16)
Live hard corals	20	(19)	4	(9)
Live soft coral	6	(11)	16	(18)
Total coral cover	26	(21)	20	(19)
Topography (m)*	2.8			

ST   Snorkel transect.
( )   95% confidence intervals.
*   Meters of additional surface area per horizontal 10 m. (a measure of surface contour).

(Dizon and Miranda 1996). Each ethnic group tends to live separately from the others. Most people depend directly on the island's natural resources for their livelihood. About 64 percent of the residents derive their principal income from fishing, 23 percent from farming, 4 percent from trading, and 9 percent from service-related occupations (Katon et al. 1999). In 1989, monthly incomes ranged from US$44 to US$66 for families who farmed or used traditional fishing methods. Family income from aquarium fishing was approximately US$100 per month.

Most people live in one of four villages on the island's coast. Typical occupations, cultural background, and family linkages are fairly homogeneous within each village but there are major differences between villages in these regards. One group of people, the Visayan aquarium fish gatherers, has never fully integrated with the rest of the island's community. Their isolation is due, in part, to linguistic differences and resentment among other community members regarding the aquarium fish gatherers' use of sodium cyanide. These population and economic conditions are prevalent in many Central Luzon fishing communities (McManus 1988).

San Salvador Island is a *barangay* of Masinloc, Zambales. The *barangay* is a smallest unit of local government in the Philippines. San Salvador has a *Barangay Council,* with one *Barangay Captain* and six Councilors, which is the island's formal governing body. Unlike many Filipino communities, religious organizations do not play a central role in local island social dynamics. Informal fishing organizations revolve around activities that require joint effort. For example, informal social networks developed around the use of certain fishing gear that required a number of people to operate (e.g., beach seines) and transportation activities that required a high level of coordination (e.g., the transport of aquarium fish to Manila). However, as of 1987, no formal fishery-related organizations such as cooperatives existed.

In 1987, upon arrival of one fieldworker, many of the island's residents considered their *barangay* poorly organized and economically underdeveloped in comparison to other nearby *barangays*. Community members cited corruption, intense political rivalries between local leaders, and a general lack of interest from government agencies in this relatively remote *barangay*. Nonetheless, in comparison to other small islands in the Philippines, San Salvador's proximity to the mainland and Manila (approximately 250 km.) makes it accessible to national-level government and nongovernmental agencies which can potentially provide funding, facilities, and technical assistance.

Although the details of fishing traditions prior to habitation of the island (approximately three generations ago) are unknown, interviews with local people provide some insight as to customs and conditions after habitation. According to residents, the island was surrounded with rich fishing grounds that amply supported residents until World War II. With the threat of starvation, occupying Japanese troops used explosives to catch fish, thus introducing blast fishing. In the late 1960s, families from the Visayan region of the Philippines began to arrive. By the early 1970s, these people were catching aquarium fish for a rapidly growing export market mainly in the United States. These aquarium fish gatherers used sodium cyanide, which damages the reef and kills juvenile fish, to collect these fish (Barber and Pratt 1997). Simultaneously, fishery development programs during the Marcos era provided loans to people for the purchase of motorized boats and highly efficient fishing equipment that contributed to overfishing. Local people maintain that their average daily fish catch declined from approximately 20 kg in the 1960s to only 1–3 kg in 1988 (Katon et al. 1999).

Currently, the San Salvador fishery is a complicated mosaic of subsistence and commercial activity on the family, municipal, national, and international scale. Approximately 75 percent of the San Salvador fishers rely on traditional methods such as nets and spears to catch fish. Most of their catch is sold in the local market in Masinloc, the nearest town, while any remaining fish is for family consumption. High quality fish, such as tuna or grouper, is often purchased in Masinloc by fish dealers who transport it to Manila for sale. Aquarium fish are transported to Manila by local fishers and then exported mainly to the United States and Europe.

Prior to the introduction of destructive fishing technology and the inclusion of these communities into an insatiable commercial market system, the fishery met the needs of the local people. Perhaps as a result of the abundance of the resources and the fact that the island area had been colonized mainly by farmers from the mainland without fisheries management traditions, strong local traditions to manage fish stocks did not exist. Open access to the resource coupled with destructive methods led to a desperate situation in which people continued to place ever-greater stress on the resource. Complaints by local fishers about the lack of fish, the negative impacts of destructive fishing methods, and their concern for their future well-being were the impetus behind the MCPSS.

THE MARINE CONSERVATION PROJECT FOR SAN SALVADOR

The MCPSS was patterned after the Silliman University Marine Conservation and Development Program (White and Savina 1987). The approach is holistic and depends heavily on the community's participation. Table 14.2 outlines the specific objectives of the MCPSS. Considering the multifaceted challenges the community and the fieldworkers faced, the MCPSS achieved significant results. A review of the methods, accomplishments, and limitations follows (See Table 14.2).

A U.S. Peace Corps Volunteer (the first author) spent one year assessing the community's needs and level of understanding of basic environmental/ecological concepts through informal interviews of residents. He studied the condition of the island's coral reef through snorkel surveys. With input from select island residents, he prepared a proposal for a community-based resource management project for financial support. The vast majority of local fishers identified destructive fishing methods and declining yields as the most important issues to address. At this point, however, only a few community members were actively involved in the drafting of the proposal since certain community leaders were allegedly involved in illegal fishing, making the issue controversial.

Subsequent to securing financial support (approximately US$10,000) from the Netherlands Consulate in Manila, the Haribon Foundation, one of the largest environmental nongovernmental organizations in the Philippines, became the implementing agency of the MCPSS. The MCPSS project was inaugurated in December 1988 and fieldwork began in January 1989. After moving to San Salvador, a Filipina community organizer (the second author) conducted a socioeconomic survey with the involvement of the community. Initially, only a few highly motivated individuals actively participated in the MCPSS while other community members expressed interest, though were reluctant to directly participate. The hesitance of some of the community

TABLE 14.2
Objectives of the MCPSS

1. To enhance the institutional capabilities of local and national governmental and nongovernmental institutions to implement a community-based resource management project, by increasing their understanding of basic marine ecology, fisheries dynamics, and resource management techniques.

2. To develop and implement a marine resource management plan based on the results of socioeconomic and environmental surveys that would establish a coral reef protected area that consisted of a sanctuary and a traditional fishing reserve area surrounding the island. The management plan's intention would be to discourage destructive fishing and to increase fish abundance, fish diversity, and long-term fish yields from the island's reef.

3. To encourage community development through the formation and strengthening of local community groups responsible for marine resource management and alternative income programs. To construct a guest/meeting house at the shore of the sanctuary for meetings, education programs, and tourism.

4. To train fishers using sodium cyanide in the use of barrier nets for the collection of tropical aquarium fish.

5. To initiate a small erosion control program along the island's heavily eroded dirt road by planting tree seedlings.

6. To replicate and extend the project to neighboring fishing communities and establish linkages with other local and national organizations concerned with marine management problems and their solutions.

members may be attributed to a historic failure of development programs on the island, the sensitive nature that the project addressed, and distrust or disinterest in the environmentalist agenda. Education programs, which highlighted the poor condition of the island's resources and the potential increased fish yields and other benefits that the MCPSS might bring about, eventually convinced more community members to support its objectives.

The ongoing education program used formal and informal approaches. Monthly education programs used slide shows, role playing, and lectures to explore basic ecological and environmental concepts and highlighted reef survey results. Field outings with children and an environmental drawing contest were also effective means to engage these future resource users. Prior to any education programs, the average score on a basic ecology/environment questionnaire for randomly selected residents was 69 percent. Fourteen months later, the average was 86 percent.

A field trip to a successful sanctuary project on Apo Island, Negros Oriental, by seven San Salvador residents was a key activity that allowed these residents to discuss the implications of marine conservation and protected areas with other Filipino fishers. As a result of their visit to the Apo Island sanctuary and discussions with residents there, the San Salvador residents formed the "Lupong Tagapangasiwa ng Kapaligiran" (LTK) or the Environment Management Committee. The LTK was the core group that educated and encouraged other residents to participate in the MCPSS.

TOWARD A MARINE SANCTUARY MANAGEMENT PLAN

During two well-attended general assembly meetings on San Salvador, community members drafted a resolution for the establishment of a 127–hectare marine sanctuary that was made off limits to fishing. Illegal or unsound fishing methods were also banned in a traditional fishing reserve area surrounding the rest of the island and the sanctuary. A large majority of the community also initially decided to ban aquarium fish gathering in the traditional fishing reserve, regardless of methods employed, because of the persistent use of sodium cyanide by some individuals. This act alienated aquarium fish gatherers who claimed to use nets supplied by the MCPSS. At this time, the community organizer focused her attention on consulting with alienated community members and conflict resolution. Ultimately they chose to abide by the ban on aquarium fishing but continued to collect elsewhere with cyanide in most cases. Some spouses of aquarium fish gatherers became very active in the MCPSS.

In July 1989, the LTK and fieldworkers presented a *barangay* resolution to the Masinloc Municipal Council and the mayor. This resulted in the unanimous approval of a municipal ordinance (Municipal Ordinance 30–89) legalizing the sanctuary and reserve. Masinloc's mayor and Catholic priest were outspoken advocates for the sanctuary and MCPSS. This ordinance provided the necessary political and legal endorsement allowing community members to enforce their *barangay* resolution with the assurance that local agencies would support them. Further support for the ordinance was assured through the 1989 election of a supporter of the MCPSS as San Salvador's *Barangay Captain*.

Subsequent alterations of the ordinance through general assembly approval included a ban on a beach seine–type fishing technique *(kunay)*, in which a long scareline of coconut fronds is dragged along the reef. The ruling on *kunay* required a series of assembly meetings and ultimately resulted in tensions between people for and against the method. The majority of the island's residents felt that the method caused overfishing and coral damage. This method, which also used very fine-meshed nets, collected primarily juvenile fish of only fifteen cm. average length. Following a petition by the *kunay* group for the intervention of the mayor as mediator, a general vote was held which banned the method in the reserve area. The one group of fishers who used the method resented the ban since they felt that their method was a traditional, nondestructive method. They also expressed frustration since they had originally supported the sanctuary resolution and now were being harmed by the agreement. While the *kunay* group stopped using this method around San Salvador, they continued to use the method on other nearby islands. Eventually, however, these surrounding communities also prohibited them from using this method in their waters, reportedly for the same reasons for which it was banned on San Salvador.

In 1990, one of the community fieldworkers applied for a Fisheries Administrative Order (FAO) from the Department of Agriculture on the community's behalf to further legitimize the municipal ordinance at the national level. At that time, Philippine law required a FAO, which is a specific regulatory statement signed by the minister of the Department of Agriculture, for the establishment of any sanctuary. For reasons that are unclear, a FAO was never granted. Perhaps the San Salvador municipal ordinance was perceived as a threat to authority traditionally held by the national government agency. The Local Government Code passed in 1991, transferring control over waters out to fifteen kilometers to the municipal government, removed the need for a FAO and further legitimized the municipal ordinance.

Eventually, interest within the national government for community-based initiatives grew steadily through the early 1990s. A number of community-based marine protected areas (including Masinloc Bay and Apo Island) were declared as part of a National Integrated Protected Areas System (NIPAS) (Presidential Proclamation No. 231). In 1993, all of Masinloc Bay was named a National Protected Seascape with zoning for different uses of the marine environment. San Salvador was declared a protected area within this zoning. Designation as a NIPAS site necessitated the establishment of a multisectoral managing board with local government, regional government, private sector, and community representation. This declaration legitimated these small marine protected areas, however it also took some control away from communities and bureaucratized decision-making processes.

The sanctuary was marked by buoys and signs written in the national language. However, the loss of buoys has been a perennial problem and enforcement of the sanctuary/reserve ordinance has been challenging. Initially, there was no regular patrol of the sanctuary since it was thought that the proximity of the sanctuary to houses allowed for easy surveillance. Typically, once a violator had been spotted a member of the LTK or the *Barangay Council* was notified. Most community members felt that it was more effective if these authority figures confronted violators. Community fieldworkers refused to become directly involved in the enforcement of the ordinance, feeling that it was an inappropriate role. If local authority figures from the island felt unable to confront a violator, they would contact the municipal government for support. A graduated sanctions system, ranging from warnings, to monetary fines, to boat impounding, was established and enforced depending on the severity of the infraction.

Of thirty-nine violations, during the first eight months after the establishment of the protected area, thirty-five were by nonresident fishers from the southern Philippines. Local residents who violated the sanctuary claimed that they did so out of economic need or temptation when large schools of fish were spotted in the sanctuary. These violators were warned and did not repeat their violations. Almost all nonresident violators claimed ignorance of the ordinance. These violators, as recommended by the municipal government, were only identified and warned. Second-time violators (all of which were nonresidents) were fined by the community environment management committee, the LTK. If violators refused to pay the fine, the case was forwarded to the municipal government's judicial system. If violators were unable to pay a fine, their catch was sold, with the proceeds used by the LTK for the maintenance of the sanctuary. In one case, local people reported a group of divers from the southern Philippines for collecting lobster from a large vessel inside the sanctuary at night. The municipal mayor ordered the confiscation of the boat until a fine was paid. Community members did not confront the violators directly, fearing that firearms were on board.

Based on records kept by local residents who enforced the ordinance, most violations (72 percent) after 1989 involved fishing in the sanctuary (Katon et al. 1999). Other violations included aquarium fish gathering in the reserve (10 percent), the use of air compressors to dive in the reserve (10 percent), blast fishing (4 percent), and the use of fine mesh nets (4 percent). Nonresidents continued to be the main violators. Violators were warned (49 percent), fined (19 percent), asked to surrender the boat and fishing gear (13 percent), and imprisoned (7 percent). In other cases fish catch was confiscated (4 percent), live fish were returned to the sea (4 percent), and an individual was shot in the leg for failing to heed the warnings of marine guards (Katon et al. 1999).

On occasion, the ordinance was not enforced. When the sanctuary and reserve were not regularly patrolled, some violators were not confronted. Also, if a person of authority was not readily available, other residents commonly chose not to confront the violator, either out of fear, apathy, or deference to those in positions of authority. It is uncertain, however, that a more formalized enforcement procedure would be consistently more effective. When a police detachment was assigned by the municipal government at the request of the LTK to protect the sanctuary, officers were bribed to tolerate violations (Dizon and Miranda 1996). The final, seemingly most effective, approach to enforcement has been the formation of a deputized group of wardens from the municipality in 1993. This group, named *Bantay Dagat* or protectors of the sea, have received training and are legally authorized by municipal authorities to apprehend violators of the protected area. The municipal government has provided the *Bantay Dagat* with funds to cover food, fuel, and a patrol boat.

Instances of dynamite and cyanide fishing have declined dramatically. Prior to passage of the MCPSS ordinance, an average of 3.2 dynamite blasts per day during the calm season in 1987 were heard along the island's western coast. Since passage of the ordinance, dynamite fishing is rare. The local aquarium gatherers accepted and respected the ban on gathering in the reserve area. The ordinance was subsequently amended to allow only free diving for aquarium fish with the use of fine-mesh nets. However, few divers collect in the reserve possibly due to their continued reliance on sodium cyanide, which they use elsewhere. Local aquarium fish gatherers have commented on the return of valuable aquarium fish to the reserve and sanctuary areas.

Through the efforts of the International Marinelife Alliance-Canada, fifty-four of the San Salvador aquarium fish gatherers (approximately 95 percent) participated in two week-long training courses on the use of barrier nets in 1990. A Haribon Foundation community organizer facilitated the formation of an active aquarium fish gatherers association whose purpose was to police its own ranks, explore potential alternative income projects and develop marketing network for net-captured aquarium fish. These community groups, however, are no longer active since the demand for net-caught fish has never been consistent and the use of cyanide results in higher yields according to local divers. In some instances, the gatherers declare that exporters demand the use of cyanide to ensure high yields.

Enforcement of the marine sanctuary and reserve has been problematic. The sanctioning of local people for violations has, at times, created considerable controversy. From 1989 to 1997, the emergence of the *Barangay Captain*, who is also the president of the Masinloc-wide *Bantay Dagat*, as the main advocate for strict enforcement of fisheries laws and the San Salvador ordinance has led to complaints by some that he is overly rigid and autocratic. Other residents appreciate this person's and the *Bantay Dagat*'s staunch commitment to enforcement. Participation in enforcement is undoubtedly dangerous. One *Bantay Dagat* member from Masinloc was murdered, reportedly as a result of his strict enforcement of the ban on the use of cyanide in Masinloc Bay.

The strategy used on San Salvador, founded on local participation, eventually attracted considerable national attention and resulted in the awarding of a prestigious national award in community development to the MCPSS in 1996. The *Barangay Captain* was awarded a national *Barangay Captain* of the Year award for his role in community development and resource management.

IMPACTS ON THE MARINE RESOURCE BASE

Underwater censuses, using a method developed by Russ (1984) and refined by White (1988), to determine fish abundance and diversity (in nineteen families) within the sanctuary and reserve confirmed that San Salvador's reef was in poor condition prior to the protected area's establishment. San Salvador had on average only 322 fish per 500 m² in May 1989 (prior to ordinance passage), followed by 431 fish for the same area in March 1990 (see figure 14.1). Fish densities increased to 460 fish per 500 m² in April 1991 and peaked at 1,200 fish per 500 m² in April 1998. A decline to 777 fish per 500 m² in June 1999 is likely due to the passage of a typhoon days prior to the survey and natural seasonal fluctuations in reef fish abundance. When only high valued target species (in eleven families) are considered, the trend is a gradually increasing one. The average fish density for the time period 1989 to 1991 period was 373 per 500 m² as compared to an average fish density of 1041 per 500 m² for the time period 1998 and 1999. This represents a significant increase in fish density between the 1989 to 1991 period to the 1998 to 1999 period (Christie and White 1994; Garces et al. 1998; Katon et al. 1999). Species richness has increased from 126 species belonging to nineteen families in 1988 to 138 species belonging to twenty-eight families in 1998 (Christie and White 1994; Garces et al. 1998). Although detailed yield studies ceased in 1990, local fishers have noted an increase of fish catch, especially of those species that are schooling and were the preferred target of dynamite fishers (e.g., fusiliers), since the initiation of the MCPSS. The coral reef itself has also begun to

FIGURE 14.1
Temporal Changes in Fish Density in the
Marine Sanctuary and Reserve of San Salvador Island

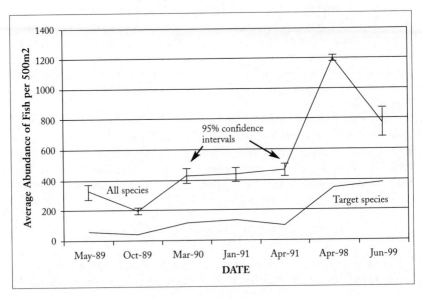

recover. Living coral cover increased from 23 percent in 1988 to 57 percent in 1998 (Christie and White 1994; Garces et al. 1998). While not quantified, the coral bleaching event of 1999 appears to have temporarily reduced living coral cover in some areas, particularly where water circulation was minimal and warm water was trapped.

In comparison to Apo Island's sanctuary, where on average 1,427 fish were counted per 500 m^2 in 1985, followed by 3,899 fish in 1986 (White and Savina 1986), overall fish abundance is still considerably lower on San Salvador. San Salvador's lower fish density in comparison to Apo Island's is possibly due to the heavy damage incurred in the past and differences in natural productivity between the sites.

COMMUNITY DEVELOPMENT AND ORGANIZATION

Community residents and fieldworkers also worked to establish associated activities to support sustainable resource management. Considerable effort was expended on the establishment of alternative income projects for residents as a means to reduce fishing effort and increase incomes. Early in the MCPSS, small groups of people on the island took out small loans to start income-generating projects. Ten families started swine-rearing projects. A fish-vending scheme involved another five families. All of these early attempts at alternative income development failed to be sustained, principally because local mechanisms for the management of these programs were very weak. Pigs were butchered at fiesta times or sold to meet immediate financial needs. Similarly, most of the small loans were never paid back (Dizon and Miranda 1996). Considerable effort by Haribon workers to this aspect of the MCPSS never resulted in effective alternative income development.

Community members constructed a sanctuary guest/meeting house on the shores of the sanctuary. It serves as a center for MCPSS-related activities and shelter for project visitors and tourists. Within the first five months from the initiation of the sanctuary, donations of more than 2,200 pesos ($100) were collected from guests and used for the continuation of the conservation efforts. Donations continue to be collected.

Community organizing, leadership skill development, networking with outside organizations, and the principle of community involvement at almost all stages of the MCPSS comprised the overall approach to implementation. The initial output of this process was the formation of the LTK, which, as mentioned, grew directly out of the Apo Island field trip experience. Participants on the field trip were those community residents most concerned with local marine resource issues. Upon their return to San Salvador, they began to assist the fieldworkers with mobilizing other residents to become involved in the MCPSS. One year after the field trip, LTK elections were held with subsequent regular elections for seven years. The size and gender balance of this committee changed continuously. Some of the most committed members were women. The responsibility of the LTK, as designated by its own members, was to develop MCPSS plans, introduce them to the community, and to encourage their involvement and support. Most MCPSS activities relied on considerable dialogue between the fieldworkers and the LTK members. For example, most of the fieldworkers' project ideas were discussed and reviewed by the LTK before actions were taken. As the leadership skills of the LTK members improved, they developed ideas independently. The LTK did not, however, make decisions for the wider San Salvador community. All regulatory decisions were made at the community level through general assemblies that were called with the support of the *Barangay Council*.

Certain key events seemed to have been decisive in reaffirming the residents' commitment to marine conservation, a phenomenon common to many social organizations when faced with adversity (Morris and Mueller 1992). One such event was the decision in 1990 of the national government to construct a large, coal-fired power plant on the mainland only approximately three kilometers from the San Salvador sanctuary. Thermal and air pollution were of immediate concern to local people and the municipal government. The municipal government and residents active in the MCPSS jointly led a movement in opposition to the plant. Rallies were organized and San Salvador leaders spoke on the issue before the national congress and ministry heads. After prolonged negotiations, the plant was approved by the Department of Environment and Natural Resources on the grounds of national economic development, but only after strict regulations and monitoring procedures involving local leaders were established as part of the environmental clearance certificate in 1993. Nonetheless, this monitoring body is only sporadically active and violations of the certificate reportedly have not spurred further action.

Besides key events such as the energy plant controversy, the participation of San Salvador residents in national and local-level environmental networks has solidified commitment. The opportunity to exchange experiences with others facing similar challenges appears to strengthen leaders' resolution. Furthermore, frequent visitation by study groups and the perception of San Salvador as a role model for community-based coastal resource management has also instilled some level of pride in island residents.

Throughout its existence, the LTK has gone through periods of relative activity and quiescence that seem to be related to member commitment, support from project staff, and local government backing (Dizon and Miranda 1996; Morris and Mueller 1992). After the formal withdrawal of full-time fieldworkers from the area workshops in 1993, Haribon occasionally organized workshops focusing on the development of new leaders, while reinforcing the commitment of the original leaders. These occasional interventions seemed to have successfully solidified resident commitment to the LTK, at least temporarily. Eventually, however, the LTK's role in marine conservation was subsumed by the *Bantay Dagat*, which focused on the enforcement of the sanctuary and reserve's regulations. Since 1997, the LTK has been largely inactive. The inactivity of the LTK has probably resulted in lowered participation in marine conservation efforts. Nonetheless, enforcement of the reserve/sanctuary ordinance continues.

ESTABLISHING A RESILIENT
RESOURCE MANAGEMENT REGIME

In 1997, the local political conditions changed considerably with the elections of a new *Barangay Captain* for San Salvador and a new mayor for Masinloc. The current *Barangay Captain*, who is the individual that held the office prior to the elections in 1989, is a social and political rival of the one that had been supportive of the establishment of the reserve and sanctuary. During interviews conducted in 2000, the current *Barangay Captain* expressed his support for marine resource management and wished that marine sanctuary enforcement was subsumed by the *Barangay Council*. The ex-*Barangay Captain* and many local residents characterized this as a ploy to relax enforcement of the sanctuary/reserve ordinance. The ex-*Barangay Captain*, who is currently the president of the *Bantay Dagat*, is unwilling to coordinate his enforcement efforts with the current *Barangay Council*.

The new mayor came forth to help resolve this issue. In June 1999, he convened a meeting of the opposing factions and made it clear he is committed to marine conservation, that the enforcement of the ordinance will continue, that the *Bantay Dagat* will oversee this enforcement through their coordination with law enforcement agencies, that the *Bantay Dagat* will be required to coordinate with the *Barangay Council* in enforcement, and that the personal rivalry between the current and ex-*Barangay Captains* should not stand in the way of ordinance enforcement.

Clearly, the past fourteen years of marine resource management on San Salvador Island is best described as a complex process that highlights the challenges of introducing resource management in difficult conditions. As a process that attempted to simultaneously address multiple development and resource management issues, such mixed responses should be expected. Research by external investigators (Katon et al. 1999) confirm this conclusion and suggest that the establishment of a co-management process involving the community and local government has been fundamental to any sustained successes. Based on extensive survey research, these investigators maintain that the following factors have supported a co-management regime: (1) stakeholder recognition of resource management problems, (2) supportive and committed local leader-ship, (3) specification and enforcement of user rights, (4) provision of legal and policy support and effective enforcement, (5) capacity building, (6) participation of partners and sense of ownership of co-management arrangements, (7) clarity of objectives, (8) positive attitude among partners toward rules and collective action, and (9) dissemination of tangible benefits.

The establishment of a strong co-management regime, which involves both community and municipal leaders, is probably the best mechanism to ensure the continuation of marine resource management in the face of constant challenges, such as the current local political rivalries (Pollnac et al. 2001; Pomeroy 1995). It is important to recognize that the establishment of this co-management process required that considerable attention be paid initially at the community level in order to raise awareness, to reach agreement about resource issues, and to strengthen community-level organizations. Attention at the community level improved the ability of the community to effectively interact with relatively powerful government agencies with some degree of parity. Thus, educational and community organizing efforts, which are the cornerstones of community-based resource management, were crucial for the development of local capacity for co-management. Co-management, based on the interaction of groups of individuals with grossly unbalanced levels of influence and power, is likely to result in inequitable social arrangements (Christie 1999; Christie et al. 2000). Eventually, inequities tend to quickly erode local support for resource management regimes, thus making their continuation unlikely.

LESSONS LEARNED

Social and environmental problems in a community such as San Salvador are complex and deep-seated. The MCPSS, despite its successes, has also had considerable difficulties meeting all of its objectives.

San Salvador provides students of community-based resource management and protected areas a rich case study by which to improve their practice. The following are some lessons that may be drawn from this case. Such an analysis is not meant to suggest that such responses are necessarily appropriate in all contexts.

Addressing multiple issues simultaneously is challenging, but possible.

At its initial stages, the primary difficulty of the MCPSS was the occasional inability of the project leaders (LTK, Barangay Council members, and field-workers) to coordinate activities among themselves and with the community. Too many activities were attempted at once and/or plans were not carried through to completion. Sometimes, these leaders took too much responsibility upon themselves without the full support of the community's residents. This may be the result of the inexperience of leaders combined with the limitations of the fieldworkers.

Membership in the voluntary community organizations requires a strong commitment to community development. While direct monetary gain is not an incentive, members do, however, enjoy some prestige through their association with the MCPSS. However, overreliance on a small group of leaders can result in "burn-out" and the narrowing of community participation.

Local political processes are influential.

Local political rivalries and social dynamics in the community have strongly influenced the implementation of the MCPSS. Prior to the MCPSS, the Barangay Council was largely inactive. The tensions between the group of community residents interested in marine resource management and the relatively disinterested Barangay Council was resolved when supportive individuals were elected Barangay Captain and mayor. The election of a new *Barangay Captain,* who is the political and personal rival of the supportive ex-*Barangay Captain,* may eventually undermine the management regime. External assistance with conflict resolution by Haribon or the mayor may be necessary if the management regime is to continue.

A degree of alienation is likely.

The profound change in attitude and behavior with the MCPSS, which encouraged some degree of alienation, especially by illegal fishers, was probably unavoidable. Differing opinions toward the MCPSS has stressed what little community unity existed prior to the MCPSS. To the degree possible, resource management plans should provide training in alternative livelihoods to destructive fishing, before alienation occurs. With this approach, alienation of the aquarium fish gatherers and kunay fishers from the MCPSS may have been avoided. In addition, workshops for local leaders stressing conflict resolution skills may be helpful. In the end, however, difficult decisions that negatively affect some people may be necessary if sustainable resource use is to be attained. This further justifies the establishment of an inclusive, transparent, and fair decison-making process that balances short- and long-term considerations.

Rapid resource recovery is possible.

Although the severely degraded environment of San Salvador precludes a rapid return to full productivity, the relative improvement in reef condition and fish abundance is dramatic. Furthermore, local fishers are encouraged by the numbers of fish in the area and the return of formerly rare forms of marine life, such as sharks, rays, and marine turtles. The continued realization of tangible benefits by fishers will likely heavily influence the future of the resource management plan.

Initial focus on the community is critical.

Community organization and education have been effective approaches in meeting the objectives of the MCPSS. It is apparent that once a community fully understands the status of its resources and begins to feel confident to act through its own institutions, meaningful and lasting achievements can be made. The process is slow since new resource management traditions are in essence being developed. In a context without any strong resource management traditions, the introduction of unsustainable fishing methods and the inclusion of the fishers into a demanding market system has led to rapidly declining fish stocks. New traditions that allow for the sustainable harvesting of resources provide a valuable and frequently welcomed alternative to these communities.

Co-management arrangements are vital to sustainability.

The long-term sustainability of the resource management regime will depend, in part, on the support of local and national governmental institutions. Their involvement provides legitimacy, a supportive policy-making environment, and, in this case, has helped lessen the potential for personal dynamics to derail the process.

External personnel and financial support is instrumental to progress, but problematic for sustainability.

Full-time fieldworker and institutional support from external agencies for the MCPSS lasted five years. This external support was instrumental in introducing new options to the community, in conducting resource and social assessments, in establishing an educational program, and supporting community organizing processes (Katon et al. 1999). It's likely that the original project duration of two years is too short a period of time for substantive changes in resource use patterns. Although it is difficult to predict exactly how long is sufficient for such change to take place, it is important for the implementing agency and fieldworkers to strike a balance between premature termination of support and community dependency on outside assistance. The proper point of termination of formal relations should be the result of a dialogue between the community, the fieldworkers, and external supporting agencies. Furthermore, recent research indicates that full-time on-site community-worker presence may not always be necessary for success (Pollnac et al. 2001). As might be expected, the strength of community organizations developed by the MCPSS waned after withdrawal of external support. Nonetheless, the management of the area's coastal resources has dramatically improved when compared to the late 1980s. Furthermore, co-management mechanisms have been established that seem to be addressing local conflicts and rivalries. These mechanisms are based on a level of interest by government institutions in resource management not previously demonstrated prior to the MCPSS.

CONCLUSION

The MCPSS is an example of a community-based program that successfully addressed the problem of a declining fishery on San Salvador Island by using a participatory process to establish and manage a marine protected area. In as complex a community as San Salvador, many difficulties arose during MCPSS implementation and after formal project termination. The strength of co-management mechanisms, which grew out of the original work at the community level, is likely to determine the long-term sustainability of this resource management regime. Whether this approach to resource management is appropriate in other less-isolated communities or will withstand the continuing pressures from an economic and social system that places continually higher demands on coastal resources has yet to be determined.

NOTE

Acknowledgments: The Netherlands Consulate and the Jaime V. Ongpin Foundation provided valuable financial resources to the MCPSS. The National Science Foundation and the International Center for Living Aquatic Resources Management (now World Fish Centre) have provided the necessary support for the continued monitoring of San Salvador. The Haribon Foundation, as the implementing agency, has provided generous personnel and logistical support. Mayor Jessu Edora and Ex-Mayor Roberto Eamilao of Masinloc have consistently supported San Salvador's community and taken seriously the problems of marine resource management. The Department of Agriculture, primarily through the efforts of Messrs. Dionisio Galeng, Ramon Miclat, and Edgardo Caroc, provided crucial program support during MCPSS implementation. Drs. Edgardo Gomez, John McManus, and Mike Fortes provided critical technical support. Most important, however, has been the inspirational commitment of San Salvador residents to marine resource management. Research for this study was conducted between 1987–1991 and in 1999.

Chapter Fifteen

THE ROAD LESS TRAVELED

Toward Nature Protection with Social Justice

STEVEN R. BRECHIN, PETER R. WILSHUSEN,
CRYSTAL L. FORTWANGLER, PATRICK C. WEST

The analysis that we present in this volume points to a critically important gap in current debates on the core approaches of international biodiversity conservation. Whereas the majority of analyses focus on objectives (the "what"), we find that many discussions fail to consider comprehensively the social and political processes by which conservation initiatives are carried out (the "how"). In other words, there exists broad consensus that biological diversity is critically threatened and that large-scale interventions are necessary for its protection. Most observers also agree that current approaches to biodiversity conservation feature significant shortcomings and thus do not provide adequate species and habitat protection. Disagreement tends to erupt when discussing the implications of these conclusions. How biodiversity protection should occur and who will enjoy the benefits or bear the burden for its impacts often are not clearly defined. We have yet to fully articulate the procedural and distributional aspects of social justice as they relate to the goal of nature protection. Throughout this volume we have discussed ways to learn from the important findings of conservationist scientists regarding species loss, encourage the most useful elements of current approaches, and construct contextually based, problem-oriented responses that are ecologically sound, pragmatically feasible, and socially just. In this concluding chapter, we revisit some of the main themes associated with this approach and propose several ideas for further inquiry that we hope will encourage greater dialogue on these issues.

CONSERVATION AS SOCIAL AND POLITICAL PROCESS

Since nature protection is a social and political process by definition, it stands to reason that our responses to the biodiversity crisis will have to focus on questions of human organization. We lay out this perspective by presenting six key concepts of social and political process, including human dignity, legitimacy, governance, accountability, learning, and nonlocal forces. By focusing on the human organizational processes associated with nature protection, those interested in conservation as well as social justice will necessarily have to reflect internally on the fundamental concepts, methods, and modes of organization that govern collective action. Fundamentally, both the "what" (the ends) and the "how" (the means) need to be negotiated and applied in context. Many of these points have been touched upon in the growing literature on participatory approaches to conservation. By synthesizing these issues we hope to provide a more integral view of conservation with social justice.

As we have noted in several chapters, the highly politicized nature of conservation and development increases both the complexity of the protection project and the corresponding incidence of conflict and resistance. In order for conservation interventions to successfully handle this degree of complexity, we have argued that the process by which nature protection is carried out must be ecologically sound, socially and politically feasible, and morally just. The most likely alternative to socially just conservation is increasing levels of resistance and conflict at all geographic scales, a situation that can derail attempts at nature protection. In what follows, we support these general conclusions by highlighting six key concepts of social and political process that emerge in this volume as well as the associated literature.

Human Dignity—Establishing a Strong
Moral Foundation for Social Process

While conservationists act upon moral arguments for biodiversity protection, they typically omit explicit discussion of such guidance for conservation as a social and political process. Many might suggest that this type of detail should be obvious and yet cases of injustice associated with conservation interventions could be interpreted as ignoring moral parameters for social action associated with conservation interventions. Indeed, conservation organizations have undertaken interventions in the name of nature protection that have had significant negative social and cultural impacts (Ghimire and Pimbert 1997;

West and Brechin 1991; Zerner 2000, chapter 2, this volume; Peluso and Watts 2001). Given these concerns, we face a series of moral questions. Who benefits from biodiversity conservation? Should biodiversity protection be granted moral superiority relative to the ideals of human welfare and dignity? If so, on what grounds? Does the preservation of basic human rights supercede the goals of biodiversity preservation? If so, in what situations? How can the ideals of human dignity and nature protection be pursued in concert rather than in opposition? When human rights and dignity are sacrificed temporarily or permanently in favor of nature protection (or vice versa), what kind of compensatory measures will be established and how will decision makers be held accountable? In addition to widely recognized sources such as international human rights programs, general guidance for answering these questions in specific contexts can be found in documents such as the 1948 Universal Declaration of Human Rights and in the growing literature on environmental justice (chapter 2).

In chapter 1, we proposed that social justice could be defined in general terms as the right to political, economic, and cultural self-determination. Subsumed within this would be the right to self-representation and autonomy. These rights imply responsibilities entailing politically constructive participation. We further posited that attempts to define social justice beyond specific cultural and social contexts risk imposing knowledge constructs incongruent with local understandings, practices, needs, and desires. At the same time, purely local definitions of justice may be too parochial to garner wide support from enough groups to allow large-scale collective action. One option is to undertake concerted dialogue and negotiation in the context of a specific intervention that can shape mutually agreeable courses of action for both conservation and human dignity. This type of deliberative approach appears to have the greatest potential for generating a legitimate process that can account for social differences as well as changing ecological and political circumstances.

Legitimacy—Constructing Authority

Given the complexity of pursuing nature protection with social justice and the urgent need to act in the face of biodiversity loss, many conservation advocates might argue that in certain cases the intrinsic rights of nature should supercede those of people. Unless carefully managed to account for historical as well as contemporary social and political factors, this approach could easily produce a backlash by those affected by protection measures, thus compromising biodiversity over the long term. At the same time, it is highly unlikely that national governments possess the resources to enforce strict protection except by extreme authoritarian practices. This is especially salient given trends in political decentralization in countries around the globe. Unlike the

moral argument presented above, this line of reasoning is pragmatic and suggests that it would be in the "enlightened self-interest" of conservation advocates to pursue socially just nature protection. On one hand, this approach is
more "cost-efficient" because it maintains the potential of government-
imposed sanctions but encourages self-enforcement and cooperation. On the
other hand, it reduces the likelihood of violent backlashes against natural
areas, by constructing broadly accepted, legitimate prescriptions.

The case studies on Colombia (chapter 5) and Ecuador (chapter 9) illustrate how a broad array of "local" actors including NGOs and indigenous and
black peoples' organizations responded to what they viewed as illegitimate
practices linked to project development and bioprospecting. In both examples,
biodiversity protection or use was initially conceived, in part, as a means of
advancing local communities politically and economically and yet each fell
short of fulfilling these expectations. As Dorsey notes in his discussion on bioprospecting in Ecuador, the political and economic forces at play surrounding
ownership and marketing of valuable species and intellectual property may
represent near-insurmountable challenges to equitable benefit sharing. At the
same time, however, the Ecuador case presents examples of apparent breaches
of ethical conduct on the part of international researchers (such as misuse and
misrepresentation of information) that served to heighten suspicion and resistance. In contrast, Wilshusen's discussion of the *Biopacífico* project in Colombia's Pacific Coastal region offers evidence that, even under circumstances of
strong local resistance, it is possible to construct a widely accepted strategy for
conservation activities. In the Colombia case, project administrators chose to
pursue a process of concerted negotiation with black and indigenous organizations in order to reformulate the project's operative plan, turning what many
considered to be a failure into a qualified success story.

Governance—Establishing Modes of
Decision Making and Power Sharing

The term *governance,* in general terms, refers to arrangements for decision
making and power sharing (chapters 3 and 10). The following questions are
fundamental to understanding social and political processes related to governance: Who decides? Based on what authority? What are the ground rules for
decision making? How will decision makers be held accountable? How will
decisions be enforced? In addition to crafting governance structures for particular interventions, practitioners need to be cognizant of the broader legal juris-
dictions within which projects are embedded (Ribot 1999). In the case of the
Biopacífico project in Colombia's Pacific Coastal region (chapter 5), for example, the process of negotiating a workable operational plan with black and
indigenous communities had to be adapted to significant institutional changes
at the national level including the promulgation of a new constitution.

Within the conservation and development literature questions of governance tend to be discussed in terms of local participation (Wells and Brandon 1992). Participation is a narrower concept that is a necessary but not sufficient component of governance. In this regard, we would need to define the parameters of participation by posing these questions: Who participates? What are their demands and expectations? What capacity do individuals and groups have to participate? Will they participate in all aspects of decision making or only selected phases? How do participants benefit from involvement? When considered in these terms, it becomes clear that questions of governance are the core of the management process. The stiff challenges of constructing strong governance structures that include full participation involve significant "start-up costs," that can stabilize power relationships over the long term (Pimbert and Pretty 1995; Wilshusen 2000).

The core of governance is authority and control. And since legitimacy is socially constructed within the bounds of existing social and cultural norms, arrangements for decision making and power sharing can be crafted in context most effectively through constant, constructive dialogue. In other words, what works in one time and place may not work in another. This is particularly true because strong tensions over legitimate action will almost always appear in the context of conservation programs. The diversity of participants makes negotiation a highly complex undertaking if we take into account potentially vast cultural, class, ethnic, gender, and other differences among participants and the often subtle power dynamics that these differences produce. Conflict and tension will subside to the extent that involved parties view decision making as legitimate. The heavy investment in building authority pays off as decision-making arrangements become institutionalized (chapters 3 and 14).

Questions of governance have taken on a more prominent role in discussion of biodiversity conservation especially given the global sweep of economic liberalization and political decentralization. While the World Bank has made explicit links between good governance and ecologically sound natural resource management, environmental organizations such as the World Resources Institute (WRI), the World Conservation Union (IUCN), and the Biodiversity Support Program (BSP), among others, have focused increasing attention on the topic (Wyckoff-Baird et al. 2000). At the same time, however, it is important to note the difference between an environmental governance agenda and an environmental conservation with social justice agenda. The former, in its support for environmentally beneficial outcomes, may or may not encourage socially just processes or outcomes (Zerner 2000a). While the concept of governance encompasses much more than "the work of governments," the economic and structural adjustments in countries around the world have had an important impact on local communities and conservation programs. Decentralization and state remodeling in Indonesia (chapter 4),

Mexico (chapter 12), and the Philippines (chapter 14) have created new opportunities and challenges for nature protection and social justice. While it is still too early to assess how devolution and joint forest management will play out in Indonesia, the case of the Yucatán Peninsula Sustainable Development network illustrates how locally initiated governance regimes can develop regional programs that link conservation, development, and justice. In addition, there are positive signs coming from marine resources management in the Philippines.

Accountability—Guaranteeing Responsibility and Performance

The idea of accountability refers to the mechanisms that participants put in place to guide and enforce agreements. In this book, we highlight two aspects of this process—responsibility and performance. The main questions to ask in this context are: (1) To what extent is each party holding up its end of the bargain? and (2) How effectively are participants pursuing their goals?

Regarding questions of social justice, we have emphasized the need for conservation and development advocates to recognize rights to self-determination as part of a proposal to incorporate social justice principles within conservation programs. Some conservation advocates react to this type of argument with frustration, as if it were nothing more than a politically correct "trump card." The perception is that attending to social justice once again will mean that humans win and nature loses; that much is given to appease humans and nature gains little. It is important to make clear, however, that the notion of rights implies responsibilities to be fulfilled. By conferring rights, the negotiating process over how to pursue nature protection can proceed based on clear expectations, commitments, rules, and agreements. Enforcement, if needed, is a perfectly legitimate undertaking when backed up by carefully negotiated agreements. A growing literature on accountability discusses the challenges of holding a wide range of social actors to their commitments. These different levels of organization include multilateral organizations such as the World Bank (Fox and Brown 1998), states (Schroeder 1999), and local authorities (Ribot 1999), among others.

A number of the case studies in this book have touched on issues related to responsibility including the chapters on Colombia (5), Belize (6), Ecuador (9), Mexico (12), and the Philippines (14). As we noted in the section on legitimacy, the Colombia and Ecuador cases center in large part on moves by local interest groups to hold national and international organizations to their commitments. In contrast, the cases from Belize and Mexico illustrate the challenges of instituting internal accountability. In Belize, community-based conservation efforts at Gales Point Manatee broke down due to conflicts stemming from differences in gender, family alliances, and party affiliation. At the same time, the Gales Point Manatee project featured no oversight or conflict resolution mechanisms to overcome these differences and hold individuals to their commitments. In Mexico, the bylaws of the Yucatán Peninsula Sustainable Development Network initially did not contemplate compliance mechanisms. As a result, when one NGO member began operating in ways that conflicted with the network's goals, the regional body had no immediate reaction. The network eventually responded to this oversight but not in time to regain the confidence of the NGO's community clients.

The second aspect of accountability—performance—refers specifically to the effectiveness of outcomes associated with action. Several appraisals of integrated conservation and development have been performed (Larson et al. 1997; Wells and Brandon 1992; Wells et al. 1999; Western et al. 1994) while others have developed guidelines for evaluation (Margoluis and Salafsky 1998). With limited exceptions, however, existing reviews of conservation programs lack an explicit framework for appraising social process (an exception is Clark et al. 2000). If conservation challenges are largely a question of human organization then we must rely on some frame for analyzing decision making and organization. This is important because even if an intervention is not apparently achieving the long-term goal of species protection, it may feature innovative organizational processes that could be applied in other contexts. We return to issues related to performance below.

Adaptation and Learning—
Institutionalizing Reflection and Self-Correction

The joint concepts of adaptation and learning appear strongly in the adaptive/ecosystem management literature (Gunderson et al. 1995; Lee 1993). These ideas also inform much of the conservation literature on participatory approaches (Borrini-Feyeraband 1996). The main question that emerges in this context is: How can we systematically adapt and learn from experience? This applies not only to management prescriptions but also to social process.

In his influential book, Lee (1993) refers to this process in terms of "compass" and "gyroscope." "Compass" suggests that conservation policy be viewed as an ongoing experiment wherein practitioners attempt to generate increasingly accurate and useable information that might advance progress toward reaching management objectives. "Gyroscope," in turn, points to democratic social process as the only legitimate way of carrying out interventions.

Regarding social process, discussions of adaptation and learning emerge in both the literature on organizations (Argyris and Schön 1987) and policy (Hall 1993; chapter 10). In addition to promoting rigorous appraisal of goals, writings on learning emphasize reflection on the appropriateness of goals (often called "double-loop learning") and approaches that individuals and organizations adopt (Argyris 1982). In this sense, conservation as social process entails continuous self-correction based on what works best in a given time and place (Brunner and Klein 1999).

For most practitioners working at the field level, the types of learning described above are a necessary byproduct of carrying out management activities in complex settings. Policy makers, on the other hand, tend to emphasize standard monitoring and evaluation procedures without reflecting on the appropriateness of goals. While learning implicitly occurs in the course of everyday management activities, it is much harder to institutionalize learning processes within program operations. Typically, the high complexity of conservation and development interventions leads to organizational routines in which managers constantly must respond to new and unexpected problems. According to the authors cited above, building in time for collective learning allows organizations to better understand and respond to this complexity.

A number of chapters in this book present examples of learning in action including the policy changes highlighted in Madagascar (chapter 11), responses to local resistance and institutional change in Colombia (chapter 5), and development of a community marine reserve on the Philippines' San Salvador Island (chapter 14). Geisler's discussion on collaborative adaptive management in the Dominican Republic (chapter 13) offers explicit elements for more inclusive and responsive policy development in situations where decision makers opt for relocation in order to protect endangered habitats. When trade-offs of this kind occur, as with the case of Los Haiteses National Park, adaptation and learning represent critical components of policy process that can allow participants to respond to unanticipated events and minimize negative social impacts.

Nonlocal Forces

There is a well-documented consensus in the literature on biodiversity conservation that nonlocal social, political, and economic forces can play a significant role in species loss as well as rural poverty (Brandon et al. 1998; Kramer et al. 1997; Terborgh 1999). This trend coincides with the literature in political ecology (Bryant and Bailey 1997; Zerner 2000). Many discussions refer to large-scale national and international commercial enterprises including pharmaceutical firms, and oil, timber, and mining companies (the so-called "resource pirates") that have strong connections to the state or political elites. It may happen, for example, that a close friend or relative of a nation's ruler receives timber concessions in recognition of loyalty. That person in turn may develop a business relationship with an international logging company, which covers capital investment in return for exclusive extraction rights. Given this alignment of political and economic interests it would be highly unlikely that the national forestry agency, NGOs, or local communities could prevent or change the logging operation. Chapter 7 on ecotourism in northern Benin illustrates this type of political dynamic where an international tourism firm used its influence with the country's Ministry of Tourism to derail its competitors' permit applications and thus maintain exclusive control of a concession near Pendjari National Park.

In addition to these types of power plays by national and international interests, nonlocal forces can refer to structural factors such as laws, treaties, economic adjustment programs, international trade, and bilateral aid projects, among others. These institutional opportunities and constraints are in many cases tied to global scale capitalist economies. In chapters 3 and 10 we present two different conceptual angles for better understanding how nonlocal, structural factors impact local conservation efforts. The first perspective (chapter 3) centers on the ways in which structural power in the form of formal and nonformal institutions, as well as discourses and ways of thinking, shape how political action occurs. In the case of "illegal" residents cultivating coffee within forest reserves in South Sumatra (chapter 4), local planters were motivated in large part by price increases precipitated by crop damage in Brazil. In Madagascar (chapter 11), a shift in global conservation strategy from ICDPs to eco-regional planning led to a restructuring of national programs that reduced investment in and participation by communities and increased the role of state agencies and national NGOs. The second perspective (chapter 10) builds on these understandings of power relationships to consider organizational outlets for constructive political action including formal organizations, international environmental governance regimes, and local common pool resource institutions. The chapters on Madagascar (11), Mexico (12), the Dominican Republic (13), and the Philippines' San Salvador Island (14) all provide examples of the challenges of crafting biodiversity conservation with social justice. A partial cross-section from the literature presents numerous other country-specific cases on the multiple layers of politics associated with conservation and development including Zambia (Gibson 1999), Tanzania (Neumann 1995), the Gambia (Schroeder 1999), India (Sundar 2000), Cambodia (Le Billion 2000), Indonesia (Li 1999), Nicaragua (Nygren 2000), Guatemala (Sundberg 1999), Ecuador (Bebbington and Perrault 1999), and Mexico (Klooster 2000).

FUTURE DIRECTIONS: RETHINKING BIODIVERSITY CONSERVATION AS SOCIAL PROCESS

Given the six key concepts associated with social and political processes presented above, we offer seven broad ideas that we hope will encourage an open and balanced dialogue on the future of international biodiversity conservation. In the second half of the book, in particular, we argue that increased human organizational capacity, in line with the elements of social and political process that we summarized above, will increase self-enforcement and dramatically reduce the need for forced compliance. While some might argue that this type of approach already has been attempted unsuccessfully, we would argue that nature protection with social justice has not yet been tried as a general strategy since integrated conservation and development has emphasized economic incentives and compensation as a means of "buying" constraint.

In general terms, what might conservation with social justice look like and what lessons can the case studies offer in this regard? Obviously, there are many different answers to these questions, but if we begin to sketch an outline of one generalized view, we might take into account seven issues, including clarification of standpoint, contextualization, power, community, organization, performance, and dialogue. While other points could be added to this list, we can start by considering how these issues intersect in the context of "doing conservation" in specific times and places. We propose that a socially just approach to nature protection advances rather than detracts from human dignity. This way of thinking about conservation does not preclude potential trade-offs or conflicts of interest between protected areas and local communities but it does elevate the goal of promoting human dignity to the same level as that of protecting species and habitats.

Interestingly, the perceived "sides" in debates on conservation—pro-people and pro-nature—make similar observations on several points (e.g., nonlocal forces mentioned above) but use them to support very different arguments. For example, as we discuss in more detail below, conservation advocates critique participatory methods (community-based conservation) because they tend to make assumptions about idealized local people living in harmony among themselves and with nature. In the majority of cases, these observers argue, local communities are internally divided, often are poorly organized, and rarely possess anything like a conservation ethic. As a general rule, therefore, it should not be assumed that they will behave in ways that protect species and habitats. Scholars and practitioners associated with political ecology and other social scientific perspectives, on the other hand, make many of the same points about assumptions regarding local communities but use the information to make different arguments about the inequities of conservation programs. While both perspectives are useful and insightful as far as they go, neither tends to consider in any detail what we might call the "pragmatic middle ground." In other words, they argue for either ecological preservation or social emancipation but do not account for what is politically possible in specific times and places. In what follows, we offer a middle course; a politically constructive proposal that satisfies three general criteria: ecological, pragmatic, and moral.

Conservation with Social Justice

If, as we noted above in the section on "human dignity," conservation and development advocates often neglect to define explicit moral parameters for social and political processes associated with specific interventions, it follows that we could focus greater attention on clarifying our collective approaches along these lines. In chapter 2, Fortwangler provides an overview of numerous international statements and agreements that join notions of human rights and environmental protection. While these documents offer general guidance, questions of social justice, like sustainability, take on practical meaning in specific contexts. In this sense, conservation and development organizations might elaborate a set of standards that can guide design, implementation, and appraisal of biodiversity programs. By clarifying its standpoint with respect to the process by which interventions will be carried out, a conservation organization defines its commitment to working in a particular place, stabilizes the expectations of all affected parties and sets the boundaries of its accountability.

Conservation in Context

Regardless of approach, conservation as a problem of human organization must account for the aspects of social and political process presented above (human dignity, legitimacy, governance, accountability, learning, and nonlocal forces). Although conservation practitioners might adopt general operating guidelines, such as the principles of social justice mentioned above, detailed action strategies will be most effective if they are negotiated by participants in a particular setting. This line of reasoning suggests that the context defines the response not vice versa. Brandon et al. (1998) and Clark et al. (2000), among others, recognize the importance of contextual problem solving in conservation given vast differences in ecological, political, and social complexity across settings. For example, protection strategies in certain times and places such as Guatemala's Petén region in the mid-1990s or Indonesia in 1997 might require immediate, emergency action on the part of government and other actors given the rapidity of land cover changes from fire or uncontrolled settlement. In other contexts, local communities may be internally divided or producer organizations (such as agricultural cooperatives) may be absent, thus posing significant barriers to the type of deliberative, participatory approach to conservation that we advocate. However, in other cases, such as in Panama's Darien region, local organizations are incipient but there appears to be strong potential for pursuing co-management agreements that encompass existing protected areas as well as parts of indigenous lands *(comarcas)* given the low intensity of environmental change. In places such as Australia and Mexico, the structure of land tenure and other legal entitlements places significant land management responsibilities in the hands of rural producers, suggesting that negotiated partnerships may be the only viable conservation strategy (Arnold 1998; Stevens 1997).

Power Dynamics, Conflict, and Domination

The conceptual analysis in chapter 3 points to diverse forms and pathways of power and domination. In particular, it brings to the fore some of the less obvious and, at times, insidious effects produced by structural manifestations of power. On one level, this type of understanding suggests directions for the empowerment of the dispossessed that goes well beyond conventional conservation with development approaches, which emphasize economic incentives and compensation (Kramer et al. 1997). On another level, however, a more comprehensive exploration of power and domination makes clear the deeply complex political, social, and economic "realities" currently entangled in the matrix of human interaction both locally and globally. In this sense we revive the term *realpolitik* (with all the usual caveats regarding the baggage that terms carry) to account for the practical and material factors that shape, in part, what is politically feasible in a given context. This complements our discussion of "social justice" above, which emphasizes ideal and moral arguments. On yet a third level, our discussion of power implies two distinct domains of justice—procedural and distributive—that are equally important but often conflated. The conservation literature typically raises issues related to distributive equity whether in terms of access and use of resources, property rights (including intellectual and genetic), tenure, or compensation. Questions of procedural justice emerge in discussions about local participation although they are not usually constructed as such. We will return to these two domains of justice below. In the final analysis, an understanding of the different modes of power as well as their interactions can inform attempts to construct conservation with social justice on all three levels.

Community Complexity

In the midst of the economic, political, and social changes brought about by processes of political decentralization, communities have received increasing amounts of attention. In this regard, Agrawal and Gibson (1999, 640) conclude that much of the mainstream conservation literature creates an image of "the mythic community" as small spatial units of cohesive, homogenous groups using locally evolved, shared sets of norms to sustainably and equitably manage resources. Regarding community heterogeneity specifically, Belsky's study of community-based ecotourism in Gales Point, Belize (chapter 6) found that the intersection of social factors such as gender, class, and political party affiliation divided community members and was largely responsible for a progressive deterioration of efforts to construct a local conservation and sustainable development enterprise. Similarly, Klooster's (2000) account of community forestry in San Martin Ocotlán in the Mexican state of Oaxaca describes how internal conflict over resource access and use continues to hamper a locally managed enterprise fifteen years after achieving devolution of management responsibilities. Prior to the Mexican state's acceptance of community-based management, outside concessionaires maintained control by exploiting internal rivalries and providing financial incentives to faithful local allies. When communities such as San Martin assumed control of forest management, a local elite had already become consolidated. According to the author, this elite group reproduced earlier forms of external domination of communal institutions through intimidation, bribes, and other means.

Conservation Organization

If conservation is primarily a problem of human organization then attending to the structures and interrelationships that sustain coordinated action should form the core of protection strategies in addition to producing ecological knowledge. For example, as Clark's (1997) in-depth analysis of an endangered species recovery program in the United States suggests, a scientific consensus on bolstering populations may be in place but organizational failures prevent concerted action. In this case, efforts to establish a captive breeding program for a newly discovered population of black-footed ferrets *(Mustela nigripes)* nearly failed due to organizational power struggles among Wyoming Game and Fish and other organizational actors.

While the social divisions noted above on communities appear at all levels of society, conservation practitioners can minimize and overcome conflict and resistance in many contexts by attending to questions of organizational and institutional crafting. Chapter 10 outlines a number of issues and alternative strategies to improve collective action in favor of nature protection. One of the central issues is collaboration. As conservation work becomes increasingly complex, practitioners face the challenge of creating and maintaining innovative organizational arrangements (Gray 1989). While increased complexity demands greater decentralization of professional effort, the need for rapid responses and precision requires greater coordinated linkages with other organizational actors (Perrow 1984). This will be difficult to do without a shared strategy, a sophisticated monitoring and communication system, and a coordinated response structure. Although there are no simple recipes for effective coordination and collaboration, project designers and other practitioners will need to account for questions of organizational structure, performance, culture, and commitment. Specially trained personnel and separate financial resources may prove central to this task, just as small groups of endangered species specialists often offer technical advice on population recovery efforts.

In general terms, the complexity and urgency of protection activities may be handled through umbrella organizational structures or networks and negotiated coordination strategies. In Mexico, the UNDP-GEF Small Grants Programme supports an innovative NGO network that successfully coordinates community-level conservation and development projects across the Yucatán Peninsula (chapter 12). At the global level, the Forest Stewardship Council (FSC) has established a forest certification regime, including flexible standards that can be adapted to local conditions (Viana et al. 1996).

Conservation Performance and Decision Process Appraisal

Evaluating how decision making occurs uncovers an event timeline that shows both missteps and successful advances. Given the decision-making history associated with a particular program, participants can trace individual and group performance as well as accountability. The importance of establishing parameters for socially just action becomes especially apparent at this stage since, in addition to project-related objectives, evaluators can examine the extent to which decision makers act in ways that promote both nature protection and human dignity.

As we note in chapter 10, conservation and development project shortfalls may result from problems of implementation rather than concept. To better understand this so-called implementation gap, practitioners need to evaluate organizational performance. Key questions that arise in this context include: Organizational performance for whom? Who defines success and failure of organizational efforts? Based on what criteria? More specifically on the nature of organizations themselves, what organizational participants, structures, technologies, and cultures are essential to promoting what specific types of conservation efforts? In sum, which organizational arrangements work and which ones do not and why?

The conservation literature is rapidly growing but lacks systematic analysis. Individual case studies comprise most of our information on people and park issues. Each author tends to use his or her own criteria for determining the relevant issues to be reviewed as well as criteria to determine success or failure. As a result it has been challenging to systematically compare the tremendous amount of information collected on people and parks issues worldwide. This has led to differing interpretations as to where we stand and where we need to go, especially regarding consensus on policy guidelines. To refine our understanding and push conservation knowledge to the next level, we need to systematically review, organize, compare, and outline what we know, what we do not and where to go next. An article in the journal *Science* by Aaron Bruner and colleagues provides an example of the type of systematic research needed (Bruner et al. 2001).

Grassroots Democratic Process and Dialogue on Conservation

Throughout this volume we have signaled the importance of concerted negotiation as a means of constructing and strengthening authority (legitimate power) at all levels. Innovative organizational arrangements, such as the community forestry association *(Walde Kelka)* in Mali mentioned in chapter 10, are fundamental to this process because they serve as "civic arenas" in which politically constructive dialogue can occur (Rudel 2000). Further, as a growing number of examples suggest, "grassroots" democratic action is not limited to the grassroots. These include the drafting of the Convention on

Biological Diversity (chapter 10) and NGO networks on Mexico's Yucatán Peninsula (chapter 12). Similarly, participatory planning was a key aspect of community-based marine protected area management on the Philippines' San Salvador Island (chapter 14). Political theorists have focused an increasing amount of attention on these issues of dialogue, mutual understanding, collective action, and social learning under the label "deliberative democracy" (Dryzek 2000; Elster 1998).

In addition to the cases presented in this volume, one organizational alternative for establishing the "civic arena" mentioned above is through continuing workshops dedicated to analyzing and testing options for the social and ecological complexities of conservation and development. Although a great number of academic and professional meetings on these themes take place every year, there remains a need for permanent interchange among key players from diverse disciplinary backgrounds. The "workshop" format could manifest itself in a variety of ways, including a series of conference meetings, roundtable discussions, etc., but the focus should center on problem solving and strategy building. Participants in diverse settings could set up multiple workshops depending on the policy arena. For example, those interested in general questions related to international biodiversity conservation might form a special task force drawing expertise from community organizations, universities, NGOs, intergovernmental organizations, and foundations, among others. More focused working teams might emerge in the context of specific country needs or projects. We expect that a combination of community groups, the conservation community, private foundations, academic institutions, and NGOs might call for and financially support a continuing series of meetings that allow critical reflection and constructive dialogue on the future of biodiversity conservation. A number of these forums already exist including a series of meetings on mobile peoples and conservation sponsored by the University of Oxford's Refugee Studies Centre, IUCN's World Commission on Parks and Protected Areas, Indiana University's Workshop in Political Theory and Policy Analysis (a key contributor to studies on common property), and the "community and conservation" working group of the Anthropology and Environment section of the American Anthropological Association (AAA).

Perhaps the best example of deliberative democracy in the context of a biodiversity conservation project appears in the case study on Colombia's Pacific Coastal region (chapter 4). With the creation of the so-called *equipo ampliado* or "expanded team," the GEF-sponsored *Biopacífico* project successfully brought together project staff and representatives of indigenous and Afro-Colombian communities to negotiate the redesign and restructuring of the entire intervention. This process involved more than simple bargaining over distribution of resources. Rather, it explored the underlying conceptualization of the project, challenging standardized understandings of nature, territory, and culture in the process. Thus, while the *equipo ampliado* served as a civic arena for concerted negotiation among diverse parties, it also developed into a constructive working group that produced innovative ideas and strategies. As such it established a new precedent for collaborative decision making throughout the region.

BEYOND THE CROSSROADS:
NATURE PROTECTION WITH SOCIAL JUSTICE

At the end of this volume's introductory chapter we suggested that the conservation community stands at an important crossroads, where one pathway appears to lead back to authoritarian protectionist practices used in the past and a second—the road less traveled—follows a course toward nature protection with social justice. We have presented a number of case studies that illustrate why this second approach is superior to the first, since it encourages politically constructive responses to highly complex problems. In contrast, the first approach—authoritarian protectionism—tends to generate social conflict and resistance and does not produce broadly legitimate, long-term protection strategies. At the same time, the "road less traveled" is more circuitous and perhaps not the best route in all situations. In other words, we are fully cognizant of the fact that conservation activities take place under highly challenging circumstances that may not always be conducive to the approach we espouse. In this concluding section, we summarize numerous advantages of pursuing conservation with social justice, with an eye toward getting beyond conservation "paradigms" and focusing on contextual problem solving.

Our discussion on social and political processes central to nature protection with social justice mirrors the structure of related analyses of "community participation," which treat local involvement as both a means and an end (Little 1994; Nelson and Wright 1995; Wilshusen 2000). When employed as a tool or a "means to an end," local participation is largely utilitarian, comprising techniques for incorporating communities in decision making in order to achieve conservation goals with greater efficiency and fairness. The underlying assumption is that participatory projects are more likely to address community needs in a manner consistent with local conditions and social norms and expectations. As a goal or an "end in and of itself," local participation becomes a process of capacity building and empowerment that seeks to improve the ability of communities to autonomously formulate, implement and sustain project activities, above and beyond nature protection objectives. The main assumption here is that self-reliant communities with strong decision-making and organizational capacities will be better able to manage and protect local natural resources. In similar fashion, we focus on conservation with social justice as both process (means) and desired outcome (end). By using social justice, however, we seek to expand the conceptual field in order to present a more comprehensive view of social and political process (the six components described above) and emphasize the moral dimension, which underlies all human action.

By including a moral argument, our discussion of three general criteria for nature protection with social justice—that interventions be ecologically sound, politically feasible, and socially just—reflects the structure of past writings on sustainable development (WCED 1987). According to Barbier (1987), sustainable development must satisfy biological, economic, and social criteria by simultaneously conserving biological riches, increasing local incomes, and promoting local social equity. Since these three goals can easily conflict in practice, existing tensions can either be circumvented through technological innovations or resolved through institutional arrangements that achieve compromises among competing resource users (Rudel 2000). In the majority of cases, technological responses are incomplete or inappropriate, leaving participants to the difficult task of negotiating workable trade-offs.

Similarly, our pragmatic view of conservation with social justice suggests that neither pure protection nor complete social emancipation can happen in most contexts. Thus, negotiated compromises need to be established on what might be called the political middle ground. At the same time, a purely pragmatic approach might easily lead decision makers to pursue the most politically convenient course of action over the short term without considering the long-term implications. For this reason, the two ideals of nature protection and social justice provide twin benchmarks for a vision of desired outcomes. As chapter 3 emphasizes, the political dimension of conservation extends beyond conventional perspectives—where one party imposes its will upon another despite resistance—to encompass institutional and cultural practices (structural power) that enable and constrain everyday action. Consequently, nature protection with social justice necessarily contemplates questions of equity but also accounts for structures of domination that continue to limit disenfranchised social groups. Regarding the organizational dimension, chapter 10 outlines a series of "design principles" for crafting complex organizations and governance regimes under conditions of social and economic change, complexity and uncertainty. While certain areas around the globe feature unstable or excessively authoritarian political environments and are thus unfavorable for deliberative democratic problem solving, the majority of sites could improve conservation and social justice outcomes dramatically by organizing and collaborating more effectively.

Yet, even though the notion of conservation with social justice bears resemblances to the contents of earlier debates on local participation and sustainable development, it differs in important ways, as we have mentioned. Most importantly, however, joining nature protection with social justice advances how we think about and respond to the social causes of biodiversity loss in at least three important ways because it moves beyond certain basic assumptions that currently dominate conservation discourse. First, it overcomes the argument that conflict over conservation is essentially a question of economics, which is based on the supposition that natural resource users refuse to accept the "opportunity costs" that nature protection programs impose. This line of reasoning typically concludes that some form of compensation will offset these costs. And yet, as several chapters in this volume illustrate, local resistance to conservation measures results from a complex array of factors such as histories of domination, nonlocal forces, and territorial control. Certainly, rural producers and their families want to advance economically but to reduce conflict to opportunity costs and equity concerns to "benefit sharing" ignores fundamental aspects of social and political process that shape nature protection outcomes.

Second, a broader conceptualization of conservation with social justice gets beyond a restricted focus on traditional or indigenous peoples with special rights. In most respects, it is highly positive that the United Nations, international NGOs such as the World Wide Fund for Nature, and others are promoting the rights of indigenous peoples through declarations and programs. Indeed, these efforts often build on years of grassroots organizing and lobbying by activist groups (chapter 2). Further, it is easier operationally to support groups with clearly defined entitlements. At the same time, however, it is important to recognize that programs favoring justice for special peoples with special rights can lead to negative, unintended outcomes unless pursued with great care. For example, given limited funds and other resources, might not a focus on special rights exclude other dispossessed groups because they do not fit into certain categories? The *caboclos* or *ribereños* of Amazonia are not formally recognized as "indigenous" peoples in the countries where they reside and yet they regularly interact with and adopt "traditional" production practices that are basically identical to those of officially sanctioned indigenous groups. Similarly, might not near-exclusive support for an indigenous group generates social divisions and perhaps even conflict with other "traditional" groups not labeled as indigenous? As the arguments of both protected areas and social justice advocates regarding community complexity suggest, most rural communities defy static categories (Zerner 2000a). Pursuing conservation based on a broad set of rights and responsibilities centered on self-determination accounts for both distributional and procedural equity for communities regardless of categories.

Third, conservation with social justice does not necessarily rely upon sustainable community development as a means of achieving protection. One of the strongest criticisms against contemporary community-based conservation approaches argues that biodiversity protection and sustainable resource use are fundamentally incompatible (Redford and Richter 1999). While some contest this assertion (Schwartzman et al. 2000), the argument points to an important conundrum about what has been referred to as "the brief, barren marriage of conservation and sustainability" (Redford and Sanderson 1992; see also Wilshusen et al. 2002). Even if we assume for a moment that economic development can occur sustainably, it stands to reason that some significant level of protection will be needed to maintain ecosystem structure and function. Approaching conservation based on principles of social justice leads to a more comprehensive definition of problems in specific contexts beyond oversimplified economic explanations. While carefully planned economic development activities might advance conservation objectives in many situations, it is also possible that they could produce the opposite effect. A more complete analysis may point to complex political and economic issues such as market access or legal discrimination that defy programmatic blueprints. Similarly, such a process may generate greater willingness on the part of resource-dependent rural communities to protect certain areas than is typically assumed.

In the vast majority of settings, as we noted above in the section on non-local forces, economic development is anything but sustainable. In what some refer to as an "age of market triumphalism" (Peet and Watts 1993), we find rapidly expanding markets, rapidly expanding (and yet often unstable) economies, and rapidly expanding resource use. While a few have profited richly from this growth, many others, ranging from the middle classes to the dispossessed, have been left to foot the bill. Indeed, the same multilateral lending institutions that fund conservation and development projects in places such as Panama's Darien region simultaneously offer loans and grants for large-scale infrastructure programs in the same places. The broad outline of social and political process that we offer in this chapter suggests that, to achieve procedural justice, questions of accountability will be fundamental to determining which groups in society are contributing to biodiversity loss and where action needs to be taken.

Beyond the actual causes of environmental change and the myriad justifications for joining conservation with social justice, the case studies in this volume uncover two trends occurring worldwide that essentially require the type of approach we propose. First, beginning in the late 1980s, many so-called "developing" countries adopted new governance structures promoting political decentralization and economic liberalization. In theory, processes of structural decentralization entail slimming down large, centralized states and devolving differing degrees of decision-making power to regional or local public and private entities. The result should be increased administrative and economic efficiency as well as improved equity. In practice, centralized states have been reduced in size but decision making has been hampered and efficiency has dropped. In many countries, state functionaries maintain authoritarian, bureaucratic political practices despite changes in organizational structure (Ribot 1999). With respect to conservation approaches, the key point is that, even if governments were to embrace state-centered, authoritarian nature protection as has been suggested to differing degrees, they have neither the means nor the capacity to do so. Most natural resource management agencies have minimal staffs that can do little more than baseline monitoring and reporting. As a result, states enmeshed in the "new world order" must rely on organizations of civil society, including local communities.

The second trend is in many ways a response to the first and constitutes the growth of civil society and grassroots mobilization. A massive increase in the number of nongovernmental organizations accompanied processes of market expansion and political decentralization in the late 1980s, leading some observers to celebrate a new era of democratic, grassroots civic action (Fisher 1998). At the same time, however, these organizations are not alien to politics and typically become important arenas of contestation and struggle vis-à-vis particular projects (Fisher 1997). NGOs, grassroots organizations, and indigenous groups, to name just a few, have developed highly effective political alliances through advocacy networks and advanced communications technology. As a result, the conservation community faces increasing demands locally, regionally, nationally, and internationally from activists who expect greater decision-making power vis-à-vis specific projects. In conjunction, these two trends—political decentralization and grassroots mobilization— leave us with the choice of critiquing one extreme of the conservation and social justice spectrum or the other (pure protection or social emancipation) or pursuing a program somewhere in the middle; one that is ecologically sound, politically feasible, and socially just. We advocate the latter approach, the one that generates a politically constructive process focused on building authority and guaranteeing reciprocity.

WORKS CITED

Abramovitz, J. 1998. Sustaining the world's forests. In *State of the world 1998*, ed. L. R. Brown, C. Flavin, and H. French, 21–40. New York: W.W. Norton.

Abu-Rafia, A. 2001. Negev's Bedouin 1948–1999: Expulsion, displacement, and forced settlements. In *Conservation and indigenous mobile peoples*, ed. D. Chatty, 202–211. Oxford: Berghahn Press.

Abercrombie & Kent. "Abercrombie & Kent." *http://www.aandktours.com/* Accessed 20 Jul 2000.

Acción Ecológica. 1996. Correspondence to Senor Ingeniero Mario Cárdenas, 25 June.

Adams, A., ed. 1962. *First world conference on parks*. Washington, DC: National Park Service.

Adams, W. M., and D. Hulme. 2001. Forum: If community conservation is the answer in Africa, what is the question? *Oryx* 35(3): 193–203.

Agbo, V. 1992. *Population environment interdependence in the northwest of Benin: Quantification of anthropological activities in the village of Tanougou*. Ann Arbor: University of Michigan, School of Natural Resources and Environment.

Agbo, V., N. Sokpon, J. Hough, and P. West. 1993. Population-environment dynamics in a constrained ecosystem in northern Benin. In *Population-environment dynamics*, ed. G. Ness, W. Drake, S. R. Brechin, 238–300. Ann Arbor: University of Michigan Press.

Agrawal, A. 1997. Community in conservation: Beyond enchantment and disenchantment. Conservation and Development Forum Discussion Paper, Gainesville, FL.

Agrawal, A., and C. C. Gibson. 1999. Enchantment and disenchantment: The role of community in natural resource conservation. *World Development* 27:629–649.

Agarwal, B. 1986. *Cold hearths and barren slopes: The woodfuel crisis in the Third World*. London and New Jersey: Zed Books.

———. 1989. Rural women, poverty, and natural resources: Sustenance, sustainability, and the struggle for change. *Economic and Political Weekly*, no. 28, 46–65.

Akama, J. S. 1999. Marginalization of the Maasai in Kenya. *Annals of Tourism Research* 6(3): 716–718.

Akama, J. S., C. L. Lant, and G. W. Burnett. 1995. Conflicting attitudes toward state wildlife conservation programs in Kenya. *Society and Natural Resources* 8:133–144.

Albert, B. 1994. Indian lands, environmental policy, and military geopolitics in the development of the Brazilian Amazon. The case of the Yanomami. *Development and Change* 23:35–70.

Alcala, A. 1998. Community-based coastal resource management in the Philippines: A case study. *Ocean and Coastal Management* 38:179–186.

Alcorn, J. B. 1993. Indigenous peoples and conservation. *Conservation Biology* 7(2): 424–427.

Alderman, C. 1994. The economics and the role of privately-owned lands used for nature tourism, education, and conservation. In *Protected area economics and policy: Linking conservation and sustainable development*, ed. M. Munasinghe and J. McNeely, 273–305. Washington, DC: IUCN and The World Bank.

Alexander, E. R. 1995. *How organizations act together: Interorganizational coordination in theory and practice*. Luxemburg: Gordon and Breach.

Alford, R. R., and R. Friedland. 1985. *Powers of theory: Capitalism, the state, and democracy*. Cambridge: Cambridge University Press.

Alliance of Taiwan Aborigines. 1993. Report of Alliance of Taiwan Aborigines presentation to the UN Working Group on Indigenous Populations. Geneva: Alliance of Taiwan Aborigines.

Alvarez, S. E., E. Dagnino, and A. Escobar, eds. 1998. *Cultures of politics/politics of cultures: Re-visioning Latin American social movements*. Boulder: Westview Press.

Amerindian Peoples Association (APA) of Guyana. 1999. Extension of Kaieteur National Park. *APA Newsletter* 1.

Arcoiris. 1996. Correspondence regarding "El Proyecto Vilcabamba" to Elizabeth Bravo, Loja. 30 May.

Areeparampil, M. 1992. Forest policy and denial of tribal rights. In *National development and tribal deprivation*, ed. W. Fernandes, 148+. New Delhi: Indian Social Institute.

Argyris, C. 1982. *Reasoning, learning, and action: Individual and organizational*. San Francisco: Jossey-Bass.

Argyris, C., and D. Schön. 1987. *Organizational learning: A theory of action perspective*. Reading, MA: Addison-Wesley.

Arnold, J. E. M. 1998. *Managing forests as common property*. FAO Forestry Paper 136. Rome: FAO.

Asher, K. 1998. Constructing Afro-Colombia: Ethnicity and territory in the Pacific lowlands. Ph.D. Dissertation, Department of Political Science. Gainesville: University of Florida.

Asiema, J., and F. Situma. 1994. Indigenous peoples and the environment: The case of the pastoral Maasai of Kenya. *Colorado Journal of International Environmental Law and Policy* 5:149–171.

Assembly of First Nations. *Charter of the Assembly of First Nations. http://www.afn.ca/ About%20AFN/charter_of_the_assembly_of_first.htm* Accessed 1 June 2002.

Associated Press. 1997. Burma using forced labor to build tourist park, exiles say. *AP wire.*

Bachrach, P., and M. S. Baratz. 1962. The two faces of power. *American Political Science Review* 56:947–952.

———. 1963. Decisions and nondecisions: An analytical framework. *American Political Science Review* 57:641–651.

———. 1970. *Power and poverty: Theory and practice.* New York: Oxford University Press.

Bailey, C. 1991. Conservation and development in the Galapagos Islands. In *Resident peoples and national parks,* ed. P. C. West and S.R. Brechin, 187–199. Tucson: University of Arizona Press.

Balick, M. 1994. Ethnobotany, drug development, and biodiversity conservation— exploring the linkages. In *Ethnobotany and the search for new drugs: Ciba Foundation Symposium 185,* ed. G. T. Prance, C. Derek, and J.Marsh, 4–17. Chichester: John Wiley.

Banfield, E. 1961. *Political influence.* Glencoe, IL: Free Press.

Barber, C., and V. Pratt. 1997. Sullied seas, strategies for combating cyanide fishing in Southeast Asia and beyond. World Resources Institute and International Marinelife Alliance. Washington, D.C.

Barbier, E. 1987. The concept of sustainable economic development. *Environmental Conservation* 14:101–114.

Barborak J. 1995. Institutional options for managing protected areas. In *Expanding partnerships in conservation,* ed. J. McNeely, 30–38. Washington DC: Island Press.

Baringa, S. 1996. A recipe for river recovery. *Science* 273:1648–1650.

Barkin, D. 2000. Social tourism in rural communities: An instrument for promoting sustainable resource management. Presented at 2000 Meeting of the Latin American Studies Association.

Barnes, T., and J. Duncan, eds. 1992. *Writing worlds: Discourse, text, and metaphor in the representation of landscape.* London: Routledge.

Barsh, R. L. 1994. Making the most of ILO Convention 169. *Cultural Survival Quarterly* 18(1):45–47.

Barume, A. K. 2000. *Heading towards extinction? Indigenous rights in Africa: The case of the Twa of the Kahuzi-Biega NP, Democratic Republic of Congo.* Forest Peoples Programme and IWGIA.

Basappanavar, C. K. 1993. Fire: The tragedy of Nagarahole. *Sanctuary Asia* 13(3):44–47.

Bates, H. 1863 (1989). *The naturalists on the River Amazon: A record of the adventures, habitats of animals, sketches of Brazilian and Indian life, and aspects of nature under the equator, during eleven years of travel.* Middlesex: Penguin Books.

Batisse, M. 1982. The biosphere reserve: A tool for environmental conservation and management. *Environmental Conservation* 9:101–111.

Bawa Village Community. 1997. Mozambique's 'Tchuma Tchato' initiative of resource management on the Zambezi: A community perspective. *Society and Natural Resources* 10:409–413.

Bebbington, A., and T. Perrault. 1999. Social capital, development, and access to resources in highland Ecuador. *Economic Geography* 75:395–418.

Becker, C. D., and E. Ostrom. 1995. Human ecology and resource sustainability: The importance of institutional diversity. *Annual Review of Ecology and Systematics* 26:113–133.

Bejar, E., R. Bussmann, R. Cruz, and C. Douglas. 1997. *Plantas medicinales de vilcabamba.* Quito: Universidad Andina Simon Bolivar.

Bell, H. 1987. Conservation with a human face: Conflict and reconciliation in African land use planning. In *Conservation in Africa: People, Politics, and Practice,* ed. D. Andrew and R. Grove, 79–101. Cambridge: Cambridge University Press.

Belsky, J. M. 2000. The meaning of the manatee: An examination of community-based ecotourism discourse and practice in Gales Point, Belize. In *Plants, people, and justice: Conservation and resource extraction in tropical developing countries,* ed. C. Zerner, 285–308. New York: Columbia University Press.

———. 1999. Misrepresenting communities: The politics of community-based rural ecotourism in Gales Point Manatee, Belize. *Rural Sociology* 64(4): 641–666.

Bendix, R. 1960. *Max Weber: An intellectual portrait.* New York: Doubleday.

Bennett, J. 1995. Private sector initiatives in nature conservation. *Review of Marketing and Agricultural Economics* 63: 426–434.

Berger, P., and T. Luckmann. 1966. *The social construction of reality.* New York: Doubleday.

Berkes, F. 1999. *Sacred ecology: Traditional ecological knowledge and resource management.* Philadelphia: Francis & Beacon.

Berkes, F., and C. Folkes, eds. 1998. *Linking social and ecological systems: Management practices and social mechanisms for building resilience.* Cambridge: Cambridge University Press.

Bernstein, H. 1996. The political economy of the Maize *Filière. The Journal of Peasant Studies* 23(2–3): 120–145.

Bilsborrow, R. E. 1992. *Rural poverty, migration, and the environment in developing countries: Three case studies.* Washington, DC: The World Bank.

Blaikie, P. 1985. *The political economy of soil erosion in developing countries.* Essex, England: Longman Scientific and Technical.

———. 1994. *Political ecology in the 1990s: An evolving view of nature and society.* *CASID Distinguished Speaker Series No. 13.* East Lansing, MI: Michigan State University Center for Advanced Study of International Development.

———. 1995. Understanding environmental issues. In *People and Environment,* ed. S. Morse and M. Stocking, 1–30. London: UCL Press.

Blaikie, P., and H. Brookfield. 1987. *Land degradation and society.* New York: Methuen.

Blaikie, P., and S. Jeanrenaud. 1996. Biodiversity and human welfare. UNRISD Discussion Paper No. 72. Geneva: UNRISD.

Blau, P., and M. Meyer. 1987. *Bureaucracy in modern society.* 3rd ed. New York: McGraw-Hill.

Bokil, M. 1999. People in protected areas: Koyna Sanctuary in Maharashtra. *Economic and Political Weekly,* 30 January.

Boo, E. 1990. *Ecotourism: The potentials and pitfalls.* Washington, DC: Island Press.

Bookbinder, M., E. Dinerstein, A. Rijal, H. Cauley, and A. Rajouria. 1998. Ecotourism's support of biodiversity conservation. *Conservation Biology* 12(6):1399–1404.

Borrini-Feyerabend, G. 1996. *Collaborative management of protected areas: Tailoring the approach to the context.* Gland, Switzerland: World Conservation Union.

———. 1997. *Beyond fences. Seeking social sustainability in conservation.* Gland: IUCN.

Bourdieu, P. 1977. *Outline of a theory of practice.* Cambridge: Cambridge University Press.

———. 1985. The forms of social capital. In *Handbook of theory and research for the sociology of education,* ed. J. G. Richardson. New York: Greenwood.

Bowen, J. R. 2000. Should we have a universal concept of "indigenous peoples" rights? Ethnicity and essentialism in the twenty-first century. *Anthropology Today* 16(4):12–16.

Brandon, K. 1993. *Bellagio Conference on Ecotourism: Briefing Book.* New York: Rockefeller Foundation Conference.

———. 1996. *Ecotourism and conservation: A review of key issues.* Global Environment Division, Biodiversity Series, Paper #033. Washington, DC: The World Bank.

———. 1997. Policy and practical considerations in land-use strategies for biodiversity conservation. In *Last stand: Protected areas and the defense of tropical biodiversity,* ed. R. A. Kramer, C. P. van Schaik, and J. Johnson, 90–114. New York and Oxford: Oxford University Press.

Brandon, K., and R. Margoulis. 1996. The bottom line: Getting biodiversity conservation back into ecotourism. In *The ecotourism equation: Measuring the impacts,* Yale Bulletin Series, No. 99, ed. J. A. Miller and E. Malek-Zadeh, 28–38. New Haven: Yale University Press.

Brandon, K., K. H. Redford, and S. E. Sanderson, eds. 1998. *Parks in peril: People, politics, and protected areas.* Washington, DC: Island Press.

Brechin, S. R. 1997. *Planting trees in the developing world: A sociology of international organizations*. Baltimore: Johns Hopkins University Press.

———. 2000. Evaluation of organizational performance in mountain forestry programmes. In *Forests in sustainable mountain development: A state of knowledge report for 2000 (IUFRO 5 Research Series)*, ed. M. F. Price and N. Butt, 439–442. New York: CABI Publishing.

Brechin, S. R., P. C. West, D. Harmon, and K. Kutay. 1991. Resident peoples and protected areas: A framework for inquiry. In *Resident peoples and national parks: Social dilemmas and strategies in international conservation*, ed. P. C. West, and S. R. Brechin, 5–28. Tucson: The University of Arizona Press.

Brechin, S. R., S. Surapaty, and L. Heydir. 1990. Population-environment dynamics and the power gap theory: Resident people protected area conflicts in South Sumatra, Indonesia. Paper presented at the Population Environment Dynamics Symposium. University of Michigan, Ann Arbor.

Brechin, S. R., S. Surapaty, L. Heydir, and E. Roflin. 1993. Protected area deforestation in South Sumatra, Indonesia. In *Population-environment dynamics: Ideas and observations*, ed. G. D. Ness, W. D. Drake, and S. R. Brechin, 225–252. Ann Arbor: University of Michigan Press.

Brechin, S. R., P. R. Wilshusen, C. F. Fortwangler, and P. C. West. 2002. Beyond the square wheel: Toward a more comprehensive understanding of biodiversity conservation as social and political process. *Society and Natural Resources* 15:41–64.

Brinkate, T. 1996. People and parks: Implications for sustainable development in the Thukela Biosphere Reserve. Paper presented at the Sixth International Symposium on Society and Natural Resource Management. Pennsylvania State University, State College.

Broad, R., and J. Cavanaugh. 1993. *Plundering paradise: The struggle for the environment in the Philippines*. Berkeley: University of California Press.

Brockington, D. 2002. *Fortress conservation. The preservation of the Mkomazi Game Reserve*. Bloomington: Indiana University Press.

Brookings Institution. 1942. *Refugee settlement in the Dominican Republic*. Washington, DC: The Brookings Institution.

Bromley, D. W., ed. 1992. *Making the commons work: Theory, practice, and policy*. San Francisco: ICS Press.

Brown, L. D., and D. Ashman. 1998. Social capital, mutual influence, and social learning in intersectoral problem-solving in Africa and Asia. In *Organizational dimensions of global change*, ed. D. Cooperrider and J. Dutton, 139–167. Thousand Oaks, CA: Sage.

Bruner, A. G., R. E. Gullison, R. E. Rice, and G. A. B. da Fonseca. 2001. Effectiveness of parks in protecting tropical biodiversity. *Science* 291:125–128.

Brunner, R. D., and R. Klein. 1999. Harvesting experience: A reappraisal of the U.S. climate change action plan. *Policy Sciences* 32:133–161.

Bryant, R. L. 1997. *The political ecology of forestry in Burma 1824–1994*. Honolulu: University of Hawai'i Press.

Bryant, R. L., and S. Bailey. 1997. *Third World political ecology*. London: Routledge.

Buck, L., C. Geisler, H. Schelhas, and E. Wollenberg, eds. 2001. *Biological diversity: Balancing interests through adaptive collaborative management*. Boca Raton, FL: CRC Press.

Burch, W. R. 1971. *Daydreams and nightmares: A sociological essay on the American environment*. New York: Harper and Row.

Burkey, S. 1993. *People first, a guide to self-reliant, participatory rural development*. London: Zed Books.

Burns, T., and G. M. Stalker. 1961. *The management of innovation*. London: Tavistock.

Cabanban, A., and A. T. White. 1981. Marine conservation program using non-formal education at Apo Island, Negros Oriental, Philippines. In Proceedings of the Fourth International Coral Reef Symposium, 1:317–321. Manila.

Calhoun, C. 1995. *Critical social theory*. Oxford: Blackwell.

Campbell J. 1999. Hutan Untuk Rakyat, Masyarakat Adat, atau Kooperasi? Paper presented at the Seminar on Legal Complexity, Natural Resource Management and Social (In)Security in Indonesia, Padang, 6–9 September 1999.

Campbell, L. M. 1999. Ecotourism in rural developing communities. *Annals of Tourism Research* 26(3):534–553.

Cárdenas, M. 1997. Correspondence to Elizabeth Bravo, in reply to letter of 10 June 1997, 18 June.

Carney, J. A. 1996. Converting the wetlands, engendering the environment: The intersection of gender with agrarian change in Gambia. In *Liberation ecologies: Environment, development, social movements*, ed. R. Peet and M. Watts, 165–187. London: Routledge.

Cater, E. 1994. Ecotourism in the Third World—Problems and prospects for sustainability. In *Ecotourism: A sustainable option?*, ed. E. Cater and G. Lowman, 69–86. New York: John Wiley.

Center for International Environmental Law (CIEL). 1999. Legal Elements of the "Ayahuasca" Patent Case. Washington, DC: CIEL.

Cernea, M. M. 2000. Risks, safeguards, and reconstruction, A model for population displacement and resettlement. *Economic and Political Weekly*: 3659–3678.

Chandrasena, U.A. 1993. The struggle for survival of an aboriginal group: The Vedda of Sri Lanka. In *Indigenous land rights in commonwealth countries: Dispossession, negotiation, and community action*, ed. G. Cant, J. Overton, and E. Pawson, 13–23. Christchurch, NZ: University of Canterbury.

Chase Smith, R. 1995. The gift that wounds: Charity, the gift economy, and social solidarity in indigenous Amazonia. Unpublished manuscript.

Chatty, D., and M.Colchester. 2002. *Conservation and mobile indigenous peoples. Displacement, forced settlement, and sustainable development*. Oxford: Berghahn Books.

Chidley, L. 2002. *Forests, people, and rights.* London : Down to Earth with Forest Peoples Programme and Rainforest Foundation.

Christie, P. 1999. "In a country without forest, no life is good": Participatory action research in the neo-liberal context of Nicaragua. Ph.D. dissertation, The University of Michigan, Ann Arbor.

Christie, P, and A. T. White. 1994. Reef fish yield and reef condition for San Salvador Island, Luzon, Philippines. *Asian Fisheries Science* 7:135–148.

————. 1997. Trends in development of coastal area management in tropical countries: from central to community orientation. *Coastal Management* 25:155–181.

————, eds. 2000. Tropical coastal management. *Coastal Management* 28(1). Theme issue.

Christie, P., D. Bradford, R. Garth, B. Gonzalez, M. Hostetler, O. Morales, R. Rigby, B. Simmons, E. Tinkam, G. Vega, R. Vernooy, and N. White. 2000. Taking care of what we have: Participatory natural resource management on the Caribbean Coast of Nicaragua. The University of Central America (Managua) and the International Development Research Centre (Ottawa).

Christie, P., A. T. White, and E. Deguit. 2002. Starting point or solution? Community-based marine protected areas in the Philippines. *Journal of Environmental Management* 66:441–454.

Clad, J. C. 1985. Conservation and indigenous peoples: A study of convergent interests. In *Culture and conservation: The human dimension in environmental planning,* ed. J. A McNeely and D. Pitt, 45–62. London: Croom Helm.

Clark, T. W. 1997. *Averting extinction: Reconstructing endangered species recovery.* New Haven: Yale University Press.

Clark, T. W., N. Mazur, S. J. Cork, S. Dovers, and R. Harding. 2000. Koala conservation policy process: Appraisal and recommendations. *Conservation Biology* 14:681–690.

Clark, T. W., A. R. Willard, and C. M. Cromley, eds. 2000. *Foundations of natural resources policy and management.* New Haven: Yale University Press.

Clarke, L. 1999. *Mission improbable: Using fantasy documents to tame disaster.* Chicago: University of Chicago Press.

Clegg, S. R. 1989. *Frameworks of power.* London: Sage.

Cohen, J. H., and C. H. Tokheim. 1994. *Smith Barney special situations research: Shaman Pharmaceuticals: Ethnobotany, biodiversity, and drug discovery.* Location Unknown: Smith Barney Inc.

Cohen M. 1995. The South African natural heritage program: A new partnership among government, landowners, and the business sector. In *Expanding partnerships in conservation,* ed, J. McNeely, 252–260 Washington DC: Island Press.

COICA. 1998. Correspondence to Adolfo Franco, First Vice-President and Legal Consultant, IAF from Mr. Antonio Jacanamijoy. March 3.

Colchester, M. 1987. *The social dimensions of government-sponsored migration and involuntary resettlement: Policies and practice.* Geneva: Commission on International Humanitarian Issues.

——. 1994. Salvaging nature: Indigenous peoples, protected areas, and biodiversity conservation. Discussion paper #55. Geneva: UNRISD.

Coleman, J. S. 1974. *Power and the structure of society.* New York: Norton.

——. 1988. Social capital in the creation of human capital. *American Journal of Sociology* 94:95–120.

Commission on Sustainable Development. 1997. *Results of the international meeting of indigenous and other forest-dependent peoples on the management, conservation, and sustainable development of all types of forests.* Leticia, Columbia.

Comstock, E. 1995. The role of private preserves in the Adirondack Park. *Adirondack Journal of Environmental Studies* 2: 32–39.

Congreso de Americanistas. 1997. *Proceedings of the 49th Congreso de Americanistas, Quito, Ecuador.* Quito: Congreso de Americanistas.

Conley, A., and A. Moote. 2001. *Collaborative conservation in theory and practice: A literature review.* Tucson: Udall Center for Studies in Public Policy, The University of Arizona.

Convention on Biological Diversity (CBD). 2000. *Sustaining life on earth: How the convention on biological diversity promotes nature and human welfare.* Geneva: CBD and UNEP.

——. 2002a. "Parties to the CBD." Available from *http://www.biodiv.org/world/parties.asp* Accessed 1 June 2002.

——. 2002b. "Article 8: In-situ conservation." Available from *http://www.biodiv.org/convention/articles.asp?a=cbd-08* Accessed 1 July 2002.

Cornelius, W. A., and D. Myhre, eds. 1998. *The transformation of rural Mexico: Reforming the ejido sector.* San Diego: Center for U.S.-Mexican Studies, University of California, San Diego.

Corntassel, J. J., and T. H. Primeau. 1995. Indigenous "sovereignty" and international law: Revised strategies for pursuing "self-determination." *Human Rights Quarterly* 17(2):343–365.

Coulter, R. T. 1994. Commentary on UN Draft Declaration on the Rights of Indigenous Peoples. *Cultural Survival Quarterly* 18(1):37–41.

Council of Europe. 1998. *Convention for the Protection of Human Rights and Fundamental Freedoms as Amended by Protocol No. 11 with Protocols Nos. 1, 4, 6, and 7.*

Cox, A., and M. Balick. 1994. The ethnobotanical approach to drug discovery. *Scientific American* 27(6):82–87.

Cox, M. C. 2001. Protected areas and population growth: Implications for protected area policy in the 21st century. Master's thesis, University of Michigan.

Cronon, W. 1995. *Uncommon ground: Rethinking the human place in nature.* New York: Norton.

Crozier, M. 1964. *The bureaucratic phenomenon.* Chicago: University of Chicago Press.

Dalton, R. 2000. Ecologists back blueprint to save biodiversity hotspots. *Nature* 406:926.

Dankelman, I., and J. Davidson. 1988. *Women and environment in the Third World: Alliance for the future.* London: Earthscan/IUCN.

DeCosse, P. 2001. Forest governance and communications under the Environment Management Support Project (PAGE) in Madagascar: Rationale and strategy. Final report submitted to the International Resources Group, Ltd. (IRG).

Deguit, E. 1989. Community organization as a methodology in implementing marine conservation programs in two islands in Central Visayas: a case study. M.A. thesis in Social Work, Asian Social Institute. Manila.

Deme, Y. 1998. *Natural resource management by local associations in the Kelka region of Mali.* IIED Drylands Programme Issue Paper. London: IIED.

Digital Freedom Network. "OGIEK.ORG." *http://www.ogiek.org* Accessed 1 June 2002.

DiMaggio, P. 1997. Culture and cognition. *Annual Review of Sociology* 23:263–287.

Dinerstein, E., D. M. Olson, D. J. Graham, A. L. Webster, S. A. Primm, M. P. Bookbinder, and G. Ledec. 1995. *A conservation assessment of the terrestrial ecoregions of Latin America and the Caribbean.* Washington, DC: The World Bank.

Dizon, J., and G. Miranda. 1996. The coastal resources management experience in San Salvador Island. In *Seeds of hope, a collection of case studies on community-based coastal resources management in the Philippines,* ed. E. M. Ferrer, L. Polotan dela Cruz, and M. Agoncillo Domingo, 129–157. Quezon City, Philippines: College of Social Work and Community Development, The University of the Philippines.

Dombeck, M. P., J. W. Thomas, and C. A. Wood. 1997. Changing roles and responsibilities for federal land management agencies. In *Watershed restoration: Principles and practices,* ed. J. E. Williams, C. A Wood, and M. P. Dombeck, 135–14. Bethesda, MD: American Fisheries Society.

Dorsey, M. K. 2001. Shams, shamans, and the commercialization of biodiversity. In *Redesigning life,* ed. B. Tokar, 320–329. London: Zed Press.

Down to Earth. 1998. Katu people refuse to move from national park. *Down to Earth Newsletter* 36.

———. 2001. Moronene people forced out of national park. *Down to Earth Newsletter* 48.

Drijver, C. A. 1992. People's participation in environmental projects. In *Bush base: Forest farm. Culture, environment, and development,* ed. E. Croll and D. Parkin, 131–145. London: Routledge.

Dryzek, J. S. 2000. *Deliberative democracy and beyond: Liberals, critics, contestations.* Oxford: Oxford University.

Dugelby, B., and M. Libby. 1998. Analyzing the social context at PiP Sites. In *Parks in peril: People, politics, and protected areas,* ed. K Brandon, K. H. Redford, S. E. Sanderson, 63–75. Washington, DC: Island Press.

DuPuis, E. M., and P. Vandergeest, eds. 1996. *Creating the countryside: The politics of rural and environmental discourse.* Philadelphia: Temple University Press.

———. 1998. *Ecotourism statistical fact sheet: General tourism statistics.* Washington, DC: Ecotourism Society.

Edwards, M., and D. Hulme. 1996. Too close for comfort? The impact of official aid on non-governmental organizations. *World Development* 24:961–973.

Ellis, D. 1989. *Environments at risk: Case countries of impact assessment.* New York: Springer.

Elster, J., ed. 1998. *Deliberative democracy.* Cambridge: Cambridge University Press.

Endicott, E., 1993. *Land conservation through public/private partnerships.* Washington, DC: Island Press.

Escobar, A. 1995. *Encountering development.* Princeton: Princeton University Press.

———. 1996. Constructing nature: Elements for a poststructural political ecology. In *Liberation ecologies: Environment, development, social movements,* ed. R. Peets and M. Watts, 46–68. London: Routledge.

———. 1997. Cultural politics and biological diversity: State, capital, and social movements in the Pacific coast of Colombia. In *Between resistance and revolution: Cultural politics and social protest,* ed. R. G. Fox and O. Starn, 40–64. New Brunswick: Rutgers University Press.

———. 1998. Whose knowledge, whose nature? Biodiversity conservation and social movements. *Journal of Political Ecology* 5:53–82.

———. 1999. After nature: Steps to an antiessentialist political ecology. *Current Anthropology* 40:1–16.

Escobar A., and A. Pedrosa. 1996. *Pacífico: Desarrollo o diversidad? Estado, capital, y movimientos sociales en el Pacífico Colombiano.* Bogotá: CEREC/Ecofondo.

Esprit, S. 1994. Dominica: Managing the ecotourism option. *Rural Extension Bulletin* 5.

Fairhead J., and M. Leach. 1998. *Reframing deforestation: Global analysis and local realities: Studies in West Africa.* London: Global Environmental Change Series/Routledge.

Faulder, D. 1997. "In the name of money: SLORC, the Thais, and two multinational oil giants are building a gas pipeline. The Karen are in the way—and that's just too bad," *Asiaweek,* vol. 42.

Fay, C., M. Sirait, and A. Kusworo. 2000. Getting the boundaries right: Indonesia's urgent need to redefine its forest estate. Paper presented at the 8th Conference of the International Association for the Study of Common Property, May 31–June 4, 2000. Bloomington, Indiana.

FEMAT. 1993. *Forest ecosystem management: An ecological, economic, and social assessment.* Report of the Forest Ecosystem Management Assessment Team. Washington, DC: US Government Printing Office.

Ferguson, J. 1990. *The anti-politics machine: Development, depolitization, and bureaucratic power in the Third World.* Cambridge: Cambridge University Press.

Fern. "About Fern." *http://www.fern.org/about.html* Accessed 1 June 2002.

————. 2001. *Forests of fear: The abuse of human rights in forest conflicts.* Moreton-in-Marsh: Fern.

Ferraro, P. J. 2001. Global habitat protection: Limitations of development interventions and a role for conservation performance payments. *Conservation Biology* 15(4):990–1000.

Ferrer, E., L. Polotan de la Cruz , and M. Domingo, eds. 1996. Seeds of hope. Philippines: College of Social Work and Community Development, The University of the Philippines. Quezon City.

Finnemore, M. 1996. Norms, culture, and world politics: Insights from sociology's institutionalism. *International Organization* 50:325–347.

Fisher, J. 1998. *Nongovernments: NGOs and the political development of the Third World.* West Hartford, CT: Kumarian Press.

Fisher, L. 1999. Beyond the Berugao: Conflict, policy, and decision-making in forest and conservation management in Nusa Tenggara, Indonesia. Unpublished Ph.D. dissertation. Ithaca: Cornell University.

Fisher, W. F. 1997. Doing good? The politics and antipolitics of NGO practices. *Annual Review of Anthropology* 26:439–464.

Forest Peoples Programme. "Who We Are." http://forestpeoples.gn.apc.org/who_we_are. htm Accessed 1 June 2002.

Forest Peoples Project (FPP). 2001. Indigenous peoples and protected areas in Africa: From principles to practice. Kigali: Forest Peoples Programme.

Fortmann, L. 1997. Voices from communities managing wildlife in Southern Africa. *Society and Natural Resources* 10:403.

Foucault, M. 1972. *The archaeology of knowledge and the discourse on language.* New York: Pantheon Books.

————. 1979. *Discipline and punish.* New York: Vintage/Random House.

————. 1980. *Power/Knowledge: Selected interviews and other writings 1972–1977.* New York: Pantheon Books.

————. 2000. *Power.* Vol. 3, ed. James B. Faubion. *Essential works of Foucault, 1954–1984.* New York: The New Press.

Fox, J. 1996. How does civil society thicken? The political construction of social capital in rural Mexico. *World Development* 24:1089–1103.

Fox, J., and L. D. Brown, eds. 1998. *The struggle for accountability: The World Bank, NGOs, and grassroots movements.* Cambridge: MIT Press.

Fox, J., and L. Hernández. 1992. Mexico's difficult democracy: Grassroots movements, NGOs, and local government. *Alternatives* 17:165–208.

Francis, C. 1996. Electronic correspondence to Elisabeth Bravo, from Carol Francis *(cfrancis@pobox1.stanford.edu)*. April 18.

Freemuth, J. C. 1991. *Islands under siege: National parks and the politics of external threats*. Lawrence: University of Kansas Press.

Freire, P. 1993. *Pedagogy of the oppressed*. 2nd edition. New York: Continuum.

Freudenberger, M., and P. Larson. 1997. The social, economic, and institutional challenges of implementing ecoregional-based conservation for WWF-US. Draft Discussion Paper. Social Science and Economics Program. Washington, DC: WWF-US.

Friedland, R., and R. R. Alford. 1991. Bringing society back in: Symbols, practices, and institutional contradictions. In *The new institutionalism in organizational analysis*, ed. W. W. Powell and P. J. DiMaggio, 232–263. Chicago: University of Chicago Press.

Fundación Arcoiris. 1997. Correspondence to Angel Paucar, Direccion de Areas Naturales, 7 Marzo. Of. No 036–FAI-97.

Fürer-Haimendorf, C. 1986. *Statement, at the Fourth International Conference on Hunting and Gathering Societies*. London.

Furst, P. 1976. *Hallucinogens and culture*. San Francisco: Chandler and Sharp.

Furze, B., T. DeLacy, and J. Birckhead. 1996. *Culture, conservation, and biodiversity: The social dimension of linking local development through protected areas*. New York: John Wiley.

GEF. 1996. Operational strategy for biodiversity conservation. Washington, DC: GEF.

Gadgil, M., and R. Guha. 1992. *This fissured land: An ecological history of India*. Berkeley: University of California Press.

———. 1995. *Ecology and equity: The use and abuse of nature in contemporary India*. London: Routledge.

Gales Point Progressive Cooperative (GPPC). 1992. Gales Point Progressive Cooperative Management Plan, Gales Point, Belize. (unpub. ms.)

Galletti, H. A. 1998. The Maya Forest of Quintana Roo: Thirteen years of conservation and development. In *Timber, tourists, and temples: Conservation and development in the Maya Forest of Belize, Guatemala, and Mexico*, ed. R. P. Primack, D. B. Bray, H. A. Galletti, and I. Ponciano, 33–46. Washington, DC: Island Press.

Garces, L., and I. Dones. 1998. An assessment of the status of coral reefs and reef fish abundance in San Salvador Island marine reserve, Philippines. Unpublished report. International Center for Living Aquatic Resources Management, Manila.

Gaventa, J. 1980. *Power and powerlessness: Quiescence and rebellion in an Appalachian valley*. Urbana: University of Illinois Press.

Gbadegesin, A., and O. Ayileka. 2000. Avoiding the mistakes of the past: Towards a community oriented management strategy for the proposed national park in Abuja-Nigeria. *Land Use Policy* 17:89–100.

Geisler, C. C. 1993. Adapting social impact assessment to protected area development. In *The social challenge of biodiversity conservation,* ed. S. H. Davis, 25–42. GEF Working Paper No. 1: UNDP, UNEP, and the World Bank.

———. 1993. Rethinking SIA: Why ex-ante research isn't enough. *Society and Natural Resources* 6:327–338.

———. 2003. A new king of trouble: Evictions in Eden. *International Social Science Journal* 175. Forthcoming.

———. 2002. Endangered humans. *Foreign Policy* 130:80–81.

Geisler, C., and R. de Sousa. 2001. From refuge to refugee: The African case. *Journal of Public Administration and Development* 21:159–170.

Geisler, C., A. Barton, and R. Warne. 1997. The wandering commons. *Agriculture and Human Values* 14: 325–335.

Geisler, C., and B. Bedford. 1998. Ecosystem management: Who's entitled? In *Who owns the land?,* ed. H. L Jacobs, 131–158. Madison: University of Wisconsin Press.

Geisler, C., and G. Daneker. 2000. *Property and values: Alternatives to public and private ownership.* Washington, DC: Island Press.

Geisler, C., and E. Letsoalo. 2000. Rethinking land reform in South Africa: An alternative approach to environmental justice. *Sociological Research Online* 3,4.

Gentry, A. 1993. Tropical forest biodiversity and the potential for new medicinal plants. In *Human medicinal agents from plants,* ed., A. D. Kinghorn and M. F. Balandrin, 13–24. Washington, DC.: American Chemical Society.

Gezon L. 1995. The political ecology of conflict and control in Ankarana. Ph.D. dissertation, Anthropology Department, University of Michigan.

———. 1997a. Institutional structure and the effectiveness of integrated conservation and development projects: Case study from Madagascar. *Human Organization* 56(4):462–470.

———. 1997b. Political ecology and conflict in Ankarana, Madagascar. *Ethnology.* 36 (2):85–100.

———. 1999. Of shrimps and spirit possession: Toward a political ecology of resource management in northern Madagascar. *American Anthropologist* 101(1): 58–67.

———. 2000. Social differentiation in resource management among women in the Ankarana region. *Taloha* 13: 239–260.

———. 2000. The changing face of NGOs: Structure and communities in Malagasy conservation and development. *Urban anthropology and studies of cultural systems and world economic development* 29(2):181–215.

———. 2002. Marriage, kin, and compensation: A socio-political ecology of gender in Ankarana, Madagascar. *Anthropological Quarterly* 75(4):675–706.

Gezon L., and B. Freed. 1999. Agroforestry and conservation in Northern Madagascar: Hopes and hindrances. *African Studies Review* 3(1): 9–29.

Ghai Y. 2001. *Public participation and minorities.* Minority Rights Group International.

Ghimire, K. B., and M. P. Pimbert. 1997. Social change and conservation: An overview of issues and concepts. In *Social change and conservation: Environmental politics and impacts of national parks and protected areas,* ed. K. B. Ghimire and M. P. Pimbert, 1–45. London: Earthscan.

————, eds. 1997. *Social change and conservation: Environmental politics and impacts of national parks and protected areas.* London: Earthscan.

Gibson, C., M. McKean, and E. Ostrom, eds. 2000. *People and forests: Communities, institutions, and governance.* Cambridge: MIT Press.

Gibson, C. C. 1999. *Politicians and poachers: The political economy of wildlife policy in Africa.* Cambridge: Cambridge University Press.

Giddens, A. 1984. *The constitution of society.* Berkeley: University of California Press.

Gomez, E., and H. Yap. 1982. Coral reef degradation and pollution in the East Asian Seas region. Marine Sciences Center, The University of the Philippines, Diliman, Quezon City, Philippines.

Gomez-Pompa, A., and A. Kaus. 1992. Taming the wilderness myth. *Bioscience* 42(4):271–280.

Gomm, R. 1974. The elephant men. *Ecologist* 4:53–57.

Goodland, R. 1982. *Tribal peoples and economic development: Human ecological considerations.* Washington, DC: World Bank.

Goodwin-Gill, G. 1983. *The refugee in international law.* Oxford: Clarendon Press.

Gordon R. J. 1985. Conserving Bushmen to extinction in Southern Africa. In *Survival International Review* 44, ed. M. Colchester, 28–42. London: Survival International.

————. 1990. The prospects for anthropological tourism in Bushmanland. *Cultural Survival Quarterly* 14(1).

Gramsci, A. 1971. *Selections from the prison notebooks.* New York: International Publishers.

Gray, B. 1989. *Collaborating: Finding common ground for multiparty problems.* San Francisco: Jossey-Bass.

Green, C. 1992. The environment and population growth: Decade for action. Population Reports, Series M., No. 10. Baltimore: Johns Hopkins University.

Greenlee, D. 1996. Personal communication, Gales Point, Belize.

Grifo, F., and J. Rosenthal, eds. 1997. *Biodiversity and human health.* Washington, DC: Island Press.

Grove, R. H. 1990. Colonial conservation, ecological hegemony, and popular resistance: Towards a global synthesis. In *Imperialism and the Natural World,* ed. J. M. MacKenzie, 15–50. Manchester: Manchester University Press.

Grueso, L., C. Rosero, and A. Escobar. 1998. The process of black community organizing in the southern Pacific Coast region of Colombia. In *Cultures of* politics/Politics of cultures: Re-visioning Latin American social movements, ed. S. Alvarez, E. Dagnino, and A. Escobar, 196–219. Boulder: Westview Press.

Guha, R. 1994. Fighting for the forest: State forestry and social change in tribal India. In The rights of subordinated peoples, ed. O. Mendelsohn and U. Baxi, 20–37. Delhi: Oxford Press.

——. 1997. The authoritarian biologist and the arrogance of anti-humanism: Wildlife conservation in the Third World. The Ecologist 27:14–20.

——. 1998. Between anthropology and literature: The ethnographies of Verrier Elwin. Journal of the Royal Anthropological Institute 4(2):325–343.

Guha, R., and J. Martinez-Alier. 1997. Varieties of environmentalism: Essays from North and South. London: Earthscan.

Gunderson, L., C. Holling, and S. Light, eds. 1995. Barriers and bridges to the renewal of ecosystems and institutions. New York: Columbia University Press.

Gustanski, J. A., and R. H. Squires. 2000. Protecting the land: Conservation easements past, present, and future. Washington, DC: Island Press.

Hackel, J. D. 1999. Community conservation and the future of Africa's wildlife. Conservation Biology 13(4): 726–734.

Haenn, N. M. 1997. "The government gave us this land": Political ecology and regional culture in Campeche, Mexico. Ph.D. dissertation, University of Indiana.

Hall, C. M. 1994. Ecotourism in Australia, New Zealand, and the South Pacific: Appropriate tourism or a new form of ecological imperialism? In Ecotourism: A sustainable option?, ed. E. Cater and G. Lowman, 196–219. New York: John Wiley.

Hammond, E. Personal comm. May 2000. 5th Conference of the Parties, Convention on Biological Diversity. Nairobi, Kenya.

Hanna, S., C. Folke, and K. Maler, eds. 1996. Rights to nature: Ecological, economic, cultural, and political principles of institutions for the environment. Washington, DC: Island Press.

Hannah, L., B. Rakotosamimanana, J. Ganzhorn, R. A. Mittermeier, S. Olivieri, L. Iyer, S. Pajaobelina, J. Hough, F. Andriamialisoa, I. Bowles, and G. Tilkin. 1998. Participatory planning, scientific priorities, and landscape conservation in Madagascar. Environmental Conservation 25(1): 30–36.

Harcourt, W., ed. 1994. Feminist perspectives on sustainable development. London and New Jersey: Zed Books.

Harper, J. 2002. Endangered species : Health, illness, and death among Madagascar's people of the forest. Durham: Carolina Academic Press.

Hecht, S., and A. Cockburn. 1989. The fate of the forest: Developers, destroyers, and defenders of the Amazon. London: Verso Press.

Hendrix, S. 1997. Bolivia's outpost of hope. Quechua Indians establish ecotourist camp, Chalalan, within Madidi National Park. International Wildlife 27 (Jan./Feb.):12–19.

Henry E. Huntington Library and Art Gallery. 1925. *From Panama to Peru: The Conquest of Peru by the Pizarros, The Rebellion of Gonzalo Pizzaro and the Pacification by La Gasca; an epitome of the original signed documents to and from the conquistadors, Francisco Gonzalo Pedro, and Hernando Pizarro, Diego de Almagro, and pacificator La Gasca, together with the original signed Ms. Royal decrees.* London: Maggs Bros.

Hernández J., A. Bidoux, E. Cortés, and J. Tresierra. 1995. "Proyecto Biopacífico: Informe final primera evaluación externa." Santa Fé de Bogotá: UNDP-GEF.

Heydir L. 1993. *Population-environment dynamics in Lahat: A case study of deforestation in the regency of South Sumatra Province, Indonesia.* Master's thesis, University of Kentucky.

Heyns, C., and F. Viljoen. 2001. The impact of the United Nations Human Rights Treaties on the domestic level. *Human Rights Quarterly* 23(3): 483–535.

Hinawi, E. 1985. *Environmental refugees.* Nairobi: UNEP.

Hitchcock, R. 1994. International human rights, the environment, and indigenous peoples. *Colorado Journal of International Environmental Law and Policy* 5:1–21.

———. 1996. *Bushmen and the politics of the environment in Southern Africa.* Copenhagen: IWGIA

———. 2002. Removals, politics, and human rights. *Cultural Survival Quarterly* 26(1):25–26.

Hitchcock, R. K., and R. L Brandenburgh. 1990. Tourism, conservation, and culture in the Kalahari Desert, Botswana. *Cultural Survival Quarterly* 14(2):20–24.

Hitchcock, R., and J. D. Holm. 1993. Bureaucratic domination of hunter-gatherer societies: A study of the San in Botswana. *Development and Change* 24(2).

Holling, C., ed. 1978. *Adapative environmental assessment and management.* London: John Wiley.

Homer-Dixon, T. F. 1999. *Environment, scarcity, and violence.* Princeton: Princeton University Press.

Honey, M. 1999. *Ecotourism and sustainable development: Who owns paradise?* Washington, DC: Island Press.

Hoppe, J. 1989. *Los Parques nacionales de la Republica Domincana/The national parks of the Dominican Republic.* Santo Domingo: Colección Barcelo 1.

Hornsborg, A. 2001. *The power of the machine: Global inequalities of economy, technology, and environment.* New York: AltaMira Press.

Horowitz, L. S. 1998. Integrating indigenous resource management with wildlife conservation: A case study of Batang Ali National Park, Sarawak, Malaysia. *Human Ecology* 26(3):371–403.

Horwich, R. H. 1996. Personal communication, Gales Point, Belize.

Horwich, R. H., and J. Lyon. 1998. Community development as a conservation strategy: The Community Baboon Sanctuary and Gales Point, Manatee projects compared. In *Timber, tourists, and temples: Conservation and development in the Maya forests of Belize, Guatemala, and Mexico*, ed. R. B. Primack, D. Bray, H. A. Galletti, and I. Ponciano, 343–364. Washington, DC, and Covelo, CA.: Island Press.

Hough, J. L. 1989. National parks and local people relationships: Case studies from Northern Benin, West Africa, and the Grand Canyon, USA. Ph.D. dissertation, University of Michigan, School of Natural Resources.

———. 1991. Social impact assessment: Its role in protected area planning and management. In *Resident peoples and national parks: Social dilemmas and strategies in international conservation*, ed. P. C. West and S. R. Brechin, 274–283. Tucson: University of Arizona Press.

———. 1994. Institutional constraints to the integration of conservation and development: A case study from Madagascar. *Society and Natural Resources* 7:119–124.

Hough, J., and M. Sherpa. 1989. Bottom up vs. basic needs: Integrating conservation and development in the Annapurna and Michiru Mountain Conservation Areas of Nepal and Malawi. *Ambio* 18: 434–441.

Hugo, G. 1995. Environmental concerns and international migration. Paper prepared for International Conference on Ethics, Migration and Global Stewardship, Center for Migration Studies, Georgetown University and Center for Advanced Studies of Ethics, Washington, DC. (13–15 September).

Huxham, C. 1996. *Creating collaborative advantage*. Thousand Oaks, CA: Sage.

Inamdar, A., H. de Jode, K. Lindsay, and S. Cobb. 1999. Capitalizing on nature: Protected area management. *Science* 283: 1856–1857.

Inter-American Foundation (IAF). 1998. Correspondence to Mr. Antonio Jacanamijoy from Adolfo Franco, First Vice-President and Legal Consultant, IAF. February 23.

International Alliance of Indigenous-Tribal Peoples of the Tropical Forests. 1999. A long struggle for our rights. *The Courier* 173 : 43–45.

International Indian Treaty Council. "Our Mission." *http://www.treatycouncil.org/home.htm* Accessed 1 June 2002.

International Labour Organisation (ILO). 1989. *Convention concerning indigenous and tribal peoples in independent countries (Convention 169)*. Geneva: ILO.

IUCN. 1980. *World conservation strategy: Living resource conservation for sustainable development*. Gland, Switzerland: IUCN, UNEP, WWF.

———. 1984. *1983 United Nations list of national parks and protected areas*. Gland, Switzerland: The World Conservation Union.

———. 1991. *Caring for the Earth: A strategy for sustainable living*. Gland, Switzerland: IUCN.

———. 1994. *1993 United Nations list of national parks and protected areas*. Gland, Switzerland: The World Conservation Union.

———. 1996. Resolutions and Recommendations, World Conservation Congress. Montreal: IUCN.

———. 2000. Confirming the global extinction crisis: A call for international action as the most authoritative global assessment of species loss is released. *http://www.iucn.org/redlist/2000/news.htm* Accessed 3 October 2000.

IWGIA. 2002. "What is self-determination?" *http:// www.iwgia.org* Accessed 1 June 2002.

Jacoby, K. 2001. *Crimes against nature: Squatters, poachers, thieves, and the hidden history of American conservation.* Berkeley: University of California Press.

Jacanamijoy, A. 1996. Amazon indigenous peoples denounce project to install ayahuasca laboratory in Ecuador. Press Release. Quito: COICA.

Jackson, C. 1993. Woman/nature or gender/history? A critique of ecofeminist "development"? *The Journal of Peasant Studies* 20(3): 389–419.

Jacobson, J. 1988. Environmental refugees: A yardstick of habitability. Worldwatch Paper No. 86. Washington, DC: Worldwatch Institute. November.

Jain, N. 1999. Trekking tourism and protected area management in the Annapurna Conservation Area, Nepal. Dissertation, School of Natural Resources, University of Michigan, Ann Arbor.

Jatun Sacha. 1997. *Posibilidades de Manejo de Sangre de Drago en la Parte Alta de la Via Hollin-Loreto.* Quito: Proyecto Gran Sumaco, Instituto Ecuatoriano Forestal de Areas Naturales y Vida Silvestre (INEFAN) and GTZ.

John, D. 1994. *Civic environmentalism: Alternatives to regulation in states and communities.* Washington, DC: Congressional Quarterly Press.

Johnson, M. A. 1997. The (wo)man in the cashew: Gender and development in rural Belize. Working paper series. Institute for Research on Women and Gender, University of Michigan, Ann Arbor.

———. 1998. Nature, progress, and place: The politics of sustainable development in rural Belize. Ph.D. dissertation. University of Michigan, Ann Arbor.

Johnston, B. R. 1997. *Life and death matters: Human rights and the environment at the end of the millennium.* London: Altamira Press.

Jordan and Associates. 1996. *Estudio de Mercado de Sangre de Drago (Croton lechleri).* Quito: Proyecto Gran Sumaco, Instituto Ecuatoriano Forestal de Areas Naturales y Vida Silvestre (INEFAN) and GTZ.

Jordon, G., and C. Weedon. 1995. *Cultural politics: Class, gender, race, and the postmodern world.* Oxford: Blackwell.

Katon, B., R. Pomeroy, L. Garces, and A. Salamanca. 1999. Fisheries management of San Salvador Island, Philippines: a shared responsibility. *Society and Natural Resources* 12(8):777–796.

Keck, M. E., and K. Sikkink. 1998. *Activists beyond borders: Advocacy networks in international politics.* Ithaca: Cornell University Press.

Kellert, S. R., J. N. Mehta, S. A. Ebbin, and L. L. Lichtenfeld. 2000. Community natural resource management: Promise, rhetoric, and reality. *Society and Natural Resources* 13:705–715.

Kelso, C. 1993. The landless Bushmen. *Africa Report* 38(2):51–54.

Kennedy, D., and M. Miller. February 23, 1996. Correspondence/Invitation to Professor Veronica Eady and attended.

Kent, S. 2002. Basarwa resettlement. *Cultural Survival Quarterly* 26(1):21–22.

King, S. 1994. Establishing reciprocity: Biodiversity, conservation, and new models for cooperation between forest-dwelling peoples and the pharmaceutical industry. In *Intellectual property rights for indigenous peoples, a sourcebook,* ed. T. Greaves, 69–82. Oklahoma City: Society for Applied Anthropology.

King, S., T. Carlson, J. Chinnock, K. Moran, and B. Borges. 2000. Issues in the commercialization of medicinal plants. In *Responding to bioprospecting: From biodiversity in the South to medicines in the North,* ed. H. Svarstad and S. Dhillion, 77–88. Oslo: Spartacus.

King, S., T. Carlson, and K. Moran. 1996. Biological diversity, indigenous knowledge, drug discovery, and intellectual property rights. In *Valuing local knowledge: Indigenous people and intellectual property rights,* ed. S. B. Brush and D. Stabinsky, 167–185. Washington, DC: Island Press.

Kirk, R. 1992. Stone of refuge; Haitian refugees in the Dominican Republic. Washington, DC: Washington Committee for Refugees.

Klooster, D. 2000. Community forestry and tree theft in Mexico: Resistance or complicity in conservation. *Development and Change* 31:281–305.

Knight, D. 1998. An enemy of indigenous peoples. The case of Loren Miller, COICA, the Inter-American Foundation, and the Ayahuasca plant. *Multinational Monitor* 19(6).

Knudsen, A. 1999. Conservation and controversy in the Karakoram: Khunjerab. *Journal of Political Ecology* 56:1–18.

Koch, E. 1994. *Reality or rhetoric? Ecotourism and rural reconstruction in South Africa.* Geneva: UNRISD.

Kohm, K. A., and J. F. Franklin. 1997. *Creating a forestry for the 21st century: The science of ecosystem management.* Washington, DC: Island Press.

Korten, D. 1990. Getting to the 21st century, volunteer action, and the global agenda. West Hartford, CT: Kumarian Press.

Korten, D., and N. T. Uphoff. 1981. *Bureaucratic reorientation for participatory rural development.* NASPAA Working Paper No. 1. Washington, DC: NASPAA and USAID.

Korten, F., and R. Y. Siy, eds. 1989. *Transforming a bureaucracy: The experience of the Philippine national irrigation administration.* West Hartford, CT: Kumarian Press.

Kothari, A., S. Suri, and N. Singh. 1995. Conservation in India: New direction. *Economic & Political Weekly.* October 28, vol. 30: 2755–2766.

Kothari, S., and P. Parajuli. 1993. No nature without social justice: A plea for cultural and ecological pluralism in India. In *Global ecology: A new arena of political conflict,* ed. W. Sachs, 224–241. London: Zed Books.

Kottak, C. 1991. When people don't come first: Some sociological lessons from completed projects. In *Putting people first: Sociological variables in rural development*, 2nd ed, ed. M. Cernea. 429–464. New York: Oxford University Press.

Kottak, C., and E. Colson. 1994. Multilevel linkages: Londitudinal and comparative studies. In *Assessing cultural anthropology*, ed. R. Borofsky, 396–412.New York: McGraw-Hill.

Kramer, R. A., C. P. van Schaik, and J. Johnson, eds. 1997. *Last stand: Protected areas and the defense of tropical biodiversity*. New York: Oxford University Press.

Kramer, R., J. Langholz, and N. Salafsky. 2002. The role of the private sector in protected area establishment and management: A conceptual framework for analyzing effectiveness. In *Making parks work: Strategies for preserving tropical forests*, ed. J. Terborgh, C. van Schaik, L. Davenport, and M. Rao, 335–351. Washington, DC: Island Press.

Kreimer, A., and M. Munasinghe, eds. 1991. *Managing natural disasters and the environment*. Washington, DC: The World Bank.

Kutay, K. 1984. Cahuita National Park, Costa Rica: A case study in living cultures and national park management. Master's thesis, School of Natural Resources, University of Michigan, Ann Arbor.

Laclau, E., and C. Mouffe. 1985. *Hegemony and socialist strategy*. London: Verso.

Langholz J. 1996. Economics, objectives, and success of private nature reserves in Sub-Saharan Africa and Latin America. *Conservation Biology* 10: 271–280.

———. 1999. *Conservation cowboys: Privately owned parks and the protection of tropical biodiversity*. Unpublished Ph.D. dissertation. Ithaca: Cornell University Press.

———. 2002. Privately owned parks. In *Making parks work: Strategies for preserving tropical forests*, ed. J. Terborgh, C. van Schaik, L. Davenport, and M. Rao, 172–188. Washington, DC: Island Press.

Langholz, J., and K. Brandon. 2001. Ecotourism and privately owned protected areas. In *The encyclopedia of ecotourism*, ed. D. Weaver, 303–314. Oxon, United Kingdom: CAB International.

Langholz, J., and J. Lassoie. 2001. Perils and promise of privately owned protected areas. *BioScience* 51(12):1079–1085.

———. 2002. Combining conservation and development on private lands: Lessons from Costa Rica. *Environment, Development, and Sustainability* 3:309–322.

Langholz J., J. Lassoie, and J. Schelhas. 2000. Incentives for biodiversity conservation: Lessons from Costa Rica's private wildlife refuge program. *Conservation Biology* 14(6): 1735–1743.

Langholz J., J. P. Lassoie, D. Lee, and D. Chapman. 2000. Economic considerations of privately owned parks. *Ecological Economics* 33: 173–183.

Larson, P., M. Freudenberger, and B. Wyckoff-Baird. 1997. *Lessons from the field: A review of World Wildlife Fund's experience with integrated conservation and development projects 1985–1996*. Washington, DC: World Wildlife Fund.

Lawrence, P. R., and J. W. Lorch. 1967. *Organization and environment: Managing differentiation and integration.* Cambridge: Harvard University, Graduate School of Business Administration.

Lawry, S. W. 1989. *Tenure policy and natural resource management in Sahelian West Africa.* Madison, WI: Land Tenure Center.

Lawson, N. 1985. Where whitemen come to play. *Cultural Survival Quarterly* 9(1):54–56.

Leach, M. 1992. Gender and the environment: Traps and opportunities. *Development in Practice* 2(1): 12–22.

Leach, M., S. Joekes, and C. Green, eds. 1995. Editorial: Gender relations and environmental change. *Ids bulletin* 26(1): 1–8.

Leach, M., and J. Fairhead. 2000. Fashioned forest pasts, occluded histories? International environmental analysis in West African locales. *Development and Change* 31:35–59.

Le Billion, P. 2000. The political ecology of transition in Cambodia 1989–1999: War, peace, and forest exploitation. *Development and Change* 31:785–805.

Lee, K. N. 1993. *Compass and gyroscope: Integrating science and politics for the environment.* Washington, DC: Island Press.

———. 1996. *Upstream.* Washington, DC: National Academy Press.

———. 2001. Appraising adaptive management. In *Adapative collaborative management of protected areas: Advancing the potential,* ed. L. Buck, C. Geisler, J. Schelhas, and L. Wallenstein, 3–26. Boca Raton: CRC Press.

Leiderman, S. 1995. Environmental refugees. *Encyclopedia of the future.* New York: Macmillan.

Leff E. 1985. Ethnobotany and anthropology as tools for a cultural conservation strategy. In *Culture and conservation: The human dimension in environmental planning,* ed. J. A. McNeely and D. Pitt, 259–268. London: Croom Helm.

Lelé, S. 1991. Sustainable development: A critical review. *World Development* 19(6):607–621.

Leopold, A. 1966. *A Sand County almanac.* New York: Oxford University Press.

Lester, J. P. 1990. A new federalism: Environmental policy in the states. In *Environmental policy in the 1990s: Toward a new agenda,* ed. N. J. Vig and M. E. Kraft, 59–79. Washington, DC: Congressional Quarterly Press.

Levitt, B., and J. G. March. 1988. Organizational learning. *Annual Review of Sociology* 14:319–340.

Levy, A., and C. Scott-Clark. 1997. Burma's junta goes green: Save the rhino, kill the people. *The Observer,* 9. London.

Lewis, J. 2000. *The Batwa Pygmies of the Great Lakes Region.* Minority Rights Group International.

Lewis, J., and J. Knight. 1995. *The Twa of Rwanda: Assessment of the situation of the Twa and promotion of Twa rights in post-war Rwanda.* Oxford: WRM and IWGIA.

Lewis, D., and N. Carter, eds. 1993. *Voices from Africa: Local perspectives on conservation.* Washington, DC: World Wildlife Fund.

Leyva, P. 1993. *Colombia Pacífico.* Bogotá: Fondo FEN.

Li, T. M. 1999. Compromising power: Development, culture, and rule in Indonesia. *Cultural Anthropology* 14:295–322.

Little, P. D. 1994. The link between local participation and improved conservation: A review of issues and experiences. In *Natural connections: Perspectives in community-based conservation,* ed. D. Western, M. R. Wright, and S. C. Strum, 347–372. Washington, DC: Island Press.

Lowry, A., and T. P. Donahue. 1994. Parks, politics, and pluralism: The demise of national parks in Togo. *Society and Natural Resources* 7(4):321–329.

Lukes, S. 1974. *Power: A radical view.* London: Macmillan.

———, ed. 1986. *Power.* Oxford: Blackwell.

MacKenzie, J. M. 1988. *The empire of nature: Hunting, conservation, and British imperialism.* Manchester: Manchester University Press.

Machlis, G. E., and W. R. Burch. 1983. Relations between strangers: Cycles of structure and meaning in tourist systems. *Sociological Review* 31(4):665–692.

Maffi, L., G. Oviedo, and P. Billy. 2000. *Indigenous and traditional peoples of the world and ecoregion conservation: An integrated approach to conserving the world's biological and cultural diversity.* Gland, Switzerland: WWF International.

Magin, G., C. Marijnissen, S. Moniaga, and C. Meek. 2001. *Forests of fear: The abuse of human rights in the forest conflicts.* Moreton-in-Marsh: Fern.

Maletsky, C. 1997. Namibia, Hai//Om case dropped. *Africa News Service.*

Margoluis, R., and N. Salafsky. 1998. *Measures of success: Designing, managing, and monitoring conservation and development projects.* Washington, DC: Island Press.

Markels, A. 1998. The great eco-trips: Guide to the guides. *Audobon* 100(5):66–69.

Marks, S. 1984. *Imperial lion: Human dimensions of wildlife management in Central Africa.* Boulder: Westview Press.

Maruyama, J. 2002. The human impact. *Cultural Survival Quarterly* 26(1):27–28.

McCarthy, J. F. 2000. Wild logging: The rise and fall of logging networks and biodiversity conservation projects on Sumatra's rainforest frontier. Occasional Paper #31, Center for International Forestry Research, CIFOR, Bogor Indonesia.

McCay, B. J., and J. M. Acheson, eds. 1987. *The question of the commons: The culture and ecology of communal resources.* Tucson: University of Arizona Press.

McChesney, J. D. 1993. Biological and chemical diversity and the search for new pharmaceuticals and other bioactive natural products. In *Human medicinal agents from plants,* ed., A. D. Kinghorn and M. F. Balandrin, 38–47. Washington, DC.: American Chemical Society.

McClaurin, I. 1995/1996. *Women setting limits: The power of gender in Belize.* New Brunswick: Rutgers University Press.

McLaren, D. 2000. Letter to Mr. Oliver Hillel, Tourism Programme Coordinator United Nations Environment Programme Division of Technology Industry and Economics Production and Consumption. 27 Oct. *http://www.twnside.org.sg/title/iye4.htm*

McLaren, D. 1998. Rethinking tourism and ecotravel: The paving of paradise and what you can do to stop it. West Hartford, CT: Kumarian Press.

McManus, L. 1988. The coral reefs of the Lingayen Gulf: a challenge to resource management. *Trop. Coast. Area Manage.* 1(2): 8–11.

McNeely, J. A., ed. 1995. *Expanding partnerships in conservation.* Washington, DC: Island Press.

McNeely, J. A., and K. R. Miller. 1984. *National parks, conservation, and development: The role of protected areas in sustaining society.* Washington, DC: Smithsonian Institution.

McNeely J. A., and D. Pitt, eds. 1985. *Culture and conservation: The human dimension in environmental planning.* London: Croom Helm.

McNeely, J. A., K. R. Miller, W. Reid, R. Mittermeier, and T. B. Werner. 1990. *Conserving the world's biological diversity.* Gland, Switzerland: IUCN.

McNeely, J. A., J. Harrison, and P. Dingwall, eds. 1994. *Protecting nature: Regional reviews of protected areas.* Gland, Switzerland: IUCN.

McNeely, J. A., and G. D. Ness. 1996. People, parks, and biodiversity: Issues in population-Eenvironment dynamics. In *Human population, biodiversity, and protected areas: Science and policy issues,* ed. V. Dompka, 19–70. Washington, DC: American Association for the Advancement of Science.

Merchant, C. 1992. *Radical ecology: The search for a livable world.* New York: Routledge.

Merton, R. K. 1936. The unanticipated consequences of purposive social action. *American Sociological Review* 1:894–904.

Mesquita, C. A. 1999. Private nature reserves and ecotourism in Latin America: A strategy for environmental conservation and socio-economic development. Masters thesis. Turrialba, Costa Rica: Centro Agronomico Tropical de Investigacion.

Meyerson, F. 1998. Guatemala burning. *The Amicus Journal* 20(3):28–32.

Meza, E. ed. 1999. Desarrollando Nuestra Diversidad Biocultural: "Sangre De Grado" y el Reto de su Produccion Sustentable en el Peru. Lima: Universidad Nacional Mayor de San Marcos Fondo Editorial.

Mies, M., and V. Shiva. 1993. *Ecofeminism.* London and New Jersey: Zed Books.

Miller, L. 3 July 1996. Fax correspondence to Elias Piyahuaje from Loren Miller.

Miller, M. 2000. Telephone interview. September 21.

Miller, J. 1999. In digger, 1999. Bioprospecting: Searching for new medicines. *Three River Confluence* (Autumn): No. 15. 1–3.

Ministerio de Agricultura y Ganadería (MAG). 1991. Autorización (Investigación Científica) (Flora Silvestre). Quito: MAG.

Momberg, F., R. Puri, and T. Jessup. 2000. Exploitation of the Gaharu and forest conservation efforts in Kayan Mentarang National Park, East Kalimantan, Indonesia. In *People, plants, and justice: The politics of nature conservation,* ed. C. Zerner, 259–284. New York: Columbia University Press.

Momsen, J. H., ed.1993. *Women and change in the Caribbean: A pan-Caribbean perspective.* Kingston, Jamaica: Ian Randle.

Montgomery, J. D., and A. Inkeles. 2000. Special Issue: Social capital as a policy resource. *Policy Sciences* 33:227–494.

Mooney, P. R. 2000. Why we call it biopiracy? In *Responding to bioprospecting: From biodiversity in the South to medicines in the North,* ed. H. Svarstad and S. Dhillion, 37–44. Oslo: Spartacus Forlag.

Moore, D. S. 1996. Marxism, culture, and political ecology: Environmental struggles in Zimbabwe's Eastern Highlands. In *Liberation ecologies: Environment, development, social movements,* ed. R. Peet and M. Watts, 125–147. London: Routledge.

Moran, E. F. 1993. Deforestation and land use in the Brazilian Amazon. *Human Ecology* 21:1–21.

Morgan, G. 1997. *Images of organization.* 2nd Ed. Thousand Oaks, CA: Sage.

Morris, A., and C. Mueller, eds. 1992. *Frontiers in social movement theory.* New Haven: Yale University Press.

Morris, B. 1987. Wildlife protection and indigenous people. *Oryx* 21:3–5.

Mortimer, D. 2001. Exploring community based natural resources management in Mali: A case study of decentralization and the Walde Kelka. Master's thesis, School of Natural Resources and Environment, University of Michigan.

Munt, I. 1993. Ecotourism gone awry. *Report on the Americas* 26(4):8–10.

Murguía, R. E. 1990. *Plan Estratégico de la Iniciativa México para el Area de Agricultura y Desarrollo Rural.* W.K. Kellogg Foundation.

———. 1998. *Informe a la Fundación Interamericana acerca de la situación de la ONGs en la Península de Yucatán.* UNDP, GEF Small Grants Programme.

Myers, N. 1988. Threatened biotas: Hotspots in tropical forests. *Environmentalist* 8:178–208.

———. 1993. Environmental refugees in a globally warmed world. *BioScience* 43(11):752–761.

Myers, N., R. A. Mittermeier, C. G. Mittermeirer, G. A. B. da Fonseca, and J. Kent. 2000. Biodiversity hotspots for conservation priorities. *Nature* 403:853–858.

Navajas H. 1995. Informe de misión: Proyecto Biopacífico COL/92/G31. Santa Fé de Bogotá: UNDP.

Nelson, N., and S. Wright. 1995. Participation and power. In *Power and participatory development,* ed. N. Nelson and S. Wright, 1–18. London: Intermediate Technology Publications.

Nepal, S. K., and K. E. Weber. 1995. Managing resources and resolving conflicts: National parks and local people. *International Journal of Sustainable Development and World Ecology* 2:11–25.

Neumann, R. P. 1995. Local challenges to global agendas: Conservation, economic liberalization, and the pastoralists' rights movement in Tanzania. *Antipode* 27(4): 363–382.

———. 1998. *Imposing wilderness: Struggles over livelihood and nature preservation in Africa*. Berkeley: University of California Press.

———. 2000. Land, justice, and the politics of conservation in Tanzania. In *People, plants, and justice: The politics of nature conservation*, ed. C. Zerner, 117–133. New York: Columbia University Press.

Neumann, R. P., and R. A. Schroeder. 1995. Manifest ecological destinies. *Antipode* 27:321–428.

Nietschmann, B. 1997. Protecting indigenous coral reefs and sea territories, Miskito Coast, RAAN, Nicaragua. In *Conservation through cultural survival: Indigenous peoples and protected areas*, ed. S. Stevens, 193–224. Washington, DC: Island Press.

Norton, B. J. 1992. Epistemology and environmental values (The intrinsic value of nature). *The Monist* 75:208.

Novellino, D. 2000. Recognition of ancestral domain claims on Palawan Island, the Philippines: Is there a future? *Land Reform: Land Settlement and Cooperatives 2000/1*, FAO.

Nygren, A. 2000a. Development discourses and peasant-forest relations: Natural resource utilization as social process. *Development and Change* 31:11–34.

———. 2000b. Environmental narratives on protection and production: Nature-based conflicts in Rio San Juan, Nicaragua. *Development and Change* 31:807–830.

OAS. 1969. *American Convention on Human Rights*. San José: Inter-American Specialized Conference on Human Rights.

———. 1997. *Proposed American Declaration on the Rights of Indigenous Peoples*. OAS.

OAU. 1981. *African Charter on Human and Peoples' Rights*. OAU.

Olsen, S., and P. Christie. 2000. What are we learning from tropical coastal management experiences? *Coastal Management* 28:5–18.

Ortiz-Crespo, F. 1995. Fragoso, Monardes, and pre-Chinchonian knowledge of Cinchona. *Archives of Natural History* 22(2):169–181.

Ostrom E. 1990. *Governing the commons: The evolution of institutions for collective action*. Cambridge: Cambridge University Press.

———. 1998. Scales, polycentricity, and incentives: Designing complexity to govern complexity. In *Protection of global biodiversity: Converging strategies*, ed. L. D. Guruswamy and J. A. McNeely, 149–167. Durham: Duke University Press.

———. 1999. Coping with tragedies of the commons. *Annual Review of Political Science* 2:493–535.

Pattullo, P. 1996. *Last resorts: The cost of tourism in the Caribbean*. London: Cassell .

Pearl, M. C. 1994. Local initiatives and the rewards for biodiversity conservation: Crater Mountain Wildlife Management Area, Papua New Guinea. In *Natural connections: Perspectives in community-based conservation*, ed. D. Western, R. M. Wright, and S. C. Strum, 193–214. Washington DC: Island Press.

Peang-Meth, A. 2002. The rights of indigenous peoples and their fight for self-determination. *World Affairs* 164(3):101–114.

Peet, R., and M. Watts. 1993. Development theory and environment in an age of market triumphalism. *Economic Geography* 69:227–253.

———. 1996. *Liberation ecologies: Environment, development, social movements*. London: Routledge.

Peluso, N. L. 1990. A history of state forest management in Java. In *Keepers of the forest*, ed. M. Poffenberger, 27–55. West Hartford, CT: Kumarian Press

———. 1992. *Rich forests, poor people: Resource control and resistance in Java*. Berkeley: University of California Press.

Peluso, N. L., M. Poffenberger, and F. Seymour. 1990. Reorienting forest management on Java. In *Keepers of the forest: Land management alternatives in Southeast Asia*, ed. M. Poffenberger, 220–236. West Hartford, CT: Kumarian Press.

Peluso, N. L., and M. Watts, eds. 2001. *Violent environments*. Ithaca: Cornell University Press.

People of Color Environmental Leadership Summit. 1991. "Principles of environmental justice." Available from *http:// www.ejrc.cau.edu/princej.html* Access 1 June 2002.

Perrow, C. 1967. A framework for the comparative analysis of organizations. *American Sociological Review* 32:194–208.

———. 1984. *Normal accidents: Living with high-risk technologies*. New York: Basic Books.

Peterman, R., and C. Peters. 1998. Decision analysis: Taking uncertainties into account in forest resource management. In *Statistical methods for adaptive management studies, land management handbook no. 42*, ed. V. Sits and B. Taylor, 119–133. Victoria, BC: Canadian Ministry of Forests, Research Branch.

Pimbert, M. P., and J. N. Pretty. 1995. *Parks, people, and professionals: Putting participation into protected area management. United Nations Research Institute for Social Development Discussion Paper #57*. Geneva: UNRISD.

———. 1997. *Diversity and sustainability in community based conservation*. UNESCO-IIPA.

Pleumarom, A. 1994. The political economy of tourism. *The Ecologist* 24(4):142–146.

Poffenberger, M. 1990a. Facilitating change in forestry bureaucracies. In *Keepers of the forest: Land management alternatives in Southeast Asia*, ed. M. Poffenberger, 101–118. West Hartford, CT: Kumarian Press.

———, ed. 1990b. *Keepers of the forest: Land management alternatives in Southeast Asia.* West Hartford, CT: Kumarian Press.

———. 1994. The resurgence of community forest management in eastern India. In *Natural connections: Perspectives in community-based conservation,* ed. D. Western and R. M. Wright, 53–79. Washington DC: Island Press.

Pollnac, R. B., B. R. Crawford, and M. L. G. Gorospe. 2001. Discovering factors that influence the success of community-based marine protected areas in the Visayas, Philippines. *Ocean and Coastal Management* 44:683–710.

Pomeroy, R. 1995. Community-based and co-management institutions for sustainable coastal fisheries management in Southeast Asia. *Ocean and Coastal Management* 27(3):143–162.

Portes, A. 1998. Social capital: Its origins and applications in modern sociology. *Annual Review of Sociology* 24:1–24.

Powell W. W., and P. J. DiMaggio. 1991. The new institutionalism in organizational analysis. Chicago: University of Chicago Press.

ROSDESAC. 1998. Proyecto para el Desarrollo Sustentable de las Comunidades Mayas de la Peninsula del Yucatán: Primer Informe de Resultados Obtenidos. Merida, Yucatán: ROSDESAC.

Rao, K., and C. Geisler. 1990. The social consequences of protected area development for resident populations. *Society and Natural Resources* 3(1): 19–32.

Rainforest Alliance. Natural resources and rights program. *http://www.rainforest-alliance.org* Accessed 1 June 2002.

Raustiala, K. 1997. Domestic institutions and international regulatory cooperation: Comparative responses to the convention on biological diversity. *World Politics* 49:482–509.

Rāval, S.R. 1994. Wheel of life: Perceptions and concerns of the resident peoples for Gir National Park in India. *Society and Natural Resources* 7:305–320.

Redford, K. H., and S. E. Sanderson. 1992. The brief, barren marriage of biodiversity and sustainability. *Bulletin of the Ecological Society of America* 73:36–39.

Redford, K. H., and B. Richter. 1999. Conservation of biodiversity in a world of use. *Conservation Biology* 13:1246–1256.

Reid, W., C. Barber, and A. La Viña. 1995. Translating genetic resource rights into sustainable development: gene cooperatives, the biotrade, and lessons from the Phillippines. *Plant Genetic Resources* Newsletter No. 102.

Reid, W. A., S. A. Lard, C. A. Meyer, R. Gmez, A. Sittenfeld, D. H. Janzen, M. A. Gollin, and C. Juma, eds. 1993. *Biodiversity prospecting: Using genetic resources for sustainable development.* Washington, DC: World Resources Institute.

Renner, M. 1996. *Fighting for survival.* New York: Norton.

Restrepo E., and J. del Valle, eds. 1995. *Renacientes del Guandal.* Bogotá: Proyecto Biopacífico/Universidad Nacional.

Rethinking Tourism Project. 2000. "Rethinking Tourism Project." *http://www2.plan-eta.com/mader/ecotravel/resources/rtp/rtp.html* Accessed 8 Aug 2000.

Revelo, N. 1994a. Regeneración natural de Sangre de Drago, Croton spp. en el Alto Napo, Ecuador. In *Etnobotanica y valoración eonomica de los recursos floristicos sil-vestres en el Alto Napo, Ecuador,* ed. Alarcon, Soldi, and Mena, 120–130. Quito: Ecociencia.

———. 1994b. Valor economico. Usos y metodos de extracción de latex Sangre de Drago, Croton spp., en el Alto Napo, Ecuador. In *Etnobotanica y valoración eco-nomica de los recursos floristicos silvestres en el Alto Napo, Ecuador,* ed. Alarcon, Soldi, and Mena, 155–175. Quito: Ecociencia.

Ribot, J. C. 1996. Participation without representation: Chiefs, councils, and forestry law in the West African Sahel. *Cultural Survival Quarterly* 20:40–44.

———. 1998. Theorizing access: Forest profits along Senegal's charcoal commodity chain. *Development and Change* 29: 307–341.

———. 1999. Decentralization, participation, and accountability in Sahelian forestry: Legal instruments of political-administrative control. *Africa* 69:23–65.

Rich, B. 1994. *Mortgaging the earth: The World Bank, environmental impoverishment, and the crisis of development.* Boston: Beacon Press.

Ridao, A., and R. Cura. 1991. Evaluation of the Marine Conservation Project in San Salvador, Masinloc, Zambales. Unpublished. ACES Foundation, Manila, Philip-pines.

Ríos M., and P. Wilshusen. 1999. Informe final de la misión evaluativa externa: Con-servación y uso sostenible de la biodiversidad en el Chocó biogeográfico (COL/92/G31). Bogotá and New York: UNDP.

Robbins, J. 2001. Regional autonomy and indigenous self-determination. *Rethinking Indigenous Self-Determination. An International Conference on the Theory and Prac-tice of Indigenous Self-Determination.* Brisbane

Robinson, J. C. 1993. The limits to caring: Sustainable living and the loss of biodiver-sity. *Conservation Biology* 7(1): 20–28.

Rocheleau, D. E. 1995. Gender and biodiversity: A feminist political ecology perspec-tive. In Editorial: Gender relations and environmental change, ed. M. S. Leach, S. Joekes, and C. Green. *Ids bulletin* 26(1): 1–8.

Rodriguez, Iokiñe. 2000 Indigenous peoples, national parks and participation: A case study of conflicts in Canaima National Park, Venuzuela. Brighton, UK: Institute of Development Studies, University of Sussex. *http://www.ids.ac.uk/ids/particip/research/institlearn/Fire%20Project%20Seminar.pdf*

Rosenthal, J. 1997. Integrating drug discovery, biodiversity, conservation, and eco-nomic development: Early lesson from the International Cooperative Biodiversity Group (ICBG). In *Biodiversity and Human Health,* ed. F. Grifo and J. Rosenthal, 281–301. Washington, DC: Island Press.

Rudel, T. K. 2000. Organizing for sustainable development: Conservation organiza-tions and the struggle to protect tropical rain forests in Esmeraldas, Ecuador. *Ambio* 29:78–82.

Runte A. 1979. *National parks: The American experience.* Lincoln: University of Nebraska Press.

Rural Advancement Foundation International and Cultural Survival Canada. 1997. *Sangre de Drago. BioPirates Log #4.* Toronto, Canada: Cultural Survival Canada.

Russ, G. 1984. Effects of fishing and protective management on coral reefs at four locations in the Visayas, Philippines (Phase II). UNEP Coral Reef Monitoring Project, Silliman University, Dumaguete, Philippines.

Russell, P. H. Indigenous self-determination—Is Canada as good as it can get? International conference on the theory and practice of indigenous self-determination, September 25–28, 2001. University of Queensland, Australia.

Saberwal, V., M. Rangarajan, and A. Kothai. 2001. People, parks, and wildlife: Toward coexistence. *Tracts for the times.* New Delhi: Orient Longman.

Sachs, A. 1995. *Eco-justice: Linking human rights and the environment.* Worldwatch Paper 127. Washington, DC: Worldwatch.

Sachs, W., ed. 1993. *Global ecology: A new arena of political conflict.* London: Zed Books.

Scheberle, D. 1997. *Federalism and environmental policy: Trust and the politics of implementation.* Washington, DC: Georgetown University Press.

Schelhas, J., and R. Greenberg. 1996. *Forest patches in tropical landscapes.* Washington, DC: Island Press.

Schelhas, J., T. Jantzi, T. Thacher, C. Kleppner, and K. O'Connor. 1997. Costa Rica: Meeting farmers' needs through forest stewardship. *Journal of Forestry* 95: 33–38.

Schiff, L. 1966. Innovation and administrative decision-making. *Administrative Science Quarterly* 11.

Schroeder, R. A. 1999. Community, forestry, and conditionality in the Gambia. *Africa* 69:1–22.

Schwartzman, S., A. Moreira, and D. Nepstad. 2000. Rethinking tropical forest conservation: Perils in parks. *Conservation Biology* 14:1351–1357.

Scott, W. R. 1998. *Organizations: Rational, natural, and open systems,* 4th edition. Englewood Cliffs, NJ: Prentice-Hall.

Selznick, P. 1984 (1949). *TVA and the grass roots.* Berkeley: University of California Press.

———. 1957. *Leadership in administration.* New York: Harper and Row.

Sewell, W. H. 1992. A theory of structure: Duality, agency, and transformation. *American Journal of Sociology* 98:1–29.

Shaman Pharmaceuticals. 1999. *Desarrollo, aprovechamiento y manejo sustentable de la especie croton lechleri (sangre de drago), Anexo No. 3: Beneficios recibidos por Ecuador en los ultimos 5 anos nivel institutional, comunitario, biodiversidad y estudiantes ecuatorianos.* Ecuador: Shaman Pharmaceuticals.

Shaman Pharmaceuticals. 1996. *Informe clinico al final del estudio, Protocolo SP-303T-A-02, Estudio doble ciego con control placebo para evaluar la eficacia y tolerancia clin-*

ica de Vivernd™ para el tratamiento de infecciones recidivantes por el virus del herpes simplex (VHS) en sujetos con el sindrome del inmunodeficiencia adquirida (SIDA). South San Francisco: Shaman Pharmaceuticals.

―――. 1998. *Informe final sobre Sangre de Drago* (Croton lechleri). Quito: Fundación Agroforestal Oriente and Shaman Pharmaceuticals.

Shiva, V. 1989. *Staying alive: Women, ecology, and development.* London and New Jersey: Zed Books.

Sherman, P. B., and J. A. Dixon. 1997. The economics of nature tourism: Determining if it pays. In *The Earthscan reader in sustainable tourism,* ed. L. France, 196–204. London: Earthscan.

Silva, E. 1994. Thinking politically about sustainable development in the tropical forests of Latin America. *Development and Change* 25:697–721.

Simon, H. 1964. The concept of organizational goal. *Administrative Science Quarterly* 9:1–22.

Simsik, M., V. Agbo, and N. Sokpon. 1993. *Farmer participation in a pre-project assessment of receptivity to agroforestry: A feasibility study in the village of Tanougou, Republic of Benin, West Africa.* Ann Arbor: University of Michigan, School of Natural Resources and Environment.

Soule, M. E. 1999. *Continental conservation: Scientific foundations of regional reserve networks.* Washington, DC: Island Press.

Spence, M. D. 1999. *Dispossessing the wilderness: Indian removal and the making of the national parks.* Oxford: Oxford University Press.

Steele, A. R. 1964. Flowers for the king: The expedition of Ruiz and Pavon and the flora of Peru. Durham: Duke University Press.

Stegeborn, W. 1996. Sri Lanka's forests: Conservation of nature versus people. *Cultural Survival Quarterly:* 16–19.

Steinmo, S., K. Thelen, and F. Longstreth, eds. 1992. *Structuring politics: Historical institutionalism in comparative analysis.* Cambridge: Cambridge University Press.

Stevens, G. C. 1989. The latitudinal gradient in geographical ranger: How so many species coexist in the tropics. *The American Naturalist* 133(2): 240–256.

Stevens, S. 1997. *Conservation through cultural survival: Indigenous peoples and protected areas.* Washington, DC: Island Press.

Stonich, S. 1993. *I am destroying the land: The political ecology of poverty and environmental destruction in Honduras.* Boulder: Westview Press.

Stycos, J., and I. Duarte. 1993. Parks, population, and resettlement in the Dominican Republic. IPAT/MUCIA Working Paper No. 16 (Oct.).

Suhrke, A. 1993. Pressure points: Environmental degradation, migration, and conflict. Occasional Paper Series of the Project on Environmental Change and Acute Conflict. International Security Studies Program, American Academy of Arts and Sciences and the Peace and Conflict Studies Program, University of Toronto.

Sugawara, K. 2002. Voices of the dispossessed. *Cultural Survival Quarterly* 26(1):28–29.

Sundar, N. 2000. Unpacking the "joint" in joint forest management. *Development and Change* 31:255–279.

Sundberg, J. 1999. NGO landscapes in the Maya Biosphere Reserve, Guatemala. *The Geographical Review* 88:388–412.

Surapaty, S. C., E. Rofin, and L. Heydir. 1991. *Studi Dinamika Kependudukan-Lingkungan Hidup diKapubupaten Lahat, Sumatra Selatan, Indonesia.* Pusat Peneli-tan Kependudukan Universitas Sriwijaya.

Survival International. 1991a. From bullets to tourists. *Survival International* (28):8–9.

———. 1991b. The tourists arrive and bam! We are dead. *Survival International* (28):6–7.

———. 1996. Parks or peoples? *Survival Newsletter* 35:1–2.

———. 2002a. UN condemns Botswana's "dispossession" of Bushmen. *Survival News. http://www.survival-international.org/bushmannews020402.htm* Accessed April 2, 2002.

———. 2002b. Terminology. *http://www.survivalinternational.org/bush%20terms.htm* Accessed 1 June 2002.

———. forthcoming. *Parks and peoples: Tribal peoples and conservation.* London.

Svarstad, H. 2000. Local interest and foreign interventions: Shaman in Tanzania. In *Responding to bioprospecting: From biodiversity in the South to medicines in the North,* ed. H. Svarstad and S. Dhillion, 145–154. Oslo: Spartacus Forlag.

Taylor, D. E. 1997. American environmentalism: the role of race, class, and gender in shaping activism 1820–1995. *Race, Gender, and Class* 5(1):16–72.

———. 2000. The rise of the environmental justice paradigm: Injustice framing and the social construction of environmental discourses. *American Behavioral Scientist* 43:508–580.

Taylor, M. 2002. Resource rights and conservation: The Ts'Exa. *Cultural Survival Quarterly* 26(1):22–23.

Tendler, J. 1975. *Inside foreign aid.* Baltimore: Johns Hopkins University Press.

———. 1997. *Good government in the tropics.* Baltimore: Johns Hopkins University Press.

Ten Kate, K., and S. Laird. 2000. *The commercial uses of biodiversity.* London: Earth-scan.

Terborgh, J. 1999. *Requiem for nature.* Washington, DC: Island Press/Shearwater Books.

Terborgh, J., C. van Schaik, L. Davenport, and M. Rao, eds. 2002. *Making parks work: Strategies for preserving tropical forests.* Washington, DC: Island Press.

Thelen, K. 1999. Historical institutionalism in comparative politics. *Annual Review of Political Science* 2:369–404.

Third World Network. 2000. Letter to Mr. Oliver Hillell, Tourism Programme Coordinator United Nations Environment Programme Division of Technology Industry and Economics Production and Consumption. *http://www.twnside.org.sg/title/iye3.htm*

Thomas, C. 1997. Public management as interagency cooperation: Testing epistemic community theory at the domestic level. *Journal of Public Administration Research and Theory* 7:221–246.

Thompson, J. D. 1967. *Organizations in action.* New York: McGraw-Hill.

Thomson, J. T. 1983. Deforestation and desertification in twentieth-century arid Sahelian Africa. In *World deforestation in the twentieth century,* ed. R. P. Tucker and J. Richards, 70–90. Durham: Duke University Press.

———. 1992. *A framework for analyzing institutional incentives in community forestry.* FAO Community Forestry Note. Rome: FAO.

———. 1995. Community institutions and the governance of local woodstocks in the context of Mali's democratic transition. Paper prepared for the 38th meeting of the African Studies Association, November 3–6, 1995, Orlando, FL.

Thomson, J. T., and K. Schoonmaker Freudenberger. 1997. *Crafting institutional arrangements for community forestry.* FAO Community Forestry Field Manual. Rome: FAO.

Trenberth, K. 1999. The extreme weather events of 1997 and 1998. *Consequences* 5:3–15.

Truong, T.D. 1990. *Sex, money, and morality: Prostitution and tourism in Southeast Asia.* London: Zed Books.

Tulio Díaz, S. 1993. Proyecto Biopacífico. *EcoLogica: Política, Medio Ambiente, Cultura* 15–16:24–31.

Turnbull, C. M. 1972. *The mountain people.* New York: Simon and Schuster.

Turner, M. 1999. The role of social networks, indefinite boundaries, and political bargaining in maintaining the ecological and economic resilience of the transhumance systems of Sudano-Sahelian West Africa. In *Managing mobility in African rangelands: The legitimization of transhumance,* ed. M. Niamir-Fuller, 97–123. London: Intermediate Technology Publications.

Tuxill, J., and C. Bright. 1998. Losing strands in the web of life. In *State of the world 1998,* ed. L. R. Brown, 41–58. Washington, DC: Worldwatch Institute.

UNCE. 1972. *Declaration of the United Nations Conference on the Human Environment.* Stockholm.

UNDP. 2000. *Human development report 2000.* New York: Oxford University Press.

UNEP. 2002. Integrating environment and development: 1972–2002. *GEO 3. Global environment outlook 3. Past, present, and future perspectives,* UNEP.

UNEP. 1974. *Patterns of resource use, environment, and development strategies.* Cocoyoc, Mexico.

United Nations. 1998. *World population prospects: The 1998 revision*. New York: United Nations.

USAID/Madagascar. 1997a. Strategic objective agreement: Annex 1, Amplified Description.

———. 1997b. Natural Strategic Agreement to Conserve Biologically Diverse Ecosystems in Priority Conservation Zones, RFA 623–98–005.

U.S. Department of Commerce. 1994. Guidelines and principles for social impact assessment. Prepared by the inter-organizational committee on guidelines and principles for social impact assessment (May. NOAA Technical Memorandum NMFS-F/SPO-16. Washington, D.C.

United States Patent Office. 1986. US Patent #5751. Washington, DC: USPTO.

———. 1993. US Patent#5,211,944. Washington, DC: USPTO.

Useb, J. 2002. Land Crisis: A San Perspective. *Cultural Survival Quarterly* 26(1):32.

Uvin, P. 1995. Fighting hunger at the grassroots: Paths to scaling up. *World Development* 23:927–939.

Uvin, P., P. S. Jain, and L. D. Brown. 2000. Think large and act small: Toward a new paradigm for NGO scaling up. *World Development* 28:1409–1419.

Vaughn, D. 1999. The dark side of organizations: Mistake, misconduct, and disaster. *Annual Review of Sociology* 25:271–305.

Vayda, A. P. 1983. Progressive contextualization: Methods for research in human ecology. *Human Ecology* 11:265–281.

Vayda, A. P., and B. B. Walters. 1999. Against political ecology. *Human Ecology* 27:167–179.

Viana, V. M., J. Ervin, R. Z. Donovan, C. Elliott, and H. Gholz, eds. 1996. *Certification of forest products: Issues and perspectives*. Washington, DC: Island Press.

Victurine, R. 2000. Building tourism excellence at the community level: Capacity building for community-based entrepreneurs in Uganda. *Journal of Travel Research* 38:221–229.

Volkman, J., and W. McConnaha. 1993. Through a glass, darkly: Columbian River salmon, the endangered species act, and adaptive management. *Environmental Law* 23:1249–1272.

Volkman, T. A. 1986. The hunter-gatherer myth in Southern Africa. *Cultural Survival Quarterly* 10(2):25–32.

von Benda-Beckmann, K. 1997. The environmental protection and human rights of indigenous peoples: A tricky alliance. In *Natural resources, environment, and legal pluralism*. Special issue: *Law and Anthropology* 9, ed. F. von Benda-Beckmann, K. von Benda-Beckmann, and A. Hoekema, 303–323.

von Humboldt, A. 2000. Nicaragua: Indigenous peoples' rights and Bosawas Reserve. *WRM Bulletin* 38:11.

Wade P. 1993. *Blackness and race mixture: The dynamics of racial identity in Colombia*. Baltimore: Johns Hopkins University Press.

————. 1995. The cultural politics of blackness in Colombia. *American Ethnologist* 22:341–357.

Waggoner, P. 1994. How much land can ten billion people spare for nature? CAST Task Force Report No. 121, in cooperation with the Program for the Human Environment, The Rockefeller University, New York.

Wagner, J. R. 2001. The politics of accountability: An institutional analysis of the conservation movement in Papua New Guinea. *Social Analysis* 45(2):78–93.

Wollenberg E., and H. Kartodihardjo. 2000. Devolution and Indonesia's new basic forestry law. Draft paper. Center for International Forestry Research (CIFOR), Bogor, Indonesia.

Walters, C. 1986. *Adaptive management of renewable resources.* New York: Macmillan.

WCED. 1987. *Our common future.* New York: Oxford University Press.

WCPPA. 1992. *Proceedings from the Fourth World Congress.* Caracas, Venezuela.

WCPA. "Local communities, equity, and protected areas (TLCEPA)." http://wcpa. iucn.org/theme/communities/communities.html Accessed 1 June 2002.

Wearing, S. 2001. Exploring socio-cultural impacts on local communities. In *The encyclopedia of ecotourism,* ed. D. Weaver, 395–410. Oxon, United Kingdom: CAB International.

Weaver, D. B. 1998. Ecotourism in the less developed world. New York: CAB International.

————. 2001. *The encyclopedia of ecotourism.* Oxon, United Kingdom: CAB International.

Weber, E. 1998. *Pluralism by the rules.* Washington, DC: Georgetown University Press.

Weber, M. 1978 (1968). *Economy and society: An outline of interpretive sociology.* Trans. G. Roth and C. Wittich. Berkeley: University of California Press.

Weber, R., J. Butler, P. Larson. 2000. Indigenous peoples and conservation organizations: Experiences in collaboration. Washington, DC: World Wildlife Fund.

Weber, W. 1991. Enduring peaks and changing cultures: The Sherpas and Sagarmartha (Mount Everest) National Park. In *Resident peoples and national parks,* ed. P. C. West and S. R. Brechin, 206–214. Tucson: University of Arizona Press.

Weiss, J. A. 1987. Pathways to cooperation among public agencies. *Journal of Policy Analysis and Management* 7:94–117.

Wells M. 1997. Economic perspectives on nature tourism, conservation, and development. *Environmental economics series, #55.* Washington, DC: The World Bank.

Wells, M., and K. Brandon. 1992. *People and parks: Linking protected area management with local communities.* Washington, DC: The World Bank.

Wells, M. P., J. Ganapin, J. Delfin, and F. Trempe. 1998. *Report of the second independent evaluation of the Global Environment Facility Small Grants Programme (GEF/SGP) 1996–1998.* United Nations Development Programme, GEF Coordination Unit.

Wells, M., S. Guggenheim, A. Khan, W. Wardojo, and P. Jepson. 1999. *Investing in biodiversity: A review of Indonesia's integrated conservation and development projects.* Washington, DC: The World Bank.

West, P. 2001. Environmental non governmental organizations and the nature of ethnographic inquiry. *Social Analysis* 45(2):55–77.

West, P. C. 1982. *Natural resource bureaucracy and rural poverty: A study in the political sociology of natural resources.* Ann Arbor: The University of Michigan Natural Resource Sociology Research Lab (monograph #2).

———. 1994. Natural resources and the persistence of rural poverty in America: A Weberian perspective on the role of power, domination, and natural resource bureaucracy. *Society and Natural Resources* 7:415–427.

West, P. C., and S. R. Brechin, eds. 1991. *Resident peoples and national parks: Social dilemmas and strategies in international conservation.* Tucson: University of Arizona Press.

West, P. C., V. Agbo, M. Simski, and N. Sokpon. In Press. Participatory action research and sustainable development: The role of eotourism in Tanougou Benin. NR&SJ Paper #2. Grand Rapids, MN: Windago Heights Press.

Western, D., R. M. Wright, and S. C. Strum, eds. 1994. *Natural connections: Perspectives in community-based conservation.* Washington, DC: Island Press.

Westing A. 1992. Environmental refugees: A growing category of displaced persons. *Environmental Conservation* 19 (Autumn):201–207.

Westley, F. 1995. Governing design: The management of social systems and ecosystems management. In *Barriers and bridges to the renewal of ecosystems and institutions,* ed. L. H. Gunderson, C. S. Holling, and S. S. Light, 391–427. New York: Columbia University Press.

Westley, F., and H. Vredenburg. 1997. Interorganizational collaboration and the preservation of global biodiversity. *Organization Science* 8(4):381–403.

Westrum, R. 1994. An organizational perspective: Designing recovery teams from the inside out. In *Endangered species recovery: Finding the lessons, improving the process,* ed. T. W. Clark, R. P. Reading, and A. L. Clarke, 327–349. Washington, DC: Island Press.

White, A. T. 1988. The effects of community-managed reserves on their associated coral reef fish populations. *Asian Fish. Sci.* 2(1): 27–41.

White, A. T., C. A. Courtney, and A. Salamanca. 2002. Experience with marine protected area planning and management in the Philippines. *Coastal Management* 30:1–26.

White, A. T., L. Hale, Y. Renard, and L. Cortesi, eds. 1994. *Collaborative and community-based management of coral reefs: Lessons from experience.* West Hartford, CT: Kumarian Press.

White, A. T., and G. Savina. 1986. Final report and evaluation for the marine conservation and development program. Silliman University, Philippines.

———. 1987. Community-based marine reserves: a Philippine first. In *Proceedings of Coastal Zone '87,* 2022–2036. Seattle, Washington.

Whyte, H. 1993. The homecoming of the Kagga Kamma Bushmen. *Cultural Survival Quarterly* 17(2):61–63.

Wilshusen P. R. 1996. Case study: Colombia Biopacífico project biodiversity conservation in the Chocó biogeographic region. New York: United Nation Development Programme.

———. 2000. Local participation in conservation and development projects: Ends, means, and power dynamics. In *Foundations of natural resource policy and management*, ed. T. W. Clark, A. Willard, and C. Cromley, 288–326. New Haven: Yale University Press.

———. 2003. Negotiating devolution: Community conflict, structural power, and local forest management in Quintana Roo, Mexico. Ph.D. dissertation, University of Michigan, School of Natural Resources and Environment, Ann Arbor.

Wilshusen, P. R., S. R. Brechin, C. F. Fortwangler, and P. C. West. 2002. Reinventing a square wheel: Critique of a resurgent "protection paradigm" in international biodiversity conservation. *Society and Natural Resources* 15:17–40.

Wilson E. 1992. *The diversity of life*. Cambridge: Harvard University Press.

Winter, M. 1997. *La gestion décentralisée des ressources naturelles dans trois pays du Sahel: Sénégal, Mali et Burkina Faso*. Ouagadougou, Burkina Faso: PADLOS/CILSS.

Wisner, G. 2001 (June 25). U.S. Patent and Trademark Office reinstates Aychuascu patent flawed decision declares open season on resources of indigenous peoples. Washington, DC: Center for International Environmental Law. *www.ciel.org/Publications/PTODecisionAnalysis.pdf*

Wolf, E. R. 1972. Ownership and political ecology. *Anthropological Quarterly* 43:201–205.

———. 1982. *Europe and the people without history*. Berkeley: University of California Press.

———. 1999. *Envisioning power: Ideologies of dominance and crisis*. Berkeley: University of California Press.

Wondolleck, J. M., and S. L. Yaffee. 2000. Making collaboration work: Lessons from inovation in natural resource management. Washington, DC: Island Press.

Woo, H. T. 1991. An assessment of tourism development in the national parks of South Korea. In *Resident peoples and national parks*, ed. P. C. West and S. R. Brechin, 200–205. Tucson: University of Arizona Press.

Wordsworth, G. 2000. Final Report (KEPEM Project): September 1997–July 2000. Prepared for USAID. Submitted by International Resources Group, Ltd.

World Alliance of the Indigenous—Tribal Peoples of the Tropical Forests. 1992. *Charter of the Indigenous and Tribal Peoples of the Tropical Forests*. Penang, Malaysia: World Rainforest Movement.

World Almanac and Book of Facts. 1999. *World Almanac and Book of Facts*. Mahway, NJ: World Almanac Books.

World Bank. 2000. *Entering the 21st century: World development report 1999/2000.* New York: Oxford University Press.

———. 2001. *Involuntary resettlement. Operational manual. OP 4.12*

WRI/IUCN/UNEP. 1992. *Global biodiversity strategy: Guidelines for action to save, study, and use Earth's biotic wealth sustainably and equitably.* Washington, DC: World Resources Institute.

WRI/UNEP/UNDP. 1996. *World resources 1996–97.* New York: Oxford University Press

———. 1998. *World resources 1997–98.* New York: Oxford University Press.

WRM. 2000a. Togo: Community rights and forest conservation. *WRM Bulletin* 36:5.

———. 2000b. India: Indigenous peoples victims of "conservation" at Rajive Gandhi National Park. *WRM Bulletin* 38:6.

———. 2002a. Ghana: Protected areas at the expense of people do not guarantee conservation. *WRM Bulletin* 57:4–5.

———. 2002b. Panamá: Protected areas vs. indigenous peoples. *WRM Bulletin* 57:15.

World Tourism Organization. 11 May 2000. World tourism results revised upwards. *http://www.world-tourism.org/pressrel/00_5_111.htm* Accessed 20 July 2000.

World Trade Organization Business Council. Nov. 1999. Catching tourists on the Web. *http://www.world-tourism.org/Internet.htm* Accessed 20 July 2000.

Wright, M. 1994. Recommendations. In *Natural connections: Perspectives in community-based conservation,* eds. D. Western, M. R. Wright, and S. C. Strum, 472–496. Washington, DC: Island Press.

Wright, P. 1997. The future of biodiversity in Madagascar. In *Natural change and human impact in Madagascar,* eds. S. M. Goodman and B. D. Patterson, 381–405. Washington, DC: Smithsonian Institution Press.

WWF International. 1996. *Indigenous peoples and conservation: WWF statement of principles.* Gland, Switzerland: WWF International.

WWF. 1997. The network of private nature reserves: Strengthening private efforts in conservation and management of natural lands and resources—project profile. Washington, DC: Worldwide Fund for Nature.

Wuthnow, R. 1987. *Meaning and moral order: Explorations in cultural analysis.* Berkeley: University of California Press.

Wyckoff-Baird, B., A. Kaus, C. Christen, and M. Keck. 2000. *Shifting the power: Decentralization and biodiversity conservation.* Washington, DC: Biodiversity Support Program.

Yanow, D. 2000. Seeing organizational learning: A "cultural" view. *Organization* 7:247–268.

Young, E. H. 1999. Balancing conservation with development in small-scale fisheries: Is ecotourism an empty promise? *Human Ecology* 27(4):581–620.

Young, O. R. 1989. *International cooperation: Building regimes for natural resources and the environment.* Ithaca: Cornell University Press

Yu, D. W., T. Hendrickson, and A. Castillo. 1997. Ecotourism and conservation in Amazonian Peru: Short-term and long-term challenges. *Environmental Conservation* 24:130–138.

Zeide, B. 1998. Another look at Leopold's land ethic. *Journal of Forestry* (January 1998):13–19.

Zerner, C. 2000a. Toward a broader vision of justice and nature conservation. In *People, plants, and justice*, ed. C. Zerner, 3–20. New York: Columbia University Press

——— . 2000b. *People, plants, and justice: The politics of nature conservation.* New York: Columbia University Press.

Zolberg, A., A. Suhrke, and S. Aguayo. 1989. *Escape from violence.* New York: Oxford University Press.

Zube E. H., and M. L. Busch. 1990. People-park relations: An international review. *Landscape and Urban Planning* 19:115–132.

LIST OF CONTRIBUTORS

EDITORS

Steven R. Brechin is associate professor of sociology at the University of Illinois, Urbana Champaign, and associate professor of environmental sociology at the School of Natural Resources & Environment, The University of Michigan, Ann Arbor. He has published widely on the human dimensions of international biological conservation, the sociology of international organizations, and global environmentalism. Professor Brechin is a member of IUCN's World Commission on Protected Areas.

Peter R. Wilshusen is assistant professor of environmental studies at Bucknell University. He completed his Ph.D. in environmental sociology and policy at The University of Michigan in 2003. His dissertation examines changing power dynamics among forestry communities *(ejidos)* in Quintana Roo, Mexico, following neoliberal reforms. His research focuses on the organizational and political processes associated with conservation and development, particularly in Latin America.

Crystal L. Fortwangler is a doctoral candidate in the Department of Anthropology and School of Natural Resources & Environment, The University of Michigan, Ann Arbor. Research interests include examining the relationships between senses of place and perspectives toward protected areas, understanding protected areas as contested places, and exploring how protected area policies can adhere to human rights principles.

Patrick C. West is currently vice president and chairman of the board of Windago Heights Inc. and editor, Windago Heights Press, a division of Windago Heights Inc. Previously, Professor West was for twenty-five years a faculty member at the School of Natural Resources & Environment, The University of Michigan, Ann Arbor. He has had a long-term interest in natural resource management and issues of social equity and justice.

AUTHORS

Valentin Agbo is professor of agricultural sciences (rural and development sociology) at the National University of Benin and holds a number of top posts within the government of Benin.

Jill M. Belsky is professor of rural and environmental sociology in the School of Forestry at the University of Montana. Her teaching and research have focused on the social analysis of rural and environmental change including sustainable agriculture, nontimber forest products, rural ecotourism, and collaborative/community conservation.

Charles E. Benjamin is a doctoral candidate at the School of Natural Resources & Environment, The University of Michigan, Ann Arbor. His dissertation research in Mali, funded by an EPA STAR fellowship, focuses on biodiversity, livelihood security, and the role of institutions and institutional change in biodiversity by local populations.

Delma Buhat is a coastal management consultant and community organizer in the Philippines.

Patrick Christie is assistant professor at the School of Marine Affairs and Henry M. Jackson School of International Studies within the University of Washington. He conducts research and teaches on social and ecological impacts of marine protected areas and integrated coastal management.

Michael K. Dorsey is a doctoral candidate at the School of Natural Resources & Environment, The University of Michigan, Ann Arbor, and a Thurgood Marshall Fellow in Residence at Dartmouth College

Len R. Garces is Assistant Scientist at the ICLARM-The World Fish Center. He is involved with the implementation of the Coastal Fisheries Projects under the Coastal and Marine Resource Research Program of the center.

Charles Geisler is professor of rural sociology at Cornell University with particular interests in comparative property systems, rights, and dispossession issues. His recent edited books include: *Property and Values* (Island Press 2000) and *Biological Diversity: Balancing Interests through Adaptive Collaborative Management* (CRC Press 2001).

Lisa L. Gezon is associate professor of anthropology at the State University of West Georgia. She has been studying the politics of resource access and management in northern Madagascar since 1990. Current research interests include the regional contexts of conservation and protected area management, including the study of productive systems and commodity chains.

Jeffrey Langholz is assistant professor of international environmental policy in the Graduate School of International Policy Studies at the Monterey Institute of International Studies. His research and teaching emphasize protected natural areas worldwide, particularly options for protecting biodiversity on non-public lands.

Raúl E. Murguía is the national coordinator for the UNDP-GEF Small Grants Programme in Mexico. He has more than twenty years of experience in conservation and development including work with UNDP, OAS, and the Mérida-based research institute, CINVESTAV

Michael Simsik is currently working as an environmental team coordinator for Cornell University Cooperative Extension in New York City and completing a doctorate in education at the University of Massachusetts, Amherst. His dissertation is entitled, "Priorities in Conflict: Livelihood Practices, Environmental Threats, and the Conservation of Biodiversity in Madagascar."

Nestor Sokpon is a faculty member with the department of agricultural economics, National University of Benin.

Alan T. White is chief of party for the Coastal Resources Management Project, Tetra Tech EM Inc., Philippines. He has written widely on the management and natural history of the Philippine coral reefs.

INDEX

315